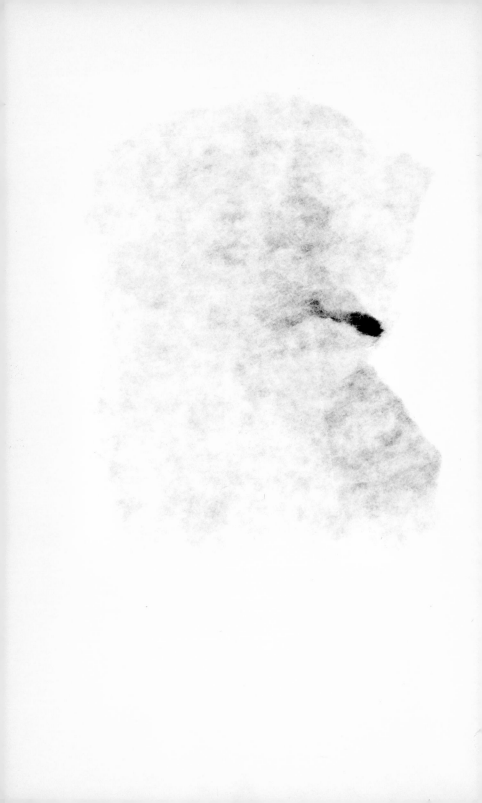

THE MESOLITHIC SETTLEMENT
OF NORTHERN EUROPE

A STUDY OF
THE FOOD-GATHERING PEOPLES OF
NORTHERN EUROPE DURING THE
EARLY POST-GLACIAL PERIOD

THE
MESOLITHIC SETTLEMENT
OF NORTHERN EUROPE

A STUDY OF
THE FOOD-GATHERING PEOPLES OF
NORTHERN EUROPE DURING THE
EARLY POST-GLACIAL PERIOD

By

J. G. D. CLARK, M.A., Ph.D., F.S.A.

Bye-Fellow of Peterhouse, Cambridge
(1932–1935)

GREENWOOD PRESS, PUBLISHERS
NEW YORK

Copyright © 1953 by Richard C. Overton

Originally published in 1936
by Cambridge University Press

First Greenwood Reprinting 1969

Library of Congress Catalogue Card Number 75-95090

SBN 8371-2579-0

Printed in the United States of America

CONTENTS

Preface   *page* ix

Introduction   xiii

Chap. I. The Natural History of the Area of Settlement   1

The retreat of the ice-sheets—Geochronology—Changes in the
mutual relations of land and sea—Alterations of climate—Post-
glacial forest development—Fauna—Summary (with table)

II. The Tanged-point Cultures   54

The Ahrensburg-Lavenstedt culture—The Remouchamps culture
—The Swiderian culture—The Komsa and the Fosna cultures of
Norway, and the survival of the tanged-point tradition in Scandi-
navia—Summary—Origins

III. The Axe Cultures of the Lowland Forest Area   79

Period I. The Lyngby culture   79

Period II. Lyngby survivals; The Maglemose culture   85

Distribution and nature of settlement—Material culture—
General considerations on material culture—Social outlook—
Chronology—Origins—Physical types

Period III. Maglemose survivals; The Ertebølle culture   136

Types of settlement—Material culture—Chronology
The Limhamn, Lihult, and Nøstvet cultures of the Scandinavian
peninsula
The Lower Halstow culture of south-eastern Britain

Summary of the development of the axe cultures   160

IV. The Art of the Maglemose Culture   162

Mode of occurrence—Techniques—Motives—Summary of chief
characteristics—Relations with Upper Palaeolithic art groups—
and with the Arctic art groups—Mutual relations of the three
art groups

v

CONTENTS

Chap. V. The Microlithic Cultures of the Sand Areas and the
            Highlands   *page* 190

            Distribution and nature of settlement—Dwelling-places—Material
            culture—Chronology—Relations with the tanged-point—and
            with the axe cultures of the Lowland Forest—The Azilian

      VI. General Summary and Retrospect   219

Appendix I. Fauna lists:
                  List A, fauna from Magdalenian and Azilian levels
                     of the caves of southern Germany   224
                  List B, fauna from sites of Period I   225
                  List C, fauna from sites of Period II   226
                  List D, fauna from sites of Period III   227

         II. Find-list of Objects of the Lyngby Culture   229

        III. List of Maglemose sites and Finding-places, arranged
              alphabetically under countries   231

         IV. Key to the distribution map (Fig. 47) of certain
              forms of bone points   245

          V. Summary of pollen-analyses correlating the Magle-
              mose culture with the development of forest history   246

         VI. List of decorated objects of the Maglemose culture   248

        VII. List of Tardenoisian sites   251

List of works to which reference is made in the text   254

Index   269

LIST OF PLATES

Plate I. (Above) Three samples of varved clay from the valley of the Kalajoki River in Ostrobothnia
(Below) Diagram of the connected clay samples, showing variations in the thickness of the varves   *facing p.* 5

II. The extinct beach of the *Litorina* Sea at Vamlingbo on the island of Gotland   *facing p.* 9

III. Fen section exposed by excavation on Peacock's Farm, Shippea Hill, Cambridgeshire   *facing p.* 37

IV. Floats of pine bark and strands of net (*in situ*) from Antrea, Finland   *facing p.* 109

V. Bone points (forms 3, 5, 6, 7, 9 and 25) from Denmark and Sweden   *facing p.* 115

VI. Bone leister prongs from Hörninge mosse, Öland Island, Sweden, compared with wooden examples from Lake Fjord, Tutilik, East Greenland   *facing p.* 122

VII. Pottery from the Ertebølle midden   *facing p.* 152

VIII. Comparison of an elk-headed stone axe from Alunda, Uppland, with a rock-engraving (style A) at Landverk, Jämtland
facing p. 186

MAP IN REAR OF BOOK

A map illustrating the distribution of the Maglemose culture, and showing the geography of Northern Europe at the beginning of the Boreal period. At the bottom of the map are shown the forest-tree pollen spectra for the key dating sites.

The sites shown on this map are listed in appendix III. The correlations with forest history by means of pollen-analysis are summarised in appendix V.

PREFACE

THE general character and scope of this book will be indicated briefly in the Introduction; in this Preface I shall say how it came to be written and express my indebtedness to the scholars of many lands whose learning and whose friendship have made possible its production. An outline of the purely archaeological side of the book was communicated to the Society of Antiquaries of London on May the 4th, 1934, but already my material was too unwieldy for publication in the form of a paper. It was furthermore clear that, divorced from its background of natural history, the archaeological story was too abstracted from reality to have very much meaning. My plan has, therefore, been to introduce the reader to the sequence of natural events in Northern Europe, as revealed by modern research, and to proceed from this to synthesise the findings of prehistory in the light of an ever-changing environment. It may be hoped that in presenting my material in this way I may not only assist archaeologists to appreciate the assistance they may derive from the related sciences of geology and palaeo-botany, both in the interpretation of their cultures and in their synchronisation, but that I may also make available to students generally the results of modern archaeological research on the food-gathering peoples of the earlier half of the post-glacial period in Northern Europe. The subject-matter of the book was covered in a course of lectures in the faculty of Archaeology and Ethnology at Cambridge during the Lent Term of 1934.

To obtain an intimate knowledge of the archaeological material, travel in the Low Countries, in Germany and in Scandinavia has been essential, and I have to thank, first of all, those who have made this possible and those who by their kindness have made it fruitful. My first view of the glories of Scandinavian archaeology was obtained when I visited Denmark and Sweden as the guest of the late Dr John af Klercker in 1929. My memories of this journey are of impressions rather than of detailed observations; I shall always remember a chance meeting with Sophus Müller in one of the Bronze Age galleries at Copenhagen, a walk on the Jära Bank in Scania—on the beach of the *Litorina* Sea, and my handling of the Ystad antler sleeve with the fine-etched cervids. At this time, also, I met Dr Arne of Stockholm and Dr Rydbeck of Lund, with both of whom I have retained close contact.

PREFACE

A second journey, made in the Long Vacation of 1933, could not have been undertaken, were it not for the generous action of the governing body of my College. Starting in Holland, I visited J. Butter of Deventer, whose collection of Tardenoisian flint implements I was able to examine, and in whose company I bicycled over the heaths of Overyssel, the habitat of Tardenoisian man. I made a passing visit to Hamburg, but it was at Kiel that I made my first prolonged stay. The services that Professor Gustav Schwantes has rendered, not only to German but, also, to European archaeology, are widely recognised; in this place I should like to acknowledge the personal kindness and attentions that he found time to pay me in Kiel. The collections at Kiel are now being re-housed in a new building more appropriate to their importance; it would be quite impossible to imagine greater facilities to the visiting student than were offered in the old building. I remember the kindness of Karl Kersten, who was working for his doctorate at that time under Professor Schwantes. From Kiel I went to Copenhagen, where Dr Brønsted, though ill in hospital, secured every facility for me in the museum; I appreciated this the more, since the extension of the museum and the rearrangement of the collections must have made the presence of an exacting student the more burdensome to the authorities. At Copenhagen, also, I met Eric Westerby with whom I visited kitchen-midden sites on Mariager Fjord. Going south, by way of Langeland Island, Laaland and Falster, I visited Berlin; the authorities at the Museum für Völkerkunde were good enough to let me examine their Mesolithic material, and have subsequently placed me further in their debt by supplying a photograph. The work of Herr Gumpert of Ansbach on the Tardenoisian drew me south to Franconia and Bavaria. Herr Gumpert was most kind and hospitable. I examined his collections and visited some of his sites in the neighbourhood of Ansbach. In studying the material from the excavations at Ensdorf I had to encounter some difficulties as it was widely scattered. Dr Pils kindly sent what he had from Vienna to Ansbach, where some had been retained by Herr Gumpert; the rest I found at the Dom Bosco monastery at Ensdorf, where I was given shelter for the night, and in the Provincial Museum at Munich, to which Professor Birkner gave me special access.

A third journey, made by road in the company of my brother during the Long Vacation of 1934, enabled me to fill in many of the gaps left by earlier journeys in Germany. I am indebted for courteous assistance at the museums of Münster, Hanover and Magdeburg; at Bielefeld Herr Adrian showed

PREFACE

me his collections; at Halle I was fortunate to meet Dr Bicker and see some of the Mesolithic material from Fienerode in the museum; finally, I have to thank Professor Reinerth for facilitating my study of his work on the Tardenoisian settlement of the Federsee, and for the courtesy of his assistants at the museums of Buchau and Tübingen.

Many museums that I was unable to visit have sent me photographs, and I should like to thank the authorities of those at Danzig, Kalmar, Lübeck and Saint-Germain in this connection. The line blocks have been made from my own drawings, in some cases of the original objects, in others of photographic or other illustrations from published sources; by this method some measure of uniformity has been achieved, which facilitates comparisons. I have, however, to acknowledge Figs. 11, 14, 13 and 73, drawn by Dr H. Godwin, the two former reproduced by courtesy of *The New Phytologist*.

I am indebted to all those whose writings are listed in the Bibliography for the material they have provided in their publications. Among the most distinguished names that I must mention are those of the Danish archaeologists: Madsen, Sarauw, Sophus Müller, Thomsen, Friis-Johansen, Broholm and Westerby; the geologists A. and K. Jessen and V. Nordmann; and the zoologist Winge. Among the Germans, Schmidt (R. R.), Schwantes, Reinerth, Gumpert, Andree, Birkner, Adrian and Zotz are prominent as archaeologists, with Weber, Bertsch, Rudolph and Gams among the natural historians. Norway can claim Shetelig, Bøe, Bjørn, Nummedal, and Brøgger (A. W.), with the geologists Brøgger (W. C.) and Øyen. Sweden has contributed the archaeologists Montelius, Lindquist, Niklasson and Rydbeck, and, among a body of brilliant natural historians, such men as Sernander, Munthe, de Geer, Anderson and von Post. Other men whose work has laid the foundations of our study are the Finnish archaeologists Europaeus and Nordman, and the geologist Sauramo; Tallgren of Esthonia; the Poles Kozlowski and Sawicki; Butter of Holland; Rahir, Hamal-Nandrin and Lequeux of Belgium; de Mortillet, Breuil, and Octobon of France. In Britain the archaeologists Burkitt, Crawford, Peake, Buckley, Armstrong, Burchell, Raistrick and Childe, and the natural historians Geikie, Skertchley, Clement Reid and Godwin, have contributed most directly to the subject.

From my association with the Fenland Research Committee at Cambridge I have experienced directly the extreme value of a co-operative approach to the problems of post-glacial history. I have been much encouraged in the

PREFACE

work of investigating the post-glacial deposits of the Fenland by Professor Seward, F.R.S., who has led the work of the Committee. The association of archaeologists, palaeo-botanists, geographers and geologists has been most stimulating, and I should like to thank especially Dr Godwin for the many talks we have had together, and particularly for reading my first chapter and making most valuable comments.

Finally I must thank my teachers. In a very real sense all those whose names I have mentioned in this preface I count among my teachers, but I must remember, especially, my friend Miles Burkitt, from whose lectures I learnt the elements of prehistory. To my professor, Dr E. H. Minns, F.B.A., I am indebted not only for help in preparing this book, but also for a benefit that oversteps the bounds of archaeology; it was under his skilful guidance that I was first introduced to the German language.

J. G. D. CLARK

PETERHOUSE
May 1935

I should like to acknowledge gratefully my indebtedness to those who have made the publication of this book financially possible. The Syndics of the Cambridge University Press very kindly undertook a substantial share of the cost, the balance of which was most generously advanced by my friends and colleagues in archaeology—Mr C. W. Phillips, F.S.A., and Mr M. C. Burkitt, F.S.A.

It is a pleasure to add that in seeing the work through the press my task has been lightened at every turn by the efficiency and understanding of the staff of the University Press.

J. G. D. CLARK

November 1935

INTRODUCTION

THIS book is concerned with the cultural development, during the earlier half of the post-glacial time, of the food-gathering peoples of the western end of the plain of Northern Europe, a region defined to the west by the mountain backbone of Britain, to the south by the highlands of Southern Germany, and to the north by the mountains of Scandinavia, but to the east lying open to the vast expanse of Russia and Siberia.

The great influence exercised by physical environment on the development of primitive cultures has for a long time been a commonplace of anthropological and archaeological research; it is less generally recognised that this environment has undergone changes in the last few thousand years so profound as to alter its influence on cultural development and so rapid as to afford a natural time-scale for the dating and synchronising of human cultures. The area of Northern Europe is one in which most has been learnt of the development of environment in the post-glacial period, and is, therefore, peculiarly favourable for such a study of Mesolithic settlement. A general account of the factors of change, the nature of the evidence from which their history can be traced, and the ways in which they are relevant to archaeology, are outlined in chapter I of the present work.

The fact that archaeological remains can be related to different phases in the history of environment by such methods as pollen-analysis, determinations of associated fauna or the relation of the finding-places to ancient sea-levels, implies the possibility of a natural chronology. In my first chapter I suggest a triple division of early post-glacial time in Northern Europe into periods I, II and III, which are used throughout the chapters that follow. This natural chronology is valuable, not only for elucidating the internal development of culture-groups, but also for synchronising cultures which have never been found in contact with one another.

Three groups of cultures, three traditions, distinguished by differences of origin and by adaptation to differing types of environment, can be recognised during the early post-glacial period in Northern Europe. The tanged-point cultures (chap. II) derive from origins distinct from those of the axe cultures (chap. III) and reflect different environments. Again, although the axe and the microlithic cultures (chap. v) possess one element in common, the former has its roots in origins more diverse than the latter and illustrates adaptation to forests in contrast with open country.

Food-gathering—hunting, fishing, fowling, and collecting—formed the economic basis of all these cultures, which therefore stand on the same general level as the Palaeolithic cultures of the Pleistocene period. Industrially, also, many features, such as the flint burin, ally them with the earlier cultures. These circumstances have led some writers to classify them as Epi-palaeolithic.[1]

On the other hand certain features, such as the flint core axe, were destined to play an important part in the Neolithic cultures of the area, which has led other writers to classify them as Early or Proto-neolithic.

A third school has sought to reconcile both these views by dividing the cultures into two groups—an earlier Epi-palaeolithic and a later Proto-neolithic group. In so far as this school recognises the inadequacy of either of the preceding outlooks it is correct, but it breaks down on the fact, amply demonstrated in this book, that the so-called 'Epi-palaeolithic' and 'Proto-neolithic' flourished contemporaneously throughout the whole of early post-glacial time and were sometimes combined in a single culture.

The school, to which most modern writers and workers belong, recognises the existence of the two elements, but insists that the cultures under discussion are best considered as forming a separate civilisation—the Mesolithic civilisation. In employing this term nothing more is implied than that the Mesolithic flourished in the main between the Palaeolithic and Neolithic civilisations in point of time; it may be emphasised that it is not intended to suggest an evolutionary stage between the two.

The origins of Mesolithic civilisation may be traced to the changes of environment associated with the close of the Pleistocene period, the contraction of ice-sheets and the replacement of tundra and steppe by forests in Northern Europe, and a progressive desiccation, caused by the northward movement of the cyclonic rain-storms, in North Africa and parts of the Near East.

The progressive desiccation of Afrasia was accompanied by a gradual degeneration of the Capsian cultures until they became microlithic in aspect, and ultimately gave rise to considerable overflows of population from North

[1] The term Epi-palaeolithic is best reserved for delayed Palaeolithic cultures, as indicated in a later paragraph of this Introduction.

Africa into South-western Europe and probably also from Palestine and Syria into South-eastern Europe. The Tardenoisian culture of our region of study finds its origin in these human overflows from the zones of post-glacial desiccation. In Northern Europe these Tardenoisian people may well have come into contact with degenerating provincial Aurignacian cultures, the two together forming our microlithic culture-group. It was these peoples who settled in sandy regions and exposed uplands, their material culture being ill-adapted to coping with forests.

On the other hand, the invasion of the plain of Northern Europe by the forests of post-glacial time gave rise to the development of the axes and adzes, at first of antler and later of flint. It was on this axe tradition, cradled in Northern Europe, that the incoming microlithic element impinged, and it was from the union of these two traditions, possibly in conjunction with elements from Magdalenian sources, that the Maglemose culture developed and flowered in the forest environment of the lowland area.

It is difficult to classify in current terminology the various tanged-point cultures that flourished in Northern Europe during the post-glacial period. It is fairly clear that those of the Low Countries, of North Germany and of Poland derive from Upper Palaeolithic cultures of which the remains are found on open stations within the same area. Apart from a slight microlithic element (which does not, however, reflect the micro-burin technique) the cultures of this group differ in no fundamental respect from those of the pleistocene period. They should properly, therefore, be classed as delayed (or 'epi' in Menghin's sense) Palaeolithic. The Fosna and Komsa cultures are even more Palaeolithic in general appearance, and they survived to a later date; to some extent, these can be regarded as even more delayed (or 'opsi' in Menghin's sense) Palaeolithic, though certain features of these Scandinavian cultures give good evidence of contact with the Mesolithic axe tradition.

The period of time during which Mesolithic cultures were dominant (the Mesolithic period, as we shall call it for short) obviously varied in length in different regions, according as they were central or peripheral to the ancient centres of food-production. In Northern Europe, where the Neolithic arts were established late, the Mesolithic period is commensurately long. On current chronology it would occupy nearly six millenia, a period rather longer than the rest of prehistoric and the whole of historic time in the area taken together. Such a span of time does not seem too great when one recalls the profound changes in geography and in animal and plant life that unfolded themselves while the cultural developments examined in this book were proceeding.

The persistence of each of the three main traditions throughout the Mesolithic and into later periods is one of the most striking features which emerges, and it is clear that no fruitful study of Neolithic civilisation in Northern Europe can be made without adequate consideration of the material examined in this book. It may, indeed, be emphasised that many of the local features of Neolithic civilisation can be satisfactorily explained only in terms of local differences rooted in the Mesolithic. The Neolithic arts were diffused among the food-gathering peoples described in the following chapters, peoples who neither vanished nor were extinguished, but who survived to form the human basis of the later civilisations.

CHAPTER I

THE NATURAL HISTORY OF THE AREA
OF SETTLEMENT

THE RETREAT OF THE ICE-SHEETS

THE withdrawal of the Pleistocene ice-sheets was an event of far-reaching importance. It produced fundamental climatic, floral and faunal changes on a grand scale; it released such vast quantities of melt-water and removed so great a stress from the earth's crust as to induce geographical changes of the first order; and it made wide stretches of Northern Europe available for the settlement of man. The retreat of the ice-sheets and the phenomena which followed in their train form the physical background to the Mesolithic settlement of man in Northern Europe, and are, therefore, fundamental to a full understanding of the cultural developments of the period.

It is generally held that the quaternary ice-age should be considered not so much as a single advance of glaciation as a series of recurrent maxima. Similarly the withdrawal of ice after the last maximum (Wurm II) was not a regular or simple process; it was a slow retrogression arrested periodically by halts and in some regions by readvances. The stages of the retreat of the Rhine glacier have been investigated on the northern slopes of the Eastern Alps by Albrecht Penck, whose conclusions have been confirmed for Switzerland and may be regarded as authoritative for the whole Alps. Penck found that the moraines of the retreating ice-sheet grouped themselves in three main series, each representing an interruption in the retrogression and even a slight readvance; at these three stadia, which he named after local sites, Bühl, Geschnitz and Daun, the snow-line is calculated to have stood respectively 900, 600 and 300 metres lower than at the present day (Penck and Brückner, 1901–9).

Similar periods of halt in the retreat of the Scandinavian ice-sheet have been recognised by Baron de Geer, Sauramo and many other workers, and these allow of conveniently sub-dividing the period of recession. The period during which the ice retreated from the north German moraines, the relics of the last glacial maximum, to the Baltic end-moraine is known as the Daniglacial period, because the recession freed from ice Denmark as well as the rest of north Germany. The next phase of recession uncovered Götland (therefore known as the Götiglacial period) and was terminated by the formation of the Fenno-Scandian moraines. The third major retreat stage, known as the Finiglacial, because it uncovered the greater part of Finland as well as large tracts of Sweden, reduced the inland ice-sheet of Scandinavia to the point when it parted into two separate areas in Jämtland; this point, known as the bi-partition of the inland ice, marks the beginning of Post-glacial[1] time in Scandinavian terminology. The successive retreat stages, interrupted by halts, are illustrated in map form by Fig. 1.

Direct correlation of the retreat stages of the north European and Alpine ice-sheets is not possible, but assuming that such major oscillations could not have merely local causes, it seems reasonable to suggest the following correlation, which may conveniently be expressed in tabular form:

SCANDINAVIA (De Geer)	THE ALPS (Penck and Brückner)
Post-glacial period	
Final stadium previous to the bi-partition of the inland ice	Daun stadium: snow-line below present level by 300 metres
Finiglacial period	Geschnitz—Daun period
Fenno-Scandian moraines	Geschnitz stadium: snow-line below present level by 600 metres
Götiglacial period	Bühl—Geschnitz period
Baltic end-moraine	Bühl stadium: snow-line below present level by 900 metres
Daniglacial period	Achen retreat period

The parallelism to be observed in the table may appear too artificial to be true, but it seems reasonable to suppose that the causes of fluctuation in the retreat of the two ice-sheets were of more than local character and in any case their distance apart is not great. There is interesting confirmation for the correlation of the Baltic end-moraine with the Bühl stadium of the Alps to be found in the various estimates made for their respective ages. The Baltic end-moraine is estimated by Sauramo (1928), on a geochronological basis, to date from roughly 18,000 years B.C. On the other hand Wright (1914, p. 158) arrives at precisely the same date for the Bühl stadium by splitting the difference between the results of Heim, who reached the figure of 14,000 B.C. from a study of the growth of the Muota delta in Lake Lucerne,

[1] This term is generally used outside Scandinavia to denote a longer period of time stretching back to the beginning of the Finiglacial period.

and of Nüesch, who dated the Magdalenian site of Schweizersbild to 22,000 B.C.

The withdrawal of the ice-sheet from Scandinavia is relevant to archaeo-

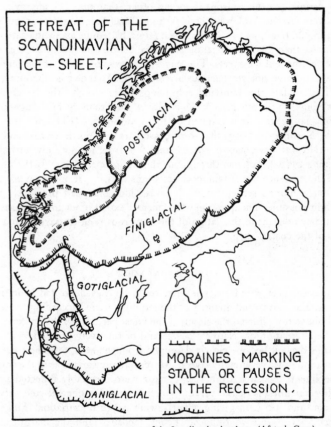

Fig. 1. Showing the retreat stages of the Scandinavian ice-sheet. (After de Geer.)

logy mainly in an indirect way through the changes of sea-level, of climate, of vegetation and of fauna which it induced. But in one respect the relevance is direct; it was only by the withdrawal of the ice that Scandinavia was

3

progressively laid open to the settlement of man. From this it follows that for any archaeological site within the region across which the ice-sheet withdrew, a maximum date can be obtained directly from its position. It is thus certain for this reason, if for no other, that the rock-engravings at Landverk (Arctic Art Group, style A) and Glösa (Arctic Art Group, style B), both in Jämtland, and at Nämnforsen (style B), Ångermanland, date from no earlier than the Finiglacial period, since before this time their sites were under permanent ice-sheets. The stages of regression north of the centre of dispersion have not yet been accurately mapped, and it is, therefore, impossible to date the Jämtland engravings more closely; the Nämnforsen engravings, on the other hand, can hardly be older than the final stages of the Finiglacial period. It is claimed by many authorities (Ekholm, 1925 and 1926; Nordhagen, 1933) that some coastal areas in north-western and northern Norway have been to some extent free from ice not only during the last inter-glacial, but also throughout the last glacial phase. If this is true (and the evidence for certain localities seems decisive) it opens up possibilities for a human settlement of the area older than had previously been thought possible. The question of the former extent of ice in Scandinavia is peculiarly relevant to the dating of the numerous rock-engravings and flint sites of the coastal strip.

GEOCHRONOLOGY

As the ice-sheet withdrew, fine mud sediment was deposited in its melt-waters. The nature and quantity of the sediment varied according to season, the bulk settling during the summer, the finest particles in the winter. Thus by the alternation of relatively coarse and of relatively fine sediment each season's deposit became clearly delimited from the next, forming a distinct lamination or varve (literally layer). Moreover, any variations in the amount of sediment deposited from year to year were inevitably reflected in the relative thicknesses of the varves, which varied as a general rule between 0·2 cm. and 3·0 cm., giving a fairly wide range of variation. Since the annual varves were continuously being deposited and the margin of ice gradually moved away northwards (except for the relatively short stadia marked by the moraines), the sediments resemble at the present time a pack of playing cards sprawling on a table, each card occurring in a definite relation to all the other cards, but all the cards resting one above the other in

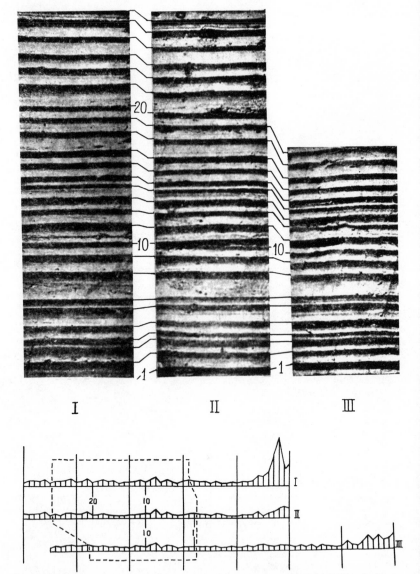

PLATE I. (Above.) Three samples of varved clay from the valley of the Kalajoki River in Ostrobothnia. Sample I is from a locality 6 kilometres and sample II 2 kilometres north-west of the
church of Haapajärvi; sample III is from 8 kilometres south-east of the same church. The
three samples connect with each other as illustrated.

(Below.) Diagram of the connected clay samples, showing variations in the thickness of the
varves. The bottom of the sections is on the right of the diagram. The dotted line encloses the
part of the samples illustrated above. (After Sauramo.)

direct vertical succession at no single place. The complete sequence of sediments can be established, therefore, only by the correlation of a number of sections situated at intervals apart. Once this can be achieved, and the number of varves between two points on the course of the retreat of the ice-sheet accurately counted, then clearly the chronology of that particular phase of retreat has been accurately established. It is the chronological potentialities of these sediments that makes them of such significance, not only for the late glacial and post-glacial natural history of Scandinavia, but also for archaeology.

The first to advance the view that there might be a close connection between the clay laminae and the annual deposition of the retreating ice was Baron G. de Geer (de Geer, 1884), and it is to this Swedish scientist that we owe the development of the whole technique of geochronology. It took de Geer twenty years before he succeeded, in 1904, in the task of correlating sections at some distance apart. In the following years he successfully linked up a series of sections, at an average distance apart of about 1 kilometre, extending from Scania to the point in south Jämtland where the inland ice finally parted into two. The wide distribution of individual varves, frequently exceeding 50 kilometres, and the regularity observed in the sequences of varves of varying thicknesses convinced him finally that his original speculations were correct, and in 1910 he was able to read his famous paper "A Geochronology of the last 12,000 years" to the International Geological Congress at Stockholm (de Geer, 1910).

The method of correlation initiated by de Geer and adopted by his followers is extremely simple (Pl. I). The vertical clay sections are cut clean, the varves are numbered and their thicknesses measured. These measurements are then recorded graphically by horizontal lines of proportionate lengths placed one above the other at equal distances against a vertical line. By connecting the unequal extremities a characteristic profile is obtained, which represents accurately the variations in the thickness of the annual sedimentation throughout the section. Correlations between neighbouring sections can then be made by visual comparison of their diagrams, the occurrence in both of a characteristic sequence of varying thicknesses acting as the connecting links. The correct distance between the sections necessary to secure a sufficient overlap can be found only by experience.

The chronological results first obtained in Sweden by de Geer related to the time taken by the ice to retreat from Scania to its point of bi-partition in southern Jämtland, a period of some five thousand years. His pupil R. Lidén was able at a later date to measure the period of time that has elapsed since the bi-partition of the ice (*i.e.* post-glacial time), on the basis of detailed work on the varve series along the Ångerman river, which gives an additional period of 8700 years (de Geer, 1928, p. 310) with a possibility of error that is not thought to exceed 100 years. The method has also been applied to Finland by Sauramo, who finds that the whole country south of the Oulu river was released from its ice-sheet in about 2800 years (Sauramo, 1929, pp. 51–6). Although the work has been done quite independently in the two countries, such correlations as have so far been made between the profiles of varved sediments from Finland and Sweden have revealed closely similar results.

At present geochronology has yielded results of approximate accuracy only, but already it has produced a natural system of chronology for the past twelve millennia that is not approached by any chronology based upon the development of human history. Leaving out of account entirely discredited systems, Egyptian chronology covers only half the period of geochronology and for its earlier stages, at least, commands far less general assent. Such chronology as there is for North-western Europe during the last two millennia B.C. depends ultimately on Egypt by a series of links, each one of which introduces an element of doubt, so that by the time one reaches the shores of the Baltic very little of value remains. In our area and for post-glacial time, geochronology holds the field, and it seems safe to predict that within the next generation it will have furnished a system of natural chronology that may have its effect on the dating of the earlier phases of human history in Egypt and the Near East. The tendency for archaeologists to date simpler cultures in peripheral areas in terms of the richer developments of the cradle-lands of higher civilisation is a natural and understandable one, but it was born of a necessity that no longer obtains. A complete reversal of the process cannot be expected until geochronology has been perfected in its home area and extended over a wider surface of the earth. Final accuracy within Scandinavia will be attained when extensive series of sediments have been correlated exactly, varve by varve, along a number of lines through different parts of Sweden and Finland drawn along the glacial retreat. The study of varve sediments in other parts of the world is already progressing, and important work has been done in the United States and Canada (Antevs, 1922 and 1925), Argentine, Chile, the Himalayas and Iceland (de Geer, 1928, p. 312). The astonishing fact is that, despite the influence of local conditions, a high degree of correlation has been observed between varve series situated in these widely separated areas and the key series in Sweden. This has suggested to de Geer and his followers that there must be some common cause of a cosmic nature, and that "varve-variation in its general features is a function of solar radiation", so that the chronology of the last twelve millennia in the history of Northern Europe has ultimately been provided by the sun.

CHANGES IN THE MUTUAL RELATIONS OF LAND AND SEA

The melting of the quaternary ice-sheet affected relative land and sea levels in Northern Europe in two distinct ways. First the release of the vast quantities of water locked up in the ice-sheet added to the volume of sea-water and tended to raise its level in relation to the land, inducing what is known as a eustatic rise of sea-level. Secondly the removal of the concentrated weight of the ice-sheet resulted in a recovery of the earth's crust or an isostatic rise of land.

Geologists vary in the weight they attach to each of these factors, but of their existence there is room for no serious doubt. To take first the eustatic factor, it will be obvious that the glacial melt-water must have added to the general volume of sea; the only field for argument concerns the proportion of this addition to the total sea-water, and its possible effect on raising the general sea-level. Albrecht Penck has calculated[1] that the melting of the ice-sheet of the northern hemisphere, covering some 490,000 square miles, would release sufficient water to raise the level of all the seas of the world by as much as 66·5 metres or about 210 feet. Antevs (1928, p. 81) estimated its volume in excess of its present size at 32,800,000 cubic kilometres, and stated that its melting would be sufficient to raise the level of the seas by as much as 272 feet. Since the excess volume of the ice-sheet of the southern hemisphere could affect the sea-level by no greater amount than 33 feet, the question of whether the glaciations of the two hemispheres were synchronous does not really affect our argument.

The isostatic theory is equally simple. The modern conception of the earth's crust as a thin skin or a floating raft makes it easy to grasp the essentials of what is meant by isostatic movement of land. The crust is con-

[1] Penck assumes that the northern ice-sheets averaged 1000 metres in thickness. On the evidence of the vertical distribution of glacial erratics and of glacially striated rocks Tanner estimates that near the centre of dispersal in Scandinavia the northern Pleistocene ice-sheet was 3570 metres thick (Tanner, 1930, p. 517).

ceived of as sinking locally under the weight of the ice-cap and recovering gradually as the load decreased with the melting of the ice. Strong presumption for this view is afforded by the fact that in the case of the Scandinavian ice-sheet the area of maximum crustal depression[1] coincides with the centre of glacial dispersal.

It will be obvious that the operation of the eustatic and isostatic factors went on side by side, and that the net result in terms of land movement and geographical evolution can be explained only by the interaction of these factors. An important distinction must be drawn between the two factors involved; whereas the eustatic rise of sea-level was constant the world over, isostatic movement varied according as the locality was central or peripheral to the heart of the glaciated area. In areas subject to the maximum depression by the load of the ice-cap the amount of recovery or isostatic movement was correspondingly greater than in the less affected peripheral areas. The net effect, therefore, of the interaction of the eustatic and isostatic factors on land and sea levels varied according to situation in relation to the centre of glaciation. Whereas in peripheral regions the sea tended to gain on the land, in more central areas the isostatic recovery of the land was always more powerful, after the initial stages, than the eustatic rise of sea-level. The fact that, for a brief period at the beginning, the sea gained on the land even in central areas is explained on the theory that, whereas the release of melt-water had an immediate eustatic effect, a certain time lag elapsed before the isostatic recovery began.

That alterations in the mutual relations of land and sea have in fact taken place in Northern Europe during the post-glacial period is manifest from evidence of two distinct kinds—that relating to the formerly greater elevation of land, and that implying a relatively higher sea-level. The occurrence of land phenomena at present under the sea affords the most satisfactory evidence of the first kind; the so-called 'submerged forests'—really peat-beds containing tree remains—to be seen at low water at many points on the British, North Sea and Baltic coasts, and the submerged peat or 'moorlog' of the North Sea bed are good examples.

Similar to this submarine evidence is that derived from deep borings or excavations in flat areas lying open to the sea. At the base of the flat region enclosed between the rivers Weser and Wümme in the neighbourhood of

---

[1] Isobases or contours of the depression have been constructed for large parts of Scandinavia, being based upon the altitudes above modern sea-level of the highest terraces.

PLATE II. The extinct beach of the *Litorina* Sea at Vamlingbo on the island of Gotland. The human figure on the left gives an idea of the scale. (After Munthe.)

Bremen a peat-bed has been found at several feet below modern sea-level (Overbeck and Schmitz, 1931). In the English fenland a peat-bed has been examined by excavation down to $22\frac{1}{2}$ feet below modern sea-level and found to contain relics of land fauna and the cultural remains of human settlement (Clark, 1934). Old land-surfaces, such as the 'Lyonesse surface' of the Essex coast, covered by modern high tides, but exposed at certain low tides, bear witness to the same phenomenon, if to a less marked degree.

The clearest kind of evidence for a period of marine transgression is that afforded by raised beaches or extinct coast-lines, such as those well known in Scandinavia and Scotland. The Jära Bank of Scania (Fig. 2), representing the coast of the maximum extension of the *Litorina* Sea and overlying a peat-bed, is an excellent example. I illustrate a stretch of the beach of the *Litorina* Sea on the Island of Gotland (Pl. II), which has been intensively

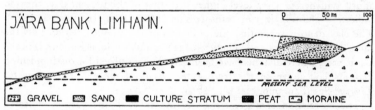

Fig. 2. Section through the Jära Bank at Limhamn, Scania, showing the position of the settlement in relation to the ancient sea-beach.

studied for the history of the Baltic (Munthe, Hede and von Post, 1924), as have also been many other parts of Scandinavia. In Britain raised beaches of this period occur outside the area with which this book is immediately concerned, but in Scotland and northern Ireland they are prominent and well known.

An equally certain indication of a sea-level higher than that obtaining at the present day is given by the inland occurrence of clays and silts deposited either by the sea or at least under marine influences. The marine nature of the deposits can be decided by investigation of minute sub-fossil organisms, such as diatoms[1] and *foraminifera*,[2] or by the occurrence of marine molluscs or even of marine mammals. The estuarine carse clays of the firths of Forth

[1] Diatoms are microscopic unicellular plants. Over 10,000 species are known to exist. Their silicious outer covering cases survive in sedimentary deposits. Some species are adapted to fresh water and others to salt; hence their value as indicators of relative salinity.

[2] *Foraminifera* are mainly marine, but some species are tolerant of brackish water.

9

and Tay, formed at a period when the Highlands were linked to the south of Scotland only by a narrow isthmus, provide a good example of this kind of evidence. They occur in thicknesses of from 10 to 40 feet, frequently overlying a thin peat bed with tree remains, and on their margins sometimes reach a height of as much as 45 feet above modern sea-level, indicating a former sea-level about 50 feet above that now obtaining (Geikie, 1881, pp. 394 ff.). In these carse clays of Scotland the remains of whales have frequently been found. Whale and seal remains have also frequently been found up to heights of 80 metres and more in different parts of Scandinavia (Sauramo, 1929, p. 58). The silt and clay deposits found overlying the lower peat-bed of the English fenland have yielded sufficient *foraminifera* to indicate access of marine water at the period of their formation, following the period of relative land-elevation or marine regression; though they do not afford evidence of a sea-level higher than that of the present day, they do indicate a phase of marine transgression (Macfadyen, 1933 (1) and (2)). The clay deposit separating the peat-beds of the Bremen region tells the same story (Overbeck and Schmitz, 1931). Similar evidence abounds in the Baltic area, where diatoms have been extensively utilised for distinguishing deposits laid down in the fresh-water *Ancylus* Lake and the salt-water *Litorina* Sea (Sauramo, 1929, p. 47).

The correlation of a great mass of evidences of the nature indicated concerned with alterations in the mutual relations of land and sea allows us to formulate certain conclusions of importance to archaeology. It should be stressed, at the outset, that much still remains obscure. The complexity of the interaction of such relatively simple factors as are described on pp. 7 and 8 is very great when we come down from theory to investigating local problems as they exist in fact. In broad outline, however, the history of the Baltic as outlined by Munthe (1910) and his collaborators and successors is fairly well established, and will be summarised briefly here as amended by Sauramo (1929, pp. 69–79) and as adopted by Nordhagen (1933):

The Baltic Ice-dammed Lake (? 8300 B.C.).

During the Götiglacial phase of glacial retreat the southern and south-western parts of the Baltic area stood far higher in relation to the sea than is now the case, forming a solid land-mass from Jutland to Småland, which together with the retreating ice-margin on the north shut off the Baltic from the sea; areas in proximity to the ice-sheet, however, were mainly under water, as for example the Swedish provinces of Bohuslän and Östergötland, the western part of Esthonia and the small extent of Finland that was yet free from the ice.

The Yoldia Sea (8300–7800 B.C.).

During early Finiglacial times the retreating ice-sheet left a breach to the north of Götland, the waters of the ice-dammed lake discharged themselves into the sea, and marine diatoms and molluscs, including among the latter *Yoldia arctica*, came in with the salt water. The solid land-mass from Jutland to Småland continued, and western Esthonia and southern Finland emerged considerably above the waters. As in the previous period the areas immediately peripheral to the ice-sheet were under water—the water through which sank the fine mud sediments that form the basis of geochronology.

The Ancylus Lake (7800–5000 B.C.).

The emergence, during the latter part of Finiglacial time, of northern Götland, of Svealand and of south-eastern Norway shut off the Baltic and converted it once more into a lake, in which abounded fresh-water diatoms and molluscs, including the bivalve *Ancylus fluviatilis*. The recovery of land which converted the *Yoldia* Sea into the *Ancylus* Lake was less rapid in areas farther from the centre of isostatic disturbance, and in these regions, the coasts of Esthonia, Latvia, Lithuania, north Germany and the Jutland-Sweden land-mass, the water gained on the land. Yet it is important to notice that, though the Jutland-Swedish land-mass had much diminished, it still afforded a land-bridge until the end of the period of the *Ancylus* Lake. At first this drained away by Lake Vänern, but finally the eustatic rise of the external sea caused a junction to be made between the Kattegatt and the *Ancylus* Lake, the level of which had risen with the accumulation of glacial melt-water.

The Litorina Sea.

The reunion of the waters of the Baltic and of the Kattegatt finally brought to an end the history of the Baltic as a lake. In the waters of the *Litorina* Sea salt-water diatoms abounded, and its greater depth seems (Wright, 1914, p. 352) to have been responsible for the fact that it was salter than the modern Baltic. Among the salt-water mollusca was the periwinkle *Litorina litorea*. The marine transgression, which reached its maximum by 4500 or 4000 B.C., was pronounced in peripheral regions but absent entirely from areas closer to the old centre of glacial dispersion. The Oslo region, eastern Svealand and Finland continued their rise from the waters, but in Denmark and south Sweden the *Litorina* beaches are stranded above the modern sea-level. The explanation advanced by Ramsay (1926) is that, whereas in regions near the old centre of dispersion of the northern ice-sheet the isostatic recovery of the land was always more rapid than the eustatic rise of sea-level, in peripheral regions the same eustatic rise had only to compete with a less degree of isostatic recovery; in central regions the sea never succeeded in gaining on the land, whereas in peripheral regions the sea won decisively and transgressed over the land.

Outside the Baltic intensive investigation of the Oslo region (Brøgger, W. C., 1901) has proved that after an early phase of depression the area has risen continuously from the sea. So far as is known this holds true for the coasts of Norway up to Finnmark, the earlier beach-lines standing at a higher level than the younger.

The evidence for the North Sea is as yet incomplete, but it shows a consistent sequence of events—a period of regression, followed by one of marine transgression. The dredging of peat off the west coast of Jutland, in the estuaries of the Weser and the Jade (Erdtman, 1928, part II; Overbeck and Schmitz, 1931) and off the coasts of the Frisian Islands has demonstrated a former greater extension of land along the sea-board from Jutland to Holland. This is supported by borings at inland sites in north-west Germany, where peat-beds are found several feet below sea-level, as for example in the Oldenbroker Moor, Oldenburg, and in the flat regions near the confluence of the Weser and the Wümme in the Bremen neighbourhood (Overbeck and Schmitz, 1931); in both the cases cited the peat-beds lying below present sea-level were covered by clays showing marine influence and regarded as equivalent to, though not necessarily contemporary with, the *Litorina* transgression of the Baltic. Similar evidence is afforded by the French coast from Normandy to Picardy and, indeed, to Brittany. The extent of the regression, which followed the Monastirien raised beaches, is estimated by Dubois (1924, p. 245 and pp. 275–6) to have been at least 30 metres on the evidence of the thickness of alluvial deposits revealed by bores at Petitville and Quillebœuf at the mouth of the Seine. At the time of the regression Dubois maintains that the English Channel could not have been very wide: "le détroit fut exondé totalement ou tout au plus occupé par un cours d'eau ou un bras de mer très étroit tels certains 'sund' danois". The cross-section of the English Channel between Dungeness and Cap Gris Nez (Hallez, 1899; Erdtman, 1928, part III) shows that a regression of 30 metres would leave an arm of the sea no more than 8 or 9 kilometres across. The modern version[1] of the Channel owes its existence to the 'transgression flandrienne',[2] which is considered to correspond to the *Litorina* transgression of the Baltic. It seems important to point out, however, that

[1] The 'Monastirien' raised beach (+11 to +15 metres) of north France clearly marks a version of the Channel. Eustatic rises of sea-level during inter-glacial phases of the Pleistocene probably gave rise to more than one earlier Channel.

[2] The Flanders-Picardy transgression certainly reached Brittany and caused the well-known submergence of the stone circles of the island of Erlanic, Morbihan (De Morgan, 1924, p. 19, fig. 6).

there is no evidence to prove that the transgression observed on the coast of north France happened at the same time as the *Litorina* transgression, though it is undoubtedly true that the sequence of events is broadly similar.

Striking evidence of regression and subsequent transgression is furnished by the 'moorlog' occurring on the floor of parts of the North Sea. According to Whitehead and Goodchilde (1909–10) it is usually found on the sand slopes of the Dogger Bank at a depth of 22 or 23 fathoms, though at the south-west end of the Bank it occurs at the top as well as on the slopes. The lumps dredged up by fishermen are sometimes as much as 5 or 6 feet long, but never more than 18 inches thick. It is described as light brown to black in colour, varying in texture from a coarse mossy deposit to a fine hard mass of a wood-like texture. It is fissile, splitting easily into laminae, and consists mainly of plant remains, stems and roots of trees, seeds, leaves and mosses, as well as the elytra of beetles.[1] The distribution of the 'moorlog' is given by Fig. 3, after Clement Reid with additions. The definite and restricted character of the distribution of the deposit seems to indicate that it was pulled up by the trawls from *in situ*; had it been merely drifted deposit its occurrence would be more haphazard. The general result of the examination of the beetle elytra (see footnote) and of the plant remains suggested to Clement Reid that "the deposit comes from the middle of some vast fen, so far from rising land that all terruginous material has been strained out of the peaty water, which probably ran, or rather stood, clear and brown. The vegetation...consists exclusively of swamp species....The sea was probably some distance away, as there is no sign of brackish-water plants, or even of plants which usually occur within reach of an occasional tide." The age of the deposit will be discussed in a subsequent section, dealing with post-glacial forest history, as fortunately the 'moorlog' is fairly rich in fossil tree pollen. A piece of archaeological evidence which corroborates Clement Reid's conclusions is the notched bone point (form 6) discovered accidentally

---

[1] G. C. Champion identified the following beetles from 'moorlog' samples obtained by Clement Reid:

Species	Natural habitats
Cyclonotum orbiculare	
Apion sp. (possibly *humile*) }	Marshes
Baris pilistriata (Steph.?)	
Chlaenius holosericeus	Fens
Philhydrus sp.	Fresh water
Donacia vulgaris (*typhae*) }	Found on *Typha* (reed-mace), etc.
D. claviceps (*menyanthides*)	
Calathus sp. (prob. *flavipes*) }	Sandy places
Notophilus sp. (*aquaticus* or *palustris*)	

13

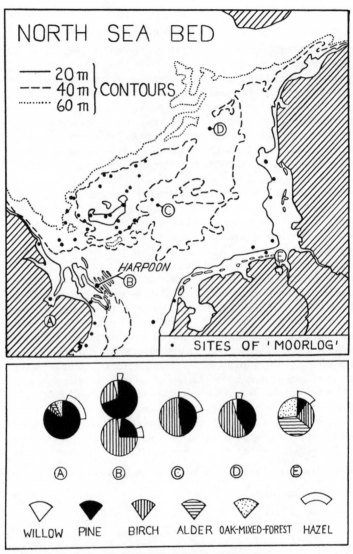

Fig. 3. (Above.) Distribution of finds of 'moorlog' from the North Sea bed.
(Below.) Characteristic pollen spectra of samples from the North Sea bed (B–D) and from marginal regions (A, E).

in a lump of 'moorlog' dredged up by the trawler *Colinda* in 1932 between the Leman and Ower Banks (Burkitt, 1932; Clark, 1932, p. 115). The point was beautifully preserved and was found in breaking open a large lump of 'moorlog' casually before it was returned to the sea; the conclusion, therefore, that the object was lost while the 'moorlog' was actually forming and while the Dogger Bank was yet a fresh-water fen, seems beyond reasonable doubt.

The 'moorlog' evidence, which fits in very well with the coastal evidence from Brittany to Jutland, is further supported by the fact that peat-beds occur in the fenland of eastern England many feet below present sea-level, beneath clay and silt deposits, showing varying degrees of marine influence. Moreover at every low tide the sea regresses from a fraction of the old landsurface off the Essex coast, sometimes known as the 'Lyonesse' surface, which at certain points is rich in archaeological remains (Warren, 1912).

More will be said about the dating of the regression and transgression, noted on both sides of the North Sea and for the Dogger Bank itself, in the section dealing with the methods of pollen analysis and their application to the dating of land and sea movements. I shall now consider briefly the chief ways in which the history of the mutual relations of land and sea are relevant to the archaeology of the area.

Of primary importance for this chapter is the chronological significance of these changes, which depends on the fundamental fact that human settlement, apart from pile-dwelling settlement of which the traces are usually easily to be detected, is possible only at or above the sea-level of the time. Where, therefore, there has been, as in Finland and Norway, a continuous emergence of the land since the beginning of human settlement, it should be clear that the maximum age of any site within the total range of regression can be gauged directly by observing its relation to sea-levels either ancient or modern.[1] It seems important to point out that, unless the site yields certain indications of subsistence by sea fish or shell-fish or is associated unmistakably with an old coast-line,[2] it is impossible to arrive at more than a maximum date for it along these lines; a site giving no evidence of having been situated at or immediately above sea-level might have been much younger than the beach at the same level in relation to modern sea-level.

A famous example of the method of dating archaeological cultures in

[1] If the history of the coast movement is known these are equally useful.
[2] The mere fact of a site being found on an old beach does not ensure this. It must show other signs of contemporaneity.

relation to post-glacial regression is afforded by the work of W. C. Brøgger (1905) in the Oslo region, who found the following sequence:

Archaeological cultures	Height of ancient sea-level above modern sea-level
Nøstvet axe culture	70 metres to
Stone axes with stump butts and circular sections—the type found at many Danish sites of the Ertebølle culture	50 metres to
Pointed butted and thin-butted axes of Megalithic type	25 metres to
Thick-butted axes and perforated battle-axes	15 metres to
By the end of the Bronze Age	0 metre

Post-glacial changes of sea-level have also thrown light on the relative dating of different styles of rock-engravings of the Arctic Art Group. A group of engravings in style B (see p. 184), for example, is found in the Oslo-Drammen region at various levels between 70 metres and 53 metres above present sea-level; it is, therefore, possible to say that they cannot by long antedate the arrival of the stump-butted stone axe, and may be much younger. Or, again, it is found in Northern Norway that engravings of the naturalistic and primitive style A occur on the average at considerably higher levels in relation to the sea than do engravings of the more schematic style B (see p. 184), the strand-line evidence thus helping to confirm the sequence indicated on stylistic grounds. The dating of the dwelling-place sites of the Fosna and Komsa cultures of the Norwegian coast will, also, largely have to depend on a study of their relationships to old strand-lines, since until now they have yielded no fauna; at present less detailed information about earlier sea-levels is available for the north-west and northern coasts of Norway, but it has already been shown from their relationship to old strand-lines that the Finnmark sites may date back to the time of an early phase of the *Ancylus* Lake (Tanner, 1930). In no part of Northern Europe has the emergence of the land from the waters been more dramatic than in Finland. At the time of the Baltic ice-dammed lake almost the whole country lay under the ice-sheet and, except for small areas on either side of Lake Ladoga, the rest lay submerged beneath the waters of the lake; from that time forward the country rose in the wake of the retreating ice, and gradually became available to human settlement. This has been of great assistance to archaeology in the determination of the relative ages of the various dwelling-place cultures of the area. Europaeus, on the basis of levels, has distinguished no less than five groups (Europaeus, 1926). Fig. 4 illustrates the distribution in the south of the coastal province of Nyland of the most primitive type of dwelling-place equipped with rough stone axes but without pottery and contem-

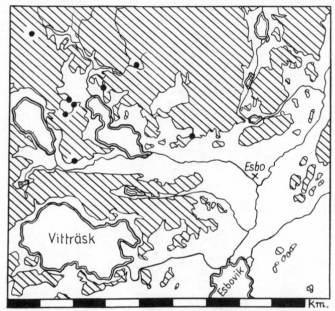

Fig. 4. Map of the district of Esbo, in the province of Nyland, Finland, showing the area above the sea at the time of the *Litorina* maximum, and the sites of the earliest dwelling-places (Suomusjärvi culture). Esbovik, shown at the bottom of the map, is an inlet of the Gulf of Finland. (After Europaeus.)

porary with the Suomusjärvi culture of western Finland; the sites all occur at or above the local level of the *Litorina* Sea at its maximum (34 m. above present sea-level), unlike the sites with cord-impressed pottery which occur below this level (Europaeus, 1922, pl. XVIII (map)).

In areas where the relations between land and sea have been more complex than in Norway and Finland greater care has to be taken in drawing

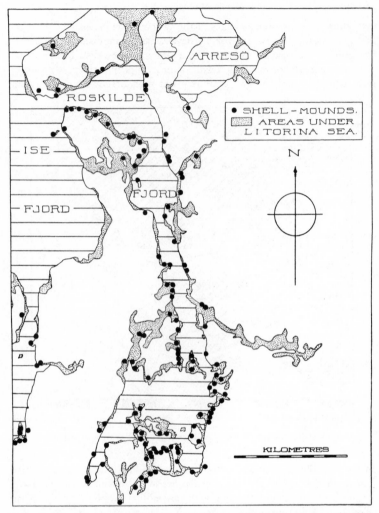

Fig. 5. Map illustrating the distribution of kitchen-middens or shell-mounds on the shores of Roskilde and Ise fjords, Zealand, Denmark. It will be observed that the great majority of the shell-mounds adhere to the *Litorina* coast-line rather than to the modern coast-line, except where these coincide. (After Milthers.)

conclusions merely from the positions of sites. Sometimes this is made possible by the adherence of midden sites to marked strand-lines as in the case of the kitchen-middens of Zealand. As illustrated by Fig. 5, which gives the distribution of these sites in the neighbourhood of Roskilde fjord, the vast majority of the middens are found on the strand-line of the maximum extension of the *Litorina* Sea, indicating that as a group they date from this period; the fact that a few are found in the area of the transgression shows that the middens belong in some cases to a later date, which is confirmed by the archaeological evidence. The distribution of dwelling-places dating from the Passage-grave period on the other hand, as given by our Fig. 6 for the Island of Gotland, shows that these are later than the *Litorina* maximum, since they occur below the coast-line of this period, except for inland sites or those situated on the north-west coast of the island where the ground is relatively high with cliffs to the sea. The relationship of dwelling-place sites to the *Litorina* maximum can also be obtained by vertical sections. The site of Brabrand Sø, Jutland, for example, now situated at the east end of the lake of Brabrand, was once on the shore of a small island at the eastern extremity of a fjord; the section (Fig. 7) shows quite clearly:

(*g*) the period of relative land-elevation of the *Ancylus* Lake period, marked by a peat bed, below modern sea-level;

(*e*) the beginning of marine transgression marked by a gravel beach;

(*c*) a further stage of transgression marked by sand;

(*d*) the maximum of the depression marked by a dark clay layer containing *Litorina litorea* and other shells typical of the interior of fjords of the *Litorina* Sea, and deposited in at least a metre of water;

(*c*) the recovery from the transgression marked first of all by sand;

(*a, b*) and finally by gravel.

Observation of the stratigraphical relationship to the dark clay layer of archaeological objects excavated from the section has confirmed the evidence of age afforded by the distribution of kitchen-middens and has given important information as to the relative chronology of separate traits of the culture. A further example of the chronological value of changes of sea-level is afforded by the Höganäs section in Scania, described on p. 40.

The chronological importance of correlating early dwelling-place sites and old sea-levels has made the accurate determinations of the situation and extent of such sites of especial significance. In cases where the site has few structural features the technique of phosphate analysis, evolved by

GOTLAND

0   5   10   15 Km.

— LITORINA COAST-LINE
--- MODERN COAST-LINE
● DWELLING-PLACE SITES
   OF PASSAGE-GRAVE AGE

Fig. 6. Map illustrating the distribution of dwelling-place sites, dating from the Passage-grave period, in the Island of Gotland, in relation to the *Litorina* and modern coast-lines. (After Munthe, Hede and von Post, 1924.)

20

Arrhenius (1930) and applied by Schnell (1932) to a number of Swedish dwelling-place sites, has been of considerable assistance. The method depends on the fact that in areas of intense human settlement the phosphate content of the soil, owing to the decay of discarded bones, tends to be considerably higher than in areas merely contiguous to such settlement, and much higher than those completely beyond the influence of settlement. It has been found, in fact, that the soil of an area of intensive settlement may contain easily as much as fifty times the proportion of phosphate as ordinary soil. The unit by which the phosphate content is measured is termed a phosphate degree and is equivalent to a yield of 1/1000 per cent. of phosphate under the action of citric acid at a strength of 2 per cent. In the investigation

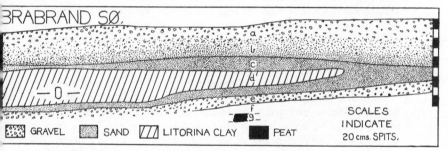

Fig. 7. Section through the site of Brabrand Sø, Jutland. Modern sea-level is indicated by –O–.
(After Thomsen and Jessen, A.)

of a dwelling-site the method followed by Schnell is to take series of soil samples at equal intervals along a series of straight lines radiating from some central point, preferably the supposed centre of settlement as indicated by objects or other features. Having obtained values for each point in terms of phosphate degrees it is possible to construct contour maps (*e.g.* Schnell, 1932, fig. 34) illustrating the varying densities of phosphate content, and these phosphate contours may then be collated with the height contours. The results can also be illustrated for any given line of samples by means of a graph, which can easily be compared directly with an accurate section of the site. By these means sites without any kind of structural feature can be accurately delimited and related to sea-level. Similar diagrams can be constructed for the frequency of potsherds, and it is reassuring to find that, where both lines of enquiry are pursued at the same site, the results have been found to be in close agreement (*e.g.* Schnell, 1932, fig. 33).

The fact that wide areas of land, which were available to human settlement during the first two periods of the Mesolithic, are now submerged beneath the sea is important archaeologically for two main reasons. In the first place it means that areas at present separated by sea formed during the mainland period of the North Sea, of Denmark, south Sweden, and of north Germany, parts of a continuous land area. This goes far to explain the remarkable homogeneity of culture found over the north European plain from south-eastern Britain to Esthonia and Poland, and from Scania and Bohuslän to Brandenburg during this period (see pp. 124 ff.). Finds of paddle-rudders (Fig. 39) testify to navigation of a sort, but it is unlikely that there was at this period much navigation, if any, across the open sea. In any case the wide distribution of specialised forms, which, in spite of undoubted local variations of culture, can frequently be noted (*e.g.* pp. 125–127), receives an adequate explanation only from the palaeo-geographical fact that the area of their occurrence formed at that time a continuous land-surface or at the least was less broken than at the present.

Secondly, the marine transgression which followed the mainland period has undoubtedly destroyed a vast amount of archaeological evidence, a fact which should be taken into account more than is normally the case in considering general questions of the origin and diffusion of culture. Although many of the inland sites of periods I and II have been lost, it is probable that sufficient evidence remains from the isolated areas of the old habitat that remain above sea-level to reconstruct their character in so far as this is archaeologically possible. The important fact, which has been sadly neglected in many archaeological speculations, is that the entire coastal culture of periods I and II has been lost for the whole extent of mainland now submerged.[1] It would be possible to take comfort from the fact that such cultures might not have existed were it not eminently probable that they

[1] This is eminently true also for the Upper Palaeolithic period. It has frequently been observed that sea fish, of the kinds which flourish near the coast, are depicted in the French Cave Art (Breuil, and Saint-Périer, 1927, p. 163), that the remains of fish occur in the cave deposits, and that sea shells were sometimes used for personal adornment. This has rightly suggested to several authors that the cave-dwellers lived in some kind of contact, either by trade or by seasonal migration, with the sea-coast. It has not been suggested from faunal studies that the occupation of the caves was of a seasonal nature, and it is, therefore, not unreasonable to suggest that the coasts supported tribes with a material culture adapted for the purpose and differing almost inevitably from that of the cave-dwellers. The fish and shells may very well have reached the caves not by any direct contact, but by a number of links, after the common manner of primitive trade.

not only existed, but flourished under conditions more favourable than those obtaining inland. That such coastal sites existed is suggested in theory by the fact that, where the basis of subsistence is limited to hunting, fishing and collecting, the sea-shore, unless for some reason unfavourable, is likely to be specially sought after. When to this is added the fact that, wherever old strand-lines exist above modern sea-level in Northern Europe, they are found to have been the foci of human settlement,[1] then it would be unreasonable to suggest that the same was not true of the submerged coasts of the old mainland. Moreover, there is good reason for believing that the coast of the old mainland between east Yorkshire and north Jutland must have been especially favourable for settlement; the influence of the Gulf Stream must have served to temper in the coastal regions the still cold climate of period I and the extremes of the continental climate of period II. Direct evidence of the nature of these submerged coastal cultures will in all probability never be forthcoming, but it is as well to recognise the gaps in existing evidence.

ALTERATIONS OF CLIMATE

During the post-glacial period the climate of North-western Europe underwent changes or fluctuations in respect both of precipitation and of temperature. I shall discuss precipitation first, because studies of this factor have given rise to the terminology currently applied to the major climate phases of the post-glacial period. According to Blytt and Sernander, after a transitional sub-arctic period, the climate of North-western Europe underwent a twice repeated cycle of warm dry 'continental' and warm damp 'oceanic' phases, which they called 'Boreal' and 'Atlantic', 'Sub-boreal' and 'Sub-atlantic'.[2] The chief class of evidence brought forward by Blytt (1882) in support of his theory related to the stratigraphy of peat-bogs, in which forest horizons, marked by tree stumps, were interpreted as indicating dry phases separating wet periods of peat-formation. Sernander (1908) reaffirmed this interpretation of bog evidence, and showed how it fitted into analogous evidence of fluctuations in precipitation, observed by other workers. A similar sequence had been noted by Hulth (1898) in certain calcareous tufa

---

[1] *E.g.* the coastal dwelling-sites of the Komsa and Fosna cultures of Norway, the Swedish dwelling-place cultures, and the early kitchen-middens of Denmark.

[2] However the theories of Blytt and Sernander are modified in the future, it is fairly certain that their terminology will survive because it has become so widely current.

deposits, in which tufa formation was temporarily interrupted by the reduction of springs and mould beds formed in their place during dry phases, and Gavelin's work on the fluctuations of lake-levels (1907) pointed in the same direction. In 1923 Gams and Nordhagen demonstrated a similar sequence of fluctuations in precipitation for Central Europe. More recently (1928) Weber has described investigations in a north German peat-bog, which confirm once again the sequence established by Sernander in the following succession:

Deposits	Conditions	Periods
Upper *Sphagnum* peat	Indicating return of damp conditions	V. Sub-atlantic
Cotton-grass peat and heather	Marking a dry phase of a millennium, during which the lower *Sphagnum* peat was weathered. The so-called *Grenzhorizont* of German workers	IV. Sub-boreal
Lower *Sphagnum* peat	Indicating the onset of damp conditions, lasting long enough for the accumulation of 8 feet of leaves and stems of *Sphagnum*	III. Atlantic
Birch-pine forest	Indicating a relatively dry period	II. Boreal

The birch-pine forest was separated from late glacial clay by sand, marl and ooze deposits, which presumably formed during the Pre-boreal period. For the purpose of this book we are only concerned with the Pre-boreal, Boreal and Atlantic phases (periods I–III).

It is possible that Sernander's fluctuations of rainfall may be connected to some extent with the geographical changes of the period. Certainly it is true that the 'continental' Boreal is largely contemporary with the period of land-elevation, whereas 'oceanic' Atlantic climate seems to have set in during the period of marine transgression in North-western Europe. Yet these changes in the relation of land and sea masses, though they may well have accentuated the fluctuations locally in peripheral regions, can hardly be counted sufficient to explain their occurrence in Central Europe. Most probably they are due to variations of solar radiation, which as Dr Simpson has shown (1934, pp. 428–9) can affect precipitation more than sufficiently to account for the phenomena under consideration.

More important perhaps than the fluctuations in precipitation are the changes of temperature which affected so profoundly the development of forests and of fauna. The curve of temperature, as conceived by Andersson (1905), Werth (1928) and many others, shows during the post-glacial period a steep rise from the cold of sub-arctic times to a maximum, from which it has receded to the present level. During the Pre-boreal (period I) the rise of temperature was slight, but during the Boreal (period II) it was rapid until it reached a maximum early in the Atlantic period, when the July temperature was $2\frac{1}{2}°$ C. higher than that of the present time; Werth (1928, p. 330) has summed up the situation by comparing the climate of northern Germany at the time of the *Litorina* Sea (period III) with that of the Rhineland at the present day. With the decline of temperature from the optimum we are not concerned as it lies outside our period.

The biological evidence for the climate curve of post-glacial time is singularly complete and unanimous in its implications. The study of marine molluscs has been especially fruitful because temperature is the chief climatic factor capable of influencing marine organisms to any marked extent. Molluscs at or near their geographical limit of distribution are particularly sensitive to changes of temperature, reacting either by a sudden increase or disappearance or else by some difference in relative size or development. Along the Skagerack there are disposed great shell-banks, which by their occurrence at varying levels above modern sea-level can easily be dated geologically in relation to land movement. By examining the molluscs of these shell-banks Antevs (1928, pp. 555–61) has been able to demonstrate the following sequence of events:

Age of shell-bank	Mollusc evidence	Temperature indicated
Period III	Several warm species, which have now withdrawn to warmer waters, e.g. *Tapes decussatus*	Warmer than to-day
Period II	Gradual invasion of southern forms	Rise of temperature to equal that of the present day
Period I	Dominant forms were those now not found south of the White Sea and the Spitsbergen Sea, e.g. *Portlandia arctica*, *Arca glacialis*, etc.	Sub-arctic temperature

Corroborative evidence for a temperature during period III in excess of that obtaining at the present day is given by the distribution of the common oyster in Norway. Whereas at the present day it is found no farther north than Lat. 66°, at the time of the climatic optimum it reached Lat. 70° (Nordhagen, 1933). Johansen (1906) has even ventured to calculate the probable July temperatures in Denmark on the basis of his studies of molluscs from successive deposits. He suggested a temperature of 8° C. for period I, 14° C.

for the middle of period II, and a maximum of 16°–17° C. for the period of the climatic optimum in period III. On the basis of the *Tapes* marine fauna of the Oslo region Andersson (1905) calculated that the maximum July temperature of period III was 2·3° C. in excess of the present time.

The evidence of land fauna suggests the same sequence of events. Johansen and Lynge (1917), working on the fresh-water mollusca of the district of Kalundborg, Zealand, traced a gradual immigration of southern forms into Denmark. The same fundamental change is shown by land mammals, cold-loving tundra and steppe species giving way to more temperate forest-dwelling forms. The common tortoise (*Emys orbicularis*) provides interesting evidence of the post-glacial warmth maximum (Bergholt, 1929). As shown by Fig. 8, the present northern limit of the common occurrence of the tortoise is a line drawn along the southern borders of Pomerania and Mecklenburg and up to the modern Danish-German frontier; fossil finds, indicated by dots on the map, have been made in recent deposits from eastern Jutland, the Danish Islands, Scania, Öland Island, and as far north as Östergötland.

The rise of temperature is also confirmed by very numerous botanical facts, both of a stratigraphical and of a distributional kind. Deposits dating from period I show very little pollen of forest trees, especially in the earlier stages, and it is certain that forests did not become significant until the temperature rose sufficiently. The late glacial clays of Scandinavia have yielded an arctic-alpine flora, *Dryas octopetala*, *Salix polaris*, *S. herbacea*, *S. reticulata*, and *Betula nana*, but the post-glacial deposits indicate the rise to importance of forest trees. The whole sequence of forest development described in the next section implies a progressive increase of temperature until period III. From his study of forest development in Sweden von Post (1924, p. 126) concluded that the post-glacial temperature maximum coincided with the peak of the oak-mixed-forests of period III.

The evidence derived from studies of the former distribution of vegetation is of two distinct kinds; it may concern horizontal distribution over wide geographical regions, or it may refer to vertical distribution on the slopes of a mountain system. Andersson's work on the distribution of the hazel in Scandinavia (1902, 1905) is the classic instance of the former type. Our Fig. 9 illustrates the substantial difference between the former distribution of the hazel, as indicated by fossil finds, and its modern distribution. Andersson calculates that since the temperature maximum of the post-glacial period the distribution of hazel has contracted by an area of some 84,000 kilometres, implying a loss of at least 2·4° C. The water-nut (*Trapa natans*) is another good example; at the present day it is found almost exclusively south of the Baltic, but as Nordhagen has illustrated (1933,

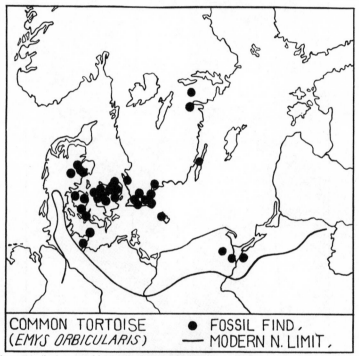

COMMON TORTOISE   ● FOSSIL FIND,
(*EMYS ORBICULARIS*)   — MODERN N. LIMIT,

Fig. 8. Distribution map of fossil finds of the common tortoise, north of the limit of present occurrence.
(After Nordhagen.)

fig. 57) it once extended to central Sweden and to southern Finland. The prickly sedge (*Cladium mariscus*) (von Post, 1925) and *Najas flexilis* (Sandegren, 1920) illustrate the same contraction of distribution since the warmth maximum. Andersson's study of relics of the elm in Scandinavia (1905) have demonstrated the same result along a slightly different line of approach. Changes in the vertical distribution of vegetation during the post-glacial

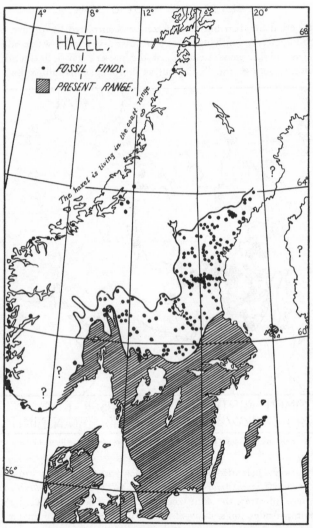

Fig. 9. Illustrating the distribution of the hazel in Scandinavia at the time of the post-glacial warmth maximum and at the present day. (After Andersson.)

28

period are well demonstrated in the mountainous parts of Central Europe. Working in a region of central Switzerland, situated at between 1500 and 2000 metres above sea-level, Keller found evidence of a tree limit during period III between 200 and 400 metres higher than that of the present day (1930, p. 285). Rudolph and Firbas, working in the Erzgebirge, found a fall in deciduous tree-levels since the temperature maximum of post-glacial time of approximately 400 metres (1924). Evidence from studies of the distribution of vegetation could be multiplied, but enough has been said to indicate that the theory of a post-glacial maximum of temperature rests upon a solid basis of biological fact.

Climate exercised its most powerful influences on man during the Mesolithic period of Northern Europe indirectly through its effect upon forest development, but in certain respects the climate changes of the period affected human settlement directly. The rapid increase of temperature which was the most marked feature of post-glacial time caused a strong drift from cave to open settlement. Man was not closely confined to caves during the Upper Palaeolithic period, nor were caves and shelters entirely abandoned during the Mesolithic; but the change of emphasis between the two periods was undeniably great. Rahir (1920) illustrated this very clearly in his study of the Tardenoisian settlement of Belgium, though the change is so striking as hardly to require demonstration. Again, the greater extremes of climate during the Boreal (period II) seem to have resulted in seasonal settlement on the plain of Northern Europe, as indicated by analysis of the fauna from typical Maglemose stations, whereas the middens of the Ertebølle folk, dating from the more equable Atlantic phase (period III), were occupied all the year round.

POST-GLACIAL FOREST DEVELOPMENT

The retreat of the Scandinavian and Alpine ice-sheets and the amelioration of climate which followed in their train made possible the rapid spread and increase of forest trees during the post-glacial period in Northern Europe. The tundra and the steppe of the late glacial period were transformed into wide forest lands, and the habitat of man and beast subjected to another great change. But the development of the post-glacial forests was neither catastrophic nor disorderly, and palaeo-botanists have been able to distinguish a series of phases or sub-periods of forest history, which, with certain reservations, are valid for the whole area of Northern Europe and afford a chronological sequence of great value to archaeology and geology. By its effect upon environment and the chronological value of its sequence of internal phases the development of forests during the post-glacial period is of the utmost importance to our subject.

The effect of the incoming of forests on the fauna of the area is considered in a separate section of this chapter. On man the influence produced more complex results; it is possible that some tribes, like the beasts, followed their old environment into other regions, but more generally the reaction took the form of cultural adaptation or else of highly selective settlement in localities unaffected by forest. The effects of the forest on the earliest civilisations of the post-glacial period were probably greater than those of any other factor of environmental change, and they will play an important part in our interpretation of cultural phenomena in following chapters.

The main factor controlling the development of the early post-glacial forests was undoubtedly climate. Trees spread and rose to dominance according as they could accommodate themselves to prevailing conditions; at first only cold-loving trees could flourish, then the warmth-loving trees came in, and ultimately dominated forests during the climatic optimum. The operation of the climatic control varied according to the geographical position of a given area or its altitude above sea-level. The climate of Central Europe tended to be more continental in character than the regions of the west and north-west, which were more susceptible to oceanic influences, and more southerly areas have generally been warmer than those farther north. Keller (1931) has shown that, during the period of the maximum of the oak-mixed-forest in north Italy and south Germany, spruce and silver-fir covered the lower slopes of the Alps and pine actually dominated the highest forests.

It is fairly certain that climate was not the only factor controlling forest development. Little is known about the refuge places of the forest trees during the last glacial phase, but the relative remoteness of the retreats of the various kinds of tree may, as Bertsch (1928) has argued, have helped to determine their order of arrival in a given locality. The same writer has pointed out that different trees vary very greatly in their speed of movement, so that in colonising new areas made available by a retreating ice-sheet slow-moving trees may well have been handicapped in favour of those more adapted to rapid migration. Finally, there is an important local qualification to the dominating influence of climate on the composition of forests. Edaphic or local topographical conditions may exercise a preponderating influence on the forest history of a given area; dense alder woods often flourish where the water-table is high, sandy wastes favour pine woods and clay lands deciduous forest.

Local variations of climate, and the operation of the non-climatic factors indicated, should all serve to induce caution in interpreting investigations of early forest history. Attempts to reconstruct past climate on the basis of such investigations are clearly beset with difficulty, and the deduction of general conclusions and correlations from local researches are matters best left to experts. Yet it is true that international research has been able to establish general drifts of forest development in North-western Europe, which reflect the known development of post-glacial climate, and afford in themselves the strongest indication that climate has been the chief agent in moulding their history. The three phases adopted in this book are:

PERIOD I. *Pre-boreal*. While the post-glacial rise of temperature was yet in its initial stage, only trees adapted to relatively cold conditions, such as willow, birch and pine, played any rôle in the composition of the forests of Northern Europe.

PERIOD II. *Boreal*. As the temperature rose towards its maximum the willow, birch and pine were reinforced by the warmth-loving forest trees, alder, and elm, oak and lime, the three components of the oak-mixed-forest. In most regions pine was dominant, but as temperature rose it gave way to the trees more favoured by the change. The end of the period is also marked over most of the area by the frequency of the shrub, hazel.

PERIOD III. *Atlantic*. The period of maximum temperature in the post-glacial period is marked by the dominance of the warmth-loving trees. Except in alpine and very northern regions birch and pine sank into relative insignificance, being replaced by alder and the oak-mixed-forest over the northern plain, by spruce in the Alpine-Carpathian area and by silver-fir on the Western Alps and the Pyrenees. During this period beech made its first appearance in Auvergne and the Jura.

Knowledge of the post-glacial forest succession was first obtained by studying the vertical succession of tree stools or forest beds, and to a lesser extent of bark, twigs, fruits and leaves, in peat-bogs. The five successive buried forests described by Skertchly (1877, pp. 165–72) for Wood Fen, near Ely, and the vegetation phases of the Scottish peat-mosses worked out by Lewis (1905–7 and 1908), are good examples of this early work. In recent years investigation has mainly been directed to the microscopic pollen grains, which under suitable conditions are found entombed in natural deposits. Pollen-analysis is able to yield results of a more precise nature than the older methods, and it has the further advantage that it can more easily and frequently be used to relate archaeological or geological phenomena to the phases of forest development. Its importance as a key to post-glacial history can hardly be exaggerated.

The idea originated with Lagerheim, while Professor of Botany at Stockholm University (Lagerheim and Witte, 1905), but the methods and technique were elaborated and put into practice by Lennart von Post of the Swedish Geological Survey (von Post, 1916). Erdtman must also be mentioned for the part he played in diffusing knowledge of the method over North-western Europe (1928). In recent years pollen-analytical investigations have been carried out in almost every country of Europe and have given rise to a vast literature.[1]

The method of pollen-analysis is possible, because under certain conditions the microscopic membranes of tree pollen survive sufficiently well for identification. The most favourable conditions for preservation are found in water-logged and unaerated deposits, whether of mineral nature, such as clays and silts, or of organic origin like peat. Forest trees do not normally grow in the immediate area of such deposits, but pollen grains are blown from neighbouring regions and become buried as they accumulate; in this way a record of the history of forest composition is preserved in the successive layers of recent deposits. The pollen grains of most of the common trees (Fig. 10) are easily identifiable after the removal of their humic content by one of the methods available,[2] though *Fraxinus* and *Salix* are almost indistinguishable. The investigation of a sample not only establishes the presence of trees, but can also be made to show their relative abundance, subject to the errors introduced by such factors as the varying pollen pro-

---

[1] *E.g.* Belgium (Erdtman, 1928, part III), Britain (Erdtman, 1928, part I; Woodhead, 1929; Raistrick and Blackburn, 1932; H. and M. E. Godwin, 1933 and 1934), Czecho-Slovakia (Rudolph, 1929), Denmark (K. Jessen, 1920), Esthonia (Thomson, 1926, 1929, 1930), Finland (Sauramo and Auer, 1928), Germany (Bertsch, 1928; Overbeck and Schmitz, 1931; Jaeschke, 1934), Russia (Dokturowsky, 1925), and Switzerland (Keller, 1928, 1929).

[2] The methods and technique of pollen-analysis have been critically described in English by Dr H. Godwin (1934), so that there is no point in my entering into detail here. It may be worth describing the two chief methods of cleaning the pollen grains:

(a) In the simple alkali treatment the sample can be examined after boiling on a microscope slide 'with a few drops of 10 per cent. KOH or NaOH'.

(b) "The newer and more complicated method is based on mild oxidation followed by acid hydrolysis. The oxidation agent is NaClO in a mixture of acetic and sulphuric acids. It is allowed to act for some hours in the cold and the residue is washed and dried with acetone and ether. The mass of material so produced is treated with 80 per cent. sulphuric acid which hydrolyses the abundant polysaccharide fraction, leaving a sample extremely rich in pollen grains." The advantage of the method is that it can be made to yield results from difficult samples.

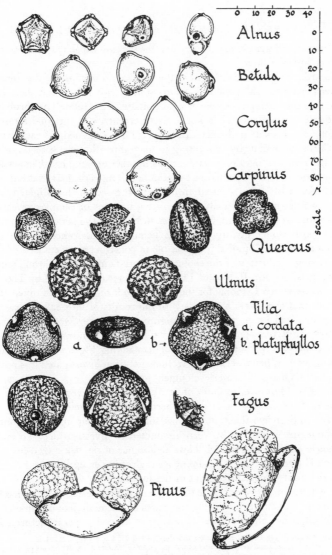

Fig. 10. Greatly magnified drawings of the commoner tree pollen grains. (By courtesy of Dr H. Godwin and of *The New Phytologist*.)

33

ductions of different kinds of tree,[1] and the varying capacity of different tree pollens to resist decay.[2]

In order to get a reliable idea of the relative proportions of different tree pollens in a given sample it is usual to count at least 150 grains, the value of each tree then being reckoned as a percentage of the total. The shrub hazel is counted separately and reckoned as a percentage of the total forest-tree pollen. In this way a characteristic spectrum is obtained for each sample. It will be clear that, by connecting in diagrammatic form a series of such spectra, representing the tree values of a number of samples taken vertically throughout a deposit, a vivid picture can be obtained of the variations in the composition of pollen content throughout the section investigated; or in other words the pollen-analysis of a vertical series of samples reveals the history of forest composition in the area throughout the period during which the deposit under investigation was being formed. When a number of sections have been studied it is possible to construct a generalised diagram illustrating the history of the evolution of forests in the area throughout the post-glacial period. In Fig. 11 I illustrate the results obtained by Thomson for north-western Esthonia for the three periods of Mesolithic time. It will be seen that the diagram accords with the results of international research as summarised on p. 31. In this figure I have expressed the individual spectra of different stages of the diagram by circles divided into sectors, and I hope this will be found useful for understanding Figs. 3 and 28, and the folding map. When a network of sections has been investigated it is possible to construct maps of forest development for given stages of post-glacial time in the area. The classic example of such a work is the investigation of 50,000 samples from 250 sections in southern Sweden carried out by von Post (1924). His maps illustrate regional differences, but also bring out the fundamental agreement between his numerous investigations. To take an instance, his map of period I shows an absence of the oak-mixed-forest; by period II (see our Fig. 12) its influence is already perceptible; by period III it is the most important element of the forests.

It will take many years before the whole of North-western Europe has been studied to the same extent as the home area of the method of pollen-analysis, but enough has already been done to give a good general picture of the

[1] E.g. *Pinus* tends to be over-represented and *Quercus* and *Tilia* under-represented.
[2] It has been established that as a matter of fact the pollen of the forest-tree dominants preserve almost equally well, though in a crumpled condition the pollen of one tree cannot so easily be identified as that of another.

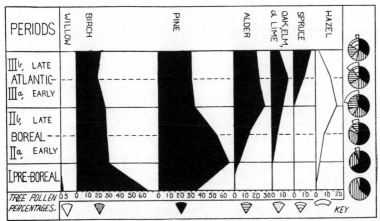

Fig. 11. Composite diagram illustrating the development of forests during post-glacial time in north-western Esthonia. (Based on Thomson.)

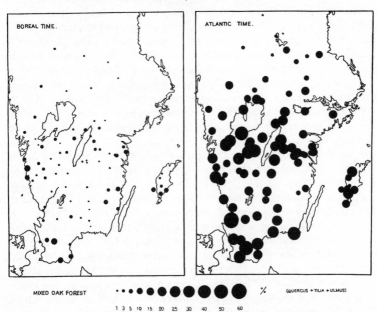

Fig. 12. Diagram illustrating the increase in importance of the mixed-oak-forest (oak, lime and elm) in south Sweden between the Boreal and Atlantic periods. (After von Post.)

35

phases of forest development over the whole area. As a result of these investigations it is possible, both to fix a vertical series, or any given point in such a series, in the general scheme established for the area, and even to correlate series from different regions. The degree of certainty is naturally higher in the former case, especially where the region has been closely investigated, but general correlations are now possible over most of the area studied in this book. From this it follows that:

(1) Any phenomena, whether geological, zoological or archaeological, which can be related to polliniferous deposits, can be dated in terms of phases of local forest succession and can, therefore, be arranged in chronological succession within a given area.

(2) Similar phenomena, even when widely separated over North-western Europe, can, when found in association with a polliniferous deposit, be related to the general history of forest development and may, within certain limits (which future work will narrow), be synchronised.

We are now in a position to date the changes of land and sea levels, described in a previous section of this chapter, in terms of forest history. For the earlier part of post-glacial time the plain of Northern Europe extended from Holderness to Blekinge and Esthonia without interruption by the sea; the southern portions of the North Sea were dry land and southern Sweden was joined by land with Jutland. The submergence of the North Sea bed and the separation of Denmark and Sweden, effected by marine transgression, have been dated by analysis of samples from vegetation now submerged beneath the sea or deep buried (often below sea-level) under recent deposits in marginal areas.

Samples of 'moorlog' from different parts of the North Sea bed at depths of between 18 and 29 fathoms have been examined by Erdtman (1924), Godwin (1933, pp. 42–4; 1934, part II, pp. 340–1) and Vermeer-Louman (1934), and their results show a close general measure of agreement. Analyses have been published of twenty samples and each revealed an overwhelming dominance of birch and pine; alder occurred only in five samples, oak in four, elm and lime in one each, and hazel, though normally present, reached high values only in four instances. It is evident that the 'moorlog' from between 18 and 29 fathoms was formed during the Pre-boreal and Early Boreal periods, and became submerged before the immigration or rise to importance of warmth-loving trees had really set in. Samples taken from nearer the margin of the North Sea date from a progressively later period; Erdtman (1928, part II, pp. 378–9) obtained spectra ranging from Pre-

Labels within image:
MEAN SEA-LEVEL (*Newlyn*)
UPPER PEAT
EARLY BRONZE AGE LEVEL
FEN CLAY
POLE MARKED IN FEET
POLLEN SAMPLES
LOWER
NEOLITHIC 'A' LEVEL
LATE TARDENOISIAN LEVEL
PEAT
SAND

PLATE III. Fen section exposed by excavation on Peacock's Farm, Shippea Hill, Cambridgeshire.

boreal to the Boreal-Atlantic transition off the east of Wangeroog, whereas closer in to Wilhelmshaven he found an Atlantic spectrum. Pollen-analysis shows decisively that most of the southern portions of the North Sea were submerged during period II, but that the peripheries were not affected until period III. The fact that most of the 'moorlog' deposits are found within two or three fathoms of 20 fathoms below modern sea-level suggests that the submergence must have affected the greater part of the North Sea bed within a short space of time; this is supported by sudden termination at much the same point of forest development illustrated by the pollen-analyses, and by the intact and undisturbed nature of the 'moorlog' deposits. The position of three samples (B, C, and D) from the North Sea bed and their pollen spectra is shown by Fig. 3. The spectrum given by the marginal sample (E) on the same figure illustrates the fact that marginal and shallow samples date from a later period of forest history.

The latest stages of the marine transgression are dated on either side of the North Sea, where peat-beds are found below deposits dating from the time of subsidence. In north-west Germany investigation of the Olden-broker Moor between Grossenmeer and Struckhausen, Oldenburg, has shown that the peat-bed underlying the clay-bed, which marks the end of the subsidence, dates from the Boreal and Early Atlantic stages of forest history; the clay-bed can, therefore, be assigned to the middle or end of period III (Overbeck and Schmitz, 1931, pp. 88–95). Similar results have been obtained in the English fenland on Peacock's Farm, Shippea Hill, near Ely. Here the ultimate stage of the subsidence is marked by a clay layer, containing *foraminifera*. The underlying peat-bed is now situated between 13 and 22½ feet below sea-level (Ordnance Datum, Newlyn), though over 20 miles from the modern sea-coast, and must have been formed during the period of relative land-elevation (Fig. 13, and Pl. III). Dr Godwin has shown that the peat-bed dates from the middle of the Boreal period until late in the Atlantic period, which puts the maximum of marine transgression at the end of period III or later. The late date of the clay-bed is confirmed on archaeological grounds by the fact that it overlay Windmill Hill pottery of the Neolithic 'A' culture of Britain (Clark and Godwin, 1935). Parallel evidence is given by the discovery of Neolithic and Beaker pottery and cooking-pits on the Essex coast between the Stour and the Blackwater on a land-surface below modern high tide (Warren, 1912). Farther north the latest stages of the marine transgression are marked by the carse clays of the

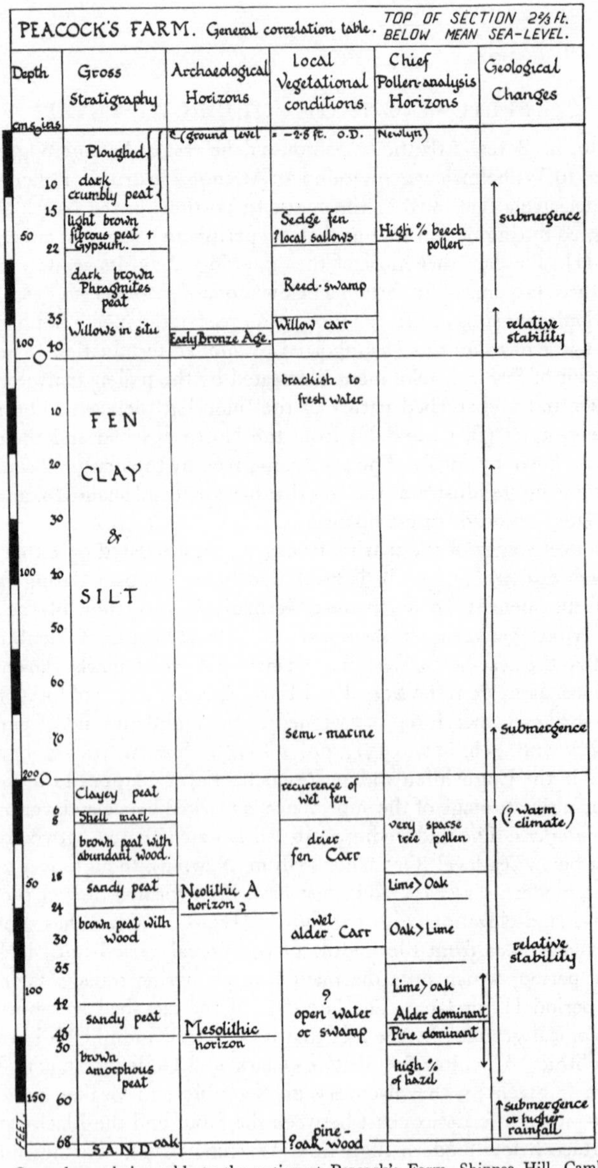

PEACOCK'S FARM. General correlation table. — TOP OF SECTION 2⅔ ft. BELOW MEAN SEA-LEVEL.

Depth	Gross Stratigraphy	Archaeological Horizons	Local Vegetational conditions	Chief Pollen-analysis Horizons	Geological Changes
cms. ins		(ground level = -2.8 ft. O.D. Newlyn)			
10	Ploughed; dark crumbly peat				
15 / 50 22	light brown fibrous peat + Gypsum.		Sedge fen ?local sallows	High % beech pollen	submergence
	dark brown Phragmites peat		Reed-swamp		
35 / 100 40	Willows in situ	Early Bronze Age	Willow carr		relative stability
10	FEN		brackish to fresh water		
20	CLAY				
30	&				
100 40	SILT				
50					
60					
70			Semi-marine		submergence
200 / 6 8	Clayey peat		recurrence of wet fen	very sparse tree pollen	(? warm climate)
	Shell marl				
	brown peat with abundant wood.		drier fen Carr		
50 15	sandy peat	Neolithic A horizon ?		Lime > Oak	
24 / 30	brown peat with wood		wet alder Carr	Oak > Lime	relative stability
35 / 100 42			?	Lime > oak	
45 / 30	sandy peat	Mesolithic horizon	open water or swamp	Alder dominant; Pine dominant	
150 60	brown amorphous peat			high % of hazel	submergence or higher rainfall
68	SAND oak		pine-oak wood		

Fig. 13. General correlation table to the section at Peacock's Farm, Shippea Hill, Cambridgeshire, England.

38

firths of Forth and Tay, which have been dated to period III by analyses of peat-beds underlying and overlying the deposit; at Forgandenny, south of Perth, peat from below 3 metres of carse clay gave a Boreal spectrum, whereas peat overlying 3·45 metres of the same deposit at Ochertye Moss, near Stirling, dated from the Sub-boreal and Sub-atlantic periods (Erdtman, 1928, part I, pp. 181–2).

The dating of the mainland period of southern Scandinavia and the correlation of phases of the development of the Baltic with periods of forest history have been achieved in much the same way. One method has been to examine submarine peat-beds as Knud Jessen has done in the free harbour at Copenhagen (1920, pp. 135–49). More fruitful, perhaps, has been the pollen-analytic examination of sections in which transgressions of the *Ancylus* Lake and of the *Litorina* Sea have both been represented; pioneer work of this kind was done on the island of Gotland (von Post, Munthe and Hede, 1924), and this has been followed up by Thomasson working in the Kalmarsund area (1927) and Lundquist in Öland Island (1928, p. 177). To illustrate how correlations are made I shall quote the section at Hoveenge, Skeldelev, in north-east Zealand, studied by Knud Jessen (1920, pp. 161–5 and p. 258). The section, the top of which was 75 cm. above modern sea-level, gave the following sequence of deposits:

	Depths from surface in cm.	Deposits	Periods of forest history
A	0– 30	Humus	
B	30– 40	*Phragmites* peat	
C	40– 60	*Litorina* mud	Period III
D	60– 95	Low-moss bog peat	
E	95–185	Calcareous *Gytje* (silt or clay) with peat layers	Period II
F	185–250	Brown *Phragmites* peat	Period I
G	250–330	Stoneless clay	Late glacial

Pollen-analysis of samples taken through deposits E–G show the development of forests previous to the *Litorina* Sea marked by deposit C. The stoneless clay yielded traces of *Betula nana* but no forest trees, and therefore dates from the late glacial time. The lower sample from deposit F (at 240 cm.) produced a few grains of willow, birch and pine pollen, indicating the very beginning of forest development in post-glacial time; a second sample from 225 cm. showed a later stage of period I with 4 per cent. willow, 41 per cent. birch, 55 per cent. pine, and a hazel value of 4 per cent.

of the whole. The three samples from layer E show a transition from a period I spectrum to a typical Boreal composition:

(*a*) At 165 cm.: 8 per cent. birch, 92 per cent. pine; hazel 7 per cent.
(*b*) At 148 cm.: 7 per cent. birch, 77 per cent. pine, 16 per cent. oak-mixed-forest; hazel 23 per cent.
(*c*) At 105 cm.: 9 per cent. birch, 61 per cent. pine, 15 per cent. alder, 15 per cent. oak-mixed-forest; hazel 23 per cent.

The *Litorina* Sea deposit is later, therefore, than period II. The section at Höganäs in Scania affords another example of botanical and geological correlation; the *Litorina* maximum, marked by a maximum frequency of salt-water diatoms, coincides exactly with the oak-mixed-forest dominance of period III (von Post, 1929). In general the Baltic evidence shows that the *Yoldia* Sea correlates with the first half of the Pre-boreal or period I, the *Ancylus* Lake overlaps with the second half of period I and covers the Boreal or period II, and the *Litorina* Sea coexisted with the Atlantic or period III.

Pollen-analysis has also been applied to the dating of faunal remains from post-glacial deposits. A particularly satisfactory instance of this is the dating of the reindeer in the Swedish province of Scania, a matter which bears directly on the dating of the reindeer antler axes of our area (Isberg, 1930). Thirty-two finds of reindeer remains have been fixed in the post-glacial time scale as follows:

Arctic-Pre-boreal (Period I)	15
Transitional (Periods I–II)	1
Boreal (Period II)	13
Transitional (Periods II–III)	3

The fact that the reindeer survived until the close of the Boreal is thus established for Scania beyond all reasonable doubt. It is very much to be desired that the method, now available, be applied more extensively to the dating of faunal remains from post-glacial deposits, as hitherto such material has been neglected or lumped together with none but the vaguest stratigraphical distinctions.[1]

The direct dating of archaeological objects or structures, when found in contact with any deposit containing sufficient identifiable pollen, is the

---

[1] Skertchly, 1877, pp. 320–2, merely lists the fauna from the peat, and the same is true of Marr and Shipley, 1904, p. 49. Before the invention and application of pollen-analysis little could, in any case, have been made of the stratigraphy, and little effort seems to have been made to record the exact finding-place of faunal remains from the fen beds.

application of the pollen-analytic method most directly relevant to this book. Recourse will frequently be made to the pollen-analytic dating of sites and of objects in discussing the chronology of the various cultures described; in this chapter, therefore, I shall confine myself to giving a few instances illustrating the practical aspect of the matter and the principles involved. It is rarely that actual monuments are found in stratigraphical relationship to polliniferous deposits, but such are not unknown; one may cite the stone-built Roman road which, in its passage over Blackstone Edge in the Southern Pennines, overlies 22 inches of cotton-grass peat (Woodhead, 1929, p. 14 and pl. II), or the group of three megalithic chamber graves and twelve Bronze Age barrows in the Kehdinger Moor, near Stade in northern Hanover, which were overwhelmed in the Sub-atlantic period by a rapid growth of *Sphagnum* peat and reappeared only after drainage had reduced this in the twentieth century A.D. (Jacob-Friesen, 1922).

More frequent and usually more important than such monuments are the debris of human settlement, especially when found *in* as opposed to merely over or under a polliniferous deposit. Many of the most important sites of period II in Northern Europe, for example Mullerup, Holmegaard, Duvensee and Broxbourne, represent seasonal settlement of favourable spots—islands or peninsulas—in fens or bogs, and it has, therefore, been possible to obtain on their peripheries good stratifications in the post-glacial deposits. Remarkable examples of post-glacial stratigraphy are being recovered in the fenland of eastern England, where the deposits of this period are found to depths of 20 feet or more in the immediate neighbourhood of well-defined settlement sites. A notable case is the site at Peacock's Farm, Shippea Hill, Cambridgeshire, where Late Tardenoisian and Neolithic A (Windmill Hill culture) debris were found stratified one above the other in a peat-bed formed during the Boreal and Early Atlantic periods and situated at between 13 and 22½ feet below sea-level (Clark, 1934; Clark and Godwin, 1935); above the clay layer overlying this lower peat-bed was an upper peat and in the base of this was found an Early Bronze Age scatter. It is not often that as many as three archaeological levels are found at one site in stratified relationship to forest development, but the correlation within an area of a number of sections each with a well-marked archaeological horizon can, by means of pollen-analysis, be made to produce a complete and consistent story. The co-operative work of Dr Reinerth and of the botanist Karl Bertsch on the Federsee in Württemberg has produced very complete and beautiful results (Reinerth, 1929; Bertsch, 1928). Here one is dealing with an inland lake at present occupying a small part only of its basin, a lake which has diminished in size progressively since an early stage of post-glacial time, and around the successive shores of which human settlement has abounded at every period; a considerable number of these settlements have been tied into the development of local forest history by pollen-analysis and the sections have been correlated to form the generalised section reproduced in our Fig. 14.

The methods of work are quite simple in character. Samples are taken at intervals throughout each section in which archaeological remains occur, the percentages for each are worked out and the usual diagram constructed to show the development of forests throughout the period represented in the section; when a number of sections, each with one or more archaeological horizons, have been worked out, it will be found that the very numerous overlaps allow them to be pieced together to form a consistent development. Once this has been achieved for a given area the stratigraphical position of archaeological remains, the character of which gives no certain evidence of date, can in itself be used, by the pollen-analytic method, to date them. A very good example of this is the wooden causeway by Oedenbühl in the south-east corner of the Federseemoor. In itself it showed no datable features, but the fact that it was found to coincide stratigraphically with the first and most marked maximum of the beech makes it possible, in view of stratigraphical relationships previously observed in the neighbourhood, to date it with confidence to the Late Bronze Age. Nor does this exhaust the possibilities of local applications of the method. It is one of the favourable factors of pollen-analysis that extremely small samples are often sufficient to give the pollen spectra requisite for stratigraphical determinations, and it frequently happens that enough material adheres to an object long removed from the ground to date it in relation to local forest development. A striking instance of this, quoted by Overbeck and Schmitz (1931, pp. 37–8), is a piece of woven material 10 cm. long, discovered near Ottersberg, east of Bremen, as long ago as 1879; some of the material was boiled and E. Schubert obtained a pollen spectrum[1] from which he was able to deduce that the material was lost in the Sub-atlantic climate period, dating, therefore, from

---

[1] The analysis gave: willow 1·3 per cent.; birch 11·3 per cent.; pine 5·4 per cent.; alder 58·7 per cent.; elm 1·3 per cent.; oak 12 per cent.; lime 0 per cent.; hornbeam 2 per cent.; beech 8 per cent.; and hazel 2 per cent. of the total forest-tree pollen.

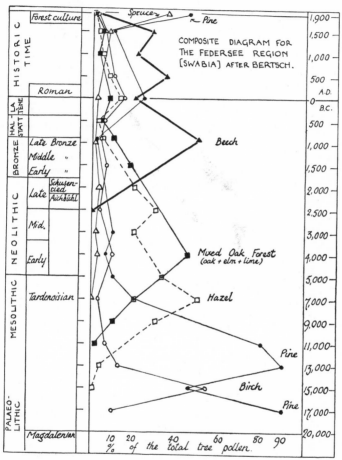

Fig. 14. Composite diagram combining numerous investigations in the Federsee region, made by Bertsch and Reinerth. (By courtesy of Dr H. Godwin and of *The New Phytologist*.)

the Early Iron Age of archaeology. In the case of heavy objects found in alluvial deposits it is frequently possible to correct by pollen-analytical methods any stratigraphical error caused by sinking. A notched bone point

43

(form 3) found in association with the forepart of the skeleton of an elk at Taaderup, Falster, Denmark, for example, was found at an Early Boreal level according to the analysis of the sample taken at its exact position of finding; analysis of a sample from inside the skull of the elk showed that the bones had sunk by as much as 20 cm. and really belonged to a later stage of period II (Ødum, 1920).

So far I have considered only the local applications of pollen-analysis to archaeology. The utilisation of pollen-analysis for the chronology of the post-glacial period of the whole of North-western Europe represents merely an extension of the same method. Just as individual sections can be correlated to give a complete history in a given region, so can regional stratigraphies be combined and correlated to form a complete history of archaeological and forest development for the whole area. The possibility of this further extension, with its great implications for archaeological chronology, rests on the essential fact that the pollen-analytic method has demonstrated drifts of forest history which hold good over wide areas of North-western Europe. Naturally there are many possible sources of error when comparisons are made between widely separated sites; due account must be taken of the geographical position of each site, of its relation to sea-level and of any peculiar local conditions. In general it can be said that the local factors operating on forest composition have been more powerful during the later periods of forest history when the various trees had made their arrival, than in the earlier periods when trees were making their first tentative immigrations; in the earlier periods, with which we are here solely concerned, the major phases, reflecting to a great extent climatic modifications, are fairly easily distinguishable in most cases. Until the whole of North-western Europe has been covered by a network of investigations, such as the Swedish Geological Survey has carried out for Scania, the finer points of chronology can hardly be established over the area as a whole on a pollen-analytic basis; on the other hand the evidence already available is sufficient to facilitate the triple division of the Mesolithic period in North-western Europe as shown on p. 31, and frequent reference will be made to this when discussing the chronology of various archaeological cultures.

Only under certain circumstances is it possible to relate archaeological strata or sites to the history of forest development by the application of pollen-analysis, but charcoal or carbonised wood is found on most sites and may sometimes be made to yield important information. Evidence for the presence of certain woods may sometimes be of value in itself; thus, in North-western Europe, oak charcoals would at once take a site out of period I, while beech would give a maximum date in period III.[1] But where sufficient samples are identified it is often possible to reconstitute contemporary forest composition in just the same way as is done by the analysis of pollen content. There are, of course, certain difficulties introduced by early man himself; to be of any value one must be certain that the charcoal reflects natural conditions and is not the selection of man. So often the carbonised wood found on a site has been selected originally for some special purpose such as hut construction, for which special properties are required. Reinerth, for instance, found huge predominances of woods with pliant stems, such as willow, poplar, alder and hazel, on many of his Neolithic sites by the Federsee;[2] the explanation of this is to be found not in any special frequency of these trees at this period—pollen-analysis has shown the contrary—but rather in the methods of hut construction favoured by the people of that time.

Reinerth's experience is important as a warning, but the investigation is worth making when, as in most Mesolithic sites, such as rock-shelters, caves, camping places, or midden sites, there is no indication that wood was used for hut construction. In these cases the charcoal from hearths is sometimes found to confirm in the most interesting fashion the evidence of forest composition obtained from pollen-analysis. To illustrate this I shall tabulate first of all the results of charcoal identification from the three most important sites of period II in Denmark—Holmegaard, Mullerup and Svaerdborg—where on the evidence of pollen-analysis pine should have been the wood most available:

Number of square metres in which the various woods occurred

Sites	Willow	Birch	Pine	Hazel	Alder	Elm	Oak	Aspen
Svaerdborg	—	3	32	6	4	2	—	—
Holmegaard	6	5	38	14	15	12	2	—

Actual number of charcoals[3]

Holmegaard	12	7	424	25	30	16	2	—
Mullerup	—	6	835	120	—	45	—	27

[1] In some areas it would indicate even later maximum dates.

[2] *E.g.* at Dullenried they accounted for 71·7 per cent. of the tree pollen, and at Taubried for 83·5 per cent. (Reinerth, 1929, pp. 63 and 91).

[3] It will be noted that very considerable numbers of charcoals have been identified. This is essential if an accurate idea of the relative proportions and apart from the mere presence of forest trees is desired.

It will be seen that by both methods of reckoning pine is shown with very high value and oak is either absent or present in the smallest quantities only. In the two cases where we have the actual number of charcoals the values of the two trees can be expressed as percentages; at Holmegaard pine accounts for 72 per cent. of the charcoal samples and oak for 2/5ths per cent., while at Mullerup pine reaches 80·8 per cent. and oak is entirely absent.

The value of this evidence from sites of period II might be minimised by the suggestion that certain woods were favoured for firewood, owing to some inherent qualities. It becomes, therefore, of interest to examine the charcoals from sites of period III in the same area. I have selected three Danish kitchen-midden sites, for which we have good charcoal evidence:

Occurrences of woods in fields 1 metre square and 0·2 metre deep

Sites	Willow	Birch	Pine	Hazel	Alder	Elm	Oak	Aspen
Ertebølle	3	67	—	6	11	74	504	40
Aamølle	—	11	—	1	—	—	21	1
Faareveile	—	11	—	4	3	6	53	2

The table reveals a state of affairs almost exactly opposite to that obtaining in the same area during the previous period; so far from being dominant in the charcoals, pine is entirely absent, whereas oak has risen from insignificance to a marked predominance over all other charcoals. This great change is hardly to be explained by any alteration in taste for firewood. On the contrary it both reflects and confirms the change of dominance from pine to oak-mixed-forest revealed by pollen-analysis.

FAUNA

The fauna of Northern Europe during the Mesolithic period is important, in that it reflects the climatic, geographical and vegetational changes, which form the subject of this chapter. The evolution of climate from period I to the warmth maximum of the end of period II and the beginning of period III, and the spread of forest trees which accompanied it, both had a profound effect on fauna, causing tundra and steppe species to give way to those adapted to forests. The general effect of the invasion of forests during the post-glacial period on the fauna surviving from the ice-age can be well demonstrated from the caves of southern Germany. The evidence collected by R. R. Schmidt (Schmidt, R. R., 1912) is summarised in list A of Appendix I, which illustrates the gradual change in fauna from the Early

Magdalenian to the 'Azilian'. Tundra species, such as the Obi and banded lemmings, the arctic fox that preyed on them, the glutton, the arctic hare and the reindeer, and steppe species, like the pika and the wild horse, give way to such forest forms as the wild pig, the brown bear, the wood marten, the beaver, the red deer and the roe deer. The gradual character of the change is illustrated by the fact that more extreme tundra forms such as the Obi lemming, last found in Early Magdalenian deposits, disappeared earlier than less extreme species as the banded lemming which persisted into the Late Magdalenian, while at the same time the forest species started to appear during the Magdalenian period, red deer going back to the Middle Magdalenian and roe deer and beaver to the Late Magdalenian. That the change was, nevertheless, a sweeping one is shown by the fact that the deposits of the Early Magdalenian and of the 'Azilian' yielded no single species in common.

The adaptation of fauna to the incoming of forests, observed by Schmidt in the caves of south Germany, can be demonstrated in ample measure for the north European plain. Indeed, since much of the faunal evidence for this area has been recovered in the open from natural deposits formed during the post-glacial period, more precision in the definition of phases of faunal development is possible.

For period I fauna is available from the caves of Remouchamps in Belgium (Rahir, 1920), and Hohlen Stein in Westphalia (Andree, 1931, 1932), as well as from the fresh-water deposits at Nørre-Lyngby in Jutland (Jessen and Nordman, 1915). In general the fauna from these sites shows on the one hand typical tundra and steppe species, and on the other species adapted to open forests. The transitional character of the fauna accords well with the fact that period I saw the first beginnings of forest migration, as tundra conditions receded for the last time. Common to all three sites are the three tundra species of reindeer, arctic hare and white grouse, while both cave sites have produced arctic fox and the wild horse of the steppes; on the other hand beaver occurs at Hohlen Stein and at Lyngby, roe deer at Hohlen Stein, and other forest species such as wild pig, red deer and aurochs occur at both the cave sites. Comparison with the Magdalenian deposits of south Germany reveals the absence at the northern sites of the pika and the glutton, but above all of both the Obi and the banded lemmings, the latter of which survived in the south German caves up till the Late Magdalenian. From this it may be inferred, more especially since they occur at more northerly latitudes, that the three sites under consideration belong to a period slightly later than the Magdalenian. More positive evidence of age is afforded by the Lyngby deposits, which, from the occurrence of reindeer, arctic hare and white grouse, must clearly be equated with Remouchamps and Hohlen Stein. The Lyngby fresh-water beds yielded two beetles, *Elaphrus lapponicus* and *Adimonia tanaceti*, naturally adapted to open forest country, as well as a single pollen grain of *Pinus silvestris*. From this and other evidence obtained by the Danish Geological Survey in 1913–14, the older view of Johnstrup and Steenstrup that the Lyngby deposits indicate a period of steppe conditions has been rendered out of date; the modern view is that they were formed "at a time when great tracts of land in Denmark were on the whole under forest growth, there being, however, just as at present, some open spaces in the form of moorland, heaths, marsh, etc...." (Jessen and Nordmann, 1915, p. 62).

The most reliable and the richest evidence for period II derives from the three famous Zealand sites of Holmegaard (Broholm, 1926–31, pp. 29–31), Mullerup (Sarauw, 1903, pp. 194–8) and Svaerdborg (Friis-Johansen, 1918–19, pp. 261–4), each of which is securely dated to this period on the evidence of both archaeology and of pollen-analysis. It is satisfactory that the determination of the fauna from each of the sites as well as of the key sites of period III has been carried out by one man, Herluf Winge of Copenhagen. The general agreement between the three sites is very close, 54 per cent. of all species being common to all three, 18 per cent. to two and 27 per cent. to one only; the disparities revealed by these figures are not very significant since they mainly involve various bird species only scantily represented, whereas out of the sixteen mammals represented no less than eleven occur at all three sites, and three others occur at two. The essential similarity, amounting in all essential facts to identity, between the faunas from the three sites justifies their consideration together. In general they show a fauna typical of forests and lakes. At each of the sites the remains of roe deer and wild pig are most abundant; beaver is also common, the Svaerdborg find being the richest ever made in Denmark, and both elk and aurochs occur at all the sites. Of the birds the crane, cormorant, great crested grebe and white-tailed eagle occur at each site. Pike remains are also found on all the sites. The fact that, out of forty-three species, two only—the long-tailed duck, which occurred at Mullerup, and the great black-backed gull, which occurred at Svaerdborg—are of definitely marine character accords well with the fact that during the contemporary *Ancylus* Lake phase of the Baltic the sites in question were farther from the sea than is now the case. The presence of the fresh-water tortoise at each of the sites reflects the warmer temperature that then prevailed, since the northern limit of the species at the present time is in north Germany (see Fig. 8). The fauna, therefore, reflects the main features of the period known from other sources, the consolidation of forests, the greater extent of land in the south Baltic, and the approaching climatic optimum. Further than this it affords information of predominantly cultural interest. Thus the occurrence of the bones of young cranes indicates that the sites were inhabited during the summer, while the predominance of fully developed roe-deer antlers suggests that they were indeed mainly inhabited at this season, if not exclusively so (Friis-Johansen, 1918–19, pp. 262–3). The bones of domesticated animals, excepting the dog, were entirely absent. An interesting detail noticed at Svaerdborg was the remarkable dearth of metacarpal and metatarsal bones of the great ruminants, the bones having been largely utilised for industrial purposes.

The absence of all the tundra and steppe species characteristic of period I and the total dominance of forest species among the land mammals fully accord with our knowledge of forest development at this period. The absence of reindeer, however, from the Zealand sites must be regarded as a local phenomenon and not as one of general validity for Northern Europe, since there is abundant evidence that reindeer continued to play an important part in many areas until the end of period II. The most striking evidence comes from the Swedish province of Scania, situated at the same latitude as and in immediate proximity to the Island of Zealand. Thirty-two occurrences of reindeer in this province have been related by pollen-analysis to the known sequence of forest development in the area and by this means the time span of the reindeer in the area is accurately known. The most important fact which emerged from this investigation is that, while in sixteen cases the bones were found to date from the Pre-boreal (period I), in thirteen cases they date from the Boreal (period II) and in three cases from the transition from Boreal to Atlantic (transition to period III) (Isberg, 1930). Other scraps of evidence confirm this decisive body of evidence; for instance the dried-up mere-beds at Kunda in Esthonia (Tallgren, 1922, p. 40) and at Skipsea, East Yorkshire, England (Godwin, 1933, p. 38), have both yielded reindeer remains from levels dated to period II on archaeological as well as on pollen-analytical evidence.[1] The fact that reindeer continued to exist in Northern Europe up till the end of period II has an important bearing on the dating of archaeological objects of reindeer bone or antler. The so-called 'Lyngby axes', for example, cannot be ascribed as a group to period I, merely because they are of reindeer antler; unless dated definitely to this period on other grounds, specific examples might equally well belong to period II.

The presence of reindeer in period II implies no contradiction of the established fact that during this period forests were well established over Northern Europe, since not only does the tundra reindeer at the present time migrate during winter into wooded country, but there is also a different race of reindeer especially adapted to woods (Wright, 1914, p. 227). The anatomical differences between the two races are not great—the tundra type tends to have large antlers in relation to its size with only a slight tendency to be palmated, while the woodland type is normally a larger beast with relatively smaller and more palmated antlers (Jessen, A. and Nordmann, V., 1915, p. 15)—and it is not possible to say to which type the remains from Boreal deposits belong.

The absence of reindeer from the Zealand sites of Holmegaard, Mullerup and Svaerdborg is accentuated by the abundance of elk at these sites, a species described as "at present a native of those northern parts of Asia, America and Europe, *not occupied by the reindeer*" (Wright, 1914, p. 230). In addition to the three important archaeological sites mentioned, the elk occurs at Kunda and Skottemarke, both dated on archaeological grounds to period II. A further carefully recorded find of elk from this period was made at Taaderup on the Island of Falster (Ødum, 1920); here the forepart of an elk was found associated with a finely toothed bone point (form 6) at a level dated to the Boreal period by pollen-analysis. Since the elk became extremely rare in period III, elk antler or bone objects are likely to date from period II.

For period III the kitchen-middens of Denmark and various settlement sites, situated on the old *Litorina* coast, yield the richest evidence of fauna.

---

[1] Reindeer is also recorded from the post-glacial deposits of the fenland of eastern England (Skertchly, 1877, p. 321). So far as is known the oldest post-glacial deposits of this region date from fairly well on in the Boreal period. As this record seems to stand on a single entry in Skertchly's list of fauna from the peat-beds of the fenland it cannot be accepted without reserve. Without doubt Skertchly's authority was Richard Owen (1846, pp. 482 and 483), who figures a bone which he describes as "a metatarsal bone, precisely corresponding with that of the existing Rein-deer, which bone was found at a depth of five feet in the fens of Cambridgeshire".

FAUNA

The sites utilised for the table in Appendix I include the kitchen-middens of Aamølle, Ertebølle, Faareveile, Havnø and Klintesø (Madsen, etc., 1900), and the sites of Bloksbjerg (Westerby, 1927) and Brabrand Sø (Thomsen, T. and Jessen, A., 1902–7). From these sites the same forest-loving land mammals occur as were present during period II, though there are important differences in the frequency of certain species. In particular both the aurochs and the elk seem to have been scarcer. The case of the elk is the more striking; it is entirely absent from all the kitchen-middens except Ertebølle, which yielded only two fragments, while Bloksbjerg yielded only a solitary tooth—only at Brabrand Sø was it at all common. A second way in which the fauna from this group of sites differs from that from the sites of the preceding period lies in the much greater frequency of marine species, of which twenty-two occur in the place of two. Among the mammals may be noted four species of seal, the porpoise, dolphin and killer whale, among the fish, spur-dog, garfish, cod and flounder, and among the birds, the scaup-duck, common and velvet scoter, eider-duck, long-tailed duck, great black-backed gull, guillemot, razorbill, great auk and gannet. The reason for this strong marine element in the fauna is that most of the Danish sites of period III were concentrated on the coast at the time of the maximum transgression of the *Litorina* Sea. A third difference is that, whereas the sites of Holmegaard, Mullerup and Svaerdborg were probably inhabited only during the summer, sufficient remains of red deer, roe deer and wild pig have been recovered from the kitchen-middens to suggest that they were occupied throughout the year (Madsen, etc., 1900, p. 115), a circumstance probably to be explained by the more equable climate of Atlantic times and by the nature of the food supply. Apart from the dog, also present at the period II sites, the bones of domesticated animals are confined to superficial layers, yielding megalithic pottery and stone forms of the Neolithic period.

SUMMARY

The history of the evolution of the natural environment of Mesolithic man in Northern Europe has been described in separate sections, arranged in what seemed to me to be their logical order. First of all I have dealt with the retreat of the ice-sheets and the system of chronology based upon their study, next with the readjustments in land and sea levels produced by this withdrawal, then with the evolution of climate, and finally with the history of forest and animal life as influenced by these changes of the habitat. I have tried to synchronise and to correlate the various aspects of environment in the course of my description, but it seemed worth while expressing the chief results in tabular form for ready reference. The same order of events is preserved in the diagram as in the description, beginning with the retreat of the ice on the left and passing on to fauna on the right. In the final column I have placed major epochs of archaeology, showing the Mesolithic divided into three periods, coinciding with the periods of climatic and forest development. Throughout the rest of the book the various periods of the Mesolithic to which I shall refer will be the time periods indicated in this table. It is perhaps worth stating explicitly that this is meant to apply only to that part of Northern Europe selected for special study in this book.

Geo-chrono-logy	Glacial eras	Land movement		Climate phases	Forest development	Fauna	Archaeology	
		Baltic	North Sea					
B.C. (2500)	POST-GLACIAL	*Litorina* Sea	Fen clay laid down	SUB-BOREAL			NEOLITHIC	
3000			Transgression of North Sea bed	Warm and moist-oceanic		Dog		PERIOD III
4000				ATLANTIC	Alder and/or oak-mixed-forest (elm, oak, lime) dominant	Forest, lake and sea forms		
				Warmth maximum Temperature (July) 17° C.		Elk rare		
5000						Reindeer absent	MESOLITHIC	
		Ancylus Lake		Temperature (July) 16°–17° C.	Birch and/or pine dominant	Dog		PERIOD II
6000				BOREAL	Alder and oak-mixed-forest coming in Hazel becomes important near the end of the period	Forest and lake forms		
				Warm and dry-continental Temperature (July) 12°–14° C.		Elk very common		
(6800)						Reindeer survived		
7000	FINIGLACIAL	*Yoldia* Sea	'Moorlog' forming	PRE-BOREAL	Birch, pine and willow the only forest trees	Mixed tundra and forest forms		PERIOD I
8000				Gradual and rapid rise of temperature from 8° to 12° C. (July)		Lemming absent		
(8300)								
9000	GÖTIGLACIAL	Ice-dammed Lake		SUB-ARCTIC	*Dryas* flora Dwarf birch and willow	Tundra and steppe forms	PALAEO-LITHIC	
				ARCTIC		Lemming		
10000								

CHAPTER II

THE TANGED-POINT CULTURES

Evidence has been accumulating during recent years to demonstrate the existence in Northern Europe during the post-glacial period of early cultures, of which the most characteristic traces that remain to us are tanged flint points of various forms. The groups in which these cultures may be divided will be considered separately, before any general conclusions are attempted. The chief sites mentioned in the text are shown in Fig. 15.

THE AHRENSBURG-LAVENSTEDT CULTURE

The Ahrensburg-Lavenstedt culture derives its name from the site of Ahrensburg, between Lübeck and Hamburg, discovered by a shoemaker of Altona, Christian Laag, and from the site of Lavenstedt, near Zeven, Hanover, found by Herr J. Müller-Brauel, but it is to Dr G. Schwantes of Kiel that archaeology owes the recognition of the new culture (Schwantes, 1928 (c)). Owing to the nature of the sites no antler, bone or wooden objects have survived, but the flint industry is highly characteristic. With the exception of nos. 16 and 28 all the specimens illustrated by Fig. 16 come from the site of Stellmoor, situated on sandy soil some 2½ kilometres south-west of Ahrensburg. The flints at Ahrensburg were exposed by ploughing, but the industry is remarkably homogeneous and is closely paralleled by that from Lavenstedt which came from deep in an ancient inland dune.

The Ahrensburg-Lavenstedt flint culture consists entirely of flake implements—axes, adzes, picks, maces and other heavy equipment being entirely absent. The most numerous objects are primary flakes, frequently of great size (*e.g.* no. 16), and generally exhibiting considerable mastery of flake production on the part of those who made them; most of the cores (no. 28) show the scars of the narrow and regular flakes required for the manufacture of microliths. The microliths themselves, which were evidently not made by the notch method, as is shown by the absence of 'micro-burins',[1] occur in three main classes:

[1] See Clark, 1932, Appendix I. The absence of micro-burins is decisive, but the fact that the pressure rings of the primary flake surface show no definite relation to the tangs of the tanged flakes affords strong confirmation. The pressure rings of the flints illustrated by Fig. 16 are mainly open towards the tips of the tanged points, but in some cases (nos. 4, 8, 18) they are open towards the tangs; had the 'notch and micro-burin' method been in use the rings would all be open towards the tip.

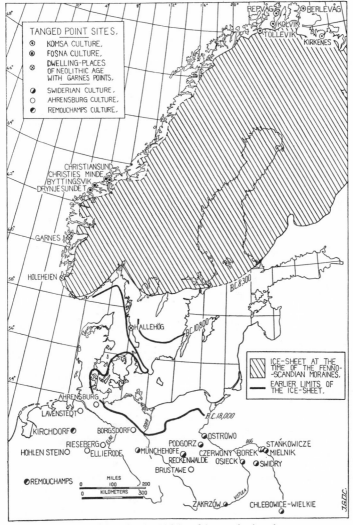

Fig. 15. Map showing the chief sites of the tanged-point cultures.

55

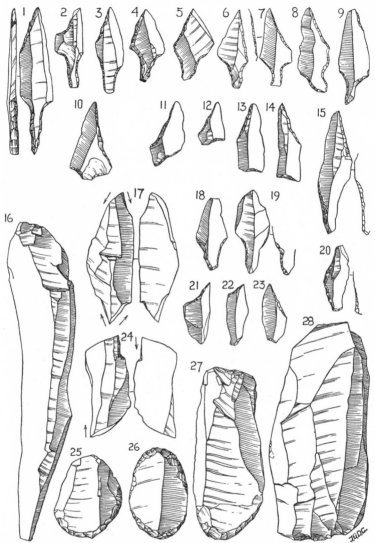

Fig. 16. Typical series of flint forms of the Ahrensburg-Lavenstedt culture. Illustrated by the author from specimens in Oldesloe Museum. Scale: ⅝.

AHRENSBURG-LAVENSTEDT CULTURE

(i) Points blunted obliquely down part of one edge, on the left (nos. 21, 22) or on the right (no. 23).

(ii) Tanged points of various forms. These are illustrated with the tangs downmost and will be so described. Variations of form occur.

The tang was normally produced by secondary flaking on both edges of the flake near one extremity, the flaking being directed from the bulbar face for both edges; in a few cases, however, the secondary flaking has been directed from the upper flake surface in the case of one edge (nos. 15, 19, 20).

The rest of the flake was sometimes left untouched (nos. 18 and 19); more generally, however, one edge was blunted obliquely, either in part (nos. 1–3, 7, 9) or completely down to the tang (nos. 4–6, 8), and either on the left edge (nos. 1–5) or on the right (nos. 6–9).

(iii) Points with concave base, the rest of the flake being blunted obliquely down part of the left (nos. 11–13) or of the right edge (no. 14).

Other flint types that occur are burins, which, though not common, are good examples of their kind (nos. 17, 24), and scrapers, of end (no. 27), horseshoe (no. 25) and double (no. 26) form.

In attempting to date the Ahrensburg-Lavenstedt culture Schwantes (1928 (c), pp. 183–93) was compelled to rely on the typology of the flint industry, since the name sites gave no relation to polliniferous deposits and were entirely lacking in faunal remains. The presence of microliths as the dominant feature of the industry suggested to him a date after the Palaeolithic, and the absence both of axes or picks and of geometric microliths and micro-burins argued for a date before the true forest period. The Ahrensburg-Lavenstedt culture would, therefore, fall into the beginning of our period I on the evidence of its lithic forms.

Since Schwantes essayed this dating his suggestion has been strikingly confirmed by the excavations in the limestone cave of Hohlen Stein, near Callenhardt, kr. Lippstadt, Westphalia, carried out by Dr Julius Andree in 1929 and 1930 (Andree, 1932 (b), pp. 21–36). Apart from a superficial deposit with Early Iron Age and modern remains, the cave yielded a homogeneous culture accompanied by a valuable fauna. The flint industry from Hohlen Stein clearly belongs to the same culture as the finds at Ahrensburg and Lavenstedt. Axes, adzes and picks are absent, the industry consisting entirely of blades, microliths, burins and scrapers. A typical series is illustrated by our Fig. 17. The three types of microlith typical of the Ahrensburg-Lavenstedt culture recur—the obliquely blunted points

57

(nos. 1–3), the tanged points (nos. 5–8) and the points with concave base, the rest of the flake being obliquely blunted (nos. 9, 10). The only form present at Hohlen Stein and absent from Ahrensburg and Lavenstedt is the

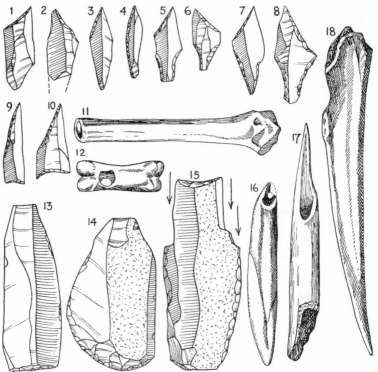

Fig. 17. Objects from Hohlen Stein, Callenhardt, Westphalia. Nos. 1–10, microliths: obliquely blunted points (nos. 1–3), tanged points (nos. 5–8), obliquely blunted points with concave base (nos. 9, 10); no. 11, bone handle; no. 12, whistle (?) or perforated reindeer phalange; nos. 13, 14, flint scrapers; no. 15, burin or graver of the transverse angle variety; no. 16, perforated wild pig's tooth; nos. 17, 18, pointed bones. (After Andree.) Scale: ⅓.

simple point blunted down the whole of one edge (no. 4). Two scrapers (nos. 13, 14) and a good example of a double angle-burin (no. 15) are also illustrated. In addition to the flints a certain number of bone objects were found, which help to fill out our picture of the Ahrensburg-Lavenstedt culture. These include a perforated reindeer phalange (no. 12), usually regarded as a whistle, of a type common in Upper Palaeolithic deposits (Déchelette, 1908, 203, fig. 82, 1), a bone handle (no. 11), a wild pig's tooth perforated for personal adornment (no. 16) and a number of pointed bone objects, of which two are illustrated (nos. 17, 18). The fauna from the mesolithic deposit is listed in Appendix I (list B); it includes both typical tundra and steppe species, such as reindeer, variable hare, arctic fox, white grouse and wild horse, and forest species, like the aurochs, roe deer, beaver and wild pig. The fauna indicates quite clearly a transitional period, when the climate had started to improve and forest was gradually invading the tundra; in other words the Hohlen Stein fauna confirms the original dating of the Ahrensburg-Lavenstedt culture made by Schwantes.

THE REMOUCHAMPS CULTURE

The general features of the Ahrensburg-Lavenstedt culture are reproduced almost completely at the Belgian cave site of Remouchamps, near Spa (Rahir, 1920). The homogeneous archaeological deposit was situated in the first chamber of the grotto and yielded two distinct hearths in recesses of the wall. Perforated shells of *Natica Parisiensis* and *Melania lactea*, together with traces of red colouring matter, were found near the hearths, and in a fissure in the opposite wall were the disturbed remains of what was evidently a ceremonial burial, also accompanied by perforated shells. Some five thousand pieces of worked flint were recovered from the excavations and a representative series of these is reproduced by our Fig. 18. The industry showed an absence of any heavy equipment and consisted entirely of flake implements. The most characteristic implements were microliths, of which 117 specimens were found of the following forms:

(i) obliquely blunted points (nos. 1–5), which, together with a few transversely blunted specimens (no. 6), accounted for 75 per cent. of the total;

(ii) points blunted down the whole of one edge (nos. 7, 8), amounting to 12 per cent. of the total;

(iii) tanged points (nos. 10–15) in a proportion of 7 per cent.;

(iv) fairly large and irregular triangles (no. 9), which accounted for the remaining 6 per cent.

In addition there occurred one true burin (no. 20) and several scrapers (nos. 16, 17, 19), but no micro-burins were present.

The flints from Remouchamps agree in general with those of the Ahrensburg-Lavenstedt culture, and in particular the characteristic tanged point is present. On the other hand the obliquely blunted form with concave base (Fig. 16, nos. 11–14; Fig. 17, nos. 9, 10) is absent, and the triangle is present. It is an interesting fact that these two points of difference recur at the sand-dune site of Kirchdorf, near Uchte, Hanover (Adrian,

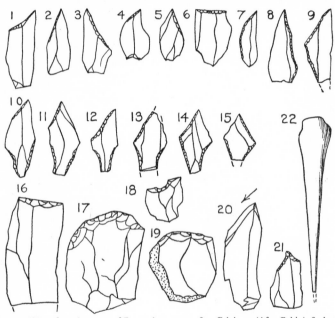

Fig. 18. Objects from the grotto of Remouchamps, near Spa, Belgium. (After Rahir.) Scale: ⅓.

1931 (a)), where microliths of the same four classes are found, together with scrapers and an angle-burin. It would, therefore, appear that the Remouchamps find represents a slightly different facies of the Ahrensburg-Lavenstedt culture.

Bone implements from Remouchamps are rare, but they include three awls (no. 22) similar in character to those from Hohlen Stein. Of more importance is a fragment of bone decorated by clusters of five pits, carried

out by the *bohrornament* technique (Fig. 57, no. 7). As we show in chapter
IV (p. 163) this type of decoration is highly specialised, and it is, therefore, significant that all other examples found in datable deposits belong
to period II. This decorated object would tend, therefore, to make the
Remouchamps industry rather later than the Ahrensburg-Lavenstedt culture
as a whole, and support for this idea may be found in the presence of the
microlithic triangle. On the other hand the evidence of the Remouchamps
fauna (see Appendix I, list B) suggests that the industry must, in large
measure, be contemporary with that in the cave of Hohlen Stein; in both the
reindeer predominates, and in addition to the variable hare, arctic fox, white
grouse and wild horse, forest forms like aurochs and wild pig are present.
It must be concluded that any time difference between the Remouchamps-
Kirchdorf[1] and the Ahrensburg-Lavenstedt cultures can only be slight, that,
if a time difference exists, then Remouchamps is certainly the later, and that
alternatively the difference in facies must be explained on the basis of
regional variation.

In any case it is clear that during period I substantially the same culture,
of which the most typical lithic form was the tanged point, extended from
Holstein to Belgium. Other traces of the culture in northern Germany are
afforded by single tanged points from Rieseberg (Hohmann, 1927, p. 204
and abb. 12, no. 2), and Ellierode (*ibid*. abb. 12, no. 1). In addition tanged
points have occurred in a number of surface finds in association with
Tardenoisian forms, as for example at Wolletz, Brandenburg, where a
tanged point was found with a trapeze and blunted-backed points (Hohmann,
1927, p. 203 and abb. 11, no. 8); at Wustrow, kr. Luchow, tanged points
occurred rarely in surface association with various forms of microliths
including trapezes (Lampe, 1926); at Kl.-Vorwerk, kr. Glogau, they occurred with typical Late Tardenoisian objects (Zotz, 1932, abb. 10); at Borgsdorf, Brandenburg, with scalene triangles and elongated crescents suggestive
of the Middle or Late Tardenoisian (Schneider, 1932, pp. 128–31 and
abb. 62–72), and at Chwalim, kr. Bomst, with triangles and trapezes
(Rothert and Dobrindt, 1934, p. 231). Whether these finds indicate the
survival of tanged-point tradition into periods II and III, or whether the
finds are mixed, it is difficult to decide, as they are all from the surface. There
is nothing improbable in the survival, and the frequency of 'mixed' finds

---

[1] Some flints illustrated by Adrian (1931 (*a*)) from Kirchdorf as trapezes appear, in reality, to be broken flakes.

makes it likely; at the same time the question must remain an open one in the absence of positive evidence.

Two alternative names have been put forward at various times to label a culture similar in many respects to that just described, but centering on the valleys of the Vistula and the Bug—Swiderian, after the site at Swidry first described by Krukowski (1922), and Chlebowician, from the site at Chlebowice published by Kozłowski (1923). I shall use the term Swiderian, partly on the grounds of priority and partly because the site at Swidry yielded a pure industry, whereas at Chlebowice there was admixture. The finds are made in sand-dune areas, and for that reason the only objects surviving are flint implements. The flint industry, like that of the Ahrensburg-Lavenstedt culture, lacks heavy equipment, consisting entirely of blade and flake implements. A series of the typical forms, from the site of Stańkowice on the Bug (Szmit, 1929), is illustrated by Fig. 19. As in the Ahrensburg-Lavenstedt culture, the tanged microlith (nos. 1–12) is the most characteristic type; in the Swiderian, however, certain new varieties of this type occur frequently and help to distinguish the culture. The forms represented by nos. 1, 4–7 and 12 are common both to the Swiderian and to the Ahrensburg-Lavenstedt cultures, but those with inverse retouch (nos. 2, 3, 8–11) occur only in the former. In the Ahrensburg-Lavenstedt industries occasional examples are found where one side of the tang of a tanged point has been chipped from the upper face of the flake (e.g. Fig. 15, nos. 15, 19); the characteristic Swiderian form, however, frequently shows flat flaking across the bulbar surface of the tang (nos. 2, 3), or alternatively an inverse retouch extending over a certain extent of the bulbar surface of the tang either on one edge (no. 8) or on both (nos. 9–11). A second difference is to be found in the absence from the Swiderian of the obliquely blunted points with concave base (e.g. Fig. 16, nos. 11–14; Fig. 17, nos. 9, 10). Other simple microlithic forms occur in the Swiderian (nos. 13, 14), but, as in the Ahrensburg-Lavenstedt culture, micro-burins are absent. The true burin is fairly common, occurring in screw-driver (no. 19), gouge (no. 20) and angle (no. 21) forms. Scrapers of various forms are also common (nos. 15–17).

In addition to Swidry, Chlebowice and Stańkowice numerous Swiderian sites are known from Poland, and the following are indicated on the map (Fig. 15):

Podgorz and Ostrowo (Kostrzewski, 1929)
Czerwony Borek and Mielnik (Szmit, 1929)
Osieck (Sawicki, 1923)
Zakrzów (Czapkiewicz, 1930)

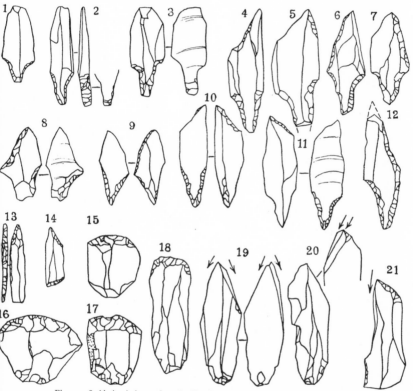

Fig. 19. Swiderian industry from Stańkowice, Poland. (After Szmit.) Scale: ⅓.

Apart from cases where admixture has occurred the flint industries conform closely to that illustrated from Stańkowice, but the three sites at Mielnik show a slightly different facies. The most notable differences are to be observed in the greater size of the implements, the greater frequency of burins and the relative scarcity of tanged points (Szmit, 1929, pp. 114–15). The difference of size could be explained by the local abundance of suitable flint, but the typological differences may indicate an earlier date.

Actually the Swiderian, though centred in Poland, seems to have extended

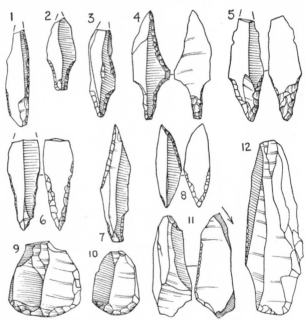

Fig. 20. Flint industry from Münchehofe, Brandenburg. (After Hohmann.) Scale: ¼.

both to the east into Germany and to the south-west into the Ukraine. The site at Münchehofe, kr. Lebus, Brandenburg, described by Hohmann (1927, pp. 186–207), certainly belongs to the Swiderian, rather than to the Ahrensburg-Lavenstedt culture. The flints described by Hohmann came from two sources, an early collection in the Muncheberg Museum, labelled as from the Klobich-See, and those collected by himself and W. Wilke in the field from what was almost certainly the original site in sand dunes

600 metres north of the Klobich-See. The material, though collected from the surface, appears to be remarkably homogeneous and free from any apparent admixture. The industry, of which the main types are illustrated by Fig. 20, was based entirely upon flakes and blades. In addition to simple kinds of microlith (no. 1) the most typical forms are tanged points, including the forms common to the Swiderian and Ahrensburg-Lavenstedt cultures (nos. 2, 3 and 7) and those forms peculiar to the former culture (nos. 4–6, 8); the presence of these latter forms indicates unequivocally the Swiderian character of the site. This is supported by the absence from Münchehofe of the obliquely blunted point with concave base, which occurs at Ahrensburg, but not on the Polish sites. The micro-burin is absent, as it is absent from all the tanged-point cultures free of Tardenoisian influence, but the true burin is present (no. 11), as well as numerous flake scrapers (nos. 9, 10, 12). Another trace of Swiderian culture in eastern Germany has been found at Reckenwalde, near Bomst (Rothert and Dobrindt, 1934, abb. 12–18). There are also indications that the Swiderian extended over part of the Ukraine, as shown, for example, by the flints from the station Smiatchka XIV published by Rudynsky (1927–30; also Zotz, 1932, abb. 3).

The age of the Swiderian is difficult to establish. The sand-dune sites from which the material has been obtained are inimical to the preservation of bone, and faunal evidence is entirely lacking. The culture has not yet been found in, or in relation to, a polliniferous deposit, so that correlation with forest history is not possible. There remains only the possibility of geological dating and of stratigraphical observations. The dunes of Poland occur within the area of the Pleistocene glaciation, but they lie outside the Baltic end-moraine, so that the mere position of the Swiderian sites can give no precise chronological information. On the other hand, when more is known of the history of the dune formation, it is possible that the flint industries enclosed in them may be closely dated in terms of geology. It has been widely noted that the dunes show alternate phases of building up and of stability marked by bands of fossil humus, and already this has afforded some stratigraphical information. A typical section is that through the dune 'Gorki' at Swidry itself, illustrated by Fig. 21, which shows two distinct humus layers. The Swiderian level was found to be in the top of the ancient wind-blown sand (layer E) below the lower fossil humus layer, which contained Neolithic and Tardenoisian remains (Sawicki, 1923, pp. 49–53). The recovery of Swiderian flints from the ancient wind-blown sand below Tardenoisian and later remains seems to be typical for the dunes of the valley of the Vistula (Sawicki, 1930). It may, therefore, be taken as established that the Swiderian, at least in its initial stages, antedates the Tardenoisian of Poland; how far, if at all, it survived is undecided.[1] Krukowski (1922, pp. 92–7) did not hesitate to suggest that the phases of dune formation and stability are similar over wide areas, reflecting the climate phases worked out for the Baltic region. The ancient wind-blown sand he correlated with a dry period (our periods I–II) from epi-glacial to Boreal, the lower fossil humus with the wet Atlantic phase (period III), and the upper wind-blown sand with the recurrence of dry conditions in the Sub-boreal period. But this is merely hypothetical and is not accepted by all workers (*e.g.* Sawicki, 1930, p. 53).

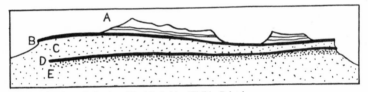

Fig. 21. Section through the dune 'Gorki', Swidry Wielkie, Poland:

A. 40–50 cm. Recent wind-blown sand with laminæ of humus.
B. 10–15 cm. Dark grey upper humus layer containing small charcoal fragments.
C. 18–100 cm. Pale yellow sand, containing charcoal.
D. 15–17 cm. Lower humus layer.
E. 100 cm. Ancient wind-blown sand, yellow in colour, but with a marked upper layer of rust colour.
(After Sawicki.) Vertical scale: 1 : 125.

THE KOMSA AND THE FOSNA CULTURES OF NORWAY, AND THE SURVIVAL OF THE TANGED-POINT TRADITION IN SCANDINAVIA

During recent years a considerable amount of research has been devoted to flint and stone chipping-places, situated on the Atlantic and Arctic sea-boards and extending from the neighbourhood of Bergen to the extreme north of Scandinavia. The more northerly sites are generally grouped together as forming the Komsa culture, which derives its name from a mountain of that name jutting out into Alta Fjord in Finnmark. The sites are all open and the culture levels are either on, or immediately below, the present surface of the ground, which means that all organic material is absent; as a consequence the archaeological remains that have survived

---

[1] Such 'evidence' as exists for this survival is derived from mixed finds, which may result from the denudation of dunes and not from culture contact or survival.

consist entirely of flint, quartz, quartzite and dolomite. It was observed by their discoverer (Nummedal, 1929) that the sites of the Alta and Porsanger Fjord regions sorted themselves out into two main groups, those below and those above the *Tapes* beach-line. With the former, the low-level sites, which yielded finely flaked crescent-shaped flints, polished slate chisels, chipped slate arrowheads, and chipped greenstone axes, we are not concerned, since they clearly belong to the Neolithic or possibly to even a later

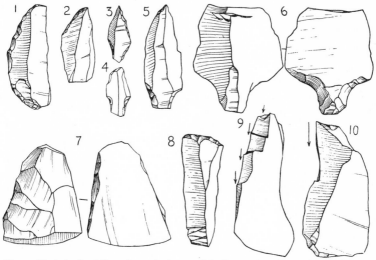

Fig. 22. Typical series of flint and stone implements of the Komsa culture from various sites in Finnmark, north Norway. Nos. 1, 4 from Stenseng; nos. 2, 5, 9 from Storbukta; No. 3 from Tollevik; no. 6 from Vedbotneidet; no. 7 from Berlevåg; no. 8 from Børselvneset; no. 10 from Russedalen; nos. 2–4, 7, 10 of flint; no. 1 of quartz; nos. 5, 6 of quartzite; no. 8 of dolomite; no. 9 of flinty quartzite. (After Nummedal.) Scales: nos. 1–4, 9, 10, ⅔; nos. 5–8, ¼.

period. The most important of the high-lying sites are situated in the neighbourhoods of Stenseng (54 and 57 metres, O.D.), and Tollevik (52–54 metres, O.D.) by Alta Fjord, Repvåg (20–30 metres, O.D.) and Kolvik (42–49 metres, O.D.) on Porsanger Fjord, and Berlevåg and Kirkenes (66½ metres, O.D.) (Tanner, 1930, pp. 463–6) farther to the east. The stone industry from these sites is substantially homogeneous, and the most typical and characterised forms are illustrated (Fig. 22). A marked feature of the industry is the skill in the production of flakes and even of blades in materials often of the most intractable nature (see Nummedal, 1930, pls. XVII, XXXVI–VIII, XLVII). Apart from a number of nodules, some of which have been rather generously interpreted as hand-axes, the lithic industry is based entirely upon flakes and (rarely) blades. Scrapers (*e.g.* Fig. 22, no. 8) are fairly common, but the most frequent type is probably the blade blunted down the whole or part of one edge (*e.g.* nos. 1, 2). Another form of particular interest is the tanged point of which typical examples are illustrated by Nummedal from the sites of Stenseng, Tollevik, Vedbotneidet and Storbukta, and by Tanner (1930, fig. 81) from Kirkenes; it occurs normally in the same form as in the Ahrensburg-Lavenstedt and Remouchamps cultures, the tang being produced by secondary flaking from the bulbar flake surface (nos. 3–5), but occasionally (no. 6) it is produced from the upper flake surface. True burins, of which I reproduce two examples (nos. 9, 10), are also typical features of the culture. In its general traits, therefore, the Komsa culture is seen to resemble the tanged-point cultures previously described. There is, however, one feature which is not paralleled in these sites, namely the presence of flake axes (*e.g.* no. 7). It must be allowed that these are frequent only at Berlevåg, only one other example occurring at Vedbotneidet, and there is no certain guarantee, in view of the superficial nature of the sites, that they belong to the culture; that their occurrence must, however, be taken into some account is suggested by the fact that they are also found on sites of the Fosna culture.

The Fosna culture derives its name from the Norwegian province of Fosna at the outlet of the fjord of Trondhjem, but typical sites are found to extend along the Atlantic sea-board from Helgeland to Sotra. In general character they resemble those of the Arctic sea-board, the sites being of an open nature and the remains consisting entirely of flint and stone. Numerous papers have been written on these chipping-places, many of which were discovered by Nummedal, but an important general study of the culture has been made by Bjørn (1929). A selection of the finished forms of the implements, all of which were of flint, from the site of Christies Minde, Kirlelandsøen, Christiansund, is reproduced in Fig. 23; the site is situated 44 metres above modern sea-level and consists of a chipping floor covered by 20–30 cm. of surface mould. The sites are usually of small dimensions, that at Byttingsvik, Gossa Island, Romsdalen, for example, having a diameter of only 5 metres. The flint types include numerous typical and quite well-made tanged points (nos. 1–5; see also Shetelig, 1922, p. 72), a few flake scrapers, a typical angle burin (no. 8), cores showing narrow flake scars (no. 6) and flake axes (no. 7). From the same site a doubtful core axe is illustrated by Bjørn, but Shetelig (1922, p. 73) illustrates a good one from the site of Drynjesundet, Vatne, Skodje.

The dating of the Fosna and Komsa cultures, which are clearly closely related, is rendered difficult by the circumstances of the sites. The absence

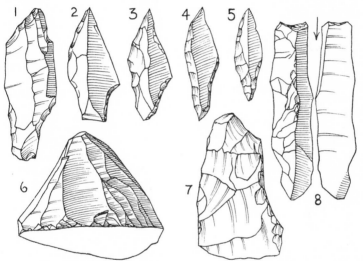

Fig. 23. Typical series of flint implements of the Fosna culture from Christies Minde, Christiansund, Norway. (After Bjørn.) Scales: nos. 1, 2, 4, 5, ¼; nos. 3, 6, 7, ½; no. 8, ⅔.

of bone precludes a dating on faunal evidence, and the fact that the sites so far discovered occur on or near the present surface of the ground eliminates a pollen-analytical or directly geological dating. There remain only the position of the sites and the typological character of the objects from them. The blunted-back points and blades and the tanged points, no less than the burins, suggest affinities with cultures of the Upper Palaeolithic, but more closely, perhaps, with the tanged-point cultures which flourished during the first period of the Mesolithic from Belgium across north Germany to Poland and the Ukraine. The presence of the flake axe on sites of both the

Fosna and the Komsa cultures, if accepted as belonging to these cultures, would certainly argue on the other hand for a later date, or at least for a survival, since the flake axe did not generally appear until period II and was not common until period III in Northern Europe. Geologically some indirect indication of the age of the cultures may be suggested by the relations of the sites to old beach-lines. It was observed earlier that on the coasts of Finnmark there was a strongly marked contrast between the sites below and those above the *Tapes* beach; the latter, with which I am here concerned, occur always between the late glacial shore-line and the *Tapes* beach and it has been suggested that they belong, therefore, substantially to the same period in the geological sense (Nummedal, 1929, p. 98). Clearly they are younger than the highest strand-line, because at the period of the formation of this beach they would have been under the sea. The fact that they occur above the *Tapes* beach indicates that they certainly can be older, and the further fact that they do not seem to occur below it suggests that they are not likely to be younger, though this depends admittedly on negative evidence.

More specific indications of date are given by the Kirkenes and Christiansund finds. At Kirkenes, on the shores of the Arctic, some typical Komsa flints were found in gravel of shores d3 and d2 of Tanner's classification (1930, p. 463), which would date them to the *Litorina* (oceanic) phase of Øyen, or in other words to our period I. The tanged flake from Christiansund (Fig. 24, no. 2) is often spoken of as 'a Lyngby point'. It certainly resembles the tanged flake from Nørre-Lyngby (Fig. 24, no. 1) and others found in Denmark and north Germany, but there seems no good reason for assigning it to the same culture. The resemblances with some of the larger tanged flakes of the Komsa and Fosna cultures are equally close, and the geographical probabilities weigh heavily in favour of regarding the Christiansund flint as belonging to one or other of these cultures. As it came from clay deposited during the Øyen's *Pholas* stage,[1] it supports the view that the Fosna and Komsa cultures were existing in Scandinavia during period I.

Whatever date is ultimately fixed by future research for the first incoming of the tanged-point cultures to Scandinavia, it is quite certain that the tradition survived unbroken, not only through periods II and III, as indicated by the flake axes, but also through the megalithic period of southern Scandinavia. Typical tanged points of flint occur in many of the dwelling-places of Norway and Sweden, dating from the passage-grave period, and

[1] Contemporary with the early stage of the *Ancylus* Lake.

before the discovery of the Fosna and Komsa cultures they were actually called after one such dwelling-place at Garnes, near Bergen, Norway. The archaeological objects from this site (Brøgger, A. W., 1913) occurred on gravel below between 15 and 20 cm. of peaty humus. The chief types are illustrated by Fig. 25 and include—in addition to the tanged flint points (nos. 6–7; see also Shetelig, 1922, p. 212), the tangs of which are formed sometimes by flaking from the upper (*e.g.* no. 6) and sometimes from the

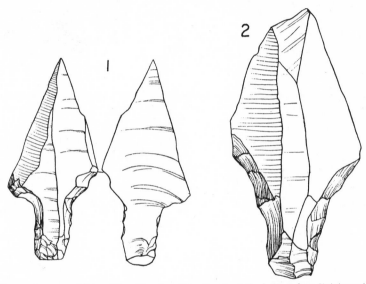

Fig. 24. Large tanged flakes of flint. No. 1 from Nørre-Lyngby, Jutland. No. 2 from Christiansund, Norway. (After Jessen, A., Nordmann, V. and Nummedal.) Scale: ¼.

lower flake surface—flint scrapers (no. 10), stone axes of various forms (nos. 4, 5, 9) and tanged slate spear- or arrowheads (nos. 1–3). A flint arrowhead with concave base also occurred but is not reproduced. The same types recur at the late passage-grave site of Holeheien, near Stavanger, (Gjessing, H., 1920 (*b*), pp. 102–10), which produced, in addition to the Garnes inventory, comb-decorated pottery and the triangular sectioned flake arrowhead with serrated edge. In the whole Stavanger region the tanged point is the commonest object on the dwelling-places after the scraper (Gjessing, H., 1920 (*b*), pp. 63–4). It is also found in many Swedish dwelling-places of the same period, of which we may quote as an instance that at Hallehög, Halland (Sarauw and Alin, 1923, pp. 98 ff. and Fig. 25,

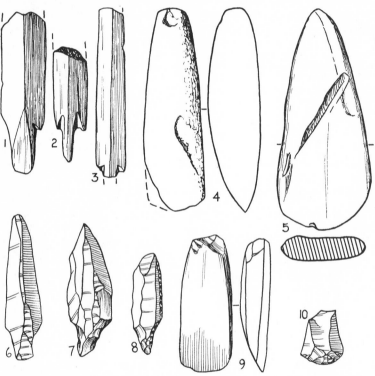

Fig. 25. Slate, stone and bone objects from a dwelling-site at Garnes, near Bergen, Norway. (After Brøgger.) Scales: nos. 1–3, 6–8, 10, ⅓; nos. 4, 5, 9, ½.

nos. 7–11). So normal, indeed, is the discovery of the tanged point at dwelling-places of passage-grave age in southern Norway and parts of Sweden that Almgren (1919) definitely referred the type to that period.

The survival of the tanged-point tradition in Scandinavia explains the presence of the flake arrowhead with tang and triangular section in the passage-graves of southern Scandinavia, though entirely absent from megalithic tombs outside the area of Nordic influence. For it is abundantly clear that morphologically the tanged point is the prototype of the triangular-sectioned flake arrowhead, as pointed out by Hohmann (1927, p. 204) and as confirmed by Schwantes; this can be clearly seen when unfinished examples of the triangular-sectioned form are examined. The latter form, the secondary pressure flaking of which is often arranged so as to produce serrated edges, is abundant in passage-graves and occurs in single-graves, but, as remarked by Almgren, is absent from dolmens and kitchen-middens. On the other hand it is found, frequently side by side with the simple tanged point of Garnes type, on dwelling-place sites from Bergen to the Island of Gotland, as for example at Holeheien (Gjessing, H., pp. 102–10), Hallehög (Sarauw and Alin, pp. 98 ff.), and Visby (Wennerstein, 1909), and Gullrum (Nihlén, 1927, fig. 68) on the Island of Gotland. It is to be assumed, therefore, that the triangular-sectioned type was evolved by the indigenous tanged-point people in southern Norway or Sweden, and was assimilated into the local megalithic civilisation during the passage-grave period.

SUMMARY

To summarise the evidence, it is clear that a group of flake cultures, characterised by tanged points and simple forms of microliths, burins and flake scrapers, flourished over the whole plain of Northern Europe from Belgium to the Ukraine during period I. The local cultures, Remouchamps, Ahrensburg-Lavenstedt and Swiderian, betray certain minor variations, but these do not affect the essential homogeneity of culture over the whole area during period I. Evidence for the local survival of the tanged-point tradition into the later periods is not yet well established, though some writers claim contact with the Tardenoisian. At any rate the main life of these cultures on the north European plain falls within our period I, and the absence of any kind of heavy equipment can be explained by the fact that during this period the immigration of forest trees had not seriously modified the tundra environment; the willow, birch and pine immigrated gradually and probably never formed more than an open and local park-land. The same general features characterised the earliest immigration of man into northern Scandinavia. The Fosna and Komsa cultures arrived fairly certainly during period I, but apparently continued through periods II and III, when they were influenced by the axe cultures from the south. Indeed the tradition survived strongly in the dwelling-place culture of the period contemporary with the megalithic civilisation of southern Scandinavia, and the tanged point gave rise to the triangular-sectioned flake arrowhead, borrowed during the passage-grave period by the megalithic folk from the aboriginal dwelling-place folk. The tanged-point tradition continued to flourish, therefore, in Norway, throughout the period of the axe cultures of the north European plain, and ultimately contributed to the megalithic civilisation of southern Scandinavia.

ORIGINS

In seeking for the ultimate origins of the Ahrensburg-Lavenstedt and kindred cultures it is natural to turn to the well-known Upper Palaeolithic site of Font Robert, a French cave site representing a special facies of the Aurignacian, and to Předmost, a Moravian loess station of evolved Aurignacian culture, since both show forms of the flint tanged point. It is, on the other hand, probable that the immediate origins are to be found in cultures, contemporary with and perhaps in part later than the Magdalenian of France, the remains of which are found in open stations in northern Germany and in northern Holland.

In 1931 a number of small flint-chipping sites, averaging about 10 metres across, were discovered along the banks of the Alster to the north-east of Hamburg, the most important of which was that of Wellingsbüttel. Similar sites have been discovered in the neighbourhood of Meiendorf, also in the neighbourhood of Hamburg. The flints from these sites, which, following Schwantes, we may group as belonging to the Hamburg culture, consist entirely of flake and blade implements with a complete absence of any heavy equipment adapted to forest conditions. A characteristic form is the shouldered or tanged point (Fig. 26, nos. 1–5) similar in many respects to that of the Ahrensburg-Lavenstedt culture, but generally larger, and often showing an oblique inverse retouch across the base (Fig. 26, nos. 4, 5) which is absent from the later culture. The Hamburg points are blunted on the right or on the left edge,[1] and the oblique blunting from the tip sometimes stops short of and sometimes joins the blunting of the tang. The various microlithic forms found with the Ahrensburg-Lavenstedt culture, the

[1] The points being regarded with the tip uppermost.

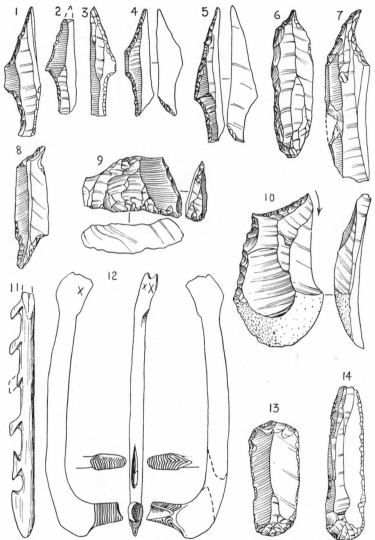

Fig. 26. The Hamburg culture from sites at Meiendorf and Wellingsbüttel. Nos. 11 and 12 are of reindeer antler. (After Schwantes.) Scales: nos. 1–8, 10, 13, 14, $\frac{3}{4}$; nos. 9, 12, $\frac{1}{2}$.

75

obliquely blunted point and the hollow-based obliquely blunted point, are absent from the Hamburg culture. The scrapers also differ (Fig. 26, nos. 13, 14), in that they are almost entirely of the end-of-blade form, sometimes double, but never of the horseshoe form. Keeled scrapers also occur (no. 9). True burins are common (*e.g.* no. 10) and the whole standard of flake and blade production is high. Another feature of the flint industry is the presence of numerous pseudo-awls[1] on blades and flakes (nos. 6–8); sometimes the point is disposed at the middle of one extremity of the flake, but more generally it is situated at one corner or else bends outwards from the middle, and frequently at both ends of the flake. These curious pointed flakes occur commonly on the Hamburg sites, but are not typical of the Ahrensburg-Lavenstedt culture. The points of difference between the Hamburg and the Ahrensburg-Lavenstedt culture are, therefore, considerable. It is significant that in every instance—the absence of microlithic forms, the dominance of end-of-blade scraper forms, the greater frequency of burins, and the presence of flakes with awl-like terminations—the special features of the Hamburg culture serve to affiliate it with the Upper Palaeolithic of Western Europe. The tanged and shouldered points recall Aurignacian forms, but the flakes with awl-like protuberances find their close analogy with the flints from the Belgian cave of Chaleux, dating from the Magdalenian period. On purely typological grounds, therefore, the Hamburg culture would best be dated to a period overlapping with the Magdalenian of France.

The sites first discovered, though remarkably pure, were of a surface character, so that no criteria, other than those afforded by typology, were available for dating. Efforts were, therefore, made to discover remains of the culture *in situ* in recently formed deposits, and this was achieved by Herr Rust in 1933 (Schwantes, 1934, pp. 62 ff.). The discovery, which was made by boring, has revealed a veritable hunting station of the Hamburg people, in which quantities of organic remains have survived intact. The remains were found to occur in the top draw of a metre of fresh-water mud (*Faulschlamm*) under a peat bed 2¼ metres in thickness. Only forty-five worked flints were recovered during the 1933 excavations, but these were sufficient to demonstrate that the site belonged to the Hamburg culture. Among the quantities of animal antlers and bones were a number showing signs of human interference, as well as several finished articles of great

[1] These objects were clearly never used as awls; their secondary flaking has all been done from the under face and they show no marked signs of use, such as is found on a real awl.

importance, made of reindeer antler. Suitable splinters for making small implements were cut out of young antlers, presumably by flint burins, and several examples of antlers from which long splinters have been so removed have been found (Schwantes, 1934, taf. 2). The two most notable reindeer antler objects from the 1933 excavations are illustrated (Fig. 26, nos. 11, 12). The barbed antler point is closely paralleled, both in the type of basal end and in the form of barbs, by another, also of reindeer antler, from Weseram in the Havelland (Stimming, 1925, p. 111 and abb. 2). The other object is shaped like a hook with a shank expanded at the top for attachment; it is curved at right angles at the lower end in which there is a slot, presumably for the insertion of a small flint or bone member. There is a biconical perforation through the basal part of the shank. The incised crosses on the expanded termination of the shank are probably ownership marks. The remarkable incised *Rillenornamentik* near the tip of the implement may have been designed in part to give purchase to the binding, necessary to secure a member to the one-sided slot. I have described the object as a hook only as an expedient; its real purpose remains obscure.

The animal most frequently represented among the bones and antlers obtained from the 1933 excavations was the reindeer, remains of which were extremely abundant; other beasts represented were wild horse, glutton, wild swan, white grouse, goose and pike. It will be noticed that forest forms were entirely absent, but equally so is the lemming, the presence of which we used in chapter 1 (p. 47) to delimit Mesolithic I from the Magdalenian of the caves. Pollen-analytical examination of the top of the fresh-water mud at the archaeological level showed that the only forest trees contemporary with the occupation were birch and pine, and of these birch accounted for 95 per cent. of the total tree pollen. A second piece of botanical evidence, this time of a negative character, was the absence of arctic plants typical of tundra conditions. The evidence of the natural chronology suggests, therefore, a date at the beginning of the post-glacial forest period, or the beginning of our period I (Pre-boreal), after the departure of the lemming and of the typical tundra vegetation, but before the environment was much affected by forest. The peat-bed overlying the archaeological level showed an increasing pine value, indicating the later part of period I and the beginning of the Boreal.

It would seem, therefore, that the Hamburg culture is slightly later than the true cave Magdalenian, but definitely earlier than the Ahrensburg-

Lavenstedt culture, to which it was probably ancestral. Traces of a similar culture have been found in the north of Holland at Elspeet. The site known as Elspeet I produced about 500 flint implements from a depth of 70–75 cm. (Popping, 1931); the industry was unmixed and included the same types of shouldered and tanged points, the same flakes with assymmetrically disposed points, as the Hamburg sites. The similarity is so close that Elspeet I can best be regarded as a station of the Hamburg culture.[1]

The origins of the Swiderian are still rather obscure, though the Mielnik sites are regarded by some as marking an earlier stage. The roots of the culture seem to go back to an Aurignacian of Předmost facies, while the flat inverse retouch, typical of many of the tanged points, is found in Solutrean levels in Jerzmanowska-Höhle (Kozłowski, 1923, taf. XII, nos. 3, 6, 9, 10, and taf. XIII, no. 4).

The Fosna culture of Norway is generally regarded as a southward extension of the Komsa culture of the coasts of the Arctic, and it seems clear that if the Komsa culture reached northern Norway in period I it can only have done so round the margin of the Scandinavian ice-sheet by way of Carelia. Bjørn (1920) supports the view that ultimately the Komsa culture derives from Central Asia, but the similarities with the Chinese finds (Boule, Breuil, Licent and Teilhard, 1928) are not really very close. It is true that the Upper Palaeolithic cultures of Siberia and China are based on flakes and blades, but the typical tanged point does not seem to occur. Whatever the origin of the Scandinavian tanged-point cultures, their main period of life was later than the Ahrensburg-Lavenstedt and Swiderian, which were supplanted during periods II and III by the axe cultures and by the Tardenoisian.

[1] Elspeet II (Popping and Bezaan, 1932) seems to represent a different culture. Some pollen analyses have been carried out, but conditions were not favourable and the results are unconvincing.

CHAPTER III

THE AXE CULTURES OF THE LOWLAND FOREST AREA

Period I

THE LYNGBY CULTURE

Before the incoming forests had to any extent modified environment the dominant cultures of North-western Europe belonged to the tanged-point group, described in chapter II. But already in period I the first traces of adaptation to forest conditions can be discerned in the reindeer antler axes, adzes and hafts of the Lyngby culture.

The handles of all three types are formed by the main branches of antlers (Fig. 27). The blades of the axes and adzes were made by cutting off the brow-tine obliquely; in the case of axes the cut was made in the same line as the handle (no. 1), and in the case of the adzes at right angles to the handle (no. 2). The haft was made from the stump of the brow-tine cut off transversely and hollowed out (no. 3). The geographical distribution of these objects is illustrated by Fig. 28. It will be observed that they have been found over the plain of northern Germany, in Westphalia, in the region of Hamburg and Lübeck, in the Havelland, and farther east into Poland; farther north they occur in Jutland, Fünen and Zealand, and in the Swedish province of Scania. It is probable that various cut reindeer antlers found in the same area and farther to the north-east in East Prussia belong to the same culture. The extension of the culture to Scania is explained by the fact that during period I, at the time of the *Yoldia* Sea phase of the Baltic, southern Sweden was connected to Denmark by a land-bridge.

A list of the reindeer antler axes, adzes and hafts, references, and other details will be found in Appendix II. All the specimens have been recovered accidentally from low-lying areas, from peat-bogs, ancient lacustrine deposits and modern rivers.

Our knowledge of the Lyngby culture apart from the reindeer antler objects is slight, but it is probable, although not certain, that various tanged flint flakes may belong to the culture. A specimen from Nørre-Lyngby, North Jutland (Fig. 24, no. 1) consists of a large flake, the bulbar end of which has been narrowed to a coarse tang by secondary flaking directed from the bulbar flake surface (A. Jessen and V. Nordmann, 1915). It came from sand forming part of the well-known series of fresh-water deposits dating from early in the post-glacial period. The fauna (see Appendix I), with its mixture of tundra and of forest forms, and the flora, which includes a grain of *Pinus sylvestris* pollen, in addition to such species as *Betula nana*

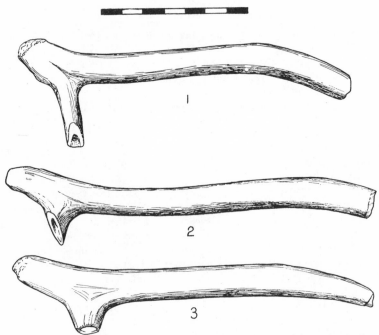

Fig. 27. No. 1. Reindeer antler axe from Langenfelde, Germany. No. 2. Reindeer antler adze from Odense, Fünen, Denmark. No. 3. Reindeer antler haft from Nørre-Lyngby, Jutland. (After Schwantes and Müller.) Scale of inches.

and *Salix polaris*, point to a date within our period I for the Lyngby flint. It is presumed that the Lyngby reindeer antler haft came from the same deposit, and the distribution of stray finds[1] of tanged flakes of similar form

---

[1] These may be accepted with caution. A tanged flake from Wentorf, nr. Hamburg, published by Schwantes (1931, abb. 1) is clearly not a Lyngby point; it has oblique secondary flaking and is probably a stray from one of the tanged-point cultures.

from Viby, Vesterborg and Bakkebölle, Denmark (Ekholm, 1925*b*), falls within that of the reindeer antler objects; the hypothesis that coarse tanged flakes[1] formed part of the equipment of Lyngby man is, therefore, a reasonable one.

The material of which the heavy equipment of the culture is made affords one method of dating. An Upper Palaeolithic date for the Lyngby axes and adzes is eliminated by the evidence of cave excavation, no single specimen having been recovered from cave deposits of the period, though they yielded an abundance of reindeer remains. Within the Mesolithic they can be tied down to the period during which reindeer are known to have inhabited the region, if we exclude the possibility that they were imported from some region where the reindeer survived until later times. We can leave out of consideration the importation of the antlers in an unworked condition, because there seems no adequate reason when other antler was available. The possibility that the finished objects were imported was adopted by Sophus Müller (1896, p. 304) as a reason for ascribing the whole class to the Danish Neolithic. Sarauw made the obvious reply (1903, pp. 303 ff.) that, in those regions of Scandinavia where the reindeer survived late, no single example of any of the types has ever been found. The Lyngby axes, adzes and hafts can, therefore, be ascribed on the evidence of their material alone to period I in north Germany and Denmark, with a possible survival to period II in south Sweden, where the reindeer endured for a longer period.

In the case of two specimens there is an approach to a geological dating, though it must be admitted that the provenance of both is uncertain. The reindeer antler haft from Nørre-Lyngby itself (Fig. 27, no. 3) was actually found on the foreshore, but it is assumed with reasonable probability that it came from the same early post-glacial fresh-water deposits as the tanged flint point found *in situ* at the same place; if this is the case the specimen dates from our period I. Another piece with claims to a geological dating is the Langenfelde axe (Fig. 27, no. 1), first noticed by Schwantes in the Mineralogisch-Geologisch Museum at Hamburg, where it lay unlabelled in

---

[1] Similar tanged flakes from Northern Ireland are outside my frame of reference, but as they will be familiar to English readers I feel I should mention them. They are found in a diatomite deposit, which occurs on both banks of the river Bann to the north of Lough Neagh. At Toome the diatomite is five feet thick and is covered by peat (Whelan, 1930). Erdtman refers the diatomite deposit to the Sub-boreal (period IV) on pollen-analytical evidence. Tanged flakes have been recovered from the lower estuarine clay at Islandmagee, dating from the middle of the Atlantic (period III) on the evidence of pollen-analysis (Burchell, 1931, 1934). The Irish tanged flakes do not seem to be earlier, on present evidence, than the end of the Mesolithic, while they seem to have continued into the Bronze Age.

a drawer with objects collected by C. Gottsche from the brickworks of Kallmorgen and Nitsch at Langenfelde. From the labels on other fossils it

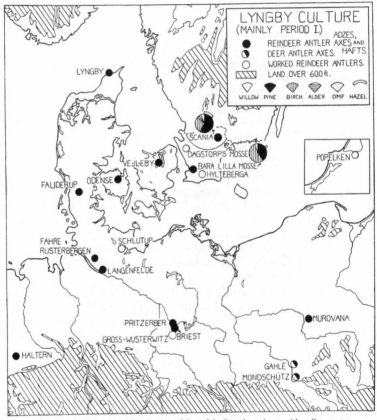

Fig. 28. Map showing the distribution of sites of the Lyngby culture, with pollen spectra for two of the finds.

is clear that in 1890 the section showed peat overlying fresh-water marl, and it is also known that in the previous year a tine of reindeer antler, artificially removed from its parent antler, was obtained from the fresh-water marl. If it is legitimate to infer that the axe came from the marl deposit, as Schwantes seems convinced, then this specimen also must date from period I, as the deposit in question dates back to the earliest *Ancylus* Lake phase of the Baltic at latest. Clearly neither the Lyngby nor the Langenfelde evidence could serve in itself as a basis for any argument, but as confirming other kinds of evidence they have some value. The Briest axe was found at a depth of 5·3 metres in Havel clay, topped by 0·7 metre of sand and humus, but this does not in itself give any certain indication of age. A reindeer antler showing signs of human work was recovered at a site near the railway station at Schlutup, Lübeck, from typical *Dryas* clay, belonging to our period I; it is probable, though not certain, that this piece belongs to the Lyngby culture.

Evidence of a more precise nature is afforded by the pollen-analytical investigation of various pieces from Scania.[1] Of these the haft from Bara lilla mosse, near Malmo, dates from period I, showing a total absence of alder and oak-mixed-forest and only a fractional percentage of hazel, while the broken specimen from an unknown provenance in Scania seems to date from the beginning of period II, giving 2 per cent. of alder, 3 per cent. of elm and as much as 14 per cent. of hazel. A worked reindeer antler, showing no definite typological character, from Hylteberga gave a definitely Boreal spectrum. In each case the pollen analysed has been obtained from samples removed from the specimens themselves. When the sample is obtained from within some cavity in a specimen, into which material is unlikely to have penetrated since its removal from the ground, this method does not in itself seem open to any serious objection. On the other hand in dealing with a relatively heavy object allowance must be made for the possibility of sinking; the pollen-analytical dating of single objects is, therefore, likely to err on the side of too great an antiquity. All the more significant, therefore, is the spectrum given by the piece from Scania, which seems to demonstrate a survival of the Lyngby culture in southern Sweden, at least, into the beginning of period II.

Taken as a whole the chronological evidence, based on considerations of raw material, geology and pollen-analysis, indicates that the main life of the

---

[1] The spectra for the Bara lilla mosse and the Scanian pieces are shown on the map. The actual figures for the three pieces are: Bara lilla mosse: willow 6 per cent.; birch 54 per cent.; pine 40 per cent.; hazel 2 per cent.; Scania: willow 6 per cent.; birch 31 per cent.; pine 58 per cent.; alder 2 per cent.; elm 3 per cent.; hazel 14 per cent.; Hylteberga: willow 5 per cent.; birch 21 per cent.; pine 60½ per cent.; alder 3 per cent.; oak-mixed-forest 10 per cent.; hazel 31 per cent.

Lyngby culture fell within our period I, though in south Sweden it seems to have lasted into period II.

The typical Lyngby antler forms have been compared by Sophus Müller (1896, p. 306) and by Schwantes (1923, p. 25) to the axe-like clubs once used by certain North American Indians. These implements were about 2 feet long, were made of reindeer antlers from which all the tines but one had been removed, and were used to "dispatch their enemies in battle, and such animals as they catch in snares placed for that purpose" (Lartet and Christy, 1875, p. 52). The same authors tell us that the implements were "called by the French voyageurs Puck-â-maugan (literally 'Strikers'), a name originating with Cree Indians of the Saskatchewan and elsewhere". The Lyngby forms can probably best be regarded as marking a transition between clubs and the specialised forms of axe and adze, and in this they are of very great significance.

The importance of the Lyngby axes and adzes in the development of culture in Northern Europe has been summarised by Schwantes in the following striking sentence: *Das Lyngby-Beil, das dem Westen fehlt, ist das älteste Beil, das wir nicht nur in Europa, sondern auf der ganzen Erde nachweisen können* (1923, p. 30). If this view be accepted, then the antler axes and adzes of period I can be considered the prototypes of the flint core axes and adzes that play so important a part in the cultures of Northern Europe during the succeeding periods II and III, and the evolution of these can therefore be claimed as indigenous. Before examining, in detail, the claim advanced by Schwantes, the alternative hypothesis may be stated for what it is worth. It is claimed by the opposite school that the Mesolithic axes and adzes of flint, and ultimately the polished flint axe, trace back their origin to the flint or stone hand-axe of the Lower Palaeolithic. But there is one fact which, in the present state of knowledge, militates as strongly in favour of the former hypothesis as it does against the theory of continuity between hand-axe and hafted axe: the Upper Palaeolithic has not yet produced a single object that can certainly be regarded as an axe or as an adze. In Western Europe, at any rate, the material cultures of the Upper Palaeolithic peoples, with flint industries based on flakes, blades and burins, appear to be conditioned by steppe and tundra environments; of heavy forest equipment there is no certain trace.[1] It is impossible to generalise with any success at this stage

[1] A possible exception is the hatchet claimed by Absolon from Předmost (Childe, 1929, fig. 4), but this has been restored conjecturally from a perforated mammoth rib and an ivory 'polisher'.

about Upper Palaeolithic civilisation outside Western Europe, but it seems to lack over the whole area of its known distribution anything that can certainly be interpreted as an axe or an adze. If, therefore, there has been continuity between the hand-axes of the Lower and Middle Palaeolithic, then it must have taken place outside the area of Upper Palaeolithic civilisation.[1]

The claim made by Schwantes that the Lyngby axe is the oldest axe (as distinct from hand-axe) in Europe seems to be incontestable, but whether or not it is the oldest in the world there does not seem to be sufficient evidence to decide; it is very possible that areas will be found where a hand-axe civilisation of Lower Palaeolithic type evolved directly into an axe culture of Campignian type. The area of axeless Upper Palaeolithic civilisation is, however, so extensive around Northern Europe that a possible direct evolution in some outlying region of the earth can hardly be invoked to account for the flint axes of period II of the northern Mesolithic. Their prototype lies, surely, in the Lyngby antler types, which from this fact derive their fundamental significance.

Mention should be made of two objects from Silesia of rather similar type but made of deer antler. In neither case were they found in datable deposits, and their attribution to period I because of their shape seems hardly justified. Their sites are, however, indicated on our map (Fig. 28), since they are frequently mentioned in the literature. As Schwantes has pointed out, the fact that they are of red-deer antler does not inhibit an early dating, more especially in view of their relatively southern situation.

Period II

LYNGBY SURVIVALS

As suggested earlier in this chapter, it is probable that the Lyngby culture survived well into the Boreal period in southern Sweden. Its influence cannot have been very significant, since this period saw the development of a new and vigorous culture, which extended over this area as well as over the whole plain of Northern Europe.

[1] It is probable that more will be learnt about the evolution of the axe when more information has been obtained on the evolution of climate and vegetation, since the axe seems to be associated intimately with forest conditions.

THE MAGLEMOSE CULTURE

DISTRIBUTION AND NATURE OF SETTLEMENT

The main feature of period II was the development and flowering on the plain of Northern Europe of a rich culture adapted to the environment of forest. Various terms have been coined to describe it. Childe (1931), rightly impressed with the transcendent influence of forest environment, would speak of the forest cultures; Lindquist (1918) and other Scandinavian authors single out a prominent feature of the culture by describing it as the bone culture; Kossinna (1921) named it the Dobbertin culture after an unimportant German finding-place. To each of these terms objection can be made on one ground or another. What is required is a label to describe a culture relatively homogeneous over a wide area, but showing local facies. This at once eliminates all the names of local sites, such as Kunda, Mullerup, Duvensee, Dobbertin or Svaerdborg, which must be used to designate the local facies of the general culture. To speak of a bone culture is misleading, since flint, stone and wood form equally important elements in the culture; flint is often, as at Broxbourne and Sandarna, the only one preserved. The term Forest Cultures has much to recommend it as a general term, but it seems desirable to use a separate label to distinguish each phase of forest civilisation of the north European plain. I propose to revert to the term Maglemose, which has the supreme virtue of being internationally current. Maglemose signifies in Danish 'big bog' and it is a common local place-name. Early writers used the term to describe the newly discovered site at Mullerup in Zealand, but it has since been extended, especially by French writers (*e.g.* Breuil, 1926), to include all sites of an analogous nature. It is in this general sense that I propose to use it, making it quite clear at the outset that in using it I make no special reference to the Zealand sites. Apart from its currency the term seems worth retaining because it expresses an important aspect of the culture, the most typical sites of which are, in fact, found in bogs and other low-lying places.

The Maglemose is found over the whole plain of Northern Europe included in our folding map, which shows the distribution of the main sites. It may be said at once that a true idea of the distribution of the culture cannot be obtained unless full appreciation is given to the contemporary geography of period II, as outlined in chapter 1. The main features are summarised on the map, in which water is indicated by blue shading. It will be seen that the coast of the present North Sea then extended from Holderness to the north of Jutland; that Jutland, the Danish Islands and part of north Germany formed a solid land bridge to southern Sweden, separating the Baltic from the North Sea; and that parts of central Sweden, western Esthonia, and Finland were submerged beneath the waters of the *Ancylus* Lake. As a consequence, the whole area from the lowland zone of Britain away into Poland and Russia and north into southern Sweden formed a single region undivided by water and, as now, unbroken by mountains.

The area richest in finds,[1] as shown by our map, is central to the whole region—Denmark and south Sweden, especially the Island of Zealand and the provinces of Scania and Blekinge. The great archaeological wealth of this area can partly, no doubt, be explained by the intensive scientific work carried out there, but its preponderance must surely indicate more than this, since intensive work has also been carried out in north Germany, the Low Countries, north-eastern France and south-eastern Britain with considerably less result. It seems likely that in fact the area indicated lay at the heart of the Maglemose culture. To the south numerous stray finds and settlement sites are found over the plain of northern Germany, in Schleswig-Holstein, Hanover, Saxony, Brandenburg, Mecklenburg, Pomerania, and East Prussia. Farther to the south-east several stray finds have been made in Poland, while to the north-east important sites have been discovered in Esthonia and a few stray finds from Finland can be related to the culture. To the south-east of the north German plain several finds have been made in Belgium, Artois and Picardy, whilst due east both stray finds and settlement sites have been discovered in the lowland zone of south-eastern Britain. It is highly probable that the southern part of what is now the North Sea was relatively well settled at this time, since the fen conditions, which are known to have obtained over the area, appear to have held peculiar attractions to the Maglemose folk, if we may judge from the situation of their sites at present visible on dry land. The dredging up of a typical barbed bone point of Kunda type (Fig. 42, no. 6) from between the Leman and Ower Banks off the Norfolk coast affords some concrete evidence in support of this supposition. To the north of the central area of the culture numerous stray finds and some important sites are found in Bohuslän, while odd pieces occur in the Oslo region, in the neighbourhood of Lake Vättern and as far north as

[1] A list of finds with references is given in Appendix III.

Dalarne.[1] The finds on Öland, which formed an island in the *Ancylus* Lake, are of particular interest, since they indicate some degree of navigation.

On the map areas over 600 feet above sea-level have been stippled in order to define more clearly the great plain of Northern Europe. It will be observed that in no single instance does a site of the Maglemose culture occur within the stippled zone. Indeed the vast majority of the sites occur within a very few feet of sea-level, and some occur below it. To the Leman and Ower barbed bone point may be added the bone objects dredged from Koldingfjord and Horsens fjord, as examples of finds from below modern sea-level. The important dwelling-site of Sandarna, near Göteborg, and the net-pricker with *bohrornament* from Limhamn both occur beneath the beach deposits of the *Tapes-Litorina* Sea. But the most typical sites, both of stray finds and of settlement sites of the culture, are found in bog and fen areas, usually on islands or peninsulas. The three famous Zealand sites of Mullerup, Svaerdborg, and Holmegaard are typical bog sites; other prominent instances are the German sites of Calbe, Duvensee and Dobbertin, and such Swedish sites as Istaby, Åmossen, Stora Dode mosse, Bare mosse, and Hörninge mosse. Indeed the bulk of the stray finds from all over the north European plain derive from bogs and fens. Other localities rich in these finds are lakes and rivers. Several pieces have, for example, been dredged from modern lakes like the Dümmersee in Hanover, the Pritzerber See in the Havelland, or Silkeborg Sø and Tissø in Denmark; more numerous than these are finds from the beds or margins of extinct lakes or meres, of which we may quote the English site of Skipsea, Dobbertin, Gohra-Worle and many other German finds from *Seekreide* or *Wiesenmergel*, and the important Esthonian finds from the lacustrine deposits near Kunda. Numerous objects typical of the culture have been dredged from rivers, as from the Thames at London, the Somme at Crouy, the Trave in Schleswig-Holstein, the Leine at Döhren, near Hanover, the Elbe at Magdeburg, and the Embach near Pernau in Esthonia; other finds have often been made on the gravel flood-plains of rivers under alluvial deposits, instances of which are given by sites in the valleys and tributaries of the Thames, Newbury and Thatcham in the Kennet, Uxbridge in the Colne, and Broxbourne in the Lea valley.

[1] The evidence in this case is a bone object decorated by a combination of two patterns typical of Maglemose art. Actually the site was under the waters of the *Ancylus* Lake in all probability until period III, and should, therefore, be regarded as a spread of the Maglemose culture into a peripheral area at a later date.

The Maglemose folk appear, therefore, to have been especially attracted by rivers, lakes and fens, which suggests that fishing and fowling played an important part in their economy. This is strongly confirmed, not only from the material remains of their equipment, as we shall show at a later stage in this chapter, but also from the faunal remains recovered from settlements (see Appendix I, list C). Pike remains are especially frequent, and on more than one occasion barbed bone points have been found embedded in pike skulls. Various species of edible water-birds, such as duck, geese, and swan, are strongly represented among the faunal remains, as well as many other bird species. The hunting of land mammals must, on the other hand, have provided the bulk of the food of the Maglemose tribes, and of these the aurochs and the elk were the most important, with wild pig, roe deer and red deer well represented. It was doubtless in the chase that the dog, found at Mullerup, Svaerdborg, Holmegaard, and Duvensee, was mainly used. An impressive victim of the Maglemose hunter is the aurochs, discovered in 1905 almost intact at Jyderup, near Vig, in north-west Zealand. The skeleton was found at the base of a peat bed 2·20 metres thick, overlain by 75–90 cm. of mould, and resting on sand and *gytje*. The peat was not pollen-analysed, but other tree remains show that it slightly antedates the full pine maximum and belongs, in all probability, to the beginning of period II. Two wounds were noticed in the seventh and ninth ribs respectively; the former, which was fresh and contained a broken flint, must have damaged the lung and was probably the one from which the beast died, whereas the latter

Fig. 29. Microliths of the obliquely blunted form from the breast of an aurochs discovered near Vig in the Island of Zealand, Denmark. (After Hartz and Winge.) Scale: ⅓.

represented an old wound that had almost healed up, the flint in this case being revealed by probing. In addition, three flint flakes, two of them obliquely blunted in microlithic style (Fig. 29), were found in the neighbourhood of the breast. The aurochs had presumably been slightly wounded on a previous occasion and, when fatally stricken, had managed to escape its pursuers. Archaeologically the find is of great importance as providing the only certain evidence for the use of microliths in composite weapons, a fact on which I shall enlarge in a further section. In addition to their fishing, their fowling and their hunting, the Maglemose people doubtless had recourse to the collection of nuts, berries and other natural fruits. The Duvensee site provided particularly good evidence of such collecting in the vast numbers of broken hazel-nuts observed there. Quantities of hazel-nuts were also found at Holmegaard, where it was noticed (Broholm, 1926–31, p. 19) that most of the shells were broken lengthwise, having been opened either from the butt-end or from the side, never from the tip.

The sites actually selected for occupation were normally on slight prominences representing islands or peninsulas in damp areas. This is well illustrated at Mullerup, where the sites of the excavations are shown (Fig. 30) to be situated on a low peninsula jutting out into the marsh. At Svaerdborg it was noticed that the areas chosen for settlement were those where the diluvial sand reached most nearly the modern surface, and at Holmegaard, again, the sites were situated on islands. Although normally in marshes and bogs, near the margins of ancient lakes, no certain traces of pile-dwellings have been found on the typical settlement sites of the Maglemose culture, a fact which suggests that they were inhabited only during the dry season of the year. It is certain that during the wet part of the year many of the more important sites could not have been inhabited, since they would have been entirely under water. Proof of this is also furnished by the faunal evidence. The roe-deer antlers show a marked predominance of fully developed examples, indicating that the occupation was predominantly in the summer, although the presence of quantities of hazel-nut shells on many of the sites shows that some settlement lasted at least until the autumn. It seems certain that the occupation of the Maglemose sites so far discovered was of a strictly seasonal nature. It seems unsafe, however, to assume that the material culture of the Maglemose people differed radically with the seasons, since there is so much material from stray finds, all of which can be correlated with the remains from the settlement sites themselves.

The fact that the settlements were usually made in damp places has important consequences to archaeology, since it implies, on the one hand the possibility of widespread pollen-analytical investigation, and on the other the survival of perishable objects of wood, bone and antler. At two kinds of site organic remains are lacking—where the floor lies near the modern surface or where a sufficient interval of time has elapsed between the abandonment of the site and the formation of an overlying deposit. It was noticed that at Holmegaard only flint objects remained on the top of the island, whereas on the lower slopes, where the debris occurred beneath a

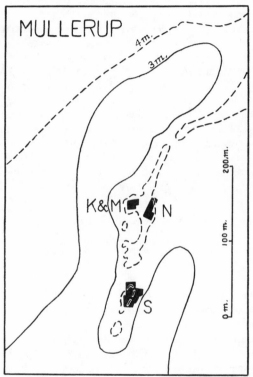

Fig. 30. Sketch map showing the situation of the sites at Mullerup in relation to heights above sea-level. S. Sarauw's excavations. K. & M. Koch and Mathiasson's excavations. N. Neergaard's excavations. (After Koch.)

layer of clay deposited in water, many antler, bone and wooden objects were recovered in good preservation.

As previously stated definite traces of piles are absent from the settlements of this period, but the site at Duvensee, to the south of Lübeck, can show some degree of artificial construction. Here Maglemose folk had settled on a slight island or peninsula in the bog, which could only have been habitable during the dry season. The actual squatting area, measuring about 5 metres across, was prepared by a floor of birch and pine bark laid on the peat, while small areas of sand and clay were brought in to accommodate a fire. It is an interesting fact that five such floors were found superimposed one above the other, giving the impression that the same site was selected for five separate seasons.

The settlements are generally very limited in extent, suggesting small social groups. The main settlement at Mullerup measured about 30 by 35 metres and the Holmegaard sites covered only a few hundred square metres. The Broxbourne and Duvensee sites could hardly have held more than family groups, both having diameters of 5 metres. This accords entirely with what one would expect in view of the economic status of the whole culture. The Maglemose people appear to have lived in small social groups, to have migrated seasonally, and to have lived on hunting, fishing, fowling and collecting.

MATERIAL CULTURE

I shall describe material culture under the headings of the chief materials employed:

A. Flint (Figs. 31–37)

For periods before pottery came into general use worked flints are of especial value to the archaeologist, since they alone of the objects of daily use are invariably preserved. Even in the case of the Maglemose culture, from which a quantity of organic remains survive, the flint industry is of great importance; not only are there rich sites of the culture, from which all organic remains have decayed, but the flints are essential in correlating the Maglemose with other cultures, such as the Tardenoisian, of which little except flint has survived. Detailed attention must, therefore, be paid to the flint work of the culture, of which I shall describe the chief types under separate headings:

(1) *Microliths* and the debris of their manufacture form an important element in the Maglemose occurring in some profusion at each of the great settlement sites—Broxbourne, Kelling, Duvensee, Calbe, Hólmegaard,

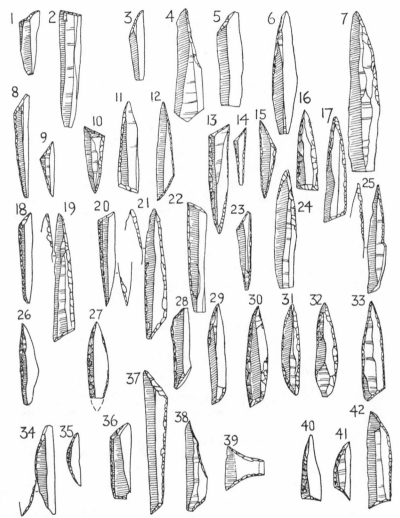

Fig. 31. Microliths from Svaerdborg, Zealand. (Drawn by the author in Copenhagen Museum.) Scale: ⅓.

93

Mullerup, Svaerdborg, and Sandarna. In certain respects there is a general similarity in the forms of microlith found on these sites; the highly evolved and often minute forms of the later stages of the Tardenoisian are normally absent. The trapeze, to take a typical example, occurs only once at all the Maglemose sites, namely at Svaerdborg (Fig. 31, no. 39), where it was found by a workman outside the regular excavation, and ranks as a doubtful find. By far the commonest forms at all stations are the simplest microlithic forms, blunted obliquely or down the whole of one edge, as illustrated by Fig. 31, nos. 1–7; Fig. 32, nos. 1–5, 7, 8; Fig. 33, nos. 1–3; Fig. 34, nos. 1–10. Certain variations may, however, be noted between different sites. For example, whereas at the English sites of Broxbourne, Kelling and Thatcham and the Swedish site of Sandarna, the microlithic forms are confined to the simple varieties common to all stations, the German site at Duvensee and the Zealand group of sites show a strong element of triangular forms. Again, as between Duvensee and the Zealand sites a distinction can be drawn in that, whereas at the former isosceles triangles predominate, at the latter sites they are replaced entirely by the scalene form. Finally, the Zealand sites as a group are distinguished by the more evolved character of their microliths; not only are the triangles frequently of very small size (Fig. 31, nos. 9 and 14), but forms such as the crescent (Fig. 31, nos. 34 and 35), the trapezoidal (Fig. 31, nos. 36–38) and possibly the trapeze itself (Fig. 31, no. 39) also occur.

The most prominent feature of Maglemose flint-work is the mass of fine narrow flakes and cores showing the scars of such flakes. As a direct result of the production of these fine flakes it was frequently necessary to rejuvenate cores by removing the whole or part of their striking platforms; in this way were produced on the one hand disc-like forms (Fig. 32, no. 13), and on the other triangular-sectioned flakes with battered keel.[1] The microliths of the Maglemose were made by the notch technique described elsewhere (Clark, 1932 (a), Appendix I), and micro-burins are, therefore, typical of the culture. In an earlier work the author, following published reports of continental material, stated that the micro-burin was absent from the Maglemose (Clark, 1932 (a), p. 103, etc.), but examination of the collections themselves has demonstrated that they do in fact exist, although previously

[1] The type occurs with many flint industries but is especially typical of microlithic industries (see Warren, Clark, etc., 1934, fig. 7, nos. 103–105; also Clark, 1934 (b), fig. 6, no. 91 and fig. 8, no. 130).

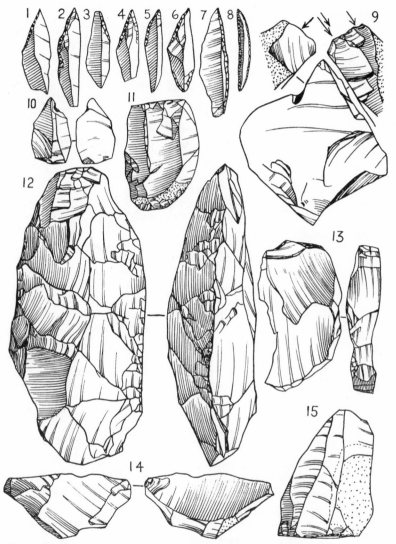

Fig. 32. Flint industry from Broxbourne, Hertfordshire, England. Nos. 1–8, Microliths; no. 9, burin; no. 10, micro-burin; no. 11, scraper; no. 12, core axe; no. 13, core trimming; no. 14, axe-sharpening flake; no. 15, core. (Drawn by the author from the originals in the Hazzledine Warren Collection.) Scale: ⅓.

unrecognised.¹ Typical examples are illustrated from Duvensee (Fig. 34, nos. 30–34), from Svaerdborg (Fig. 35, nos. 13–16) and from Mullerup (Fig. 35, nos. 20–23). In excavating the chipping-floor at Broxbourne Mr Warren was careful to keep a look out for micro-burins and he found them in some numbers (Fig. 32, no. 10). It is, therefore, probable that they really occurred on other sites of the same culture in England, but escaped observation. Of particular interest are the asymmetrically notched points, representing the stage before the separation of microlith and of micro-burin, which occur fairly commonly at Svaerdborg and at Mullerup (Fig. 35, nos. 4–8, 18, 19).²

It is possible that single microliths were attached to the tips of shafts to serve as arrows or darts, though it must be admitted that we have no direct evidence for this. On the other hand it seems certain that they were also used as the members of composite implements or weapons, being inset into wood and possibly also into bone. The class of bone points with slots, described below, are frequently found with flint insets, but in every case the flints are plain primary flakes without trace of secondary flaking; though usually of microlithic proportions these flint insets have never yet been found with the typical steep microlithic secondary flaking. It seems probable that the hafts into which microliths were mainly inset were of wood, the relatively soft nature of the haft necessitating the steep, blunting, secondary flaking. The fact that the hafts were, mainly at least, of wood is the chief reason why they have never yet been found; had the hafts been of bone they would surely have been discovered, just as have the slotted bone points with flint-flake insets. The discovery of three flint flakes, two of them microliths (Fig. 29), in the breast region of the Vig aurochs demonstrates the use of composite weapons. Francis Buckley's discovery near White Hill on the South Pennines, to which reference will be made in chapter v, supports the view that microliths were inset into wooden hafts.

(2) *Burins* of types found in Upper Palaeolithic cave deposits are typical of the Maglemose culture, though by no means common. From Broxbourne there is a good example of the single faceted type (Fig. 32, no. 9) and another

---

¹ The micro-burin has not yet been published from any of the Zealand sites, nor was it at first recognised from Duvensee. Dr Schwantes has, however, just published micro-burins from Duvensee (1934, abb. 94).
² These have been illustrated and published, but their significance has not been recognised. To regard them, as one writer has done, as tanged points is surely impossible, when it is realised that the 'point' consists, in fact, of the bulbar end of the flake.

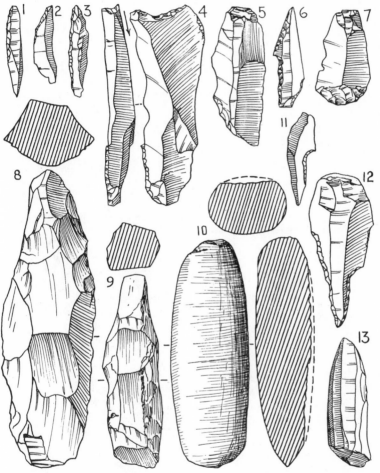

Fig. 33. Flint and stone types from Sandarna, Bohuslän, Sweden. (After Niklasson.)
Scales: nos. 1–6, 11, 12, $\frac{1}{3}$; nos. 7, 8–10, 13, $\frac{2}{3}$.

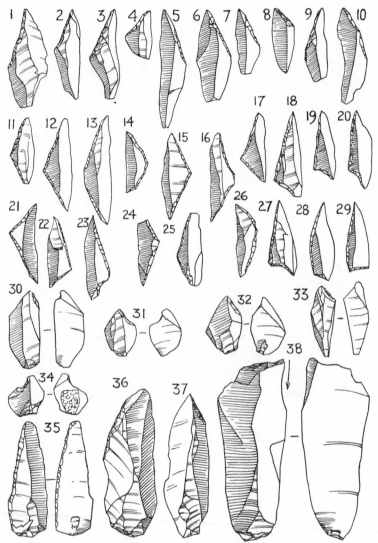

Fig. 34. Microliths (nos. 1–29), micro-burins (nos. 30–34), points with blunted backs (nos. 35–37), and angle-burin (no. 38) from Duvensee, near Lübeck. (Drawn by the author in Kiel Museum.) Scale: ¼.

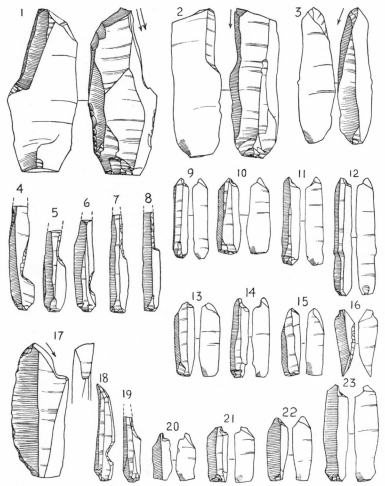

Fig. 35. Nos. 1–16 from Svaerdborg; nos. 17–23 from Holmegaard; nos. 1–3, 17, true burins; nos. 9–16, 20–23, micro-burins; nos. 4–8, 18, 19, unfinished microliths and micro-burins. (Drawn by the author in Copenhagen Museum.) Scale: ⅝.

of the double polyhedric type (Warren, Clark, etc., 1934, fig. 9, no. 117). Burins also occurred on the open site of Kelling (Clark, 1932 (*a*), fig. 29, nos. 18, 19). Duvensee produced the transverse straight angle-burin illustrated by Fig. 34, no. 38. The new Swedish site of Sandarna was closely investigated for burins, but produced only one good example, a transverse concave angle-burin (Fig. 33, no. 4). From the Zealand sites no burins have hitherto been published, but working through the collections I found from Svaerdborg the single-faceted and the two single-blow burins illustrated by Fig. 35, nos. 1–3, respectively, while the material from Holmegaard produced an oblique convex angle-burin (Fig. 35, no. 17). Although specimens may have been rejected among waste flakes from the Zealand sites, owing to the fact that they were not apparently recognised, the evidence from Broxbourne, Duvensee and Sandarna, where burins were actively sought after, suggests that they were never common in the Maglemose equipment. That they were nevertheless typical of the culture is shown by the fact that they occur at all the major sites and in a great number of varieties; among the eight burins cited no less than six varieties are represented. The burin, therefore, played an integral part in the culture of the Maglemose people. It is probable that it was used largely in the production of the bone and antler objects, which bulk so considerably in the material equipment of this people. The engravings on bone and antler objects are normally so fine in character as to suggest that they were made by a finely pointed implement rather than by a burin. It is, on the other hand, likely that certain exceptional pieces, such as those from Svaerdborg, Romsey or the Thames (see chapter IV, p. 162), heavily incised in the Upper Palaeolithic manner, were engraved by burins.

(3) *Scrapers* on flakes occur at all the main sites of the culture and generally in some numbers. The chief variations in the form of flake scraper found on Maglemose sites are illustrated by Fig. 36, nos. 1–5.[1] It is notable that convex, concave and straight end-of-blade scrapers are almost entirely absent from all the key sites of the culture, a few isolated examples (Fig. 36, no. 10) only occurring. The small 'thumb-scraper' is also absent. Core scrapers occur sparingly at some stations, as at Broxbourne (Warren, Clark, etc., 1934, fig. 5, no. 74) and at Sandarna (Niklasson, 1934, fig. 55).

[1] The following details of scrapers from Svaerdborg in the Copenhagen Museum may serve to illustrate this statement. No 'thumb-scrapers' and only three straight end-of-blade scrapers (cf. Fig. 36, no. 10) occurred. Out of 184 flake scrapers 15 were of the same type as Fig. 36, no. 1, 44 as no. 2, 87 as no. 3, 30 as no. 4, and 8 as no. 5.

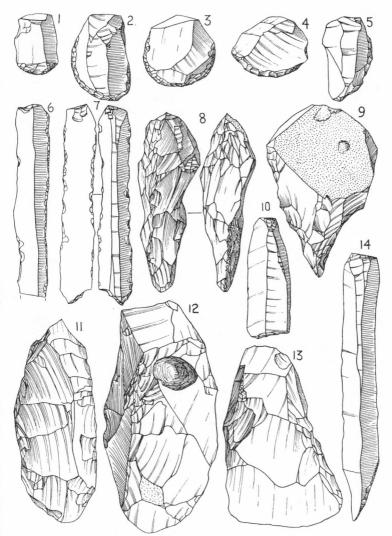

Fig. 36. Flints from Svaerdborg (nos. 1–7, 10–14), Holmegaard (no. 8) and Mullerup (no. 9), Zealand. Nos. 1–5, flake scrapers; no. 6, edge-trimmed blade; no. 7, used blade; no. 8, core awl; no. 9, flake awl; no. 10, transversely blunted blade; nos. 11, 12, core axes or adzes; no. 13, flake axe; no. 14, obliquely blunted blade. (Drawn by the author in Copenhagen Museum.) Scale: $\frac{2}{3}$.

(4) *Awls* are so rare on most of the sites of the culture that their absence or infrequency constitutes a characteristic trait. They are absent from Kelling, Broxbourne, Thatcham and Svaerdborg. From Holmegaard there are four awls on rough flakes and two core awls (Fig. 36, no. 8), and from Mullerup four flake awls (Fig. 36, no. 9), in the collections at Copenhagen. As a general rule the awls on blades, characteristic of the Ertebølle culture, are entirely lacking in the Maglemose. The only exception is given by Sandarna, where thirty-five specimens occurred (Fig. 33, no. 12), though all of these may not belong to the period II level.[1]

(5) *Points with blunted backs*, but retaining their bulbs of percussion, are never abundant, but their occurrence is so general that they must be considered an integral part of the culture. I illustrate typical specimens from Duvensee, Sandarna and Svaerdborg (Fig. 34, nos. 35–37; Fig. 33, no. 5; Fig. 36, no. 14).

(6) *Axes, adzes, picks and chisels of core type* (*kernbeil*) form as fundamental an element in the lithic equipment of the Maglemose as the microliths, and reflect the forest environment of the habitat. They are found on all the major stations from which any quantity of flint-work has been recovered—at Broxbourne (Fig. 32, no. 12), Kelling, Thatcham, Skipsea, Calbe, Duvensee (Fig. 37, nos. 4, 5, 8), Holmegaard, Mullerup, Svaerdborg (Fig. 36, no. 11 and 12) and Sandarna (Fig. 33, no. 8). All varieties and forms have been chipped down from nodules, and their edges are formed by the intersection of two or more primary flake scars, usually, on one face at least, transverse to the main line of the axe. The transverse blow necessary to produce this edge gave rise to a typical by-product in the form of the axe-sharpening flake (see Clark, 1932 (*a*), p. xxii). This was first observed on axes from the English sites of Peacehaven and Kelling, and it also occurred at Broxbourne (Fig. 32, no. 14). Searching through the material from Duvensee at Kiel I discovered typical examples,[2] one of which is illustrated (Fig. 37, no. 1). The edge of a transversely sharpened axe had the advantage of being sharp and effective when new, and though doubtless quickly blunted, was easily renewable by the removal of another transverse sharpening-flake.

[1] Occupation of the site continued as the beach built itself up and flint and stone objects typical of the Ertebølle culture occur at higher levels. Awls on the end of blades are extremely typical of the Ertebølle culture.

[2] Schwantes has since published two specimens (1934, abb. 96).

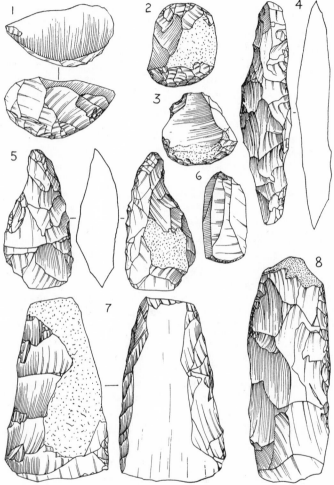

Fig. 37. Flints from Duvensee, near Lübeck. No. 1, axe sharpening flake; nos. 2, 3, 6, scrapers; no. 4, chisel; nos. 5, 8, core axes or adzes; no. 7, flake axe. (Drawn by the author in Kiel Museum.) Scale: ¾.

AXE CULTURES OF THE LOWLAND FOREST AREA

Variations in the form of this group of core implements sometimes suggest varying uses; axes tend to be symmetrical in section and adzes asymmetrical, rod-like forms with a pointed end may be regarded as picks, and light narrow forms (Fig. 37, no. 4) may well be chisels, but too much attention need not be paid to these determinations, which are largely subjective. The use of individual pieces of this group of chipped core implements can be decided for certain only when they are found mounted in their hafts. Towards the butt-ends these implements are frequently bruised (see Clark, 1932 (*a*), fig. 2, no. 4) to reduce wear on the haft, which took the form as a general rule of a sleeve, either of antler or of wood, into which a wooden handle was inserted. It is impossible to be sure of the relative extent to which wood was used for sleeves, as conditions have seldom allowed of its preservation, but the example from the Elbe-Trave canal shows that wood was employed as well as antler. No specimens of flints set into sleeves complete with wooden shaft have been found, but the wooden handle of the Höganäs antler axe was recovered in fragments and this was of birch wood (Rydbeck, 1929, fig. 56).

(7) The so-called *flake axes* (*grand tranchet*, *spalter*, *skivespalter*) occur on certain Maglemose sites, but never in any quantity, always being far outnumbered by core axes (*kernbeil*), a situation to be reversed in the succeeding Ertebølle culture of period III. The *spalter* is absent from the English sites of period II; at the German, Danish and Swedish sites of the same period it occurs relatively to the core axes in small numbers.[1] The *spalter* does not seem ever, in its true form, to have been found in a haft or sleeve, in spite of conditions at many sites favourable to the preservation of antler or wood.[2] The size of many examples of the type also makes one doubt whether they were really used as axes at all. The German term *spalter*, meaning 'cleaver', is probably more accurate than the term 'flake axe'; but, since the English equivalent is normally applied to a larger kind of implement altogether, I shall employ the German. I illustrate typical *spalter* from Duvensee (Fig. 37, no. 7), Svaerdborg (Fig. 36, no. 13) and Sandarna (Fig. 33, no. 9).

[1] Among the material examined at Hamburg and at Kiel I counted 6 *spalter* from Duvensee as against 20 core axes. At Copenhagen I counted from Svaerdborg 3 as against 20, and from Holmegaard 2 as against 44. From Sandarna Niklasson noted (1934, pp. 136–7) 46 core axes and a maximum of 4 possible flake axes, of which two only were anything like typical.
[2] The example illustrated in an antler haft from Bøgenaes, Roskilde fjord, is not very typical (Friis-Johansen, 1918–19, fig. 39).

MAGLEMOSE STONE IMPLEMENTS

B. Stone (Figs. 33, 38)

The chief types made of stone, other than flint, are:

(1) Unperforated pebble axes (*geröllebeil*), consisting of natural pebbles of oval section and elongated form, the surfaces improved locally by pecking, and the cutting edge produced by grinding from either face. So far, the type has only been found associated with Maglemose culture in Sweden, where it occurred at Sandarna from the early level (Fig. 33, no. 10).

(2) A perforated adze of fine-grained gneiss, oval in section, with one face rather flatter than the other, and a cutting edge produced by rubbing or grinding (Fig. 38, no. 6). The only example came from Holmegaard.[1] It clearly represents an imitation of the precisely similar antler adze forms which are common on Maglemose sites.

(3) Quartzite pebbles with countersunk hollows for thumb and fore-finger. The abrasion of their edges indicates that they were used as hammers. One comes from Mullerup (Sarauw, 1903, fig. 15) and another from Svaerdborg (Fig. 38, no. 4).

(4) Various forms of perforated mace-heads:

(*a*) A quartzite pebble with hour-glass perforation from Svaerdborg (Fig. 38, no. 5).

(*b*) A more complex form with two tapering projections at opposite points on a circular body with hour-glass perforation (Fig. 38, no. 2) comes from Kungsladugård, nr. Göteborg, from mud at between 1·2 and 1·5 metres below surface; it dates on pollen-analytical evidence (von Post) from early in period II, and the diatom investigation made by Halden and Sandegren established that it antedates the *Tapes* transgression. An un-finished example of the same type comes from the Sandarna section at a level dating from the end of period II or the beginning of period III (Fig. 38, no. 1). There is insufficient evidence for fixing the life of the Kungsladugård type, but it certainly dates from period II.

(*c*) A more complex cross-shaped form with no distinct 'body' and direct perforation (Fig. 38, no. 3) is probably to be associated in its origins with the Maglemose culture, though probably most examples are younger. One

---

[1] Unfortunately this was found by peat-diggers on the east site before the controlled excavations by the National Museum were undertaken. As no single object was observed during the excavations in the peat layer overlying the culture stratum, it is reasonable to accept the perforated adze as contemporary.

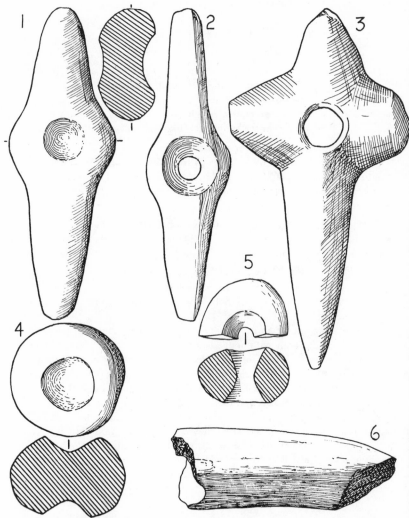

Fig. 38. Stone types of the Maglemose culture. No. 1 from Sandarna near Göteborg; no. 2 from Kungsladugård, Göteborg; no. 3 from Skarås, Sogndal, Norway; nos. 4, 5 from Svaerdborg; no. 6 from Holmegaard. (No. 1 after Niklasson; no. 2 after Sarauw and Alin; nos. 3, 6 after Gjessing, H.; nos. 4, 5, Copenhagen Museum.) Scales: nos. 1, 3–5, ½; no. 2, 4⁄7; no. 6, ⅔.

from Stala, Bohuslän, is finely incised with the net pattern characteristic of Maglemose art.

(5) Miscellaneous stone objects include:

(a) Three quartzite rubbers from Holmegaard (Broholm, 1926–31, p. 42) may have been used to sharpen the cutting edges of antler axes and adzes.

(b) An oval quartzite pebble from Broxbourne retains one face as natural surface, but the other and more convex face is artificially pecked, and the edge of the stone is abraded from use (Warren, Clark, etc., 1934, fig. 9). Its purpose remains obscure.

C. WOOD (Fig. 39; Pl. IV)

The three Zealand sites were particularly suited to the preservation of wood, but of these Holmegaard is the only one to produce any wooden objects of moment. The simplest are four ends of rods, pointed and hardened by fire, which probably served as pikes (Broholm, 1926–31, figs. 31, 32). Two club-like objects, the handles formed by the lower ends of branches, the heads by the junctions of branches and trunks (Broholm, figs. 33, 34), were probably used as throwing-sticks, similar to those of the Australian aborigines (Franz, 1928, fig. 6). Wood was sometimes used in place of antler to provide sleeves for the insetting of flint axes or adzes; such a perforated wooden sleeve, containing a flint adze, was dredged from the Elbe-Trave canal near Mölln (Schwantes, 1934, abb. 97). Half of a pear-shaped wooden plaque from Holmegaard (Broholm, 1926–31, fig. 36) is of interest as it shows indications of two perforations having been made by fire; some of the traces of fire observed on the wooden objects from Holmegaard result from the primitive method of hardening wood in fire, but such evidence as this suggests that fire was also employed as a method of carpentry. Traces of fire were also observed on the willow paddle-rudder from Holmegaard (Fig. 39, no. 2), which is closely matched by a better preserved example from Duvensee (Fig. 39, no. 1). These two paddle-rudders seem to be the oldest examples of their kind yet discovered in the world, and they afford important evidence for navigation during period II. The occurrence of pollen-analytically dated finds from this period at Hörninge mosse and Källingemöre mosse, situated in that part of Öland which formed an island in the *Ancylus* Lake, certainly suggest that there must have been navigation,

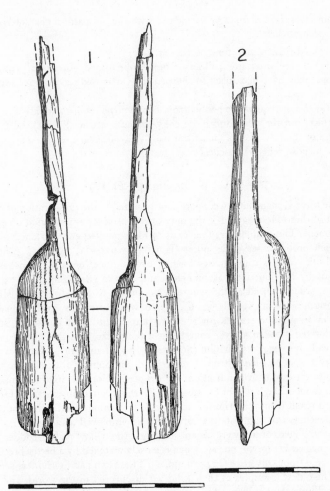

Fig. 39. Wooden paddle-rudders from Maglemose sites. No. 1 from Duvensee; no. 2 from Holmegaard. (After Schwantes and Broholm.) Scales in inches.

PLATE IV. Floats of pine bark and strands of net (*in situ*) from Antrea, Finland. (After Pälsi.)
Scales in centimetres.

at least in inland waters, during this period. More direct evidence than this is given by the dug-out canoe from beneath the carse clays of the Tay at Friarton brickworks, Perth (Geikie, 1879). The position of this canoe, which rested on a thin peat-bed under 10 feet of estuarine silt and 1 foot of overlying humus, dates it fairly satisfactorily to period II,[1] in which case it must rank as the oldest boat yet discovered in North-western Europe. About 10 feet of the canoe were found intact, but neither prow nor stern were sufficiently preserved to give any certain indication of their form. The dug-out portion of the canoe was 6 feet long, and had been excavated with the help of fire. The greatest measurement of the canoe across its gunwales was 3 feet. The tree from which it was made is recorded as Scottish fir. The continuity of land which characterised the period diminishes the importance of navigation as a factor in the diffusion of culture, but it is interesting to have certain evidence that navigation was not unknown at this time.

The discovery of a fishing-net at Korpilahti, in the parish of Antrea, Viborg, Finland (Pälsi, 1920), affords a remarkable instance of the preservation of perishable substances over a long period of time. The discovery was made in some low-lying meadows that had recently been drained, and the remains lay on the surface of pale grey mud (*Lehmgrund*) under between 80 and 90 cm. of plough-soil, peat and clay. The find consisted of a group of sink-stones and of eighteen pine-bark floats, perforated at one end (Pl. IV) and arranged in a crescent at an angle of about 40° to the scatter of stones. Under twelve of the stones were observed traces of plant-fibre, doubtless used to secure them to the net, which had decayed entirely except for a few knots found under four of the floats. The net itself was made of double-threaded cord made of coarse-fibred plant bast, but it was not possible to elucidate the type of knot or mesh employed, from the fragments that remained. The dating of the net depends upon the phytopalaeontological investigations by Lindberg, who puts the net well back in the *Ancylus* Lake phase of the Baltic. This early dating has been disputed by some (Alio, 1922, pp. 7, 8) on the ground that certain elk-bone and stone objects found in the neighbourhood must be of later date on archaeological evidence, but recent reinvestigation of the site has confirmed the early date.[2] This evidence for

---

[1] Erdtman (1928 (I), pp. 181–2) states that the peat-bed underlying the carse deposits dates from the Boreal period. The only woods noticed by Geikie in the shallow peat-bed, in which the canoe was found, were pine and birch.

[2] I have to thank Dr C. A. Nordman for this information in a recent letter.

net-fishing in period II is of particular interest, since the net pattern is characteristic of Maglemose art.

D. Amber (Fig. 57, nos. 10, 11)

Evidence for the utilisation of amber in the Baltic region, during period II, is afforded by the flat, tongue-shaped pendant, perforated for suspension through the narrower and thicker end, from Svaerdborg (Broholm, 1926–31, fig. 66). Three pendants, decorated in the pitted technique, characteristic of period II, come from unknown, but almost certainly Danish, provenances. Two amber pieces from Resen Mose, Jutland, may well belong to this period, judging from their decoration. Three amber beads, perforated by conical holes at either end, were obtained with antler and bone objects dating from periods II and III from Havel clay; two of these were from Grosswusterwitzer See and one from Pritzerber See (Stimming, 1925, p. 116 and abb. 222–4).

E. Animal teeth (Fig. 40, no. 10)

Wild animal teeth were used, both for personal adornment and as implements. Fifteen perforated animal teeth were recovered at Svaerdborg—five bear canines, five otter canines, two aurochs incisors, one wild cat canine, one wild boar incisor, and one deer incisor; there seems to have been no special preference for any particular beast. In the case of teeth used as implements only those kinds were selected which were readily adaptable to the purpose in mind. Wild boars' tusks were occasionally set into antler sleeves as adze blades (Friis-Johansen, 1918–19, p. 342), but their chief use was as knives, examples of which occurred at Holmegaard, Mullerup and Svaerdborg. From the last-mentioned site a number of beaver incisors was found, split lengthwise, polished on the inner face and provided with bevelled edges (Friis-Johansen, 1918–19, fig. 71).

F. Antler and bone (Figs. 40–4; Pl. V)

Antler and bone played an extremely important part in the life of Maglemose man, and the situations in which he lived have ensured the preservation of a considerable number of objects made from these materials.

MAGLEMOSE BONE-WORK

(1) Of particular importance are the various types of axe and adze and the sleeves for the insetting of flint axes and adzes:

(*a*) Antler axe or adze blades without perforation (Fig. 40, no. 5) occur generally but never commonly at Maglemose stations, *e.g.* at Mullerup (Sarauw, 1903, fig. 17), at

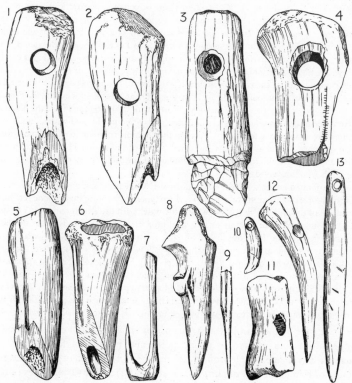

Fig. 40. Antler and bone objects of types commonly found on Maglemose sites. Nos. 6, 8, 9 from Muller-up, and nos. 1, 3–5, 7, 10–13 from Svaerdborg. (After Sarauw, Friis-Johansen, Broholm, Madsen and others.) Scales: nos. 1, 6, 8, 9, 12, ⅓; nos. 2–4, 11, ⅔; nos. 5, 7, 13, ½; no. 10, ⅔.

Svaerdborg (Fig. 40, no. 5), and from Pritzerber See (Stimming, 1925, abb. 185). Schwantes (1934, abb. 119) illustrates a markedly celtiform example from Gr. Rönnau, Schleswig-Holstein.

(*b*) Axes or adzes made from large tubular bones (Fig. 40, no. 6). The cutting edge of this type, which is of comparatively rare occurrence, is formed by cutting the bone obliquely; the haft was let into the articular end of the bone in which a perforation was sunk. It occurs at Mullerup (Fig. 40, no. 6), Svaerdborg (Friis-Johansen, 1918–19, fig. 47), Holmegaard (Broholm, 1926–31, fig. 21), and Gohra-Worle (La Baume, 1933, taf. 5, *d*).

(*c*) Perforated antler adzes (Fig. 40, no. 1) are of common occurrence during period II, but axes of similar type (Fig. 40, no. 2) are very rare.[1] Both types are made from the lower portions of antlers, the cutting edges have been produced by cutting the antler obliquely at the desired point, in the case of adzes at right angles to and in the case of axes in the same line as the perforation. The adze form is so rare in period III that it can be used with a high degree of probability as a type fossil for period II. It occurs at the three chief Zealand sites, at the pollen-analytically dated site of Stora Dode, Scania, in association with slotted bone points (Bring, 1921, fig. 6), at several sites in the Havelland (Stimming, 1925, abb. 186–8,) from the river Leine, near Döhren, and from the Thames at Hammersmith. Axes occur rarely in closed finds of period II, and when found loose are more likely to belong to period III, when they become common in closed finds. One single specimen, found at Höganäs and dated to the end of period II from diatom and pollen analyses, is of interest, as a certain amount of the original wooden handle, in this case birch wood, survived.

(*d*) Perforated antler sleeves are typical of the Maglemose stations and absent from those of the Ertebølle culture of period III. Two types can be distinguished, one retaining the crown of the antler (Fig. 40, no. 4) and the other with the crown removed (Fig. 40, no. 3). Both types occur in more or less equal proportions.[2] The objects inset into these haft were generally of flint, but in one instance from Svaerdborg the blade itself was of red-deer antler and in another from the same site a wild boar's tusk served the purpose (Friis-Johansen, 1918–19, fig. 40, and p. 342). In the case of one of the antler sleeves from Holmegaard part of the wooden handle remained (Broholm, 1926–31, fig. 13), sufficient to show the simple method adopted to prevent the sleeve working loose. One end of the wooden handle was left considerably thicker than the perforation in the sleeve, the slim part of the handle was pushed through it, and the sleeve wedged tightly.

(2) A type of antler object, the purpose of which is not at once apparent, is the antler tine worked to a fine point and perforated for hafting. I illustrate a typical example from Svaerdborg (Fig. 40, no. 12); others were found at Holmegaard (Broholm, 1926–31, fig. 23) and at various sites in the Havelland (Stimming, 1925, abb. 193–5).

(3) A large and indefinite class includes branches of antlers with large perforations but not further adapted for use. They are often highly decorated

---

[1] *E.g.* out of 43 specimens from Svaerdborg 97·7 per cent. are adzes. From period III sites the percentages are reversed, adzes accounting for no more than 5·5 per cent. (out of 18) from Ertebølle and nothing at all (out of 23) from Brabrand Sø.

[2] Out of 23 specimens from Svaerdborg 11 retained the root, and from 12 it had been removed.

with geometric engravings, and were, therefore, of some moment to their owners; in some cases they recall the *bâtons de commandement* of the Upper Palaeolithic. I illustrate decorated examples from Mazowsze and Ostrolęka, Poland (Fig. 62, nos. 4 and 5) and from Kl. Machnow, near Berlin (Fig. 59, no. 4); others were found at Svaerdborg (*e.g.* Broholm, 1926–31, fig. 54), and a fine specimen was dredged from the Trave (Schwantes, 1934, taf. 4).

(4) Small bone handles seem to have been in fairly common use. Examples from Mullerup and Svaerdborg are illustrated (Fig. 62, no. 6; Fig. 59, no. 2). They also occurred at Holmegaard (Broholm, 1926–31, fig. 29), as well as loose at Refsvindinge, Fünen (Sophus Müller, 1918, fig. 18) and elsewhere.

(5) The so-called elbow-bone dagger, made from an animal cubitus, occurs rarely in the Maglemose culture, though extremely abundant on sites of the Ertebølle culture. I illustrate the only specimen from Mullerup (Fig. 40, no. 8); another single specimen occurred at Holmegaard (Broholm, 1926–31, p. 64).

(6) A rare type is the centrally perforated aurochs toe-bone or phalange from Svaerdborg (Fig. 40, no. 11), which seems to occur only once in the Maglemose culture. Perforated reindeer phalanges are common in the Upper Palaeolithic of the caves, and the type also occurred at Hohlen Stein in a deposit dating from period I. The reindeer phalanges, which are usually perforated nearer one extremity, are often interpreted as whistles; the aurochs phalange, on the other hand, which is considerably larger and is centrally perforated, is sometimes regarded as a small hammer.

(7) Bone awls or bodkins (Fig. 40, no. 9), useful in leather-work, are found fairly commonly on Maglemose sites, but the fine-eyed needles of the Upper Palaeolithic are absent.

(8) Barbless bone fish-hooks are a marked feature of the material equipment of Maglemose man. It is noticeable in Denmark that the hooks of period II are generally larger and coarser than those of the Ertebølle sites. The hooks of the Zealand sites were secured to the line by means of a swelling at the top of the shank (Fig. 40, no. 7). Numerous hooks have been recovered from the Havel clay and these were secured in three distinct ways, by an expansion, a perforation or an indentation of the top of the shank (Fig. 43, nos. 10–12); it should, however, be remembered that the Havel material belongs in part to period III. Barbless bone hooks are found widespread over the area of the Maglemose culture, as at Kulm and Neugut in

East Prussia (La Baume, 1933, taf. 5 e, f) or at Reddis in Pomerania (Lissauer, 1887, p. 47), but cannot certainly be referred to period II unless geologically dated. A quite special form of barbless hook occurs at Pernau, Esthonia, in which the shank is enormously expanded laterally; two forms of attachment were employed, perforation and expanded top for looping (Fig. 45, nos. 8, 9).

(9) A class of bone objects known by the Swedes as *nätstickor* appears to have been of some importance, as a high proportion of the examples recovered are lavishly decorated. The term is applied to two separate classes of implement, which do not seem to have very much in common:

(*a*) The first, a narrow bone, obtusely pointed at one end and perforated at the other end, may very well have been used in net-making, though some German writers (Stimming, 1925, p. 113; Schwantes, 1934, p. 105) refer to them as fish-scaling knives (*fischschuppmesser*). A typical example was found at Svaerdborg (Fig. 40, no. 13); it is decorated by some feeble incised chevrons and the perforation is worn in such a way as to suggest that the implement was used for plaiting by a backwards and forwards movement (Broholm, 1926–31, p. 110). Another specimen with traces of chevron pattern comes from a depth of between 6 and 7 feet in Källingemöre mosse, Öland Island, and is dated pollen-analytically to period II. An example decorated all over with parallel lines of drilled pit ornament (Fig. 57, no. 1) was found under the Jära Bank near Limhamn, Scania, and is, therefore, dated on geological grounds to period II. A plain piece from Oslo, geologically dated to the same period, is closely matched by similar implements from Late Bronze Age sites in Northern Britain (Covesea and Heathery Burn); Childe (1935 (*a*), p. 171) interprets these as netting-needles. Specimens decorated with pit ornament from Odense, Fünen (Fig. 57, no. 5) and Mendrienen, East Prussia, and the fine piece from Travenort, Schleswig-Holstein (Fig. 61, no. 1), decorated with chequer and net patterns, can safely be dated to period II on account of the types of decoration found on them. Another decorated net-pricker was found at Fernewerder in the Havelland, associated with a barbless bone hook and some barbed bone points.

(*b*) The second type, included under the heading *nätstickor* by many writers, is less common; it consists of a socketed implement with spatulate end and is usually highly decorated. A famous example from Bohuslän is decorated by an elaborate net-pattern (Fig. 59, no. 3), and another from

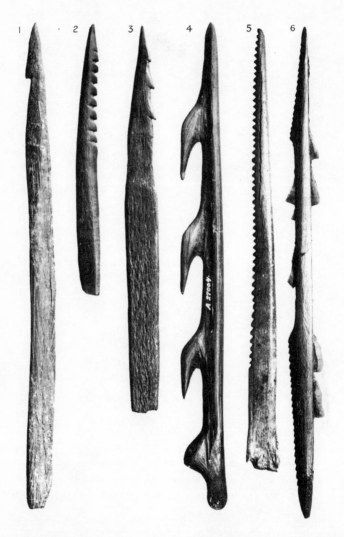

PLATE V. Nos. 1–4. Group of barbed bone points (forms 5, 6, 7 and 9) found, together with an antler axe and a perforated dog's tooth, in a bog at Løjesmølle, in the parish of Rerslev, Zealand, Denmark. Copenhagen Museum, nos. A 27002, A 27004, A 27001, A 27003.

No. 5. Notched bone point (form 3), from peat below salt-water *Litorina* clay, at Istaby bog, Mjällby, Blekinge, Sweden. Stockholm Museum, no. 13181.

No. 6. Slotted bone point (form 25) from Bussjö mosse, Bromma, Scania, Sweden. Dated pollen-analytically to period II. Stockholm Museum, no. 13075.

Scales: nos. 1–4, $\frac{9}{14}$; nos. 5, 6, $\frac{3}{4}$.

Sollerön, Dalarne (Fig. 62, no. 3), shows a combination of the two commonest patterns of Maglemose art, the linear chevron and the oblique
barbed line. The use of this type is problematical.

(10) The last class of bone object to be described—the bone point—is
probably the most important fossil of Maglemose culture. It is important
because it was made in a great variety of forms; a study of the distribution
and associations of these forms can, therefore, be made to yield peculiarly
valuable information about the history of the culture. Before discussing the
use to which these objects were put, or considering their distribution, it is
necessary to distinguish and label the chief forms. It is admittedly impossible to provide a scheme of classification that accounts for all the
secondary variations to be noted on individual pieces, but I hope that the
scheme adopted will be found sufficiently precise without being too pon-
derous for practical use. A diagrammatic key to the chief types distinguished is given by Fig. 41, on which each of the main forms is given a
number. Reference can always be made to individual forms by means oi
these numbers for purposes of tabulation, but where several different forms
belong to the same group I have distinguished them by site names.

A more detailed impression of the different forms can be obtained by
studying Figs. 42–45 and Pl. V and their underlines, which illustrate series
of bone points from Britain, France and Belgium, from the Havelland, from
Denmark and south Sweden, from the north German plain, and from
Esthonia. Illustrations of the broad slotted points will be found on Figs.
61, no. 8, and 62, no. 1.

Many writers constantly refer to the group of bone points as a whole,
and to individual types in particular, as 'harpoons', although the forms of
most of them are ill-adapted to the purpose and there is positive evidence to
suggest their use as the prongs of fish-spears (or leisters) and of bird-catchers.
Friis-Johansen (1918–19, p. 322) went out of his way to point out the error
of interpreting the Mullerup type of barbed point as a harpoon, but the loose
application of the term has continued. It is possible that the Törning type
(form 9) with its large recurved barbs was sometimes used as a harpoon, and
it is interesting in this connection that the type is often furnished with a
considerable perforation in the base for securing to the line. Apart from
this it is likely that most of the other forms were hafted for use, singly as
javelins or fish-spears, or in groups for fish-spears or bird-catchers. The
faunal material from Holmegaard, Mullerup and Svaerdborg is singularly

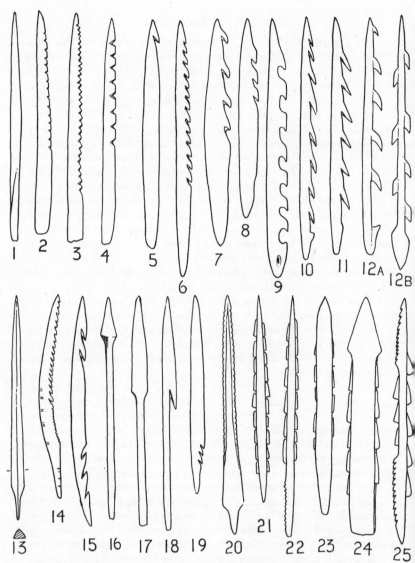

Fig. 41. Diagrammatic key to the chief types of bone point of the Maglemose culture.

116

complete, but it has yielded no scrap of evidence of any beast for which harpoons would be practicable. These sites, and others similar to them, were occupied seasonally, during the summer and early autumn, and it may well be that during the winter the Maglemose tribes migrated to the coast to

Table of the main forms of bone point of the Maglemose culture

Plain points of circular section. No. 1.

Notched points
- Simple notches. Duvensee type. No. 2.
- Triangular notches, leaving triangular teeth. Istaby type. No. 3.
- Triangular notches, spaced apart. Dobbertin type. No. 4.

Single-barbed points. No. 5.

Barbed points
- Finely toothed by oblique notches. Kunda type. No. 6.
- With convex barbs. Mullerup type. No. 7.
- With convex angular barbs. Pritzerber type. No. 8.
- With large recurved barbs. Törning type. No. 9.
- With pointed but slightly convex barbs. Gohra-Worle type. No. 10.
- With sharp triangular barbs. Sorbehnen type. No. 11.
- Single and double barbed with stem of circular section. Havel type. Nos. 12 A and B.

Tanged point of triangular section. No. 13.

Barbed leister prong, bowed but with straight basal portion. No. 14.

Bow-shaped point, barbed at either end. No. 15.

Conical tipped point. No. 16.

Lanceolate points
- Plain. Pentekinnen type. No. 17.
- Single barbed. Lohusu type. No. 18.
- Finely toothed towards the base. Pernau type. No. 19.

Flat tanged point, finely notched on both edges. No. 20.

Slotted points with flint insets
- Plain and narrow. Stora Dode type. No. 21.
- Ditto, but indented near the lower end. Svaerdborg type. No. 22.
- Broad and flat. Copenhagen type. No. 23.
- Ditto, but with lanceolate tip. Søholm type. No. 24.
- Narrow type finely barbed on one edge. Bussjö type. No. 25.

harpoon seals, whales, dolphins and the like. As the coastal sites of period II are under the sea at the present time, evidence of this winter culture is never likely to materialise.

Positive evidence for the use of the bone points found on the summer

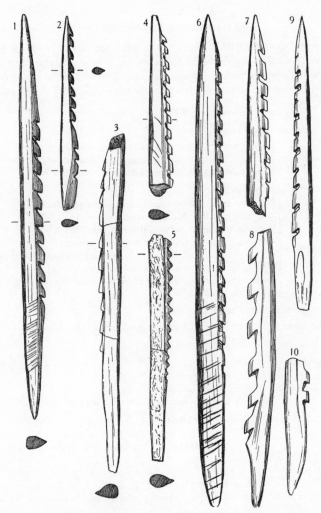

Fig. 42. Notched and barbed bone points from south-eastern Britain, north-eastern France, and Belgium. No. 1 (form 6) from Hornsea and no. 2 (form 6) from Skipsea, Yorkshire; no. 3 from the Thames at Battersea; no. 4 (form 6) from the district of Royston, Hertfordshire; no. 5 (form 3) from the Thames at Wandsworth; no. 6 (form 6) from the North Sea between the Leman and Ower Banks; no. 7 (form 6) from the river Escaut at Wichelen, Flanders; no. 8 from Béthune, Artois; no. 9 (form 6) from Béthune; no. 10 (form 6) from near Brussels. (After Breuil, Clark and Haase.) Scales: nos. 1–5, $\frac{2}{4}\frac{1}{0}$; nos. 6, 10, $\frac{3}{4}$; no. 7, $\frac{3}{8}$; no. 8, $\frac{1}{2}$; no. 9, $\frac{9}{20}$.

settlements of the Maglemose people is necessarily incomplete, but it is nevertheless highly suggestive. The discovery of groups of points closely packed together has occurred fairly often; at Mullerup itself,[1] a group of eight was accidentally discovered in 1896, another group of six came to light during Sarauw's excavations (Sarauw, 1903, pp. 241–2), and a group

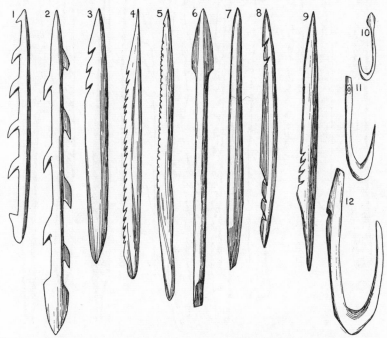

Fig. 43. Bone points (forms 12 A and B, 8, 6, 2, 17, 1, 15, 19) and hooks with various devices for attachment, dredged from the lakes and rivers of the Havelland, Brandenburg. (After Stimming.) Scale: ⅔.

of seven was discovered during a later excavation (Friis-Johansen, 1918–19, p. 323, note 1). The fact that the points were found in groups, closely packed together, certainly does not suggest their use as harpoons. To Sarauw the positions of the individual points of the group discovered by him suggested

[1] Three finely barbed points of Kunda type, found closely packed together at Svedstrup, Zealand, afford further evidence of the same kind (Sarauw, 1903, p. 249).

that they were hafted to form an eel spear. It may be hazarded that certain types of bird-catcher, in which bunches of barbed points are bound at the

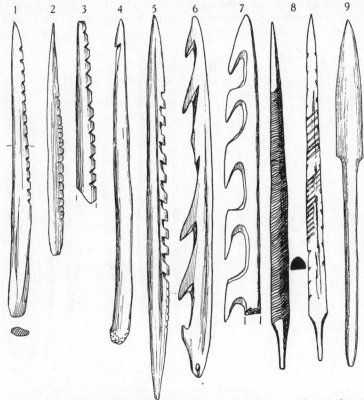

Fig. 44. Bone points from north Germany. No. 1, Duvensee (form 2); no. 2, Calbe-a-M. (form 2); no. 3, Dobbertin (form 4); no. 4, Dobbertin (form 5); no. 5, Szirgupönen (form 6); no. 6, Gohra-Worle (form 10); no. 7, East Prussia (form 9); no. 8, Szirgupönen (form 13); no. 9, Pentekinnen (form 17). Scales: nos. 1–7, 9, $\frac{1}{2}$; no. 8, $\frac{2}{3}$.

top or in some cases half-way down a wooden shaft, might also meet the evidence. The two most recent finds from Mullerup were composed entirely of single-barbed points (form 5),[1] but the find of 1896 was composed of two

[1] One of the points from Sarauw's excavation was too far damaged for accurate determination.

with one barb (form 5), three with two barbs, one with three and two with four barbs (form 7). This last group illustrates that different forms of point may not only be of the same age, but may also be used as units of a single implement.

A pair of barbed bone points (Fig. 46, nos. 1 and 2), found close together on fresh-water clay (*snäckgyttja*) below 1·7 metres of peat, at Siretorp, near

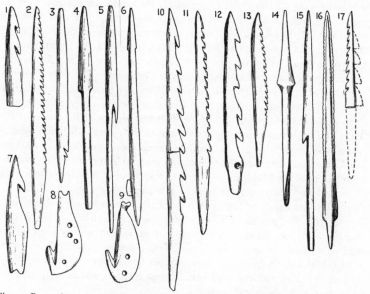

Fig. 45. Bone points and hooks from Esthonia. Nos. 1–9 from Pernau (forms 6 (2), 19, 17, 18, 21, 5); nos. 10–17 from Kunda (forms 6 (4), 16, 18, 20, 25). Scale: ⅓.

Mjällby, Blekinge, Sweden (*Fornvännen*, 1913, p. 271), certainly suggest use as the prongs of a leister or fish-spear. The position in which they were found, and the remarkable similarity in their forms, both suggest that they formed opposite and complementary parts of the same implement. A slight constriction is noticeable, rather more than an inch below the lowest barb, and the mark of the haft is still visible. A very fair idea of the way in which they were hafted is given by a leister, now in the Ethnological Museum at Copenhagen, used in modern times in regions bordering the north of

Hudson's Bay (Fig. 46, no. 3). Traces of binding in the form of horizontal and parallel markings at the lower end are still visible on a barbed bone point from Fäls mosse, near Lund, Sweden, and the oblique graffiti, seen to advantage on the Hornsea and Leman and Ower barbed points, are clearly designed to give purchase to binding.

In the case of two points (form 14) from Hörninge mosse, Öland Island, both pollen-analytically dated to period II, the form itself is eloquent of its use (Pl. VI, nos. 1 and 2); there can be no reasonable doubt that these two pieces formed the prongs of a leister. I illustrate on the same plate (no. 3) the prongs of a wooden salmon-spear from a grave at Lake Fjord, Tutilik, East Greenland, excavated by John Rymill and now in the University Museum of Archaeology and Ethnology at Cambridge. The close similarity in the general forms of the pieces from Hörninge mosse and the external prongs of the specimen from East Greenland is too apparent to require stressing. It is interesting to observe that the profiles of the barbs of the Greenland leister agree exactly with those of the typical Mullerup type of barbed bone point, though there can be no real connection between the two. The Greenland leister seems to have been used for salmon catching, but the main quarry of the Maglemose fishermen was the pike, remains of which are of general occurrence on the sites of this period (see Appendix I, list C). P. W. Thomson records (1930, p. 239) that an old man, who worked as a boy digging the deposit of lake-chalk (*Seekreide*) from which the Kunda material has been obtained, declared that he remembered a large pike's skull with a bone point sticking into it. It is elsewhere stated (*Ymer*, 1907, p. 453) that a finely barbed point of Kunda type (form 6) from a depth of 1·2 metres in Esperöds mosse, Tranäs, Scania, Sweden, was found in intimate association with a pike's skeleton.

That bone points were occasionally hafted singly for use as javelins or fish-spears is strongly suggested by the discovery in the bog of Aamosen, in the parish of Rerslev, Zealand, of a barbed bone point of Mullerup type, said to have been found complete with a wooden shaft which rapidly disintegrated on exposure (Friis-Johansen, 1918–19, p. 322). The conical tipped point (form 16) is used to-day in northern Russia for shooting fur animals without damaging the skins (Childe, 1935 (*b*)).

Evidence for the use of the slotted bone points with flint insets (forms 21–25) is lacking, though they are frequently referred to by German writers as bird-arrows. It is worth noticing that the small flint flakes inset into these

1   2   3

PLATE VI. Nos. 1, 2. Bone leister prongs from Hörninge mosse, Öland Island, Sweden. Kalmar Museum, nos. 602, 603. No. 1 has been dated pollen-analytically to period II. Scale: $\frac{3}{5}$. No. 3. Wooden salmon spear prongs from a grave at Lake Fjord, Tutilik, East Greenland. Collected by John Rymill. University Museum of Archaeology and Ethnology, Cambridge, no. 33. 840. Scale: $\frac{2}{5}$.

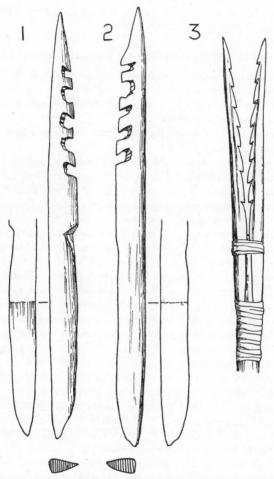

Fig. 46. Illustrating the use of barbed bone points as leister prongs. Nos. 1, 2. Pair of barbed bone points from Siretorp, Mjällby, Blekinge, Sweden. (After *Fornvännen*.) No. 3. Bone leister prongs, mounted on wooden shaft, from the northern Hudson's Bay region. (After Rau.) Scales: nos. 1, 2, $\frac{11}{16}$; no. 3, $\frac{1}{2}$.

points never show any sign of secondary flaking, and, when isolated, are indistinguishable from other primary flakes.

GENERAL CONSIDERATIONS ON MATERIAL CULTURE

Having described the material culture of Maglemose man in detail, we are now in a position to appreciate how it reflects:

(*a*) the modes of subsistence of the people and the natural environment in which this subsistence was won; and

(*b*) the substantial homogeneity of culture over the whole plain of Northern Europe during period II.

There is no indication that the Maglemose people practised agriculture or herded domesticated animals for food; carbonised grains and such implements as sickle flints are absent, as are also the bones of domesticated animals (other than dog). Among the flints there is no trace of polishing, and, in spite of the phenomenally favourable conditions for preservation, no single potsherd has survived.[1] On the other hand the quantities of wild animal remains utilised for implements or discarded as waste bear witness to hunting, and fish-hooks, net-prickers, nets and the prongs of leisters and bird-catchers show that fishing and fowling played an important part in daily life. The forest, which, as Childe (1931) was the first to show, to a great extent dominated the environment, is reflected on the one hand by the extensive use of wood for handles, hafts of composite implements, sleeves, clubs, javelins, paddle-rudders and dug-out canoes, and on the other by the abundance of heavy equipment adapted to dealing with it, such as axes, adzes, clubs and maces of flint, stone, bone, antler and wood.

The dominant impression one receives from a study of the geographical distribution of individual traits of the culture is one of homogeneity over an extensive geographical area. The degree of homogeneity is such, moreover, as can only be explained on the basis of the geographical changes described in our first chapter. The plain of Northern Europe extending from south-eastern Britain to Poland and Esthonia formed a unity in period II in a truer sense than it does to-day, when Britain is separated from the Continent and the Baltic forms an arm of the open sea. Local variations of culture can be

[1] If the Maglemose people used pottery it is reasonable to assume that we should have found it, in view of the favourable conditions prevailing at the more important sites. The absence of pottery from a culture with Upper Palaeolithic antecedents will not surprise anyone other than those who claim pot-making as a Palaeolithic art in Western Europe.

recognised, but these are subservient to the features homogeneous and general over the whole area.

The best illustration of this is to be found in the distribution of the various forms of bone point. I have not attempted to illustrate on my map (Fig. 47) the distribution of every type, but only of those of general significance. A key to the map will be found in Appendix IV. It will be seen that certain forms occur generally over almost the entire area of distribution of the culture, and so afford the most straightforward indication of its homogeneity. The barbed bone point of Kunda type (form 6) is found over the whole area from south-eastern Britain and north-eastern France in the west, to Esthonia and Poland in the east and south Sweden in the north, and the various forms of the slotted bone point (forms 21–25) are almost equally widespread, being absent from Britain, though occurring farther north in Sweden. The evidence of pollen-analysis shows that the slotted type is on the whole later than the Kunda type of barbed point, and the absence of the former from Britain is explained by this fact and not by any difference of culture; by the time the slotted type had come into use the marine transgression had covered most of the North Sea bed, but the land-bridge to Sweden was still intact, permitting the diffusion of the type in that country. Other forms of point have more local distributions, but the very manner in which these distributions overlap each other in every variety of way argues for the homogeneity of the culture of which they are fossils. Certain forms (11, 13 and 16–20) are not found outside the region extending from the Havelland to Esthonia; within this region some, like the Pentekinnen or Pernau types, occur intermittently over the whole area, whereas others are confined to certain localities within the area—form 16 to East Prussia and Esthonia, form 11 to East Prussia, and form 20 to Esthonia. The Havel type of barbed point (forms 12 A and B) is found scattered over the area from Hanover to East Prussia and so overlaps with the previous group. Within the area of this overlap, the central portions of the north German plain, is found the notched point of Duvensee type (form 2). The Törning type (form 9) is found in Poland, East Prussia, Schleswig-Holstein, Denmark and Sweden, form 10 is found only in Pomerania, East Prussia and south Sweden, the broad forms of the slotted bone point (forms 23, 24) occur only in Zealand and south Sweden, and the famous Mullerup type itself (form 7) is confined to the Danish Islands of Zealand and Bornholm. Finally, one may note the occurrence of a distinctive form locally at widely separated points in our area,

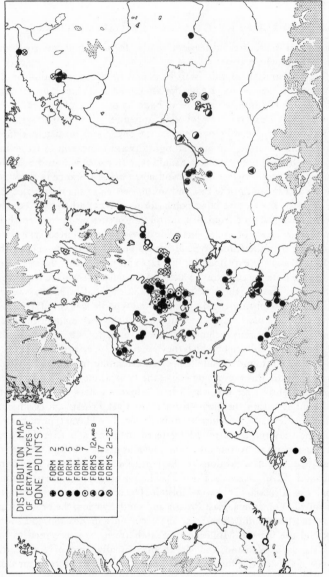

DISTRIBUTION MAP
OF CERTAIN TYPES OF
BONE POINTS:

● FORM 2
◐ FORM 3
✖ FORM 5
● FORM 6
◉ FORM 7
◕ FORMS 12A AND B
◀ FORM 17
⊗ FORMS 21-25

Fig. 47. Map of the plain of Northern Europe (stippled area over 600 feet above mean sea-level), showing the distribution of the chief forms of the Maglemose bone points.

indicating to my mind some community of culture; the Istaby type of point with triangular notches and teeth (form 3) is found only in the Swedish province of Blekinge[1] and in the Thames at Wandsworth.

Our study of the techniques and motives of Maglemose art in chapter IV (especially p. 174) illustrates once more the homogeneity of the culture province. The drilled pit ornament is spread over the wide tract from Belgium to Esthonia and reaches south Sweden in the north. Objects with decorated cracks have been dredged from the Somme and excavated in Zealand. Specialised patterns like the net pattern and the chequer are found in Sweden as well as in north Germany and Denmark, and identical combinations of simpler motives are common to Poland, Sweden, Denmark and north Germany. Motive i occurs in the drilled technique only twice, once in Jutland and once in Esthonia. The opposed triangles (motive w) are also found twice only, in Jutland and in south Sweden. Instances could be multiplied to tell the same story.

SOCIAL OUTLOOK

Evidence of the social outlook of the Maglemose people is necessarily meagre, but certain scraps of information can safely be inferred from the archaeological material that has survived. The size of single communities must have been relatively small, since large concentrations of population, where subsistence rests purely on a hunting, fishing and collecting basis, are economically impossible. Direct evidence for small communities is given by the size and character of the settlements themselves. It is also safe to infer that the Maglemose people migrated seasonally, since the settlements so far investigated were inhabited only during the summer and autumn months (see over p. 90). Evidence of the religion of these small groups of hunters and fishers is slight. Their art, which is described in chapter IV, was almost entirely of a geometric order; it shows no evidence of hunting magic, such as we know from the Upper Palaeolithic cave art, but was more likely the product of boredom. Although, therefore, their art shows that their prowess as hunters and fishers earned them sufficient leisure to be bored, it throws very little light on the motive forces of their religion. There are, however, some interesting biomorphic designs, which are frequently found on pendants, and it is possible that these may be inter-

[1] From Istaby (3) and Lörby bogs, near Mjällby, from the Mjällby district, and from Väby.

preted as fertility amulets. There is no burial that can safely be ascribed to the Maglemose people, but human bones have frequently been found haphazard on settlement sites. At Mullerup Sarauw found (1903, p. 198), mixed with the ordinary debris of settlement, the thigh-bone and finger-bone of an adult and the lower jaw of a youth; Friis-Johansen (1918–19, p. 264) noticed fragments of human skull in the deposit at Svaerdborg, and Niklasson (1934, p. 142) discovered the left tibia of a man at Sandarna. This mixture of odd human bones with debris of settlement suggested cannibalism to Franz (1927, p. 14), and he further pointed to the fact that the thigh-bone from Mullerup showed definite signs of cutting. The circumstances are certainly suspicious, although not everybody will regard them as conclusive. There is a certain amount of circumstantial evidence for cannibalism from the Upper Palaeolithic deposits in the Belgian caves (Rutot, 1907), but interpretation is always difficult.

CHRONOLOGY

The dating of the Maglemose culture in the sequence of events of post-glacial natural history rests upon a wealth of evidence. This is due, in large measure, to the low-lying character of the sites most favoured by Maglemose man. On the one hand the culture can be related to the history of land-movement and on the other to the history of forest development, both of which are outlined in chapter 1. In that chapter the period of post-glacial time, with which this book is concerned, was divided into three phases, and it is to the second of these that the Maglemose mainly belongs.

Period II, especially during its earlier stages, was one of marked continentality in that part of Europe inhabited by Maglemose man, and considerable areas now under the sea were then dry land. The most direct geological evidence, therefore, for dating the Maglemose culture to period II is the discovery of typical objects in such areas under the sea. The barbed bone point of Kunda type dredged from between the Leman and Ower Banks some 25 miles from the coast of Norfolk is in this respect typical. Other examples are given by objects dredged from fjords in the east coast of Jutland—the antlers decorated by drilled pit ornament from Koldingfjord and the decorated antler object from Horsens fjord. Evidence no less convincing is that of finds made beneath marine deposits dating from period

III. These deposits may consist of old sea banks or beaches, or of silts or clays containing marine organisms. The main culture stratum of the important and typical dwelling-place at Sandarna, near Göteborg, underlay such a sea-bank, and a bone net-pricker, decorated by the typical drilled pit ornament, was found under the famous Jära Bank at Limhamn, Scania. The perforated and decorated antler axe from Höganäs, Scania, was found to occur well below the period of the *Litorina* maximum, as indicated by the studies of diatom frequencies made by Halden, and on this evidence it is dated to the end of period II. The perforated stone mace from Kungsladugård was dated to before the *Tapes* sinking by Halden's and Sandegren's work on the diatoms. The notched bone points (form 3) from Istaby, Blekinge, occurred in a peat bed below salt-water clay dated geologically to the *Litorina* phase of the Baltic (period III), and the bone net-pricker from Oslo was lost at the period previous to the *Tapes* sinking.

The Höganäs axe and the Kungsladugård mace were also dated to the same period by the palaeo-botanical method of pollen-analysis, which forms the second and perhaps the more important class of natural historical evidence. The pollen-analytical method is more valuable because it is more frequently and more universally applicable. Since the method is a modern one that has not been extensively applied outside Sweden until after the Great War, it is only the more recent finds that have been investigated pollen-analytically, except in so far as traces of deposit adhering to specimens has made possible the tentative dating of single pieces long after their discovery. A very considerable number of finds have been investigated, however, since the sites normally occur in situations peculiarly favourable to the preservation of tree pollen. It has been found that in every case where conditions have been satisfactory the pollen-analytical evidence dates objects and sites of Maglemose culture to period II. The evidence from eight settlement sites and from sixteen single objects is tabulated in Appendix IV, together with references, and the pollen spectra, expressed as sectors of circles, are illustrated at the bottom of the folding map. As a general rule it will be seen that the analyses show high values for birch and pine and hazel, the components of the oak-mixed-forest and alder being present but seldom to any very great extent; in fact the analyses point to period II as defined in our chapter I. Naturally there is a wide variation between the pollen spectra for different sites, since period II covered a long period of time, during which the composition of forests was undergoing constant change. Moreover the sites investigated extend over a considerable geographical area, over which the composition of forests can never have been identical.

When more correlations have been made between cultural remains and post-glacial forest history, and when the course of this history is more accurately known over the whole area of the Maglemose culture, it should be possible to sub-divide the period and to arrange the various sites in some kind of chronological sequence. At present the evidence is not available for working out the chronology of the culture in any detail, though certain facts merit some attention. The system of Knut Stjerna (1911) was based on purely archaeological evidence of a restricted kind. His view that the barbed points of Kunda type (form 6) are younger than the typical Mullerup points (form 7) can hardly be maintained to-day. With our greater knowledge of the distribution of the Maglemose culture it has become clear that the Mullerup variety, almost confined to the island of Zealand, is restricted, whereas the typical Kunda form of point is found widespread over the whole area of the culture. The Mullerup form appears, therefore, on the broad view, as a special and local variety, which for this very reason is likely to be younger rather than older than the more generally spread Kunda form. The group find of Løjesmølle (Pl. V, nos. 1–4), in which each of the three main Danish varieties of barbed point is represented, serves to indicate that the various forms overlapped in time, and it may be remembered in this connection that the site of Mullerup itself produced a point of Kunda type (Sarauw, 1903, fig. 30). On the other hand the finds of points exclusively of certain kinds within a small island like Zealand imply some difference in the main lives of the different forms; at Skottemark, for example, 14 points were found all of Kunda type (form 6), whereas at Svaerdborg the two excavations produced 274 points, all of which were of the single-barbed and Mullerup varieties (forms 5 and 7). I suggest that it is more likely on archaeological grounds that the Mullerup variety of the Maglemose culture is younger than the Kunda, at least in origin. I also suggest that the notched bone point of Duvensee type (form 2) is also in origin earlier than the Mullerup form, since the microlithic forms found at Duvensee were markedly less evolved than those from the Mullerup stations of Zealand.

The relatively later date of these stations is supported definitely by the results of pollen-analysis. Comparison of the pollen spectra of samples from the culture strata of Mullerup, Svaerdborg and the two Holmegaard sites will show how close is the mutual agreement, emphasising the contemporaneity of the sites, the objects from which are themselves so uniform. All four are definitely younger than Duvensee, where birch and pine account for 95 per cent. of the total forest tree pollen. The evidence from the ancient lake deposits of Kunda shows, that at the period when the typical finely barbed points (form 6) were in use, alder and the oak-mixed-forest had made less inroad on the birch and pine dominance than they had when the Mullerup stations were flourishing. The typical Kunda point from between the Leman and Ower Banks came from 'moorlog' showing a spectrum typical of an early stage of period II, considerably earlier than that to which the Mullerup stations belong. On the other hand the Kunda points from Taaderup in the island of Falster and from Hörninge mosse in Öland Island seem to date from much the same period as the Mullerup stations. Pollen-analysis gives one further hint of some importance, which also agrees very well with the archaeological evidence. Slotted bone points of the narrow forms have been dated pollen-analytically from Bussjö mosse, Hylteberga, Stora Dode mosse (2), Svaerdborg and Åmossen (3), and in each case they are found to belong to the later stages of period II; it is evident that they came into use later than the period of the Duvensee station, and that, while occurring rarely at Svaerdborg, they did not become common until the end of the period.

ORIGINS

Analysis of the Maglemose culture suggests that certain elements can be traced ultimately to Upper Palaeolithic civilisation, whereas others were called forth to meet the exigencies of the new environment of the Mesolithic period. Under the former heading we may consider the microlithic and burin elements, the bone points and many of the motives of the art, whereas the heavy equipment of the culture, certain types of fishing apparatus, nets and hooks, and the drilling apparatus, fall under the heading of Mesolithic innovations, and derive in part from an earlier stage of the axe civilisation.

I shall discuss these innovations first, because they form the central thread of a whole civilisation of which the Maglemose culture is one expression. The axe and adze forms of period II derive from the reindeer antler prototypes of the Lyngby culture of period I along two main lines of development:

(i) The blade or head was made to articulate with the handle, which now formed a separate entity. The articulation was sometimes direct, but often it was effected indirectly by the use of a sleeve of antler or wood. The blade, heads and sleeves were perforated for the insertion of the handle.

(ii) The blade, though sometimes still formed of antler, was frequently translated into bone, flint and stone.

The perforation of stone was also applied to quartzite pebbles producing primitive maces, which gave rise in Sweden to more complex forms (Fig. 38). It is possible that the bow-drill was devised to facilitate the perforation; at any rate it seems to have been in use at this time, and gave rise to a special technique of decorating bone by drilling, discussed in chapter IV. The habitat of Maglemose man was such that we need hardly wonder that he devised new methods of fishing with hook and line and with net. The net in turn gave rise to the most important and characteristic motive of his art, the net-pattern (see p. 170).

Of the elements of Upper Palaeolithic origin, some were perhaps derived more or less directly from an Upper Palaeolithic source in Western Europe, while others trace their origin indirectly to Upper Palaeolithic sources, probably in North Africa. The most important item of the latter category, which I propose to deal with first, is the microlithic element of the Maglemose culture. I must anticipate chapter V by claiming that this microlithic element differs in no way, either in the forms of the actual microliths or in the technique of their production, from that which forms the central feature of the middle stages of the Tardenoisian. The micro-burin itself, the 'type fossil' of the Tardenoisian, has been shown to occur in Maglemose industries in England, north Germany and Denmark, on the very classic sites of the culture (see p. 96). This important element of Maglemose culture must presumably trace its origin to the same source as the Tardenoisian, namely the evolved Upper Palaeolithic cultures of North Africa and possibly also of Palestine.

Whether the burin derived from the Tardenoisian source or directly from the Upper Palaeolithic of Western Europe it is hardly possible to say. It is tempting to trace the origins of some forms of bone points from Late Magdalenian sources, especially as they occur in the Hamburg culture of the beginning of period I. But for the strongest indication of a Magdalenian contribution to the make-up of the Maglemose culture I must point to the art, described in chapter IV. Of the three elements which seem to have gone to the making of the Maglemose culture, the Magdalenian is probably the least important, but it added colour to a culture already rich from the coalescence of the axe and adze tradition of period I in the north and of the microlithic element common to the middle stages of the Tardenoisian.

PHYSICAL TYPES

A considerable amount of human skeletal material has at various times been ascribed to the Maglemose people by different writers, but very little of it is admissible as evidence. It is an unfortunate but undoubted fact that ancient human bones, and skulls in particular, have tended to exercise an effect on the judgment of scholars only too often of the most baleful nature; hypotheses and theories have been elaborated on evidence that no impartial investigator could for one moment admit as valuable, and anthropometric ingenuity and patience has exhausted itself on material without any certain relevance to the question in hand. It would be a task as melancholy as it would be tedious to consider these theories; I shall therefore content myself with detailing the chief material that has passed as evidence, and with attempting to isolate what is likely to be valid.

Kossinna's Dobbertiner folk, so-called after an unimportant finding-place of three bone points in Mecklenburg, were considered by him to represent what he called the *Vorfinnen* (Kossinna, 1921 and 1926). His chief material consisted of four finds of brachycephalic skulls, no single one of which can satisfactorily be dated to period II by any ordinary process of human judgment. Considerable importance was attached to so-called *Homo Kiliensis* (c.1. 79·05), which consisted of the skeleton of a youth of between ten and twelve years of age, recovered during the Great War by dredging at Poppenbrugge, near Meinersdorf, Kiel. The section in the neighbourhood of the dredging consisted of peat overlying a mud deposit (*Faulschlamm*), in the base of which occurred the chalky deposit of an ancient lake, and under which rested the basal diluvial strata. Kossinna assumed that the skeleton came from the mud deposit, because he considered its preservation in the peat-bed to be impossible. The stratigraphical provenance of *Homo Kiliensis* depends upon an assumption that does not bear scrutiny. The Neanderthaloid traits discerned by Kadner (1925) have been explained by Reche

133

(1925, p. 176) as normal infantile characteristics. The Dömitz skull (c.i. 79·8) was dredged from the bed of the Elbe and there seems no particular reason for ascribing it to the so-called Dobbertiner race. The skull from Spandau (c.i. 88·4), a moor find from near the mouth of the Spree, is better documented, but the evidence hardly suggests a date in period II of the Mesolithic. The skull was obtained in 1881 from a clay or mud deposit (*Moorschlamm*) under peat and sealing the bases of wooden piles driven into the underlying gravel and sand. From between these piles came a number of bronzes dating from period II of the Bronze Age. It is true that the bronzes may have sunk into the mud and that the piles may have been driven through it, but it would be strange if the skull was in no way connected with the structure. In any case, among the red-deer antler and bone objects, described by Kossinna (1921, p. 16) as associated with the skull, is a type of perforated antler axe (cf. Fig. 55, no. 1) which cannot be earlier than Mesolithic III and may be a good deal later. Finally there is the well-known skeleton (c.i. 86·36) discovered in a crouched position at a depth of 1·8 metres in pebbly sand at Plau in Mecklenburg. The dating of this burial depends entirely upon the character of the grave goods, consisting of a perforated antler axe, a pair of boar's tusks, and perforated deer's teeth, accompanied by red ochre. It is possible that these might date back to period II, but it is equally possible that they might be considerably later; Schliz ascribes the burial to the Neolithic, but it is difficult to see on what evidence any accurate dating of the find is possible.

Two dolichocephalic skulls from the Pritzerber See in the Havelland have received detailed attention from Reche (1925). They were dredged, together with two complete and two fragmentary human jaws, and a vast quantity of bone and antler objects, from the blue Havel clay, which was overlain by a certain thickness of whitish-grey marl, between 30–40 cm. of sand and from 20–30 cm. of mud. The observation of Stimming, who recovered the material from the dumps of the mechanical dredgers, is confirmed by the fact that Reche found traces of Havel clay in the cavities of the skulls. Unfortunately this stoneless clay, which overlies glacial valley sands, cannot be accurately dated by geological or palaeo-botanical means, and the antler and bone objects from it belong to periods I, II and III of the Mesolithic. That the Pritzerber skulls belong to the Mesolithic is probable, but it seems hardly possible to decide to which sub-period they belong. Skull no. 1 has a cephalic index of 71·5 and a capacity of 1450 c.c., and skull no. 11 an index of 71·1 and a capacity of 1260 c.c. They resemble one another closely and are considered by Reche to be typically Nordic, with relations on the one hand to the Chancelade skull and on the other to skulls of the cord and band ceramic folk of Silesia and Bohemia.

Attention has of recent years been redirected to a discovery at Stångenäs in the parish of Bro, Bohuslän, Sweden, dating back to 1843. The find consisted of two skeletons, their heads almost touching and their bodies extended at an angle of about 125° one to the other. They were discovered accidentally by gravel-diggers in a shell-bank, which has recently been dated on geological grounds (Hägg, 1924) to period II. If these skeletons are really contemporary with the shell-bank, they provide us with important material for reconstructing the physical type of Maglemose man, but on this question there is an element of doubt. The find was an accidental one, but Sven Nilsson visited the site and actually removed some of the bones which he observed in position; his observations, which must be treated with respect, are to the effect that the shells overlying the skeletons were definitely undisturbed. This implies that the skeletons were incorporated into the shell-bank during its formation. Hägg (1924) explains this by the hypothesis that they represent the corpses of drowned individuals. That two individuals should be drowned and incorporated in the shell-bank in such close proximity makes a coincidence that is hard to believe, and raises doubts as to the accuracy of Nilsson's observation; to that extent, therefore, the Stångenäs material must be accepted with reservation. It appears that Nilsson was only able to extract certain bones from the local collector, a defective cranium, a femur, a tibia, an ankle-bone and a heel-bone, and these are the only ones to survive. The skull was dolichocephalic (c.i. 71·9) and shows powerful brow-ridges. The limb-bones suggest that one of the individuals was about 180 cm. in height. Fürst (1925) regards the cranium as of proto-Nordic type.

When all is said and done the only human skeletal material that can without doubt be referred to Maglemose man is that recovered from Mullerup, Svaerdborg and Sandarna. The Mullerup material consists of a damaged thigh-bone and a finger-bone of an adult, and the lower jaw of a child. Svaerdborg produced another lower jaw of a child, fragments of human skull and some odd bones. The material from Sandarna is still more meagre, consisting of a single human limb bone. Nielsen (1921) studied the children's jaw-bones from Mullerup and Svaerdborg and claimed the lack of chin development as a primitive feature; other writers, however, seem to be agreed that this feature is characteristically infantile (Rydbeck, 1934, p. 36). The only skeletal material that can be relied upon is thus singularly unhelpful. We cannot, *pace* Kossinna, speak with any certainty about the physical type of Maglemose man.

Period III

MAGLEMOSE SURVIVALS

The main feature of period III is the development of coastal cultures in the centre of the area under the stimulus of the *Litorina* marine transgression. But the development of these cultures did not bring to an end entirely the tradition of the Maglemose culture, which not only underlay much of the new cultures, but also continued to flourish almost free from external influences in peripheral regions. With the isostatic rise of land nearer the centre of origin of the Scandinavian ice-sheet new areas of land became available for settlement, for example in central Sweden, and into these new areas were pressed a certain number of Maglemose people. A trace of this movement is furnished by the bone object with socketed butt and spatulate edge, decorated by a combination of finely incised barbed lines and linear chevrons, from Sollerön, Dalarne. The form of the object,[1] and the technique and patterns of the decoration, are typically Maglemose, but its finding-place lay, in period II, under the waters of the *Ancylus* Lake.

The most complete evidence for the survival of the Maglemose tradition in a relatively pure form comes from the regions of Stavanger and Bergen in south-west Norway. The find of Viste, near Stavanger, carries on the tradition, at least, until the period of the Ertebølle civilisation of Denmark. The site consists of a rock shelter situated $3\frac{1}{2}$ metres above the *Tapes* strand-line, with which it was probably contemporary (Brøgger, A. W., 1908).[2] The fauna included remains of seventeen kinds of wild animal, among which were found many forest species such as elk, beaver and wild pig, as well as twenty-eight species of bird, twenty-two of which were water-birds, eight species of fish and many shell-fish. Evidence of the forest, which probably reached this area later than Scania or Denmark, is provided not only by the fauna but also by charcoals of aspen, birch, pine, oak and alder. The shell-

---

[1] A precisely similar piece decorated with the typical net pattern comes from Bohuslän.
[2] Though only $3\frac{1}{2}$ metres above the *Tapes* line, the site is 17 metres above modern sea-level.

fish, seal bones, water-fowl and fish support the view that the site was contemporary with the *Tapes* strand-line. The culture stratum enclosed numerous hearths and cultural remains, including a quantity of bone and antler work, flint and stone work, and a few sherds of pottery. Among the Maglemose forms were a slotted bone point, a broken point with recurved barbs and an unperforated celtiform antler axe or adze. A bone awl and a barbless fish-hook might belong equally to the Maglemose or to a later tradition, but the fragment of polished greenstone axe and the potsherds, which include a bent-out rim, point at the earliest to period III. We have in Viste, therefore, a delayed Maglemose, slightly diluted with influences from the later dwelling-place cultures and dating from no earlier than the period of the *Litorina* maximum.

There is good evidence that the tradition persisted to a much later period even than this. Two of the slotted bone points of the type found at Viste have been obtained from Høilandsvandet, to the south of Stavanger, from clay deposited after the lake had become separated from the sea, and, therefore, date from after the *Litorina* maximum (Brøgger, A. W., 1909(*b*)); indeed Brøgger estimates that they must be regarded, on the geological evidence, as contemporary with the earlier stages of the megalithic civilisation of southern Sweden. The rock-shelter find of Ruskenesset, near Bergen, carries on the tradition to an even later period (Shetelig, 1920). The fauna suggests that hunting and fishing formed the main basis of subsistence, but a certain number of domestic animal bones were found and imprints of grain were observed on several sherds. A fragment of barbed bone point, a barbless fish-hook and a bone awl are types which go back to Mesolithic II, but the barbed fish-hook, the tanged slate point, flint daggers and flint arrowheads of the concave base type, no less than the indications of domestication of animals and of agriculture, all point to a later date. The flint types, indeed, point to the final stage of the megalithic civilisation of the south of Scandinavia, but the most eloquent evidence of a late date is given by fragments of bronze.

The continuity of tradition revealed by these Norwegian sites has been interpreted in two ways. Either it indicates the survival of hunting tribes, throughout the megalithic period and into the Bronze Age, or else, as A. W. Brøgger (1926) has argued, the sites represent merely the hunting stations of tribes, which had to some extent absorbed the new methods of life. The evidence from Ruskenesset certainly supports this explanation for the later sites, the remains from which can, therefore, be regarded as representing only one aspect, possibly seasonal, of the material culture of the people.

THE ERTEBØLLE CULTURE
TYPES OF SETTLEMENT

Of the new developments of culture on the coasts of the *Litorina* Sea the most vigorous was that situated at the heart of the area in Denmark and Schleswig-Holstein. The term Kitchen-Midden culture which is often used to describe this culture is open to the double objection that some of the most important sites of the culture are not kitchen-middens, and that not all kitchen-middens in the area belong to this culture. I shall, therefore, use a site name, Ertebølle, to describe the culture dominant at the time of the *Litorina* maximum in Denmark and parts of north Germany.

The marine transgression, which affected regions peripheral to the centre of the Scandinavian ice-sheet at this period, brought the strand-line in parts of Denmark and south Sweden above that of the present day. The sites of the Ertebølle culture contemporary with the *Litorina* maximum in these areas are found, therefore, to adhere to a coast-line slightly above modern sea-level, as shown by our Fig. 5. This is fortunate for archaeology, as it means that in this area the investigation of the sites is greatly simplified. On the other hand, farther south, the transgression did not bring the strand-line as high as modern sea-level, so that many coastal sites may now be below the waters of the Baltic. The well-known German site of Ellerbek, near Kiel, provides an excellent example. The deposits at the bed of Kiel fjord have been studied by Weber (1904) and more recently by Tidelski, who found a series of fresh-water deposits formed in the beds of ancient lakes. In the base of the deposits remains of birch and pine were dominant, but by the time that man settled round the edges of the lakes the oak-mixed-forest had risen to the chief place. The present fjord was not created until the *Litorina* Sea broke into the area covering the ancient lakes and their settlements of Ertebølle man. To-day these settlements occur at depths ranging down to 24 feet below sea-level, as illustrated by Fig. 48. The finds were made by dredgers from various sites and are probably not strictly contemporary, though they include all the typical features of the Ertebølle culture. It is probable that coastal sites of the culture extended along the contemporary coasts of Mecklenburg, western Pomerania and Rügen (Beltz, 1910, p. 13), but are now below water. At least it is certain that flint material, *spalter* and the like, that might very well belong to period III, is found fairly commonly

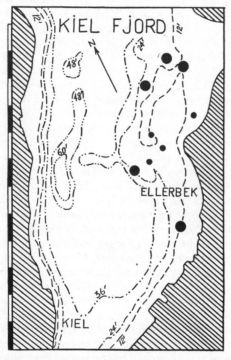

Fig. 48. Map of Kiel fjord, showing the distribution of sites and finds of the Ertebølle culture made by dredging off Ellerbek. The large dots indicate the main sites; the small dots mark the finding-places of single objects. The contours mark depths in feet below modern sea-level. (After Weber.) Scale of hundreds of metres.

near the modern coast. Beltz (1910) mentions such finds from the neighbourhoods of Rostock and of Neu Bukow, Klinghardt (1927) describes workshops with core axes and *spalter* at Lietzow, Rügen, and some good illustrations of the finds from this last site are given by Voss (1880, sect. II, taf. 1–4). These traces must, however, be used with caution, as none of them are geologically or botanically dated, and this type of flint-work had a long life.

The kitchen-midden sites of Denmark are so well known that I shall spend little time describing them. Isolated examples were investigated and published in early days, as for example Sølager, near the mouth of Roskilde fjord (Steenstrup, 1869) and Meilgaard in eastern Jutland (Madsen, 1888), but our detailed knowledge of this type of site derives from the systematic excavations carried out by a group of workers on a settled plan between 1893 and 1897. This magnificent publication (Madsen, Müller, S., Neergaard, Petersen, Rostrup, Steenstrup and Winge, 1900) deals with five kitchen-middens of period III—Ertebølle, Havnø and Aamølle in Jutland, and Klintesø and Faareveile in northern Zealand. The middens stretch along the contemporary shore-line and frequently extend to over a hundred yards in length, though seldom more than a fifth of this in width and normally only from 3 to 5 feet thick.[1] They are composed almost entirely of the debris of food, mostly shells of edible shell-fish (*Ostrea edulis*, *Litorina littorea*, *Cardium edule*, *Mytilus edulis*, and *Nassa reticulata*), but also of the bones of wild animals (see Appendix I, list D). Stone hearths, with which are associated charcoals and cultural remains, occur throughout the middens. The mammalian remains prove, as indicated in chapter 1 (p. 51), that the kitchen-middens, unlike the Maglemose stations, were frequented at all seasons of the year. It would appear that, while still hunting and to some slight extent fishing in the hinterland, the strong attraction of an easy food supply drew Ertebølle man to settle on the coast throughout the year. Whereas in period II the coast was far away and Maglemose man hunted and fished in the forests and lakes of a great plain stretching from Britain to Siberia, in period III the transgression of the sea had reduced and split the area forcing a new feature of environment on the attention of man.

The middens have their interest, but from a stratigraphical point of view they have not the significance of certain other sites, which show a sequence of natural deposits. The site at Brabrand Sø (Thomsen and Jessen, A., 1902–7), near Århus, Jutland, is placed at the eastern end of an inland lake, which at the period of the *Litorina* maximum formed the eastern extremity of a fjord. The section (Fig. 7) illustrates the post-glacial history of the region, and the well-defined stratification makes possible a valuable correlation between this history and the development of culture. First there is

[1] The Ertebølle midden was 141 metres long and nowhere more than 20 metres wide or 1¾ metres deep.

indication of a period of relative land-elevation with a thin peat-bed below a sea-beach, both of which are under present sea-level; then followed a gradual submergence, indicated in its earlier stages by the sand layer and culminating in the clay layer, deposited at the period of the *Litorina* maximum; finally the process is reversed, the clay gives way to sand and this, in turn, to gravel beach. The clay layer which was deposited under about one metre of water contained quantities of shells, typical of the fjords of the period, and representing a natural accumulation, not an artificial mass of shells rejected from meals. This deposit is important to archaeology, because it enables us to date various traits and phases of culture in relation to the *Litorina* maximum. A secondary point of interest is that it preserved a number of wooden artifacts, which have perished in the kitchen-middens.

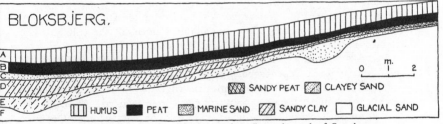

Fig. 49.   Section through the site of Bloksbjerg a few miles to the north of Copenhagen.
(After Westerby.)

A second site of the period which merits a separate description is that of Bloksbjerg on the east coast of Zealand to the north of Copenhagen (Westerby, 1927). Bloksbjerg formed during period III an island in a fjord, which is now fossil; to-day it forms a low eminence dominating marshy flats. The stratification is illustrated by the section shown in Fig. 49. Here, as at Brabrand Sø, the maximum of the *Litorina* transgression is well marked, coinciding with the top of the clayey sand layer (E) and the whole of the sandy clay layer (D), which latter contains quantities of shells of molluscs typical of the *Litorina* fjords. The marine sand layer (C) was deposited as the land began to rise in relation to the sea. Knud Jessen has found that at the junction of layers E and D the pollen of the trees of the oak-mixed-forest still shows admixture with pine pollen, but that through layer D the percentage falls considerably before the continued advance of the oak-

141

mixed-forest. Archaeological events can, thus, be correlated both with land-movement and with the development of forest composition.

MATERIAL CULTURE

The traits of the Ertebølle and Maglemose cultures are broadly similar but differ in detail and in importance. Core axes or adzes and *spalter* form an important element in both cultures, but, whereas in the older culture the former are many times more numerous than the latter, in the younger culture the proportions are almost exactly reversed.[1] Microliths are also common to both cultures, but, whereas only one trapeze or *petit tranchet* arrowhead has come from the Maglemose stations,[2] this is almost the sole microlithic type found on Ertebølle sites. A handful of microliths obliquely blunted or blunted down the whole of one edge and a small narrow scalene triangle were found at Bloksbjerg (Westerby, 1927, fig. 23), but in comparison with the mass of *petit tranchet* arrowheads from the site they form a very insignificant proportion of the microlithic element of the culture.[3] The various forms of *petit tranchet* found at Ertebølle are illustrated by Fig. 50, nos. 1–8. Out of a total of 444, which I counted in the National Museum of Antiquities at Copenhagen, I found 7 examples of the triangular form (no. 2) and 26 examples with oblique flake-edge (no. 1). It was interesting to notice that in 10 instances only was any cortex retained. At Bloksbjerg Westerby (1927, pp. 78–80 and fig. 22) found the oblique form rather more common. Several finds of *petit tranchet* arrowheads, showing the character of their hafting, have been made in Northern Europe (Fig. 51). In the case of specimens found respectively at a depth of between $2\frac{1}{2}$ and 3 metres in a peat-bog at Tvaermose, Eising Sogn, Ginding Herred, north Jutland (Müller, S., 1917, p. 149), and in Petersfehner Moor, Oldenburg, the shaft .or foreshaft was of wood and the binding material of animal sinew. The shaft of the specimen from a peat-bog at Vissenberg, Odense, Fünen, engraved by Madsen and reproduced by Evans (1897, p. 409, fig. 344), was also of wood, but in this case the binding was of 'fine bast-fibre'. The type of chisel-ended arrow was specialised in Egypt for the shooting of birds,

[1] In the National Museum at Copenhagen, for example, I counted 268 *spalter* and only 20 core axes from Brabrand Sø; from Meilgaard I found 133 *spalter* and only 11 core axes. Compare with these figures those quoted on p. 104, note 1, for the proportions from Duvensee, Holmegaard, Svaerdborg and Sandarna. From the site of Langø on Fünen (Broholm, 1928) only 25 core axes were obtained as against 265 *spalter*.

[2] As I stated on p. 94, the trapeze from Svaerdborg was not found in systematic excavations.

[3] By no means all the types illustrated as microliths by Westerby can really be counted as such.

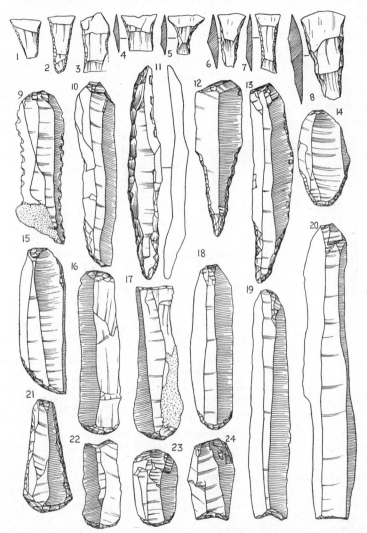

Fig. 50. Flint types of the Ertebølle culture. All are from the Ertebølle midden except no. 9 from Vester Ulslev and nos. 15 and 21 from Godsted. (Drawn by the author in Copenhagen Museum.) Scale: ⅔.

and it is possible that the Ertebølle people also used them for the same purpose; quantities of bird bones figure in the fauna lists of their sites (Appendix I, list D).

Flint scrapers abound in the Ertebølle culture, but they differ very greatly in character from those of the Maglemose. The squat horse-shoe scrapers typical of the earlier sites are rare; only two examples from Ertebølle approach the form (*e.g.* Fig. 50, no. 14). Oblique scrapers on flakes or

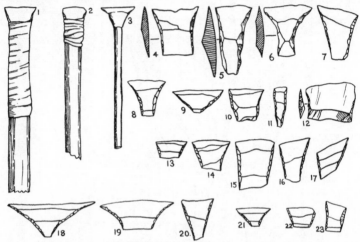

Fig. 51. Nos. 1–3 illustrate the method of hafting trapezes or *petit tranchet* arrowheads: no. 1 is from Tvaermose, north Jutland; no. 2 from Petersfehner Moor, Oldenburg; and no. 3 from Egypt (Middle Empire). Nos. 4–23 illustrate the wide diffusion of the type in Europe and North Africa: nos. 4–7 are from Ertebølle, Jutland; no. 8 is from Svaerdborg, Zealand; nos. 9–11 come from Wangford, Suffolk; no. 12 is from Selmeston, Sussex; nos. 13–17 are from Zonhoven, Belgium; nos. 18–20 from Capsian middens in Algeria; no. 21 is from Mugem, Portugal; and nos. 22, 23 are from Słochy Ogrodinki, Poland. Scale: ⅞.

blades (Fig. 50, no. 15) occur in both cultures rather infrequently, but the end-of-blade scraper is the typical Ertebølle type. The end-of-blade scrapers occur in the convex (Fig. 50, no. 18), transverse (no. 20) and concave (no. 19) forms, as well as in combinations of these (nos. 16, 17, 22). The finest specimens sometimes reach the length of 6 inches, whereas others (nos. 23, 24) are considerably shorter.[1] The sides of a certain number are

[1] From Ertebølle, for example, I counted at Copenhagen only 2 specimens of the approximately horse-shoe form, 26 scrapers with oblique edge, and no less than 402 end-of-blade scrapers, of which 130 were convex, 105 transverse or straight, 151 concave, and 16 combinations of the foregoing.

trimmed, presumably to facilitate hafting (no. 21). Sufficient attention has not been paid to the remarkable skill in the production of flint blades shown by many of the scrapers (*e.g.* no. 20). In this respect the Ertebølle culture stands closer to the Upper Palaeolithic than does the Maglemose.

Flakes and blades were sometimes used for cutting and sawing. I illustrate a coarsely serrated flake (Fig. 50, no. 9) and a flake with one edge partly blunted for the finger, the opposite one carrying a thin band of lustre (Fig. 50, no. 10).

Westerby noticed the occurrence of burins at Bloksbjerg (1927, pp. 72 ff. and fig. 20), but they were also common, though hitherto unobserved, on the classic stations of the Ertebølle culture. In working through the collections at Copenhagen I expected to find a few burins, but was astonished to find great numbers of typical specimens. I illustrate a few of these on Fig. 52. Single-blow (nos. 6, 7) and *bec de flûte* forms (no. 5) occur, but most of the specimens I was able to identify were angle-burins (nos. 1–4, 8 and 9). It is probable that this is due to the fact that the other forms have mostly been discarded,[1] the angle forms having been preserved because of their ordinary secondary working. Many of the angle-burins have been re-sharpened (*e.g.* no. 4), and others have burin blows on both sides of one end (no. 3) or at both ends (no. 1). Burins are found in the Maglemose, but always rarely; in the Ertebølle culture they are definitely common. Here again the younger culture stands typologically closer to the Late Palaeolithic. The presence of burins in the Ertebølle culture demonstrates how real is the thread of continuity between the whole series of Mesolithic cultures and those of the Late Palaeolithic.

Core awls and awls on coarse flakes are found rarely, as on Maglemose stations, but pseudo-awls on the end of blades are a new development.[2] The simple form with one extremity of the flake pointed (Fig. 50, no. 13) is found abundantly; the varieties pointed at both ends (no. 11) or with a scraper edge at one end (no. 12) are rare.

The stone types show, on the one hand, a continuity with the Maglemose, as in the quartzite maces with hour-glass perforation, two of which occurred in the Ertebølle midden (Fig. 53, no. 2), and on the other, new departures such as the round-butted pecked axe with ground edge (Fig. 53, no. 5) and

[1] In the Brabrand Sø report it is stated rather ominously that most of the waste (*sic*) flakes were discarded (Thomsen and Jessen, 1902–7, p. 164), and further (p. 180) that only about one-third of the 30,000 flints were retained.
[2] Absent from all Maglemose stations except Sandarna.

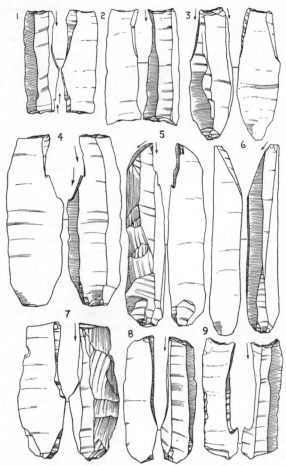

Fig. 52. Burins of various forms: except for no. 4 from Brabrand Sø, all come from the Ertebølle midden. The Copenhagen Museum numbers of the Ertebølle specimens in the order in which they are illustrated are: E. 136, E. 1510, E. 5a, E. 8345, E. 5837, E. 1867, E. 6446, E. 7260. The Brabrand Sø specimen is no. B. 412. (Drawn by the author in Copenhagen Museum.) Scale: $\frac{5}{8}$.

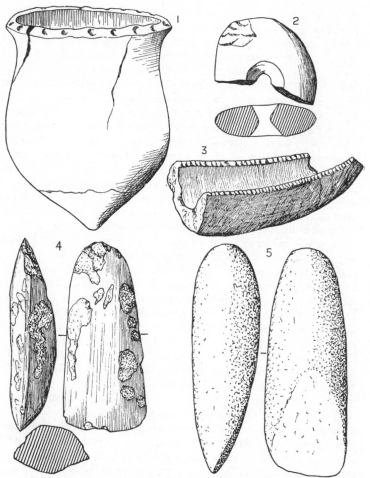

Fig. 53. Pottery and stone types of the Ertebølle culture. Nos. 1, 5 from Brabrand Sø; no. 2 from the Ertebølle midden; no. 3 from the Faareveile midden; no. 4 from Bloksbjerg. (Nos. 2 and 5 drawn by the author in Copenhagen Museum (nos. E. 8070 and B. 136); the others after Thomsen, Madsen and others, and Westerby.) Scales: no. 1, $\frac{1}{4}$; nos. 2 and 3, $\frac{3}{8}$; no. 4, $\frac{1}{2}$; and no. 5, $\frac{3}{4}$.

the partly polished stone axe of Limhamn type (no. 4). Five of the round-butted stone axe or *walzenbeil* were found at Brabrand Sø; of the three with cutting edges relatively intact all were slightly gouged. They occurred well down in the section, but were absent from the last third; in other words they occurred down to the deposits dating from the *Litorina* maximum, but not below it. At Bloksbjerg the *walzenbeil* and the Limhamn axe both occurred in the same section, which affords decisive evidence for the sequence of these types in Denmark. Westerby found that, whereas each of the four Limhamn axes occurred in layer C—and three of them high up in this layer—the seven *walzenbeil* extended down to layer E, dating from an early stage in the *Litorina* transgression. C. A. Nordman's view (1918) that the *walzenbeil* derives from the Limhamn axe seems to be invalidated by this new strati-graphical information from Bloksbjerg. The section also demonstrated that the thicker butted *walzenbeil*, which occurred both in layer E, antedates the narrower butted form, a fragment of which came from layer D and four of which came from layers B and C. The *walzenbeil* forms an integral part of the Ertebølle culture and occurs at the kitchen-middens of Havelse, Sølager and Meilgaard, as well as at Brabrand Sø and at Bloksbjerg. I have called the *walzenbeil* a new departure, but it is nevertheless essentially an indigenous product of the northern forest civilisation. If Maglemose man could fabri-cate the maces of Kungsladugard type or the perforated stone adze of Holmegaard, there is no reason to believe that his successor could not have made the *walzenbeil*. A primitive version, indeed, of this type came from the main culture layer at Sandarna, in the shape of a pebble with ground cutting edge (Fig. 33, no. 10). The idea of pecking probably arose from improving such pebbles, and the technique of polishing was one with which Maglemose man was familiar in his antler and bone work.

The *Litorina* clay layer at Brabrand Sø produced numerous wooden objects, about which there has been some difference of opinion. There can be no reasonable doubt that the asymmetrically curved object illustrated on Fig. 54, no. 1 represents a throwing-stick. It is probable, as Franz has argued (1928), that the other objects illustrated on the same figure are also throwing-sticks of differing forms, though originally interpreted as the prongs of fish-spears. Sixteen examples of the forms shown by nos. 2–4 were obtained from Brabrand Sø; ten of these were identified as of hazel. A fragment, of what Thomsen regarded as a bow with restricted termina-tions, is interpreted by Franz as a club. In this case it would seem that

Thomsen's explanation is the more probable, especially as this object was one of the two found to be of ash wood. The quantities of *petit tranchet* arrowheads characteristic of the culture indicates that the Ertebølle people

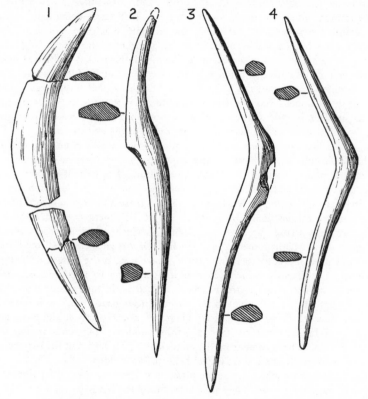

Fig. 54. Wooden throwing-sticks from Brabrand Sø, Jutland (after Thomsen).
Scales: in plan, $\frac{1}{3}$; in section, $\frac{1}{2}$.

must have used bows. Part of the hazel wood handle of a perforated antler axe also came from the clay deposit at Brabrand Sø; 59 cms. of the handle survived and it measured 2·2 cm. in diameter.

The perforated antler axe is typical of the Ertebølle culture, whereas adzes of similar type are extremely rare.[1] This exactly reverses the proportions as found on Maglemose stations. The perforated antler sleeve for containing a flint, which was characteristic of the Maglemose, is absent from the Ertebølle culture. On the other hand, at this time, a new type of perforated antler axe made its appearance. Instead of being perforated through the antler near its stump, the perforation is driven through the stump of a branch of the antler, so giving a socket to the handle (Fig. 55, no. 1); sometimes, as in the example illustrated, this socket is situated near one end of the implement, but in other cases it is found at the middle (*e.g.* Schwantes, 1934, abb. 125). At Brabrand Sø this socketed type was found only in the upper levels of the implementiferous part of the section, showing that it came in only at the *Litorina* maximum.[2] The type made up rather more than a half of the perforated antler axes of the culture.

Of barbed bone points only a few examples are known from sites of the Ertebølle culture, and most of these are coarse heavy objects quite different from anything found in the Maglemose culture. The base of a point with recurved barbs and a perforation is recorded from the midden of Sølager (Steenstrup, J., 1869, pl. XIII, no. 9), though there is no certain record of its stratigraphical position. The stratified site of Bloksbjerg has yielded three barbed points (Fig. 55, nos. 7–9), none of which resemble closely types known from Maglemose sites in Denmark. Of these no. 8 comes from layer E and probably antedates the *Litorina* maximum, no. 7 comes from the transition to D and E, which is more or less contemporary with the maximum depression, and no. 9 is from layer C, which is definitely later than the maximum. No. 9 resembles in its size, and in its bent form, the specimen from Ellerbek (Fig. 55, no. 10). There are also records of slotted bone points of the narrow type (form 21) from middens; fragments of four or five are said to have come from the midden at Nivaagaard, but the two from Kassemose really came from gravel beneath the midden.

Barbless fish-hooks of bone were found at Ertebølle (four), Meilgaard, Bloksbjerg, and Langø. They are a legacy from the Maglemose, but tend to be smaller on the Ertebølle sites.

[1] There were none at Brabrand Sø, where 23 perforated axes were found. Ertebølle produced only 1 adze as compared with 17 adzes.
[2] The following table illustrates the situation:

Spits	3	4	5	6	7	8
Base of antler type	–	1	1	2	6	1
Socketed type	3	7	2	–	–	–

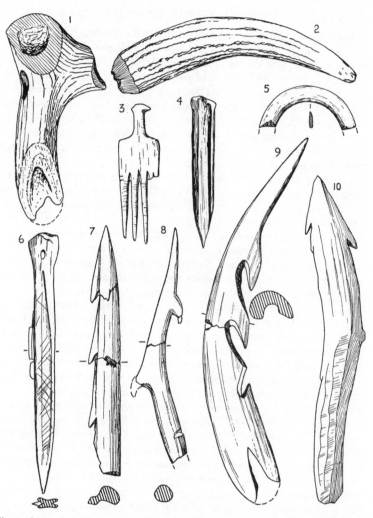

Fig. 55. Some antler and bone types of the Ertebølle culture. No. 1 from the Havnø midden; nos. 2, 4 from the Ertebølle midden; nos. 3, 5 from Brabrand Sø; nos. 6–9 from Bloksbjerg; no. 10 from Ellerbek (after Madsen and others, Thomsen, Westerby and Kossinna). Scales: nos. 1, 10, $\frac{3}{8}$; nos. 2–9, $\frac{1}{2}$.

Bone combs, which are known from Ertebølle, Brabrand Sø, Meilgaard (five) and Sølager, appear for the first time in the Ertebølle culture. They are mostly handled, as in the example illustrated (Fig. 55, no. 3), but sometimes the back is curved and perforated for a string. Another new type is the bone bracelet from Brabrand Sø (Fig. 55, no. 5). These bracelets were made from discs removed from scapulae; two loose discs and six scapulae (three aurochs, one elk, one deer, one wild pig), from which discs had been wholly or partially removed, were found at Brabrand Sø. The scapulae occurred down to the middle of the clay deposit and show that the bracelets go back to the period of the *Litorina* maximum.

The most important new feature of the Ertebølle culture is the presence of pottery of a distinctive type (Pl. VII). The paste was mixed with coarse grit and was built up into pots by the coil method. The pottery is generally black in core and the surface is normally brown or grey in colour; the pink or red colour indicative of high firing is rare, and where it does occur, may be due to use over a fire rather than to the process of manufacture. The surface was sometimes left uneven, but frequently it was burnished by a pebble until it was quite shiny. The beaker with pointed base and outcurved rim (Fig. 53, no. 1) is one of the two chief forms, good examples occurring at Ertebølle, Brabrand Sø, Langø, Ellerbek and Rüder Moor, Schleswig-Holstein; the rim was sometimes straight as in a smaller pot from Rüder Moor (Schwantes, 1934, abb. 133). These beakers were sometimes as much as 18 inches high. Their relatively great size and poor firing made them specially liable to crack; funnel-shaped holes, sunk from the outside of the pot after firing, were probably designed to carry strings for holding together cracked pots. The other chief form is an oval saucer with curved base (Fig. 53, no. 3), found in the Faareveile kitchen-midden and at sites at Brabrand Sø, Bloksbjerg (Westerby, 1927, fig. 40), Langø (Broholm, 1928, fig. 20), Godsted, Vester Ulslev and Koldingfjord (Copenhagen Museum). Mathiassen (1935) regards these as blubber lamps. Many of the beakers and saucers are plain, but both forms are sometimes decorated by finger or finger-nail impressions disposed along the top of the rim.

This pottery is of so general occurrence at sites of the Ertebølle culture that it must surely be regarded as an integral trait. There has been a tendency on the part of some writers (Franz, 1927, pp. 19–20) to count it a late feature, but the stratigraphical evidence does not entirely support this view. At the midden of Ertebølle sherds were recovered from no less

PLATE VII. Pottery from the Ertebølle midden. (Photo. National Museum, Copenhagen.)
Scales: nos. 1, 2, 4, c. $\frac{7}{16}$; no. 3, $\frac{1}{3}$.

ERTEBØLLE POTTERY

than 635 places, and it is clearly stated in the report that they occurred in the same way as flint and other artifacts in association with hearths (Madsen and others, 1900, p. 76). Sherds were found down to the bottom of the midden; if they were rarer in the basal levels, so also were other classes of object. The stratigraphical record of the excavations at the midden at Meilgaard also show that sherds occurred down to the base (Madsen, 1888, p. 306). It is true that at Bloksbjerg the pottery was all obtained from layers B and C, above the sandy clay deposit of the *Litorina* Sea, but only 34 sherds were found. At Brabrand Sø sherds were found in 86 places; although the majority certainly dated from immediately after the *Litorina* maximum (spits 3–5), seven finds were made well down to this level (spits 6–7).

An analysis of the material culture of Ertebølle man suggests how greatly he was indebted to his predecessors in the same area. Certain features of the Maglemose tradition disappeared or diminished greatly in importance, as antler sleeves and adzes, barbed bone points, microliths other than trapezes, and micro-burins, but in general the main forms of the earlier culture persisted in the later: flint axes and *spalter*, perforated quartzite maces, perforated antler axes, barbless bone hooks, burins, and slotted bone objects with flint insets. Most of the new forms represent only simple developments from the inherited tradition; the *petit tranchet* arrowhead is the natural descendant of the earlier forms of microlith, the socketed perforated antler axe is merely an elaboration of the older form perforated near the base of the antler, the *walzenbeil* finds its prototype in the *geröllebeil* of Sandarna, and the crude barbed points descend from the most characteristic bone objects of the Maglemose culture. The only features that appeared for the first time in the Ertebølle culture without any obvious roots in the Maglemose are the bone combs and bracelets, and the pottery, which seems to be typical of the middens dating from the *Litorina* maximum and occurs down to this level in other stratified sites. Comparisons are difficult for the less material aspects of culture, as so little is known, but the engraving of conventional patterns affords some scope. We are here confronted with a characteristic situation—continuity between the two cultures, but a marked difference of emphasis. The art of the Ertebølle culture was both scarcer and poorer than that of the Maglemose (see chapter iv), but such examples as do exist afford important links with the earlier culture. A perforated antler axe from Brabrand Sø shows an incised lozenge pattern (Maglemose art, motive *q*) and some lines in *ornementation pointillée*, and Langø yielded a broken perforated antler axe with typical, though poorly executed *bohrornament*.

CHRONOLOGY

The most important evidence for the chronology of the Maglemose was obtained by pollen-analysis; in the case of the Ertebølle culture, the chief sites of which were situated on the coast, evidence relating to changes of sea-level assumes the chief place. The kitchen-midden sites of the culture in Denmark date beyond reasonable doubt from the period of the maximum extension of the *Litorina* Sea; this is demonstrated, both from their topographical position in relation to the known sea-coast of this period, and from the shells of which they were composed. The map of middens around Roskilde fjord (Fig. 5) illustrates the situation more clearly than words. But, if the culture represented in the midden of Ertebølle can be dated from the *Litorina* maximum and the period immediately succeeding, there is also evidence of a stage of culture of intermediate type that dates from the years preceding this event. At Bloksbjerg and at Brabrand Sø the maximum extension of the *Litorina* Sea is clearly marked in the sections, and both sites confirm that the novel features of the Ertebølle culture, combs, bracelets, pottery, perforated antler axes of the socketed type, *walzenbeil* and Limhamn axes, date back only to this period. In the lower levels of the Brabrand Sø section, where these types were absent, the Maglemose tradition is found unmixed; none of the perforated antler axes of socketed type were found in the bottom four spits, which yielded on the other hand 9 out of the 11 examples of the Maglemose type perforated through the base of the antler.

Little has survived from the lower levels at Brabrand Sø and Bloksbjerg; yet it is clear, that between the end of the Boreal period (period II) and the maximum extension of the *Litorina* Sea, a length of time elapsed during which cultural development must have proceeded. The Ertebølle culture, as represented by the material from the name site, does not antedate the *Litorina* maximum, but, as I have laboured to demonstrate, many of its elements have descended directly from the Maglemose. Many of the differences between the two cultures are differences of proportion; others have been brought about by the evolution of common traits. The intermediate period should, therefore, give evidence of these transitions in cultural development. The stratigraphy of the antler axe forms in the Brabrand Sø section does show such a transition, and such other evidence as exists points in the same direction. Westerby (1933) has recently published an account of various sites in Jutland and Zealand,[1] which occur at between 3 and 5 metres below the level of the *Litorina* Sea at its maximum extension and show a typological development transitional between the Maglemose and Ertebølle cultures. The sites show a low percentage of *spalter* in relation to core axes and adzes, and a series of microliths illustrating the evolution of the *petit tranchet* arrowhead from earlier forms of microlith. These sites help to fill the gap between the Maglemose culture, where the *petit tranchet* hardly existed, and the Ertebølle, where it formed almost the sole microlithic type.

To the early part of period III may also be assigned the flint-chipping sites, situated on low hillocks sloping down to the river Gudenaa in Jutland (Friis-Johansen, 1918–19, pp. 274–7 and figs. 25–27; Schwantes, 1928 (c), pp. 224–6). The sites are of surface character, but they are generally accepted as yielding a homogeneous industry. The flints include core axes, *spalter*, and microliths of types ranging from the normal Maglemose forms to the trapeze, typical of the Ertebølle culture. Closely analogous sites have been found on sandy and loamy eminences along the banks of the Trave, especially in the neighbourhood of Oldesloe, in Schleswig-Holstein (Sonder, 1928; Schwantes, 1928 (c), pp. 222–6). Here, again, the sites are superficial in character, but their relatively small size, and their reduplication in well-defined regions, suggests that they represent a true industry and not a mixture. In two ways the Oldesloe industry is transitional between the Maglemose and the Ertebølle cultures; the proportion between core axes and *spalter* is approximately intermediate, and, in addition to the trapezes or *petit tranchet* arrowheads (some of them markedly oblique), other microlithic forms occur, such as the triangle and the crescent.[2] The Oldesloe sites also produce burins, scrapers and perforated quartzite maces of the type common to the Maglemose and the Ertebølle cultures.

The evidence of these transitional industries supports the view, to which one is driven by the mere comparison of the Maglemose and Ertebølle cultures, that the later culture was to a large extent the product of indigenous development. There is one feature of the Ertebølle culture, in particular,

[1] Kolindsund, Jutland, sites to the west of Sandy Bro and to the north-east of Gisling Bro, both on Lammefjord, Zealand, and others on Sidingefjord, Zealand.

[2] I examined the material from a site known as Brennermoor bei Oldesloe in the local museum. I found that core axes occurred in relation to *spalter* as 2 to 3; at the Maglemose sites the proportion was more like 20 to 1, and at the Ertebølle sites the reverse. Again, whereas in the Ertebølle culture trapezes account for nearly the whole microlithic element, at Brennermoor they amounted to three-quarters only.

which is difficult to account for on this hypothesis; it is hard to think that pottery was invented separately and independently by the strand-loopers of the *Litorina* coasts. It must surely have been made, either under the influence of another culture, either by direct contact or by spreading from a distance, or else as a result of some ethnic movement. The last possibility is difficult to examine, owing to the scarcity of the skeletal material available. Not only is the material of the indigenous Maglemose people too negligible to afford a basis for comparison, but the remains attributable to Ertebølle man are equally scanty. Burials, it is true, have been recorded from no less than five kitchen-midden sites, at Ertebølle itself, at Aamølle, Fannerup, Holbaek and at Kassemose, but Rydbeck's review of the evidence (1934, pp. 41–51) has shown that no single one of these skeletons can certainly be attributed to the Ertebølle people; indeed it seems certain, in most cases, that the skeletons date from the Neolithic period, having been inserted into the superficial layers of abandoned middens. Several crania were dredged from the submerged sites in Kiel fjord, near Ellerbek, but all of them are too defective for exact measurement, though Kossinna (1921, p. 26) says they are probably dolichocephalic. The identification of the Maglemose culture with broad-headed *Vorfinnen* and of the Ertebølle with long-headed proto-Nordics, made popular by Kossinna (1921, 1926), has generally been rejected as fantastic. The only well-authenticated skull from period II, that from Stångenäs, was long-headed.

Direct evidence for or against an ethnic movement is wanting, but the cultural continuity is so great that it is safe to say that if such a movement occurred it was not a very important one. The idea of making pottery can hardly have been communicated by direct contact with Neolithic civilisation in Denmark or north Germany; the Ertebølle ware goes back to the period of the *Litorina* maximum, which antedates the Neolithic in those regions, and such indications of Neolithic civilisation as have occurred in middens of Ertebølle man have been confined to superficial deposits. The idea must have spread either from the south or from the south-east from the areas of Europe, where Neolithic civilisation was first established.

THE LIMHAMN, LIHULT, AND NØSTVET CULTURES OF THE SCANDINAVIAN PENINSULA

The main life of the Limhamn-Lihult dwelling-place cultures of Sweden lies in a later period when they absorbed influences from the megalithic and boat-axe civilisations, but their origins are to be found in period III. The most important site is that of Limhamn itself, where the dwelling-place is situated on the Jära Bank, the ancient beach of the *Litorina* Sea (Fig. 2). Rydbeck (1928) has shown that there were two distinct phases of settlement, the earlier contemporary with the Ertebølle culture, the later showing the same cultural basis but with finer pottery and stray flint types of the megalithic period. The cultural material obtained by Kjellmark (1903) from the lower level shows the closest affinities to that of the Ertebølle culture. The pottery is coil-built and occurs in the forms of pointed-based pots and shallow elliptical bowls. It is normally plain but is sometimes decorated by crude stab-marks over the body of the pot. The flint types are also closely similar, flake axes or *spalter* (30) greatly outnumbering core axes (12), and transverse arrowheads (52) being very common. The typical partly polished greenstone axe of the culture is illustrated by Fig. 53, no. 4; it occurred in the Danish kitchen-midden sites of Sølager and Klintesø as well as at Bloksbjerg, where the type occurred rather high up in the section.

Kjellmark (1904) mapped a number of coastal sites of the Limhamn culture, but most of them belong to the Neolithic period. The same tradition, modified by contacts with Neolithic civilisation, is to be found over wide areas of Sweden, where it is often, as at many of the dwelling-places on the Island of Gotland studied by Nihlén (1927), accompanied by traditions of an earlier phase of the axe civilisation, as evinced by the bone types. The dominant stone-axe form of the Lihult sites on the west coast of Sweden more nearly resembled the flint core axe and was generally less completely polished than the Limhamn axe. The volcanic stone axes of the Nøstvet dwelling-places of southern Norway were often completely unpolished and their relation to old sea-levels suggests that in origin the culture dates to a period before the *Litorina* maximum.

THE LOWER HALSTOW CULTURE OF SOUTH-EASTERN BRITAIN

The British counterpart of the Ertebølle culture of Denmark is that of Lower Halstow, so-called after the site in North Kent investigated by Burchell (1924, 1925, 1927 and 1928). The site lies on the south shore of the estuary of the Medway, and on the extreme edge of the sunken channel of that river. Two floors were excavated, both of them resting on London Clay and overlain by a few inches of peat and up to 6 feet of marsh clay; samples from the clay immediately underlying the floor level and from the peat immediately above it have been pollen-analysed by Erdtman and show quite clearly that the culture dates at earliest from period III, oak being the dominant tree.[1] The investigation of the more southerly floor demonstrated that the floors were earlier than a flint industry, including leaf arrowheads, and probably of Neolithic age. The Lower Halstow culture can, therefore, be regarded with some confidence as the contemporary in age of the Ertebølle culture of Denmark.

Unfortunately nothing but flint and stone has survived from either site, so that comparison with the Danish culture must be made on somewhat restricted ground. In general the flint industries have much in common, both being composed of a heavy element of axes or adzes, a microlithic element, flake axes or *spalter*, scrapers and burins. In detail, however, they diverge in almost every particular. The core axe or adze element is commoner at Halstow than the flake axe, which on the Ertebølle sites easily dominates, and it includes a special form, the 'Thames pick' (Fig. 56, no. 8), which is extremely rare on the Danish sites; the microliths found at Lower Halstow are all of the simplest forms (nos. 1–2), whereas those from the kitchen-middens are almost entirely of the evolved trapeze or *petit tranchet* form; scrapers at the Ertebølle sites are abundant and frequently on blades, but at Halstow they are rare and on flakes; and lastly burins are rare at Halstow and abundant at Ertebølle. The only stone type from Halstow was the quartzite pebble with counter-sunk hollows (no. 3), which belongs to the same family as the hour-glass perforated quartzite maces of the northern forest cultures.

[1] The clay sample gave: P. 2½ per cent.; B. 7½ per cent.; A. 14½ per cent.; U. 5½ per cent.; Q. 61 per cent.; T. 9 per cent. The peat sample gave: P. 1 per cent.; B. 4 per cent.; A. 3 per cent.; U. trace Q. 89 per cent.; T. 2 per cent. (Burchell, 1934, p. 371.)

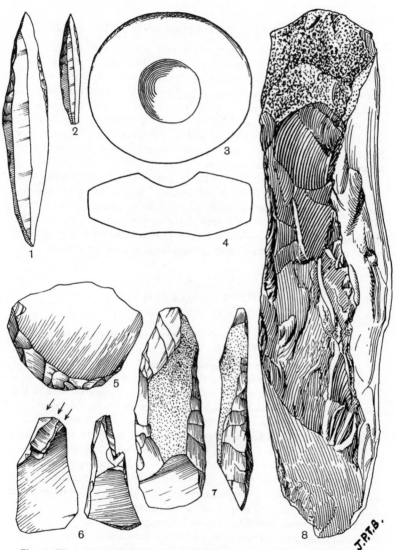

Fig. 56. Flint and stone implements of the Lower Halstow culture (after Burchell and Clark). Scales: no. 1, $\frac{2}{7}$; nos. 2, 8, $\frac{1}{3}$; nos. 3–7, $\frac{2}{3}$.

Lower Halstow is contemporary with and analogous to the Ertebølle culture, but differs more fundamentally than Broxbourne differed from Duvensee. In period II the closeness of the relationship between bone and flint industries from Britain and those of the plain of Northern Europe was such as to reflect, and even to confirm, the land connection across the southern portions of the present North Sea. The local divergences of culture that can be noted, both in the axe and in the microlithic civilisation (see p. 206) during period III, as surely reflect the marine transgression and the geographical tendencies of the time.

The typical pick of the culture, with its frequently sub-triangular section, is not only found in abundance in the Thames Valley as its name suggests, but also occurs in most parts of south-eastern Britain, where flint is abundant, as on the South Downs. There is little doubt that in such areas the so-called 'Campignian' tradition survived as long as flint-working itself (excluding of course such specialised versions as strike-a-light or gun-flint manufacture).

SUMMARY OF THE DEVELOPMENT OF THE AXE CULTURES

The axe tradition was cradled in the centre of our area of study, in Denmark, north Germany and southern Sweden, in response to the stimulus of the development of forests. The Lyngby culture flourished during period I, but survived in south Sweden into the succeeding period.

The Maglemose culture arose in period II from a coalescence with the axe tradition of the previous period of two other elements, the microlithic Tardenoisian element and some vestiges of Magdalenian artistic tradition. It flourished over the whole uninterrupted plain of Northern Europe from Britain to Esthonia and Poland, and from southern Sweden to central Germany; over this whole province it preserved a high degree of homogeneity, reflecting in this way the geography of the period. Subsistence was based on hunting forest game, collecting, and fishing in inland waters, and extremities of climate induced seasonal settlement.

The Maglemose tradition survived throughout period III and also through the Neolithic period in many parts of Scandinavia, either relatively pure as in parts of Norway or mixed with the newer culture forms of the axe civilisation of period III. The new developments of period III tended towards the growth of local cultures, reflecting once again the contemporary geographical changes. At the centre of our area the Ertebølle culture developed from the Maglemose by way of intermediate stages, such as those of Oldesloe, Gudenaa River, Kolindsund and the lower levels of Bloksbjerg and Brabrand Sø. The forest still formed the background to human activities, but settlement was mainly attracted to the new sea-coasts. The early dwelling-place cultures of the Scandinavian mainland, Nøstvet, Limhamn and Lihult, were closely allied to the Ertebølle culture, and formed the basis of the Arctic culture of the Neolithic period. In Britain the equivalent culture was that of Lower Halstow, which differed widely from that of Ertebølle, and survived into the Neolithic period. The 'Campignian'[1] style of flint-work, found over northern Germany and France and southern England, wherever flint was common (*e.g.* in flint-mining regions), persisted as long as flint-axe production itself.

[1] I see no justification for speaking of a Mesolithic Campignian culture in my area. The site of Le Campigny itself is generally dated to the Neolithic period.

CHAPTER IV

THE ART OF THE MAGLEMOSE CULTURE

MODE OF OCCURRENCE

The art of the Maglemose culture consists very largely of engravings on small objects, most of which are implements of daily use, including perforated antler hafts, axes and adzes, bone points with flint insets, bone net-prickers and a perforated stone mace. Antlers, plain or perforated, were often prepared by scraping and polishing and decorated without being adapted to any special purpose. Four decorated amber pendants may have been used for personal adornment, though the biomorphic designs on two of them suggest the possibility that they were amulets. Apart from a crude amber figurine from Jutland (the only sculpture belonging to the art group, it is incised with geometric patterns) and the decorated antlers mentioned above, there seems to be no trace of 'art' dissociated from objects of use, adornment or superstition.

TECHNIQUES

The engravings were made by three distinct techniques, those of direct incision, pricking and drilling. Of these the commonest and least specialised method was that of incision, which was normally done with an exceptionally sharp object, producing so fine a line that the patterns are often difficult to distinguish.[1] The fineness of the incision is a typical feature of the art, but rare examples of heavier incision are known. It is worth remarking that this heavier type of incision is confined to two motives, linear and single chevrons (motives h and x). It is found on objects from Svaerdborg (LII)[2] and Holmegaard (IX), as well as others from the Thames (VI) and from Romsey (XXXIX), both of which are included in the art group only by conjecture.

The method of engraving by pricking with a finely pointed instrument, leaving fine cuneiform dots, is well described by the French as *ornementation pointillée*. One of the best examples is that shown by Fig. 61, no. 8, a bone

---

[1] Perhaps the patterns were made visible by rubbing in some dark substance, as is done by Esquimaux in rather similar incised bone-work.

[2] The Roman numerals in brackets refer to the list of decorated objects in Appendix VI, where bibliographical references may also be found.

point with flint insets from Copenhagen (III). The motives executed in this technique are mainly simple arrangements of straight lines. They do not include any of the favourite geometric patterns, but a biomorphic design on a bone handle from Refsvindinge (XXXIII) is done by this method.

The third method of decoration is also the most remarkable. The designs in this case are made up of small holes or pits of regular shape, which have evidently been produced by the rotation of a pointed object (see Fig. 57). The German term *bohrornament* expresses very well the character of this decoration made by drilling. The pits are so regular that it seems hardly possible they could have been made by a drill rotated directly by hand. Sophus Müller (1896, pp. 99–101) made practical experiments and arrived at the conclusion that the work must have been done by a bow-drill. A scraped and polished rib-bone from Mullerup (Sarauw, 1903, fig. 36) with a natural curvature and notches on either side of one end may very well be the broken bow of such an apparatus. Rather similar pitted ornament is made by the bow-drill among certain Esquimaux. Müller also showed that the work could be done equally well with a drill of flint or bone, though more rapidly with the former. A strong hint that the drill normally used was of bone may be gleaned from a study of the decorated antler from Silkeborg Sø (XL). As Müller himself remarked, the numerous pits which go to form the complex pattern increase in size gradually from 0·0005 metre near the base to 0·0025 metre towards the tip. One explanation of this might be that the drill tip became blunter as the decoration was carried up the antler. But, if this is so, the drill must have been of bone to wear out so quickly.

The drill technique of decoration is so specialised that it is of particular value as a culture fossil. It is a type of decoration which seems to be associated with the bow-drill, and it appears to have originated in the Mesolithic period, perhaps with the introduction of that apparatus. Parallels have been cited from the French caves, from Gorge d'Enfer (Lartet and Christy, 1875, B, pl. XIII, fig. 13c) and from an Aurignacian station near Sergeac (Didon, 1912, fig. 1, no. 10), but in no case are the pits sufficiently regular to indicate the same technique of work. The palaeolithic site of Malta, Siberia, has produced objects with pit decoration (Salmony, 1931, taf. I, nos. 3, 4, 6), but once more the parallel is not satisfactory.

Most of the pieces decorated with the typical drilled pit ornament are

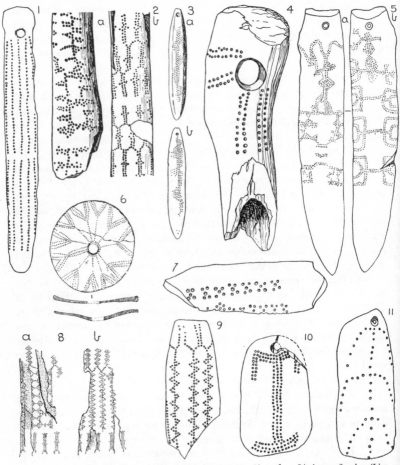

Fig. 57. Selection of objects decorated by drilled pit ornament. No. 1 from Limhamn, Sweden (List no. XXIII); no. 2 from Koldingfjord, Jutland (List nos. XX and XIX); nos. 3, 6 from the Havel region, north Germany (List nos. VIII and VII); no. 4 from Svaerdborg, Zealand (List no. XLIV); No. 5 probably from Fünen (List no. LX); no. 7 from Remouchamps, Belgium (List no. XXXIV); no. 8 from Silkeborg Sø, Jutland (List no. XL); no. 9 from Pernau, Esthonia (List no. XXXII); nos. 10, 11 from Denmark (?) (List nos. LXIII and LXII). Scales: nos. 3, 6, 8, $\frac{3}{18}$; nos. 2, 4 $\frac{5}{12}$; no. 1, $\frac{1}{2}$; nos. 5, 11, $\frac{5}{9}$; nos. 7, 9, 10, $\frac{5}{8}$.

loose finds, but there are several dated finds and most of these belong to period II. There is, it is true, one find which seems to be earlier; the cave of Remouchamps produced a fragment of bone with clusters of five pits (Fig. 57, no. 7), which is associated with a fauna typical of period I. The Maglemose settlement site of Svaerdborg produced a perforated antler adze and a bone handle (XLIV, XLV), both with the typical decoration, and a bone net-pricker with parallel lines of pits came from under the Jära Bank in the neighbourhood of Limhamn (XXIII). These three examples are certainly from period II. The only other certainly dated piece comes from the period III site of Langø, Fünen (XXII). Out of the large quantity of bone-work surviving from Ertebølle sites the Langø piece is the only example of the technique, and it is interesting to observe that the execution and the design are both poor. The Langø find affords interesting confirmation of the continuity of tradition between the Maglemose and the Ertebølle cultures, but it seems fairly certain that the technique had ceased to be common in period III.

The densest area in the distribution of the technique, as illustrated by Fig. 58, is Denmark, which is situated in the centre of the province. Jutland has yielded five pieces, Fünen two, Zealand two, and three others come from unknown Danish provenances. South Sweden has yielded one piece, another comes from the Esthonian site of Pernau, East Prussia gives one piece, two come from Havel clay in Brandenburg, and another from Remouchamps, Belgium. As Breuil (1926) has already pointed out the Maglemose tradition is also strongly displayed in the technique and style of decoration of a group of perforated antler hafts described by d'Acy (1893) from northern France. Unfortunately none of the French pieces are datable on geological or other grounds, but their distinctive bow form (seen in side profile) marks them off from the normal Maglemose hafts and their general appearance suggests a late date. I have been unable to study all of them at first hand, but some at least display the drilled pit decoration and the motives (obliquely barbed lines and chevrons on lines) and their arrangement in lines often tied together at one end support Breuil's opinion most emphatically. The drill technique is found, therefore, over almost the whole province of Maglemose culture, and serves to accentuate once more the cultural unity of the whole of the north European plain during period II. No example has yet been found in south-eastern Britain, but such a discovery is almost to be expected.

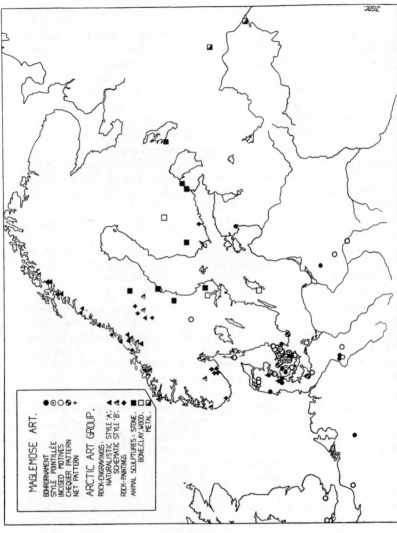

MAGLEMOSE ART.

BOW-ORNAMENT ● ◐ ○ ◓ ←
STYLE POINTILLÉE
INCISED MOTIVES
CHEQUER PATTERN
NET PATTERN

ARCTIC ART GROUP.

ROCK-ENGRAVINGS: NATURALISTIC STYLE 'A'. ▲
SCHEMATIC STYLE 'B'. ◢ ◆
ROCK-PAINTINGS.
ANIMAL SCULPTURES: STONE. ■ ◨
BONE, CLAY, WOOD.
METAL.

16DC.

Fig. 18. Map showing the distribution of the Maglemose and Arctic art groups. Numbers within circles indicate reduplication of finds,

MOTIVES

It will be convenient to consider the motives of the art under three separate heads. In a number of cases the art consists of no more than the improvement or accentuation either of cracks or of scars on the surface of the object decorated. Perhaps the best known example of the former is the perforated antler haft from Svaerdborg (LI) (Fig. 59, no. 5), in which a crack extending from the end of the haft towards the neighbourhood of the perforation is accentuated by short incisions, some extending right across, others being confined to one edge. A second example (IV), described nearly a century ago, comes from the Somme at Crouy; this haft, found five or six hundred miles away, differs only in the slightest degree from the Svaerdborg piece, in that all the incisions without exception extend right across the crack. In describing the French piece Picard (1836–7, p. 240) interpreted the incisions as a method of facilitating the binding of the haft. If this be the right interpretation, then the incisions must be regarded as utilitarian and not as decorative in character. Against this view may be cited precisely similar incisions disposed round the edges of the scars caused by the removal of tines from antlers, which could not conceivably be explained as a technical device of any description; one of these (LVII), which we illustrate (Fig. 59, no. 8), comes from a fresh-water deposit of *Ancylus* age near the Hôtel de Taarbaek, and the other, of the same age, from Horsø (XIII). It would seem that, while the utilitarian explanation advanced by Picard could possibly apply only to the antler hafts, the general similarities both in the actual style of incision and in the way it is disposed warrant the assumption that an explanation equally applicable to both categories is likely to be nearer the truth. Probably the decoration really has a psychological explanation. Both a crack and a scar must be accounted blemishes on an object; perhaps the craftsman sought to nullify them or, as it were, to incorporate them by bordering them with his own handiwork. This explanation is hypothetical and is adopted with due reserve.

In a second category may be grouped the various geometric motives. The explanation of most of these patterns and their relation to the lives of the people who designed them is, and must inevitably remain, obscure. I shall, therefore, restrict myself almost entirely to an objective study of the patterns as culture fossils. I have distinguished some twenty-four motives, and shall

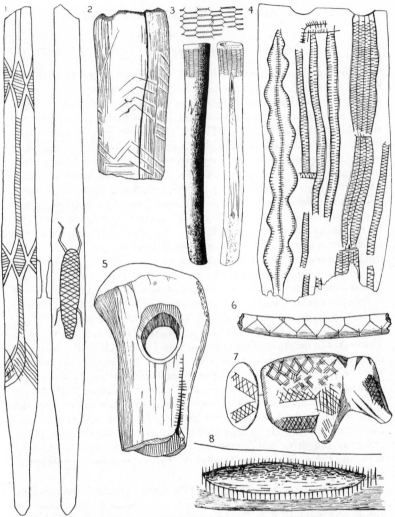

Fig. 59. No. 1 from Langeland Island (List no. XXI); nos. 2, 5 from Svaerdborg, Zealand (List nos. LII and LI); no. 3 from Bohuslän, Sweden (List no. I); no. 4 from Klein-Machnow, north Germany (List no. XVII); no. 6 from Mullerup, Zealand (List no. XXVIII); no. 7 from Resen Mose, Jutland (List no. XXXVI); no. 8 from Taarbaek, Zealand (List no. LVII). Scales: no. 3, $\frac{5}{18}$; no. 4, $\frac{5}{18}$; nos. 5, 8, $\frac{5}{9}$; no. 7, $\frac{5}{6}$; nos. 1, 2, 6, $\frac{5}{8}$.

refer to them by the small letters used to designate them on the key illustration (Fig. 60). The following motives occur:

a–d Variations of the barbed line: the barbs may be oblique or at right angles to the main line, and they may or may not be confined to one side.

e–g Variations of the shaded band: the shading may be oblique, vertical or both.

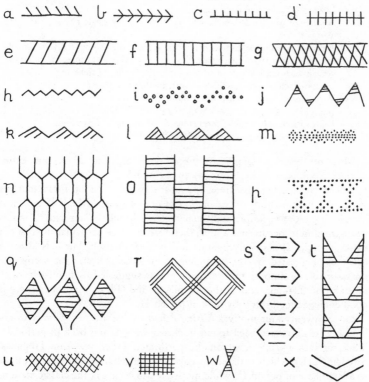

Fig. 60. The chief geometric art motives of the Maglemose culture.

h–m Variations of linear chevrons: plain; crossing and recrossing a straight line; with each angle transversely shaded; shaded obliquely on one side, sometimes alone and sometimes based on a straight line; based on a pair of straight lines, the latter placed back to back.

THE ART OF THE MAGLEMOSE CULTURE

n Net-pattern: in its simplest form as illustrated but showing many minor variations.

o Chequer-pattern: minor variations occur in the character of the shading and the form of the chequer.

p Two lines of solid triangles spaced apart and opposed, the apexes of the triangles being connected by lines across the interval.

q, r Lozenges, shaded and reserved.

s A series of parallel dashes flanked on either side by single chevrons at slight intervals.

t A pair of parallel straight lines connected at equal intervals by transverse straight lines, the upper right angles formed by the original straight lines and the transverse lines being marked off to form the right angles of right-angled triangles, hatchured and not contiguous one with another at any point.

u, v Variations of cross-hatched lines: the lines are either oblique or cross at right angles.

w Pair of hatchured triangles formed by the intersection of two lines.

x Single chevrons often placed one above the other.

Most of the more important pieces decorated with these and other motives are illustrated by Figs. 57, 59, 61 and 62.

Before considering the time and space distribution of these motives something may be said in explanation of one of them. Many of the most popular motives are simple and uncharacterised, but the net-pattern is less widespread in its occurrence and is, therefore, of more particular interest. It exists not only as a strictly geometrical pattern in itself, but it is also, on occasion, suggested by the arrangement of other patterns; it seems not unreasonable to suppose that this motive was suggested by familiarity with nets and net-making, and as the Korpilahti find (Pl. IV) indicates there is good evidence for fishing by nets in period II.

Of the twenty-four motives distinguished twelve are tied down chronologically, as they have been found in closed finds dating back to period II. Thus motives *a–d* all occur on the perforated antler axe from Höganäs, Sweden (XIV), which is dated on palaeo-botanical and geological grounds to a late phase of period II, while motive *a* also occurs at the classic stations of Mullerup and Svaerdborg (Fig. 62, no. 6, and List no. L) dating back rather earlier in the same period, and motive *c* also occurs at Svaerdborg (XLIX). Motive *e* occurs on a perforated antler tine from Holmegaard (X) which dates from the same period as Mullerup and Svaerdborg. Motive *h* occurs at each of the three major Zealand stations of the period, at Holmegaard (IX), at Mullerup (Fig. 62, nos. 6, 7) and at Svaerdborg (XLVII, XLVIII). Motives *k* and *l* both occur at Svaerdborg (XLVI and XLVII), motive *n* at Mullerup (Fig. 59, no. 6) (XXVIII), motive *q* at Höganäs (XIV), motive *r* on a perforated antler axe of *Ancylus* age from Horsø (XII), and motive *x* on an antler handle from Svaerdborg (LII). Motives *a*, *b*, *c*, *d*, *e*, *h*, *k*, *l*, *n*, *q*, *r* and *x* all, therefore, date back to period II on evidence of the strongest nature. In the succeeding period only one survives, motive *q* on a perforated antler axe from the dwelling-site of Brabrand Sø, Jutland; the motive is rendered rather poorly but is important as an indication of continuity.

Three more motives can be tied down almost certainly to period II, since they are executed in the drilled technique which flourished chiefly in this period. Motives *i*, *m* and *p* occur in this technique on an antler from Silkeborg Sø, Jutland (Fig. 57, no. 8), and motive *i* also occurs on a bone fragment from Pernau, Esthonia (Fig. 57, no. 9), both in the same technique.

Six other motives can be dated more or less certainly, since they are found on the same pieces as other motives already dated to period II. Thus motive *g* is found with motive *r* on an amber figurine from Resen Mose, Jutland (Fig. 59, no. 7), and motive *j* occurs with motive *n* on a net-piece from Bohuslän, Sweden (Fig. 59, no. 3). Motive *o* occurs on a perforated antler from Kalundborg, Zealand (Fig. 61, no. 3) with motive *d*, and on a net-pricker from Travenort, Holstein (Fig. 61, no. 1) with the two dated motives *l* and *n*. Motives *u* and *v* both occur on the same object from Kalundborg, Zealand (Fig. 61, no. 3), together with motive *d* and with motive *o* belonging to the same period; motive *u* also occurs on two occasions with two motives dated certainly to period II, namely at Ostrolęka, Poland (Fig. 62, no. 5) with motives *h* and *l*, and on a bone object with flint insets from Denmark (LXIV) with motives *a* and *k*. Finally, motive *w* occurs with motives *d* and *n* on an antler object from Horsens fjord, Jutland (Fig. 61, no. 7) (XI), and also with motive *o* on the famous perforated antler haft from Ystad, Sweden (Fig. 61, no. 6).

We are left with three motives each of which occurs only once in the art, namely *f*, *s* and *t*. Motive *f* occurs on a bone object from Stensby (XLIII), which has a biomorphic design incised on the opposite face; this biomorphic design has no exact parallels but it falls into the same class as others belonging to the art group and may legitimately be used as a link by which to connect

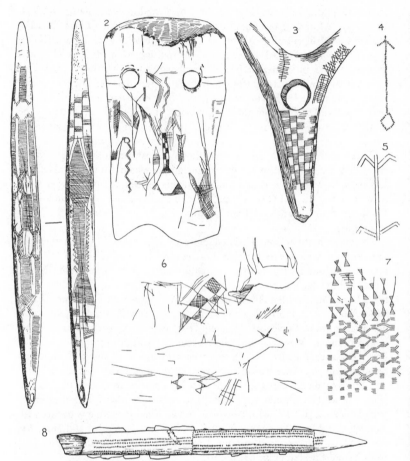

Fig. 61. No. 1 from Travenort, Holstein (List no. LVIII); no. 2 from Skalstrup, Zealand (List no. XLI); no. 3 from Kalundborg, Zealand (List no. XVI); no. 4 from Refsvindinge, Fünen (List no. XXXIII); no. 5 from Stensby, Zealand (List no. XLIII); no. 6 from Ystad, Sweden (List no. LIX); no. 7 from Horsens fjord, Jutland (List no. XI); no. 8 from Copenhagen (List no. III). Scales: no. 2, $\frac{5}{16}$; no. 3, $\frac{1}{2}$; nos. 1, 6, $\frac{5}{9}$; nos. 4, 5, 7, 8, $\frac{5}{8}$.

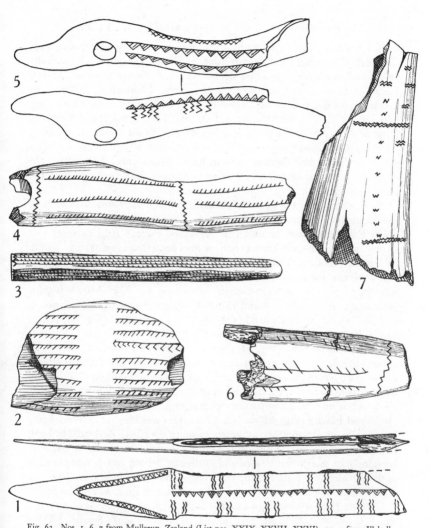

Fig. 62. Nos. 1, 6, 7 from Mullerup, Zealand (List nos. XXIX, XXVII, XXVI); no. 2 from Illebølle, Langeland Island (List no. XV); no. 3 from Sollerön, Sweden (List no. XLII); no. 4 from Mazowsze, Poland (List no. XXIV); no. 5 from Ostrołęka, Poland (List no. XXXI). Scales: no. 5, $\frac{1}{4}$; no. 3, $\frac{1}{3}$; no. 4, $\frac{1}{2}$; nos. 2, 6, 7, $\frac{2}{3}$; no. 1, $\frac{1}{4}$.

motive f, although admittedly not with complete certainty. Motive s occurs on a bone net-pricker from Fernewerder, kr. Westhavelland, north Germany (V), found in a loose association with bone points (forms 1, 5 and 7) and a bone fish-hook belonging typologically to the Maglemose culture: the association is not well enough established to rank as certain evidence but, taken in conjunction with the form of the object decorated, it is sufficient to allow of the tentative inclusion of the motive in the art we are considering. Motive t is admittedly more doubtful, as it is found only on an amber object without other datable decoration from Resen Mose, Jutland (XXXV); the object is, however, one of a pair of amber pieces from the same bog, the second (XXXVI) having datable ornament.

As a general rule the geometrical motives found engraved on objects of the Maglemose culture are scattered indiscriminately over the whole of the north European plain, although in peripheral regions such as south-east Britain and north-east France only a few decorated objects are found. In illustration of the relative homogeneity of this art province may be cited first of all the distribution of two of the more uncommon and characteristic motives of the art, the net-pattern (motive n) and the chequer-pattern (motive o); the former is found in south-western Sweden (Fig. 59, no. 3, and List no. XXX), in Zealand (Fig. 59, no. 6), in Jutland (Fig. 61, no. 7), and in Holstein (Fig. 61, no. 1), and the latter in south Sweden (Fig. 61, no. 6), in Zealand twice (Fig. 61, nos. 2, 3), and in Holstein (Fig. 61, no. 1). A further indication is the occurrence of combinations of two simpler patterns on the same piece; thus motives a and h are found combined on objects from Sweden (Fig. 62, no. 3), Zealand (Fig. 62, no. 6) and Poland (Fig. 62, no. 4), while motives h and l occur together on pieces from Zealand (Fig. 62, no. 1) and Poland (Fig. 62, no. 5). These instances illustrate a remarkable community in art motives as between south Sweden, Zealand, Jutland, Holstein and Poland. Outside this area the art occurs only sparsely in Brandenburg, north-east France and south-east Britain, but motives in each of these regions form part of the stock common to the whole area. Thus the complicated-looking pattern on a perforated antler from Klein-Machnow, near Berlin (Fig. 59, no. 4), consists simply of an arrangement of motive c which is found in Zealand (List no. XLIX) and in south Sweden (XIV), the perforated antler haft with the crack accentuated by transverse incisions from the river Somme (IV) is exactly matched by another from Svaerdborg (LI), and the heavily engraved single chevrons (motive x) from southern

England (Thames (VI), Romsey (XXXIX)) find a close parallel at Svaerdborg (Fig. 59, no. 2).

The third category in which the motives of the art may be grouped is biomorphic; it is concerned with motives obviously based on some form of life, but except in one instance showing very little approach to a naturalistic rendering. We may first of all consider a group of designs symbolic of human figures. These occur in each of the three techniques, incised on a pointed bone from Stensby (Fig. 61, no. 5), in the *style pointillé* on a bone handle also decorated with motive *a* from Refsvindinge (Fig. 61, no. 4), and in the drilled technique on a net-pricker from Fünen (Fig. 57, no. 5), and on two amber pendants from Denmark (?) (LXII, Fig. 57, nos. 10, 11). Thus, although none of the specimens come from geologically dated deposits, they are referable to period II on the grounds of technique of execution, of associated ornament and on the form of object decorated. There is some variety in the designs but they all have in common a vertical line for the trunk and some indication of arms and legs; little or no attempt has been made to indicate the head, this being indicated in two cases simply by an extension of the vertical trunk line, and in two others by the perforation of the object decorated. An interesting feature of Fig. 57, no. 11 is the arc which intersects the trunk about its middle. Wernert (1920) has drawn some interesting comparisons between this group and some of the figures in the Spanish rock-paintings; the example last mentioned with the protrusions at the middle of the trunk (Fig. 57, no. 11) is paralleled closely by a painting in the grotto of Garcibuey, Salamanca (Wernert, 1920, fig. 11), and the more simplified symbol shown by Fig. 57, no. 10 is matched by a painting at Los Gavilanes, near Fuencaliente, Sierra Morena (Wernert, 1920, fig. 15).

A second group of biomorphic designs is based on animal forms. Some of the interpretations placed upon conventional patterns in this art are of a purely subjective character, but I shall confine myself here to cases where the animal character is evident and objectively apparent. A broken bone implement with a flint inset from Langeland Island (Fig. 59, no. 1) has on one face a design including hatchured lozenges (motive *q*) and on the other a creature of almond form, the head being indicated by a slight constriction, the body being cross-hatchured, and the limbs stretched out behind and in front; the kind of creature represented must remain conjectural. Wernert has pointed out that on one of the fragments of antler decorated with drilled pit ornament from Koldingfjord (Fig. 57, no 2 *a*) a row of stylised stags can

THE ART OF THE MAGLEMOSE CULTURE

be clearly seen; in two cases these are quite distinct, the stags being represented in the regardant aspect, but the representations gradually become
incorporated into the net-like pattern until no longer recognisable. The more
recognisable examples suggested to Wernert some rock-paintings at Cogul,
near Lerida, Catalonia (Wernert, 1920, fig. 2). The perforated antler from
Skalstrup (Fig. 61, no. 2) has in addition to the chequer-pattern (motive *o*)
some faintly incised lines which have been variously interpreted; these
include two irregular bar-chevrons, one of them being shaded, which
possibly represent serpents or eels, and what looks very like the greater part
of a fish—the head is missing but the tail is fairly clear. The impression one
gains from this piece is that someone has been idling and incising with a
very fine point various patterns, some of them based on living forms. The
drawings ignore each other completely and are for the most part obviously
unfinished. Similar in style is the decoration on the famous perforated
antler haft from Ystad (Fig. 61, no. 6); here again one has the same impression of somebody's idle moments. Characteristically enough the two
famous cervids are placed back to back and looking in opposite directions;
moreover one of them is very incomplete and the head of the other one has
been spoilt by irregular hatchuring. Stress is often, and rightly, laid on the
naturalistic drawing of the two cervids, but it will be observed that the out-
lines are very angular when looked at closely. The most important fact to be
noticed is that the animals were clearly drawn at the same time as various
geometrical patterns including the chequer-pattern (motive *o*), found on the
Skalstrup piece and typical of the art group as a whole, and opposed hatched
triangles (motive *w*), found on a piece from Horsens fjord. The Ystad
engraving was once ascribed by Montelius (1906, p. 19) to a late phase of
the Neolithic, but the occurrence of these patterns, the close similarity of
style with the Skalstrup piece and the fact that the type of implement on
which the engraving is made became extinct in period III should be
sufficient to anchor it in period II.

SUMMARY OF CHIEF CHARACTERISTICS

Before passing on to comparisons, I shall recapitulate briefly the main
features of the art, which is mostly found on objects of daily use, mainly
of bone or antler, but also on objects of adornment and possibly on amulets.
The commonest technique employed is extremely fine incision, but in some

cases the patterns are formed by fine dots (*style pointillé*), and in others by regularly formed pits probably made by a bow-drill. There is very scanty evidence for sculpture in the round. The motives of the engravings are almost entirely geometric and include, in addition to a number of simple patterns, some rather more characterised ones such as the net-pattern, which clearly relates to an aspect of the economic basis of the culture, and the chequer-pattern. In the arrangement of the patterns two features are characteristic, the tying together of narrow panels of decoration at either end giving the effect of a rudimentary net-pattern (XXXII and LVIII) and the interruption of simple linear patterns running the length of an object either by blank zones (XV, XXIII, XXXVIII, LIII, LIV) or by a line or lines at right angles (III, XVII and XXIII). The only good example of naturalism, the cervids on the antler haft from Ystad (LIX), is of less significance than has sometimes been thought; it was obviously made by somebody normally accustomed to purely geometric patterns. A certain number of animal forms can be discerned, so highly conventionalised as to be unidentifiable, and in particular the art can show a considerable series of extremely interesting conventionalisations of male figures.

RELATIONS WITH UPPER PALAEOLITHIC ART GROUPS

An art style is characteristic of a culture and betrays individual features peculiar to itself. It is nevertheless important to see whether some of the traditions and background of the Maglemose art cannot be traced to an earlier civilisation. With this in mind we may very well consider the engraved bone and antler objects from the Upper Palaeolithic deposits of Europe. The two chief styles of this region, styles which overlap in distribution, but which are easily recognised as distinct, are those, broadly speaking, of Western and of East and Central Europe. Since the Maglemose and the Eastern Palaeolithic styles are both markedly conventional and even geometrical, whereas the Western style has a strong naturalistic element, the comparison might be thought to lie more closely in that direction. Yet the most remarkable examples of the Eastern style, the Předmost woman (Obermaier, 1925, fig. 100), the Cyril Street, Kiev, engraving on mammoth ivory, and the extraordinary Greek key-pattern motives on mammoth ivory from Mézine (Volkov, 1912, fig. 13; 1931, pls. XVI–XVIII, XXII–XXV), are as distant from the style and feeling of the Maglemose art as they are from that of the Western Upper Palaeolithic. Moreover, and to this I attach more importance, the one really common and simple pattern of the Eastern art, the disjointed herring-bone, is entirely absent from Maglemose art. It would seem, therefore, that the comparison between these two art groups breaks down completely. We must look elsewhere for the Palaeolithic antecedents of Maglemose art.

Before instituting comparisons between the Western Palaeolithic and the Maglemose art groups it is important to stress that within the former there was a progressive tendency from naturalism towards conventionalisation, and that our comparison would naturally lie with the latest and most conventionalised stages of the Palaeolithic art. The progressive degeneration or development of naturalistic engravings towards simple geometric patterns has been traced in the rich material of the Magdalenian cave deposits by Breuil (1905, 1906) and by Burkitt (1925, pp. 233–4 and pl. XXXI).

The closest analogies existing between the two arts are to be found in their motives, and in particular in the geometric patterns which predominate in Maglemose art. To illustrate this I shall tabulate some examples of the motives common to the two art groups, designating these according to the scheme adopted on pp. 169–70 and illustrated by Fig. 60.

Geometric motives of Maglemose art	*Some examples from Western Cave Art of Magdalenian age*
Motive *a*.	Le Placard (Breuil, 1912, fig. 18, no. 9). Thaingen (Schmidt, 1912, taf. XXXII, no. 4).
Motive *b*.	Gourdan (Breuil, 1912, fig. 40, no. 9). La Madeleine (Breuil and St-Périer, 1927, fig. 75, no. 1).
Motive *c*.	Bruniquel (*ibid.* 1927, fig. 23, no. 13). Lespugue (St-Périer, 1927, fig. 17). Marsoulas (Breuil, 1912, fig. 27, no. 3).
Motive *d* (with motive *b*).	Grottes des Fées, Marcamps (*ibid.* 1912, fig. 25, no. 6).
Motive *e*.	Bruniquel (Breuil and St-Périer, 1927, fig. 29, no. 5).
Motive *f*.	Saint-Marcel (Breuil, 1902, fig. 5 *c*).
Motive *g*.	Laugerie-Haute (Breuil and St-Périer, 1927, fig. 23, no. 11).
Motive *h*.	Grotte des Espélugues (Piette, 1907, pl. XIV, no. 1). Le Placard (Breuil and St-Périer, 1927, fig. 25, no. 5; fig. 26, no. 7; fig. 27, no. 7). Thaingen (Schmidt, 1912, taf. XXXII, no. 5).
Motive *k*.	Saint-Marcel (Breuil, 1902, fig. 5 *c*).

PALAEOLITHIC AFFINITIES

Geometric motives of Maglemose art	*Some examples from Western Cave Art of Magdalenian age*
Motive *q*.	Laugerie Basse (Breuil and St-Périer, 1927, fig. 21, no. 5; fig. 23, no. 19).
Motive *r*.	Laugerie Basse (*ibid.* 1927, fig. 22, no. 2; fig. 23, nos. 6 and 18). La Madeleine (*ibid.* fig. 23, no. 15; fig. 26, no. 4; fig. 72, no. 3). Raymonden (*ibid.* fig. 26, no. 3).
Motive *u*.	Marsoulas (Breuil, 1912, fig. 27, nos. 5, 6).
Motive *x*.	Bruniquel (Breuil and St-Périer, 1927, fig. 59, no. 3). Espélugues d'Arudy (Piette, 1907, pl. LXXXV, no. 8).

This table, which does not pretend to completeness, shows that a very fair proportion of the geometric patterns of Maglemose art are to be found also in Magdalenian art. In dealing with such simple patterns caution must be exercised in attaching weight to comparisons, but it may be emphasised that we are considering not isolated patterns, but the main stock of geometric patterns of two cultures. It is interesting to note that the barbed line and zig-zag motives, found combined on Mesolithic pieces from Denmark, Sweden and Poland, also occur together on the same object at Le Placard (Breuil and St-Périer, 1927, fig. 26, no. 1). That the patterns common to the Magdalenian and Maglemose cultures are virtually absent from the Eastern Palaeolithic art is surely some confirmation of the value of the comparison we have made. It is true that the two most characteristic patterns of Maglemose art, the net-pattern and to a lesser extent the chequer-pattern, are both absent from the Palaeolithic art, but allowance must be made for some modifications. The introduction of the net-pattern may very well be due to the use of nets for fishing, for which there is no evidence from Palaeolithic deposits. In the same way the new drilling method of executing patterns on antler and bone, for which we could produce no sound parallels from Palaeolithic art, seems to have arisen from the use of a boring apparatus for which there is equally no evidence from that period.

If we are right in assuming some continuity in the traditions of the two art groups on the basis of this evidence, it certainly helps to explain the traces of naturalism which are found in the Maglemose art. The fish on the Skalstrup piece and the cervids on the Ystad haft show just those indications of 'lateness' that one would associate with the last survivals of a naturalistic tradition. Naturalism had already, on the bone engravings of the Mag-

dalenian, given way to a large extent to conventionalisation; in the Maglemose art it barely survived at all.

There remains one element of Maglemose art to be considered, namely
the biomorphic designs described on p. 175. Affinities have been traced
between these and certain paintings of the Spanish art group III by Paul
Wernert (1917, 1920), but there are obvious difficulties in the way of
accepting these as a sound basis for a community of tradition. The first
difficulty is that, whereas the paintings are found in Iberia, the engravings
are far away on the shores of the Baltic. This is not in itself fatal, because the
microlithic element of the Maglemose culture cannot be distinguished from
certain phases of the Tardenoisian, which almost certainly reached Northern
Europe to some extent from the extreme south-west and probably ultimately
from North Africa. More important is the chronological difficulty. The
conventional human figures or biomorphs from the district of Fuencaliente
in the Sierra Morena, with which Wernert wishes to compare the Maglemose pieces, belong to what Burkitt classes as Spanish art group III (1925,
pp. 290ff.). But most authorities agree that this art group certainly survived
until the introduction of metal in Iberia, and there seems to be no positive
evidence for thinking it old enough to have any connection with Maglemose
art. Obermaier (1925, p. 329) claims that the Sierra Morena designs
belong to an early tradition and were made by people of Late Capsian culture, but his chief evidence for this, the comparisons with Azilian painted
pebbles, is generally disputed. It is, therefore, difficult to accept any real
connection between the Maglemose biomorphs and the Spanish paintings,
although it may be emphasised that, should the chronological difficulty be
removed by future research, there seems nothing inherently impossible in
the theory.

RELATIONS WITH THE ARCTIC ART GROUPS

It now remains to see what relations, if any, existed between the Maglemose
art and that of the Arctic cultures of northern Scandinavia (for distribution
see Fig. 58), since many writers have claimed a genetic relationship between
the two. The Arctic art groups consist mainly of rock-engravings and of
loose animal sculptures, belonging to a hunting people for whom a great
antiquity has sometimes been claimed. Some account of the group will be
given and special attention will be paid to the chronology before returning
to the question of a possible relationship with Maglemose art.

The Arctic engravings were not at first distinguished from those of the Bronze Age, found particularly in Bohuslän. Credit is due in large measure to Gustaf Hallström for recognising the distinct character of the group and undertaking systematic field-work (Hallström, 1907, 1908, 1909). The first co-ordination of the existing evidence from Norway was made by Haakon Shetelig (1922 and 1926), but additional survey work in the field has been carried out since by G. Gjessing (1932), Bøe (1932) and Engelstad

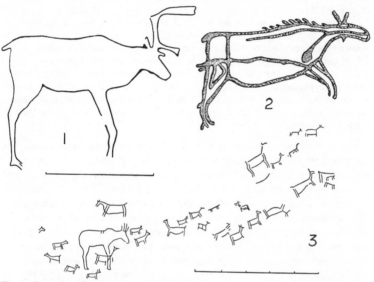

Fig. 63. Engravings of the Arctic art style in Norway. No. 1, Style A engraving at Böla; no. 2, Style B engraving at Gjeithus; no. 3, Style B engraving at Bogge. (After Shetelig.) Scales in metres.

(1934). A complete list of sites with most of the essential details has been published recently by A. W. Brøgger (1931). The existence of these sources makes a detailed discussion of the art group unnecessary, but it is essential to emphasise the distinction between the two main styles:

Style A, or the naturalistic style (Fig. 63, no. 1). The animals are shown in profile, internal features such as eyes or body mouldings being omitted from the design. The beasts are often shown on a large scale, and generally singly or in small groups. Where the rock was peculiarly soft, as at Hell, immediately south of Trondhjem fjord, the technique was one of direct incision, but the technique peculiar to style A was that of grinding into the rock-surface (*Schleiftechnik*), found at Sagelven, Leikines, Klubba, Landverk, Sletjord and Fykanvatn. The pecking technique was also used on a certain number of engravings of this style at Böla, Bardal, Strand and Forselv. The naturalistic style is found exclusively on the sea-board of Norway, north of latitude 63°, and in the central Swedish province of Jämtland (Landverk).

Style B, or the schematic style. Includes engravings of various styles, which for present purposes may be considered together, their treatment being distinct from the naturalism of style A.[1] The beasts are usually shown with four legs, instead of two, and internal features are often indicated (Fig. 63, no. 2). A convention often found is the continuation of both pairs of legs up to the back-bone (Fig. 63, no. 3). As a general rule the beasts are shown on a much smaller scale than those of style A, and are frequently found in large groups, as at Vingen where nearly 800 were found. The only technique employed is that of pecking. The style is mainly found in southern Norway, as at Ekeberg, Åskollen, and Gjeithus in the Oslo region, and Vingen and Bogge in the south-west, but also farther north at Evenhus in the Trondhjem region and even so far as Tennes, the most northerly site of the whole art group. The style also occurs in the Swedish province of Jämtland as at Glösa.

The underlying character and motive of the art group seems to be the same for both the styles which we have just distinguished. We have to deal with the art of hunting and fishing tribes, featuring the big game of land and sea, reindeer, elk, bear, whale, halibut and sea-bird. The whole complex of ideas associated with agriculture, found on the Bronze Age rock-engravings of Bohuslän, is lacking; there are no representations of domesticated animals or plough-scenes, no traces of a solar cult, such as 'ships' or sun-discs, and no scenes with bronze weapons. The motive force of the Arctic art was probably hunting magic; at least it is certain that the art was the work of people whose economy was bound up with hunting and fishing. It has been suggested by A. W. Brøgger (1926) that many of the manifestations of hunting culture may be explained on the hypothesis of seasonal changes of the economic life of the same people; that the rock-engravings may have been made by bronze-using folk while on hunting expeditions. In our view such a dualism between completely differing stages of economic development is hardly conceivable. The chronological question must be solved on its own merits, but we hold firmly to the view that the Arctic art was the product of a purely hunting people, belonging in origin to the pre-

---

[1] Authors are not agreed on the internal sub-divisions of style B, and as these are not relevant to our argument I have refrained from discussing them.

megalithic settlement of Scandinavia. In style and in content of ideas the Arctic art differs almost as widely from the Bronze Age art of Bohuslän as the limitations of primitive technique allow.

The only direct archaeological evidence for the dating of the art is found at Bardal, where profiles of elks in the naturalistic style A are overlaid by typical Bronze Age engravings. Hallström considered this superposition sufficiently conclusive to assign the north Norwegian engravings to a period anterior to the Bronze Age; in particular he noted that the naturalistic engravings showed greater signs of weathering (Hallström, 1908, pp. 62–8). A. W. Brøgger, on the other hand, has pointed out (Brøgger, A. W., 1926, pp. 101–2) that, like so much archaeological stratigraphy, the superposition indicates merely a sequence of events and tells us nothing of the period of time that elapsed between the two periods of engraving; he further points out that the later series of engravings do not belong to the earliest phase of the Bronze Age, so that the dating of the naturalistic engravings to a period anterior to the Bronze Age is not necessitated by the evidence. Brøgger's contentions are sound in so far as they minimise the significance of the superposition as such, but they do not invalidate the original observation of Hallström on the relative weathering of the two sets of engravings, indefinite and subjective though this may be.

There is one remarkable feature common to almost every example of the Arctic rock-engravings, and that is their nearness to fjords, rivers, lakes and waterfalls. Many workers have, accordingly, suggested that the chronology of the art might be established by using the evidence of land-movement, the history of which is for some regions well known. This line of approach can yield valuable results but certain snares must be pointed out. It is too often assumed that individual engravings were made immediately above sea-level and calculations are sometimes made on this basis. In reality it is safe to assume only that the engravings were not made under the sea; they might have been made at any distance above it. A local complication is introduced by the position of rock-surfaces suitable for engraving; at some places such surfaces are available only at a considerable height above sea-level. Yet much of the area of the distribution of the art is a desolation of rocks with many surfaces planed smooth by glaciers, and conclusions based on a study of many engravings widely distributed are unlikely to be affected by this factor. Where a group of engravings are found only above a certain height above sea-level and good rock-surfaces occur below this level, it is probable that they were made at a time when these rocks were not available. One could not argue much from one or two instances, because, as previously stated, engravings might have been made at any heights above sea-level, but where one is comparing two groups differing in style it seems legitimate to attach some importance to differences in relation to sea-level that are at all constant.

As stated above in chapter I, the Oslo region underwent an almost continuous process of elevation from the waters of the *Yoldia* Sea. This has enabled Brøgger to correlate the successive archaeological occupations of the region with varying extents of this emergence. In the neighbourhood of Oslo and Drammen there occurs a famous group of style B engravings and these range between 53 and 70 metres above modern sea-level (Åskollen at 56 m., Ekeberg at 54 m., Gjeithus at 53 m., and Skogerveien at 70 m.).[1] As Brøgger correlates the Nøstvet culture with a fall in the level of the sea from 70 to 45 metres above modern sea-level, it is certain that the engravings cannot be older than this culture, which belongs to the beginning of our period III; it is always possible that the engravings are younger, but it is something to know that they cannot be older. Less is known of the history of land-movement on the western and north-western coasts of Norway, but it is interesting to observe that in this region engravings of style A (Bardal, 42 m.; Böla, 66 m.; Fykanvatn, 95 m.; Klubba, 55 m.; and Sagelven, 44 m.) are normally found at considerably higher elevations than those of style B (Bogge, 22 m.; Evenhus, 32 m.; Vingen, $8\frac{1}{4}$–$9\frac{1}{2}$ m.), suggesting that rock-surfaces available during the dominance of style B were still under water while style A was flourishing. The neighbourhood of Nordfjord has been particularly studied from a geological point of view by Kaldhol (1912), and this has enabled Bøe (1932, p. 39) to estimate that the Vingen group of style B engravings cannot be older than the latest kitchen-middens and the earliest dolmens of Denmark; here, again, it must be conceded that they might be younger.

It has been shown, therefore, that the engravings of style B are not earlier than period III of the Mesolithic and that some may very well be later, but that the engravings of style A may, and probably do, belong to an earlier period. The priority of style A, based on purely geological considerations, is supported by the fact that the engravings of style B represent in the words of Shetelig *un travail plus réfléchi*. The antiquity of the earlier style is difficult

---

[1] Authors vary slightly on the question of levels. I have followed A. W. Brøgger, 1931, except for Vingen, which is more precisely given by Bøe, 1932.

to assess with accuracy, but it is interesting to note that many of the sites occur well above the *Tapes* line (Gjessing, 1932, pp. 71–2) and may very well be older than the period of the *Tapes* Sea, which would put them well back to period II. The situation of the Landverk engraving in relation to the retreat stages of the Scandinavian ice-sheet shows that it cannot be older than this period.

A certain number of paintings, of which the distribution coincides closely with that of the engravings, has survived in south and west Norway, in Jämtland and in southern Finland. Traces of paint on the engraving of Leiknes show that the two mediums were sometimes combined. Stylistic evidence would suggest that the surviving paintings are contemporary with style B; this is confirmed by the find in the cave of Solsem in north Trondhjem, where the schematic human figures were revealed only by the excavation of a deposit which yielded a bone bird figurine of east Baltic type and a slate arrowhead of the Arctic dwelling-place culture, both contemporary in age with the megalithic civilisation of southern Scandinavia (Petersen, T., 1914).

Of more importance are the animal engravings studied by Oscar Almgren (1906, 1907 and 1911), since they belong to the purely naturalistic tradition of style A. Figurines of elks in burnt clay came from the dwelling-place of Åloppe in Sweden, which dates from the early passage-grave period of Denmark (Almgren, 1906, figs. 43, 44), and a bone comb with an animal's head was obtained from the dwelling-place of Gullrum in Gotland island, dating from the passage-grave to stone-cist transition period (Nihlén, 1927, fig. 78). To much the same period belong the numerous slate knives with elk-head terminations from dwelling-places of the Arctic culture in Sweden.[1] Even more remarkable are the animal-headed perforated stone axes from Russian Carelia,[2] Archangel, Olonetz, Finland[3] and Sweden,[4] which sometimes reached, as in the case of the examples from Säkkijärvi and Alunda, a high degree of artistic excellence in difficult materials. A class of mace is also found where the animal's head itself is perforated, as the bear's head from Antrea and the elk's head from Hvittis in Finland (Almgren, 1907, fig. 28, and 1911, fig. 3). A wooden ladle[5] with a handle formed

---

[1] *E.g.* from Delsbo, Helsingland (Almgren, 1907, fig. 4), Åsele, Lappland (*ibid.* fig. 5), and various sites in Ångermanland.
[2] *E.g.* Petrosavodsk and Padosero (Aspelin, 1877, figs. 71 and 76).
[3] *E.g.* Säkkijärvi and Antrea (Almgren, 1911, figs. 2 and 4).
[4] *E.g.* Alunda, Uppland (Almgren, 1911, fig. 1).
[5] The wood is given as *Pinus cembra*.

by an elk's head in the same style has survived from Laukaa, Tawastland, Finland (*Reallexikon*, III, taf. 125, *a*). Finally it may be mentioned that various animal-headed objects of metal clearly belong to the same style; I shall quote only the copper dagger with elk-head termination from Seïma in the old government of Nijni-Novgorod. The extraordinary similarity in style between the Seïma dagger and the elk-headed stone axe from Säkkijärvi has been stressed by Tallgren (1920), who explains the grooves on the stone example as copies of those on the metal piece. Whether this is so or not, it seems clear that there cannot be any great difference in date between the two pieces. As Reuterskiöld has shown (1911) the animal-headed implements and weapons were clearly the work of a people closely dependent on hunting, and he is probably right in connecting the naturalistic sculpturing of weapons with ideas of magic or luck. The elk and the bear were the big game of the region, and it is the heads of these beasts that figure in the sculptures.

Many students have observed close stylistic resemblances between these naturalistic animal sculptures of Sweden, Finland, Russian Carelia and the Fatyanovo culture area, and the rock-engravings of style A in Norway and Sweden (Brøgger, A. W., 1926, p. 210). It may be objected that the resemblance is based only on the fact that both are naturalistic, and that a naturalistic rendering of animals is so often found among peoples subsisting on the chase as to constitute no adequate basis for cultural relationship. But the resemblances in this case are stronger than vague analogies. I illustrate on the same plate (Pl. VIII) the head of one of the elks engraved on rock by the Ånnsjöns in Jämtland, and a sculptured axe from Alunda in Uppland. The similarity of treatment is to my mind too real to avoid the conclusion that there is some cultural connection between the engravings and the sculptures. As is shown by the distribution map (Fig. 58) the geographical spread of engravings and sculptures is continuous from Norway to central Russia with an overlap in central Sweden. If the cultural relationship is a real one it adds another argument to the late dating of style A, since the sculptures are datable with some certainty to the megalithic period of Denmark and south Sweden. If geology suggests period II as the earliest date for the rock-engravings of style A, archaeology certainly encourages the view that the tradition was active in period III and even later.

But many writers, following the lead of Hallström, have insisted on the close analogies claimed to exist between the Scandinavian engravings of

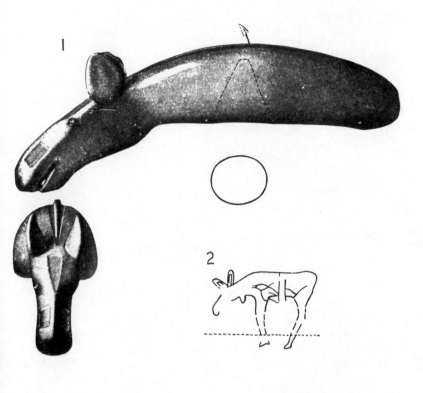

PLATE VIII. No. 1. Elk-headed stone axe with incomplete perforation from Alunda, Uppland, Sweden.

No. 2. Rock-engraving (style A) at Landverk, Jämtland, Sweden.

Scales: no. 1, *c.* $\frac{2}{3}$; no. 2, $\frac{1}{44}$.

style A and certain engravings dating from the Upper Palaeolithic of Western Europe. If this is correct we are faced with a survival of artistic tradition for a period of time which seems hardly credible, especially when we consider that the analogies can rest only with the earlier stages of cave art. This circumstance has not always been appreciated at its full value, but it is a fact that the only Upper Palaeolithic engravings, on which any close comparison can be made, belong to an early phase of the art antedating such ideas as perspective or the suggestion of form by devices of shading. The best analogies can be found, perhaps, at Pair-non-Pair in the Gironde (Burkitt, 1925, pl. IX, D), where the engravings belong to the earlier part of the Aurignacian, being covered by deposits dating from the Late Aurignacian.

The length of life necessitated for the tradition, if any connection be accepted between the Aurignacian art and style A of the Arctic art, is so immense that it would in any case be difficult to admit; one could indeed only admit it in the face of analogies so close and so detailed as to demand some continuity of tradition. But the detailed analogies adduced by Hall-ström and Shetelig do not in my view bear examination, and we are not, therefore, called upon to strain our credulity to bridge the huge gap of years separating the two art groups. A general similarity may be admitted, but since both art groups reflect the economic desires of tribes living by the chase, the naturalistic represen-tation of big-game animals cannot in itself constitute a very remarkable or valuable basis for comparison. A de-vice of draughtsmanship sufficiently specialised to afford a sound basis for

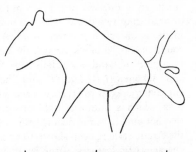

Fig. 64. Rock-engraving at Fykanvatn, Norway, illustrating a time-saving device of draughtsman-ship; the trunk and limbs are common to two beasts. (After Hallström.) Scale of metres.

comparison is the trick of adding the head of one beast to the rear of another in such a way as to produce two beasts; examples of this occur at Fykanvatn (Fig. 64) and Bardal (Hallström, 1908, fig. 22). The instances cited by Hallström (1908, pp. 78–9), as parallels from cave art, are mainly super-positions of the kind which abounded at that period, but which have nothing but a superficial resemblance in common with the labour-saving device of the Arctic art. Another 'parallel' cited from the Palaeolithic art by Hallström is that of the heads of two ruminants in near proximity and looking in opposite directions; in this case the two heads are the only common factor, the body of the pair being entirely absent and with it the whole point of a possible comparison. A second feature of the Arctic art for which detailed parallels are claimed in the Palaeolithic art is the occurrence of rough signs, including linear chevrons, on the bodies of animals; Hallström compares the signs on a bison from La Mouthe (Rivière, 1901, fig. 2) with those on one of the cervids at Hell (Hallström, 1908, fig. 20). Actually, however, the 'chevrons' on the Hell engravings are misinterpreted; they are not isolated geometric patterns or signs placed on the body of the beasts, but, on the contrary, represent merely the extension of the leg lines drawn up to meet the spine. The real geometric signs found at Hell and again at Forselv (Gjessing, 1932, pl. X, 23) are hatchured lozenges; these do not occur on, but only near the beast in the Arctic art, and from the Palaeolithic art they are entirely absent. Not only, indeed, are the supposed detailed parallels between the art groups unsound, but most of the special features of the Arctic art group are missing from the older group. The short-hand device of producing two beasts with a common body, to which reference has been made, is one such feature. Another is the occurrence of a kind of band round the bodies of elks, which characterises both styles of the art; it is found in style A at Landverk (Hallström, 1907, fig. 15) and in style B at Glösa and Åskollen (*ibid.* fig. 12; and Shetelig, 1922, p. 136). A technique of engraving special to style A is the method of grinding the outline into the rock, which is unknown in the cave art of the west. It can be said, therefore, that not only have the detailed affinities between the Upper Palaeolithic and the Arctic style A been shown to be mistaken or illusory, but important and characteristic features of the latter have been found to be absent from the older art. The argument for connecting the two art groups on the basis of their detailed affinities must be dismissed as unsound.

The Palaeolithic hypothesis cannot completely be ruled out of consideration so long as there is room for doubt about the antiquity of style A in Scandinavia, but it seems to us extremely unlikely. In our view the affinities of style A lie rather with the sculptures found over a wide area from Sweden to central Russia and contemporary with the megaliths of Denmark; some of the engravings may date back to period II, but the bulk of them belong to period III or later.

AFFINITIES OF MAGLEMOSE ART

MUTUAL RELATIONS OF THE UPPER PALAEOLITHIC, MAGLEMOSE AND ARCTIC ART GROUPS

Something must now be said of the mutual relations of the three art groups of which this chapter has treated. The original theory of these relationships is well illustrated by Hallström's suggestion (1908, pp. 74–8) that the Ystad antler-haft engraving of cervids forms a link between the Upper Palaeolithic and Arctic art groups. This, in my opinion, indicates a complete misunderstanding of the real situation. It has been shown that any affinities that the Arctic style A may have with Upper Palaeolithic art are with an early phase (Early Aurignacian), whereas the affinities of the Maglemose art are clearly with the latest phase (Magdalenian). The suggestion that the Maglemose art could be in any way intermediate between the Upper Palaeolithic and Arctic groups is, therefore, unthinkable. But it has further been shown that the Palaeolithic affinities of the Arctic group are not so close as some Scandinavian writers have suggested, and, indeed, that the acceptance of any kind of connection between the two groups involves chronological difficulties of so grave a nature as to make it extremely unlikely. The Magdalenian affinities of the Maglemose art are of a detailed nature, and, though the latter has characteristics of its own, there is at least a reasonable probability—in this case open to no chronological objection— that there has been some real cultural connection. As regards the relationship between the Arctic and the Maglemose art groups it is probable that none has ever existed. The Maglemose art became virtually extinct, so far as is known, in the Atlantic period, whereas there is no positive evidence that the Arctic art group of engravings and sculptures pre-existed this period.

CHAPTER V

THE MICROLITHIC CULTURES OF THE SAND AREAS AND THE HIGHLANDS

DISTRIBUTION AND NATURE OF SETTLEMENT

It is well to make clear at the outset that the Tardenoisian is considered in this book strictly in relation to the area of Northern Europe selected for special study. In the case of the Maglemose culture the whole area of settlement is included within this zone, but the Tardenoisian extends much farther afield in South-western Europe and North Africa. I shall describe, therefore, not the Tardenoisian as a whole, but the Tardenoisian settlement of the region. The name 'Tardenoisian' is derived from the original finding-place of Fère-en-Tardenois, Aisne, France, discovered by A. de Mortillet (1896), but it is now used to describe a culture of which the name site represents only one phase.

The distribution of the Tardenoisian within our area is illustrated by Fig. 65. The two densest areas of settlement in Britain are enclosed in rectangles on the main distribution map, and are illustrated separately by Figs. 66 and 67. Apart from eastern Britain, sites are distributed over northern France, Belgium and Holland, the southern fringe of the plain of northern Germany, Franconia and Württemberg, almost the whole of the loess-free areas of Poland, and eastwards into the Ukraine (Alio, 1922, p. 6).

Traces of Tardenoisian man are mostly found on sandy soils; a better example of geological control over human settlement could, indeed, hardly be found. I illustrate on Fig. 66 the distribution of sites in a part of south-eastern England which has been investigated relatively intensely. They are found at intervals along all but the eastern end of the Lower Greensand belt (which loops round the Weald), on the Tunbridge Wells sand and on two small patches of Woolwich Beds sand on the South Downs. Apart from a site on gravel, immediately to the north of Farnham, all the forty-eight sites indicated on the map are situated on sand. Particularly striking is the fact that even small isolated areas of sand a few acres in extent, like the patches of Woolwich Beds sand on the South Downs east of Brighton, were settled. The same control has been observed for Lincolnshire, where the famous

Fig. 65. Map showing the distribution of Tardenoisian settlement in the area of study. N.B. The mapping of the very numerous Polish sites has not been attempted.

FIG. 67

FIG. 66

TARDENOISIAN SITES

LAND OVER 600 FT. ABOVE SEA-LEVEL.

FÈRE-EN-TARDENOIS.

ENSDORF

ANSBACH

FEDERSEE

SCUNTHORPE

CRESWELL

PEACOCK'S Fm.

LAKENHEATH

ZONHOVEN

R.MAAS

R.RHINE

R.EMS

R.WESER

KULLER BRUCH

FIENER BRUCH

FREISACK

R.ELBE

R.SPREE

R.ODER

R.WARTA

R.WISTULA

R.DANUBE

R.OISE

191

Scunthorpe sites occur on blown sand, and other sites in the county occur on the Spilsby sandstone and on Lower Greensand (Phillips, 1933, pp. 116–19). The most prolific Tardenoisian sites of East Anglia are found in the dunes between Lakenheath and Wangford, and on sand hillocks, now wholly or in part submerged by the post-glacial deposits of the fens. The name site of the culture and most other sites in northern France are situated on sand. Dursin (1931) has remarked that the great majority of the numerous sites of Belgium and Holland are sand sites. Adrian has shown (1934, pp. 113–14, and abb. 2) that in the neighbourhood of Bielefeld the numerous Tardenoisian sites are found on the southern sand-covered slopes of the Teutoburger Wald and are absent from the loam-covered northern slopes. Over the north German plain the majority of the sites are found in dunes blown up from the diluvial valley sands of the Weser, the Aller, the Elbe, the Spree and the Oder (Keilhack, 1917). Bicker has published an instructive map of the Tardenoisian settlement of the Fiener Bruch, situated between the Elbe and the Havel; no less than twenty-six sites have been found on sand dunes on its northern margin (Bicker, 1934, abb. 1). Farther east the dunes of the valley of the Vistula have yielded a great number of sites; on my map those on the middle course of the river have not been indicated, as they have not been accurately mapped. The generalisation made by Coutil that the sites of Tardenoisian man are mainly to be found on sand (Coutil, 1912, p. 308) has been supported in striking fashion by subsequent discoveries.

The close inter-relation between Tardenoisian settlement and sand is further underlined by the absence of sites on contiguous deposits. This is illustrated on a local scale by Fig. 66, where the South Downs and the Weald clay lands are sterile. On a wider scale our main distribution map shows that north of the main sand areas of Germany, the forested regions inhabited by Maglemose man were unoccupied by the Tardenoisians. Or, again, the loess belt, immediately to the south of the chief areas of Tardenoisian occupation in north Germany, shows hardly a trace of settlement. I have not mapped the Polish sites as a whole, but the dense Tardenoisian settlement of the country is almost confined to sand areas, being absent in marked fashion from the loess lands. To quote Kostrzewski (1931, p. 400): *L'industrie tardenoisienne est bien richement représentée en Pologne, et celle est connue par quelques centaines de gisements situés dans toutes les provinces de notre pays, à partir de la Haute Silésie, la Petite Pologne et la Volhynie jusqu'aux*

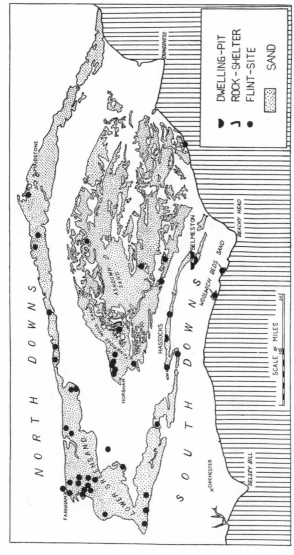

Fig. 66. Map of Sussex, with parts of Kent, Surrey, Berkshire and Hampshire, showing the relationship of Tardenoisian settlement to sand formations.

bords de la mer Baltique et aux frontières de la Lithuanie, excepté seulement les territoires fertiles du lœss au sud de la Pologne.

But Tardenoisian settlement in our area was not confined to sand; quite a large number of sites are found on high ground. Raistrick (1933) has shown that the numerous sites of West Yorkshire, England, are found as a general rule at elevations of between 1000 and 1500 feet above sea-level,[1]

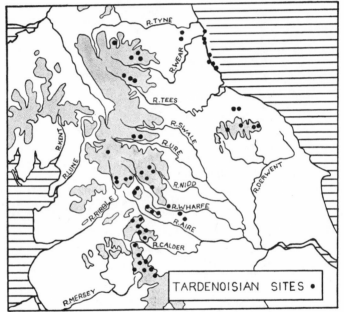

Fig. 67. The distribution of Tardenoisian sites in the north of England. Stippled areas are over 1000 feet above sea-level. (After Raistrick.)

and Petch (1924) has done the same for the Pennines near Huddersfield. This evidence is summarised by our distribution map (Fig. 67). A similar group of high-lying sites is found in Franconia, south Germany, where Herr Gumpert has made his valuable investigations. In the immediate neighbourhood of Ansbach the sites are found on plateaus capped by sandstone (*Blasensandstein*) at elevations ranging between 450 metres (1476 feet) to

[1] Raistrick points out that many sites may occur above this level, being obscured by peat.

520 metres (1705 feet); valley settlements in the neighbourhood are un-known. Other surface sites in Franconia are Hohlefels, Holzheim and Lichtenfels, all at elevations between 400 and 600 metres above sea-level; rock-shelters and caves in the neighbourhoods of Pottenstein and Ensdorf are similarly situated. Herman Stoll has discovered a group of sites in the Ostschwarzwald, centring on Nagold, which are situated in exposed positions at elevations ranging from 519–610 metres (1703–2034 feet) above sea-level; other sites in the same region are known from the neighbourhoods of Tübingen and Stuttgart. Farther south, in Württemberg, a group of sites has been investigated by Reinerth on the margins of an earlier version of the Federsee. As is demonstrated on Fig. 68, the diminution in the size of the lake has been progressive from the period immediately succeeding the melting of the quaternary ice-sheet to the present day.

The distribution of Tardenoisian settlement is peculiarly informative. The first point that arises is that by settling either in sand-dune areas, on exposed rocky situations, or by the margins of lakes, the Tardenoisians avoided the necessity of coping with dense forest; for this reason their material culture, in marked contrast to that of the Maglemose people, lacks the heavy equipment of axes and adzes. Secondly their areas of settlement—sand areas and exposed situations on hills or mountains—were entirely unadapted to primitive agriculture; this not only supports the view suggested by a study of their material culture, that they subsisted without agriculture, but it further renders highly probable their survival on their poor territories well into the Neolithic period. The loess grounds, along which the earliest agri-culturalists of the area—the Danubians—first advanced, must have been empty;[1] the Mesolithic folk, dwelling on grounds less desirable agricultur-ally, would not have been disturbed until such a time as pressure of popula-tion caused the Neolithic peoples to spread into the poorer zones. The Federsee settlement suggests that fishing, as well as hunting and collecting, played its part in the economy of the Tardenoisians.

DWELLING-PLACES

The mouths of caves and the shelter of overhanging rocks provided the chief homes of Upper Palaeolithic man; in the more temperate climate of the Mesolithic period they played a less important rôle, giving way almost

[1] This agrees with the well-known rarity of weapons in the Danubian peasant culture (Childe, 1929, p. 47).

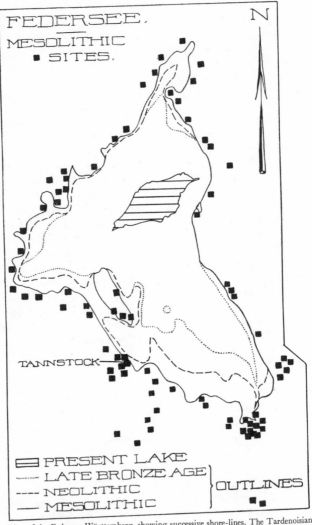

Fig. 68. Map of the Federsee, Württemberg, showing successive shore-lines. The Tardenoisian sites are situated on the earliest of these. (After Reinerth.)

entirely to open sites. Traces of Tardenoisian culture have, however, been found in England in the mouth of Mother Grundy's Parlour, Creswell, a limestone cave in Derbyshire (Armstrong, 1925), and also under the shelter of a 20 foot wall of Lower Tunbridge Wells Sand at Balcombe, Sussex (Clark, 1934, pp. 422–3). In Belgium an early stage of the Tardenoisian has been found in the cave of Chaleux (Rahir, 1920),[1] and in the grottoes at Montaigle a later stage has been found in the upper levels; two small emplacements, showing a fairly advanced stage of the culture with trapezes, occurred under the shelter of the rock containing the caves of Bay-Bonnet in the valley of the Vesdre (Lequeux, 1923, pp. 50 ff.). In Germany a primitive microlithic industry comes from the cave of Martinshöhle, near Letmathe, Westphalia (Schmidt, 1912, p. 90). At Wüste Scheuer, near Döbritz, Thuringia, a number of microlithic triangles and crescents were recovered from a disturbed deposit, containing material ranging from mammoth's teeth to Slavic sherds. Traces of typical Tardenoisian culture have been yielded by several rock-shelters and caves in Upper Franconia; two strata, overlying a Magdalenian deposit, against a rock-shelter at Rennerfels, near Pottenstein (Gumpert, 1931), have produced a few triangular microliths and a micro-burin; traces of Tardenoisian industry were found in the basal deposits by the rock-shelter of Geisskirchfels; and a rock-shelter in a broad valley known as "der Breit", in the neighbourhood of Pottenstein, has given a rich Tardenoisian of developed character with trapezes, triangles, crescents, points with concave base and micro-burins (Gumpert, 1929, abb. 8). As a final instance I may quote the rock-shelter at Ensdorf on the Vils in the Oberpfalz, where a rich Tardenoisian stratum, showing development from Early to Middle and from Middle to Late Tardenoisian, occurred above Early Tardenoisian and Magdalenian deposits (Gumpert, 1933).

In many of the examples quoted the indications of Tardenoisian culture were so sporadic as to indicate occasional visits; only in a few cases, such as the shelter at Ensdorf, is there indication of any prolonged occupation. The majority of the sites are found in the open air and so reflect climatic conditions more favourable than those of the Upper Palaeolithic period. Of the open-air sites the greater number give no certain indication of the types of dwelling occupied, though it has been noticed generally by investigators all

---

[1] The material from Chaleux was not obtained in stratigraphical relationship; the two industries were sorted out of the large material known to have come from the cave.

over Europe that surface finds of microliths and flint-chipping debris are frequently found in concentrations suggesting hut emplacements. At Badger Slacks (site 2), situated on the Pennines in the Huddersfield area, at an elevation of 1350 feet, Francis Buckley found traces of what he interprets as a wind-break shelter of wood and heather (Buckley, 1924, pp. 1–3); over 600 chert and flint implements, including microliths, micro-burins, burins and scrapers, were concentrated within a roughly circular area of 4 square yards, around one half of which was observed a semicircle of birch and ling charcoals.

Especially when he settled a region of soft rock, Tardenoisian man often inhabited 'pit-dwellings', or rather dwellings of which 'pits' or '*fonds de cabanes*' are usually the only surviving trace. The earliest example recorded was that discovered and excavated by H. S. Toms (1907) on the Lower Greensand at Hassocks, Sussex, England; the pit was 2½ feet deep, had a diameter of approximately 6 feet, and contained over 2000 worked flints, including 70 microliths and a core axe with transversely sharpened cutting edge (see Clark, 1932 (*a*), fig. 44). On the same formation, a few miles to the east, at Selmeston, traces of a settlement of similar pit-dwellings have been found; most of the dwellings were probably destroyed by sand-diggers but two pits and the remains of a third were excavated. Pit 1 was most clearly defined and proved to be oval in form with maximum diameters of 8 × 15 feet; it was overlain by 4 feet of top soil, was sunk into the undisturbed Lower Greensand to a maximum depth of 3¾ feet, and contained more than six thousand worked and calcined flints. Of pit 2 only a trace was found, but pit 3 produced more than one thousand five hundred flints. Most of the typical forms from pit 3 are illustrated by Fig. 71, which also gives the leading microlithic forms from pit 1. Fragmentary hazel-nut shells were recovered from pits 1 and 3. Another pit-dwelling has been found near Loughton in Epping Forest by Mr Hazzledine Warren (Clark, 1932 (*a*), pp. 62–3).

Similar pit-dwellings have been recorded from Belgium. Rahir (1924) has described one with a diameter of 2 metres and a depth of 60 cm. sunk into *roche psammitique* at Sougné in the valley of the Amblève; it contained a thousand worked flints and some charcoal. Lequeux (1923, pp. 67–9) has described a group of seven shallow hut emplacements, extending only from 15 to 30 cm. below plough level with diameters of between 2 and 3 metres, at Wegnez in the valley of the Vesdre; the pits contained numerous worked flints[1] and quantities of charcoal. At the upper station of Roche-aux-Faucons, in the valley of the Ourthe, Lequeux investigated three pit-dwellings with diameters of between 2 and 3 metres and depths of *c.* 70 cm. The bottoms of the pits, which were excavated in clay, were reddened by fire, the worked flints[2] and charcoal occurring above this sterile burnt layer. The important feature of the Roche-aux-Faucons site is the occurrence of traces of burnt clay daub, suggesting the character of the superstructure of the dwelling (Lequeux, 1923, pp. 104–5).

The first Tardenoisian dwelling, other than a cave or rock-shelter, to be discovered in Germany was that found by Gumpert (1927, pp. 14–25) at Eyb, some 2 kilometres to the east of Ansbach in Franconia. The pit-dwelling was sunk through a thin sandstone layer (*Sandsteinbank*) to a depth of $\frac{3}{4}$ metre into the underlying clay; it was oval in plan (3 m. × 3·30 m.) and was lined with sandstone blocks, which had the appearance of careful arrangement. In the centre of the pit was a hearth with quantities of spruce charcoal. The only artifacts were three flakes of flint and one of quartzite; one of these shows traces of secondary flaking, but none of them seems to betray features of a peculiarly Tardenoisian character. The situation of the site, and the absence of pottery or artifacts of late date, have convinced many authorities that the dwelling-place was inhabited by Tardenoisian man. The evidence is not really conclusive, though the balance of probability seems to rest with Gumpert's view. More satisfactory evidence of pit-dwellings has been recovered by Reinerth and his assistants at Tannstock on the borders of the Federseemoor, near Buchau, Württemberg (Reinerth, 1929, pp. 50–7). Here we have a settlement of thirty-eight huts, which showed up as dark discolorations of the diluvial loam immediately underlying the plough soil; the huts were mainly oval in plan (3·2–3·7 m. long by 1·8–2·1 m. wide) and some 30 cm. deep. Reinerth considers that the huts belong to two distinct periods, so that the settlement was in reality quite a small one at any given time. Many of the huts were linked one to another by forecourts, in some cases three being so joined together. Hearths were found in many of the huts; as a general rule they were found near one side of the hut plan and sometimes they were defined by a ring of pebbles. Traces of a framework of branches have been recovered from the settlement in a good state of pre-

[1] One of these pits contained 759 flints (149 showing traces of fire), 78 blades, 14 cores, 4 microliths, 6 micro-burins, 3 burins, 5 scrapers and 1 hammerstone.
[2] A typical hut emplacement yielded 1620 flakes (732 burnt), 135 blades, 7 cores, 54 microliths, 1 scraper and 1 hammerstone of quartzite.

servation, suggesting that the huts themselves were formed of tree branches covered with reeds. It will be remembered that traces of wattle and daub construction were observed on the Belgian site at Roche-aux-Faucons. A series of the flint types, and the only bone type from the Tannstock dwellings, is illustrated by Fig. 70. A few sherds of unidentifiable and featureless pottery were also recovered, but the extent of the site and the extreme shallowness of the pits make it difficult to accept them as contemporary.

It is evident, from the evidence cited, that Tardenoisian man constructed dwellings for himself, sometimes mere wind-breaks, but where practicable huts with branch frames covered with reeds or wattle and daub, as well as occupying various natural shelters. In every case the flints from such artificial dwellings have represented a fairly developed stage of the culture. In contrast with this the only Early Tardenoisian material associated with a dwelling has come from caves or shelters. The cave continued in use throughout the Mesolithic and into the Iron Age, but the more temperate climate favoured settlement in the open.

MATERIAL CULTURE

Evidence relating to the material culture of early man is subject to the selective influences of the natural forces of decay. The settlement of Maglemose man in damp places, where natural deposits have accumulated rapidly, has ensured the preservation of quantities of objects made from perishable materials, such as wood, antler or bone. On the other hand the sand dunes and highland areas, favoured by Tardenoisian man, have been highly destructive of all but the least perishable evidence. Wooden objects have nowhere survived, and only from a few favoured sites have we any bone objects. Of the undisturbed cave or shelter sites only Ensdorf has produced much evidence of worked bone; this includes the tips of two pointed objects, a bone fragment with signs of sawing, three bow-shaped pins of fine ribbones polished to points (the only complete specimen is illustrated by Fig. 69, no. 28), a bone fragment with incised lines, and numerous fragments of bird bones, broken off at either end. That the bird-bone fragments were, in some cases at least, used as hafts for microliths, is suggested by the discovery of the flint illustrated by Fig. 69, no. 27, set in one of them. Menghin (1927, abb. 2, no. 10) illustrates a microlithic triangle set into a short length of tubular bone from the middens of Tebessa, Algiers. Two red-deer antler tines from Ensdorf show signs of use at their extremities, but no other worked or used antler pieces were recovered. The only other object of bone or antler associated with Tardenoisian man in the area is the plain bone point (Fig. 70, no. 1) from one of the huts at Tannstock on the shore of the

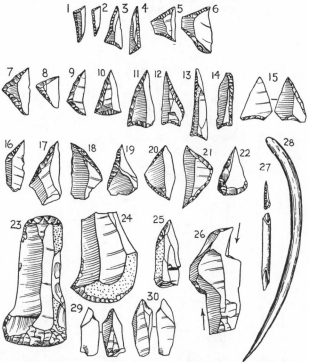

Fig. 69. Tardenoisian industry from the cave of Ensdorf, Bavaria. Nos. 1–6, microliths from the top of the main Tardenoisian stratum; nos. 7–15, from the middle of the stratum; nos. 16–22 from the base of the stratum; nos. 23–28 from the main stratum. (After Gumpert, and from the originals.) Scale: ⅓.

ancient Federsee. Evidence of bone and antler work is meagre, but sufficient material has survived from Ensdorf to make it improbable that the culture was characterised by distinctive antler or bone forms. Antler axes or adzes, and antler or bone points or harpoons, are absent.

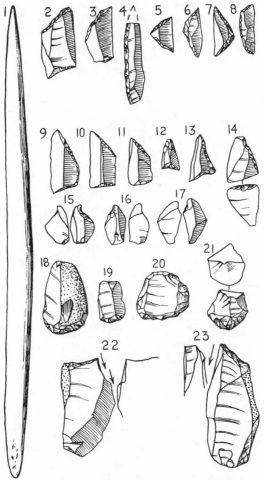

Fig. 70. Objects from dwelling-place at Tannstock, Federseemoor, Württemberg. No. 1, bone point; nos. 2–14, microliths; nos. 15–17, micro-burins; nos. 18–21, scrapers; nos. 22, 23, angle-burins. (Drawn by the author in the Federseemoor Museum at Buchau.) Scale: ⅔.

TARDENOISIAN MATERIAL CULTURE

The only objects to survive in any quantity or variety are those made of flint or stone, and of these the most characteristic and important are microliths. The manufacture of these objects, which are frequently less than a centimetre long, required a special technique of work, and the by-products and wastage of manufacture are characteristic. The fine narrow flakes necessary for the production of microliths, and the fluted cores from which these were removed, occur in profusion on the chipping-floors. The dressings from such cores, necessary to provide a clean striking platform, consist either of disc-like slices from the base or of flakes of triangular section and battered keel, removed from the edge of an old platform. The removal of the bulbar ends of flakes involved in the production of microliths was normally done by the notch technique, a by-product of which is the 'micro-burin'. Examples of the stage preliminary to the separation of microlith and micro-burin are frequently found[1] (Fig. 71, no. 69). The actual number of flakes converted into microliths formed a very small proportion of those produced, as reference to the statistics of the contents of certain pit-dwellings will show (p. 199).[2] At the same time they are of predominant importance to archaeologists, since they were made into so many distinctive forms. I shall not discuss these in detail, as they have been described elsewhere (Clark, 1934), but I must indicate them briefly. The simplest forms are those blunted obliquely down part of one edge, or down the whole of one edge; oblique or transverse blunting[3] across the base of these types adds other forms. More evolved forms are triangles, crescents, lozenges, rhomboids, trapezes and points with concave base. The only direct evidence for the method of hafting microliths, most of which are too small to have served as individual tools, is that from Ensdorf, quoted above. Yet, while it seems likely that single microliths were hafted in this way, it is also fairly certain that they were mounted in large numbers as units of composite implements. Francis Buckley, who is a most careful observer, recorded a find of thirty-five

[1] *E.g.* From Hastings, Sussex (Clark, 1932 (*a*), fig. 59, no. 47); Darlaten, Hanover (Adrian, 1931, abb. 3, no. 1850); Ansbach, Franconia (Gumpert, 1927, abb. 142, nos. 1 and 6); Roche-aux-Faucons, Belgium (Lequeux, 1923, fig. 32, nos. 5–7); Słochy Annopolski (site II), Poland (Szmit, 1929).
[2] Raistrick (1933, p. 194) has stressed this fact. It has to be remembered, however, that, whereas many finished microliths must have been shot away or lost in use, the flints from chipping represent very largely the wastage of manufacture.
[3] I use the word 'blunting' advisedly. The secondary flaking of microliths was devised not to sharpen but to blunt the edge of the primary flake. The tip and the primary flake edge were intended for use; the blunted edge formed in some cases a finger rest, and in others it served to minimise wear on the haft, which was probably in many cases of wood. This 'blunting' flaking, which is often almost vertical, is one of the most marked and typical features of microlithic flint-work.

minute microliths of sub-triangular and trapezoidal form at White Hill on the Pennines near Huddersfield, which suggest such an interpretation; the flints lay under 6 inches of peat at a depth of 1 inch in sand, and they were spaced out in a single straight line at intervals of between $1\frac{1}{2}$ and 2 inches. The evidence of the Vig aurochs, fully discussed on p. 89, makes it certain that the simple form of microliths, at least, were used as barbs of weapons. Fishing seems to have played an important part in the economy of some groups of Tardenoisian people, as for example those who settled the ancient shores of the Federsee; it is not fantastic to suggest that single microliths were sometimes hafted to form the tips of primitive fish-hooks. The method of hafting the trapeze, which is the same as the *petit tranchet* arrowhead, is well known (Fig. 51).

True burins are typical of the culture, though they rarely occur in large numbers on one site. I illustrate examples from dwelling-pits at Tannstock (Fig. 70, nos. 22, 23) and Selmeston (Fig. 71, nos. 32, 68), and from the cave of Ensdorf (Fig. 69, no. 26).[1] Convex scrapers are generally common, but do not help archaeology very much; where flint is scarce, as on the Scottish sites (Clark, 1932 (*a*), fig. 28, nos. 21–23) or by the Federsee (Fig. 70, nos. 18–21), the scrapers tend to be small, but where the raw material is more plentiful the ordinary horseshoe form is common (Fig. 71, no. 27 and Adrian, 1931, abb. 5). Pointed flakes retaining their bulbs, but showing steep secondary flaking, are often found on Tardenoisian sites (Fig. 71, no. 50), and finely serrated flakes (Fig. 71, no. 31) also occur. Awls, unless some microlithic forms were used for this purpose, are uncommon.

It is notable that axes, adzes or picks of flint are normally entirely absent, as are also the same types in antler or bone. The Tardenoisian shows no adaptation in its pure form to forest environment, thus verifying the evidence obtained directly from a study of the regions chosen for settlement. It is true that at certain sites in Britain and in Belgium a slight axe element can be distinguished, but this does not affect the main point and its significance will be discussed at a later stage.

Hammerstones are often found on the chipping-floors, and a roughly circular piece of quartzite with a pecked depression in one face from Roche-

---

[1] Burins occur on most open sites with a good bulk of material. *E.g.* on broad and narrow blade sites of the Pennines (Clark, 1932 (*a*), fig. 6, no. 12 and fig. 9, no. 40); on the sites in the valleys of the Ourthe, Vesdre and Amblève (Lequeux, 1923, fig. 8, no. 34; fig. 10, nos. 34, 35; fig. 22, nos. 2, 3); and on the sites in the neighbourhood of Ansbach (Gumpert, 1927, abb. 83).

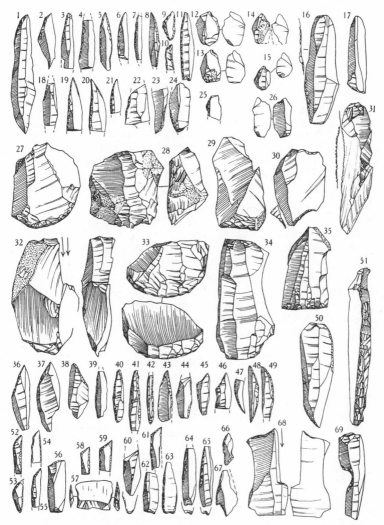

Fig. 71. Flints from pit-dwellings in Lower Greensand at Selmeston, Sussex, England.
Nos. 1–35 from pit 3; nos. 36–68 from pit 1; no. 69 loose. Scale: ⅔.

aux-Faucons (Lequeux, 1923, fig. 27, no. 1) probably served as an anvil. A number of quartzite objects are recorded as having been dug up from a rich flint chipping-floor on Blackdown, Hampshire (Clark, 1932 (*a*), pp. 73–4 and fig. 38); the flints had not been disturbed when they were excavated, and, though immediately below the surface, they were tightly packed together. It is possible that the quartzites were dropped on the site at a later date, though more likely that they were contemporary. They consist of a tongue-shaped pebble abraded at one end, a flat circular pebble some $3\frac{1}{2}$ inches in diameter with hour-glass perforation, and a ring $1\frac{3}{10}$ inches across and directly perforated by a hole $\frac{1}{2}$ inch across. The second of these is similar to the simple quartzite maces of the forest cultures. Stone axes of any type seem to be entirely absent from the culture.

Pottery is another important absentee. Its absence from the extremely numerous sites in Britain, the Low Countries and Germany can hardly be explained on the hypothesis that it has decayed, since over this area the natural conditions at different sites have been so various. In particular the finding of burnt clay daub at Roche-aux-Faucons (Lequeux, 1923, pp. 105–6) suggests that, had pottery been present, it would also have survived. Certain claims have been made for Tardenoisian pottery in Germany, but in no case do they seem to be well justified at present. Max Schneider's 'Binsen keramik' would command more attention if his account was more scientific (Schneider, 1932). Reinerth found a few featureless sherds in some of the dwelling-pits at Tannstock (Reinerth, 1929, p. 55), but, since the pits were only from 15 to 30 cm. deep below plough level and covered a good area, it would be risky to accept the pottery as contemporary. One may hazard the suggestion that if Tardenoisian flints are found, in the future, associated with pottery, this will prove to have been borrowed from another culture complex. It would be curious, if the Tardenoisians made a distinctive pottery of their own, that we have not by this time found it.

Over the whole area included in our map (Fig. 65), and indeed far beyond this, a remarkable degree of uniformity in culture is to be observed, until the latest stage, when local variations become apparent. In Britain the influence of the Early and Middle stages of the Tardenoisian, as found in Belgium, is clear (Clark, 1932 (*a*), p. 94), but between our Late Tardenoisian and that of the mainland there are marked differences. The trapeze never became common in the British industries, and the lanceolate point with one face pressure-flaked (Fig. 72, no. 3), so typical of the Late Tardenoisian of Belgium and Holland, is entirely absent; on the other hand certain forms, such as that illustrated by Fig. 71, no. 67, seem to be peculiar to Britain. The community to be found between Britain and the Continent in the earlier stages and the variations in the latest period may perhaps be explained in terms of land-movement. By period III Britain was, in all probability, separated from the Continent. Some evidence of navigation is afforded by the fact that four Tardenoisian sites have been found in Federseemoor, on land which must have formed an island in the contemporary lake (Fig. 68); it is, however, improbable that serious navigation on open water was practised. One may mention here, as an instance of early commerce, the distribution of Wommersom quartzite. This fine grey-brown quartzite, which is highly tractable, occurs naturally only at one locality, half a kilometre south-west of the church of Wommersom, a few miles to the east of Tirlemont, Belgium (Dursin, 1931, pp. 391–2), where nodules are exposed on the surface detached by weather; yet thousands of pieces have been found on Tardenoisian sites scattered over the whole of Belgium and southern Holland. The trade seems to have been confined to the later stages of the Tardenoisian, and it is interesting to find that no polished axes, barbed and tanged arrowheads or other types of later cultures have been identified as of this material.

CHRONOLOGY

Unscientific excavation and fortuitous disturbance of deposits in caves or under rock-shelters has destroyed much of the evidence of stratification, but, wherever a Tardenoisian stratum has been found in relation with one of Upper Palaeolithic age, it has been the younger. At Mother Grundy's Parlour, Creswell, a poor Tardenoisian overlay a developed provincial Aurignacian. Under the Rennerfels shelter, near Pottenstein, two strata with traces of Tardenoisian overlay a thick stratum dating from the Magdalenian, being separated therefrom by an 80 cm. sterile layer. And, finally, at Ensdorf the following section was obtained:

10 cm. Humus.
10 cm. Culture stratum with pottery—probably Hallstatt.
20 cm. Sterile layer—accumulation due to weathering of the rock-shelter.
45 cm. Dark culture stratum with hearths—Tardenoisian.
25 cm. Erosion layer, mostly of angular gravel.
20 cm. Culture stratum—Early Tardenoisian.

25 cm. Erosion layer, mostly of angular gravel.
35 cm. Culture stratum of Magdalenian age.
50 cm. Stony diluvial deposit.
85 cm. Stoneless loam.
　　　 Dolomite rock.

The post-palaeolithic age of the Tardenoisian strata at Creswell and at Ensdorf is confirmed by the nature of the fauna, which is markedly of the forest type. The Creswell stratum gave horse, ox, bison, red deer and pig, while Ensdorf gave red deer, roe deer, pig, fox, squirrel, badger, hare, marten, and various rodents, birds and fish.

Three main phases of the Tardenoisian culture itself have been identified in Belgium (Fig. 72):

(1) A Lower or Early Tardenoisian, as represented by the lower level at Zonhoven (Hamal-Nandrin and Servais, 1909). The microlithic forms are of the simplest—points blunted obliquely or down the whole of one side, and triangles.

(2) A Middle Tardenoisian found on many sites in the valleys of the Amblève, Ourthe and Vesdre (Lequeux, 1923). Here the microlithic element of the culture is most richly developed. The simple types continue, but the triangles tend to become smaller and more regular, and crescents, hollow-based points, and a few rare trapezes make their appearance.

(3) An Upper or Late Tardenoisian found on or near the surface at Zonhoven and commonly in Campine (Hamal-Nandrin and Servais, 1909; Lequeux, 1924). In this final stage the microlithic forms of the Middle Tardenoisian continue in use, but the trapeze becomes the dominant type. In addition, small lanceolate points (Fig. 72, no. 3) with shallow secondary flaking over one convex face and occasionally to a less complete extent on the flatter face become common.

The three phases have never been found in Belgium stratified one above the other, though at Zonhoven the late or final stage overlay the Early Tardenoisian. The early phase is known to belong to an early stage of the Mesolithic owing to its close resemblance with the Remouchamps material, dated to period I on the grounds of associated fauna; the later or final phase is known to have overlapped (at least) with the Neolithic, since at Zonhoven itself trapezes were found chipped from flakes removed from polished axes of flint. It is assumed, with a reasonable degree of probability, that the phase typologically intermediate between the Early and Late Tardenoisian belongs to a period between the two.

The Ensdorf section tells a similar story. Between the main Tardenoisian

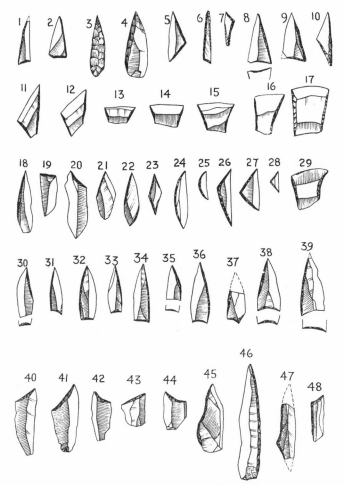

Fig. 72. Stages of the Belgian Tardenoisian. Nos. 1–17, Upper Tardenoisian from Zonhoven (Upper level). (After Hamal-Nandrin and Servais.) Nos. 18–39, Middle Tardenoisian from the valleys of the Amblève, the Ourthe, and the Vesdre. (After Lequeux.) Nos. 40–48, Lower Tardenoisian from Zonhoven (Lower level). (After Hamal-Nandrin and Servais.) Scales: nos. 1–17, $\frac{3}{8}$; nos. 18–39, $\frac{2\frac{1}{4}}{8}$; nos. 40–48, $\frac{4}{9}$.

stratum and the Magdalenian is a poorly represented but typical Early Tardenoisian, in which the only microlithic forms present are obliquely blunted points. The main Tardenoisian stratum, which is 45 cm. thick, produced over 2000 worked flints as well as a few bone objects, much animal debris and two stone-circled hearths. Where the deposit was undisturbed by hearths or other circumstances, Herr Gumpert found it easily divisible into three vertical zones for excavation, the upper and the lower being grey in colour and the middle black. In the black central zone the microlithic forms were typical of the Middle Tardenoisian (Fig. 69, nos. 7–15) with small geometric triangles and hollow-based points; but in the lower zone the microlithic forms—obliquely blunted points and rough triangles (*ibid*. nos. 16–22)—were typical of the Early Tardenoisian, and in the upper zone the further diminution in the size of the triangles and the presence of a good proportion of trapezes (*ibid*. nos. 1–6) pointed towards the Late Tardenoisian. The Ensdorf section supports, therefore, the succession of the Tardenoisian phases, first established in Belgium.[1]

The pollen-analytic method may be expected to assist in the future towards a more exact knowledge of the phases of Tardenoisian culture in different regions, but the habitats of the people make its application difficult. Two good examples of correlation with forest history have, however, been published and these throw some light on the chronology of the culture. At Peacock's Farm, Shippea Hill, Cambridgeshire, a section cut through recent peat and clay deposits (see Pl. III) resting on the flanks of a sand-ridge settled by early man gave the following stratification:

Levels below modern sea-level (O.D. Newlyn)	Natural deposits	Cultural remains
−2¾ feet to −6½ feet	Upper Peat-bed	Early Bronze Age at −6 feet
−6½ feet to −13⅛ feet	'Buttery Clay' (containing *foraminifera* and marking a stage of relative land subsidence)	
−13⅛ feet to −21½ feet	Lower Peat-bed	Neolithic A (Windmill Hill culture) at −15 feet, Tardenoisian at −17 feet
At 21½ feet	Sand	

N.B. The section is summarised in tabular form in Fig. 13.

[1] It is probable that this succession holds good for Britain, though stratigraphical information is deficient. It has long been recognised that two markedly different phases of Tardenoisian exist on the Pennines, one corresponding to the Early Tardenoisian of Belgium, and the other contemporary in all probability with the middle and late phases of the culture (Clark, 1932 (*a*), p. 26).

From this section it will be seen that, when the site was inhabited by Tardenoisian man, the land stood at a considerably higher elevation than is now the case. In previous chapters we have shown that at the beginning of period II much of the southern part of the North Sea was a vast fresh-water fen, over which the sea has subsequently transgressed; in some parts of Denmark the maximum of this marine transgression fell in the middle of period III and coincided with the Ertebølle culture, but evidently the maximum, as

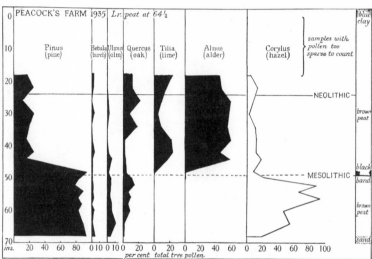

Fig. 73. Pollen diagram through the lower peat-bed with Neolithic and Tardenoisian levels at Peacock's Farm, Shippea Hill, Cambridgeshire, England.

marked in the southern part of the fen basin of eastern England by the buttery clay deposit, was considerably later, dating at earliest from the very end of period III. Pollen-analysis of the Lower Peat-bed by Dr Godwin has shown that its lower part dates from the later stages of the Boreal (period II), the transition to the Atlantic (period III) occurring immediately above the Tardenoisian level. In the diagram (Fig. 73) the transition from period II to period III is clearly shown by the striking change over from pine to alder dominance and the incoming of lime among the forest trees; the later stages of period II are also marked by high values for the shrub hazel. The micro-

THE MICROLITHIC CULTURES

lithic material (Fig. 74), obtained from the excavation and dated closely to the transition from period II to period III, shows a fairly advanced stage of the Tardenoisian culture, and is paralleled in Britain by the later Tardenoisian material from beneath the dunes between Lakenheath and Wangford. The evolved character of the microliths (*e.g.* nos. 62–64) shows that they fall into the later stages of the culture; in Britain they might be classed

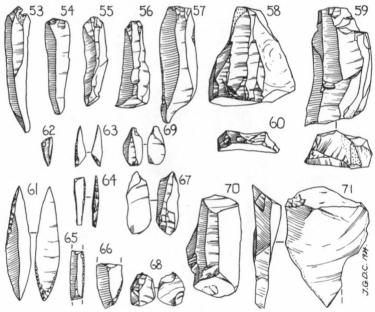

Fig. 74. Tardenoisian flints excavated from Peacock's Farm, Shippea Hill, Cambridgeshire, England. Scale: ⅝.

as Late Tardenoisian,[1] but typologically they resemble those of the Middle Tardenoisian of Belgium.

The second reliable correlation[2] is that made by Bertsch and Reinerth by

[1] The upper or final Tardenoisian of the Continent seems to be absent from England. Our Late Tardenoisian resembles more the Middle Tardenoisian of the Belgians.

[2] One cannot rely very much on the analyses of the Rhinluch site, near Freisack, Brandenburg (Bertsch, 1928, pp. 33–4; Stoller, 1927), because the samples were taken so near the surface and contained too little pollen for reliable interpretation.

the Federsee in Württemberg. Here some traces of Tardenoisian material were found in peat. The analyses made by Bertsch show that the culture flourished on the margins of the lake during the latter part of period II. The Tardenoisian level succeeds the maximum of pine but antedates the oak-mixed-forest maximum, and coincides with a hazel value equal to more than four-fifths of the total forest tree pollen. Assuming that the flints found in the peat belong to the same phase of the Tardenoisian as that represented at Tannstock, this evidence seems to fix a date towards the end of period II for the Middle Tardenoisian of south Germany, in which I should include most of Gumpert's finds from the Ansbach region and the central industry from the Upper Tardenoisian culture stratum at Ensdorf.

RELATIONS OF THE TARDENOISIAN WITH THE TANGED-POINT CULTURES

The history of the Tardenoisian during period I and the beginning of period II is obscure. There is not, indeed, any certain evidence for its existence before period II, but it is possible that the Early or Lower Tardenoisian, which at Ensdorf underlay a Middle Tardenoisian similar to that dated to the latter half of period II in the Federsee area, goes back to that time. The flint industry from Remouchamps, found with a fauna typical of period I, has sometimes been classified as Early or pre-Tardenoisian, but I have shown that its tanged points ally it with the Ahrensburg-Lavenstedt culture of the tanged-point civilisation. Typologically the Remouchamps culture stands between the Early Tardenoisian of Zonhoven and the Ahrensburg-Lavenstedt culture; it includes the microlithic forms of the one and the tanged points of the other. In the present state of knowledge one cannot be certain how far this relationship can be explained generically, or how far it must be ascribed to regional variations.

There is some reason for thinking that in periods II and III a more easterly group of tanged-point people, the Swiderians, survived on treeless dunes and mixed with the Tardenoisians, but it would be wrong to argue from this that there is any generic connection between the cultures.

THE MICROLITHIC CULTURES

The habitats of Maglemose and of Tardenoisian man in Northern Europe differed profoundly, and this fact doubtless contributed largely to the differences in their material cultures. Speaking generally the Maglemose culture is by far the richer of the two; this is partly no doubt due to the fact that it has survived more intact than the Tardenoisian, which is normally found on sites peculiarly unfavourable to the preservation of all but the least destructible materials, though sufficient cave finds have been made to indicate that the bone and antler equipment of the Tardenoisians cannot compare with that of Maglemose man. However, much of the equipment associated with the Maglemose and absent from the pure Tardenoisian, such as axes and adzes of flint, stone, bone and antler, is due to adaptation to forest conditions, and traces its descent from the Lyngby culture of period I. The art of the Maglemose also finds no parallel in the Tardenoisian.

When the great differences existing between the two cultures have been conceded there still remains an underlying common element, to which I wish to draw special attention. An integral part of the Maglemose culture, whether found in south-eastern England, north Germany, Denmark or Sweden, is the microlithic element with all its attendant by-products. This in itself provides an important link between the cultures, but additional weight is lent to this by the fact that the micro-burin, the 'type fossil' of the Tardenoisian according to the orthodox view (Saint-Périer, 1922), also occurs at such typical Maglemose sites as Broxbourne, Svaerdborg and Duvensee. This point, which is a new one, has been established in detail on pp. 94 ff. The microliths from Maglemose stations do not differ either in their mode of production or in their forms from those of the Tardenoisian. This does not alter the fact that the two cultures are separate, belonging to different civilisations and cradled in different environments, but it does show that there is a strong common element. It is not, indeed, always very easy to draw the line between the two cultures when, as in south-eastern Britain and Belgium, one finds a very slight axe element in otherwise microlithic industries. Is the presence of this element on the Lower Greensand sites of Sussex, from the dwelling-pits at Hassocks and at Selmeston, for instance, to be interpreted as an indication of culture-contact and admixture, or does it represent some kind of continuity between the two cultures?

RELATIONS WITH MAGLEMOSE CULTURE

This question of the microliths and micro-burins in the Maglemose culture is one of the very highest importance, because it shows that, while certain elements of the culture are common to the axe tradition going back to period I in the north of Europe, yet at the same time it cannot easily be regarded any longer as a purely northern growth among purely northern people. A strong element must find its origin in common with that of the Tardenoisian, which is found over the greater part of Europe from the Ukraine to Spain as well as over northern Africa. The similarity in culture and in the typological sequence of microlithic forms—for example the lateness of the trapeze—over this wide area has been interpreted as indicating either movements of people from North Africa under stress of climatic change or a common evolution of culture over the whole area of distribution from a common stock under common changes of natural environment. It seems likely that there is truth in both these views, but that neither of them alone can provide an adequate explanation. It seems fairly certain that the indigenous Upper Palaeolithic cultures of North-western Europe contributed to the microlithic civilisation of the Mesolithic; the process of modification has been traced in detail in the upper beds of the Grottes des Enfants, Mentone, at Mother Grundy's Parlour, Creswell (Armstrong, 1925), and at King Arthur's Cave, Ross-on-Wye (Taylor, 1927). At the same time there are certain peculiar features of the Tardenoisian, such as the micro-burin, which are common to the whole area of its distribution, but which could hardly arise independently. Moreover, a similar sequence of development, with the trapeze becoming more frequent in the later stages, is found over the whole area, suggesting a community of culture which can only be explained on an ethnic basis. One would conclude, therefore, that, though the indigenous population contributed locally to the new civilisation, it was due primarily to ethnic movement under stress of the climatic changes which characterised the post-glacial period. The source of these invasive influences is often sought in North Africa, but Miss Garrod's work in Palestine suggests that population may also have overflowed from the eastern end of the area of desiccation.

The microlithic element common to the Maglemose and the Tardenoisian cultures allows of a chronological correlation independent of that already established on the basis of environmental phases. We have already shown that the Early Tardenoisian dates from the end of period I or the beginning of period II, that the Middle Tardenoisian dates from the latter part of period II, and that the final Tardenoisian is contemporary with period III. The microlithic element of the Maglemose sites of Broxbourne, Duvensee and Sandarna, which date from about the middle of period II, includes only the simple forms characteristic of the earlier phases of the Tardenoisian, whereas the later Zealand sites at Holmegaard, Mullerup and Svaerdborg have produced microlithic forms, such as scalene triangles, crescents and points with concave base, more closely approximating to those of the Middle Tardenoisian of Belgium. The microlithic element continued in the Erte-bølle culture of period III, when it consisted almost entirely of trapezes, and this, again, forms a parallel to the final Tardenoisian of Belgium, northern Germany and Poland, in which the trapeze played an important rôle. There is thus a strong typological parallelism between the internal development of the element common to the axe and the microlithic culture-groups of periods II and III.

THE SURVIVAL OF THE TARDENOISIAN

The chief areas settled by Tardenoisian man in Northern Europe, sand-formations and dunes, and exposed hill-tops on hard rock, were precisely those least suited to agriculture, and, therefore, least likely to be disturbed by the earliest agriculturalists. Indeed, Tardenoisian man seems positively to have avoided the loess regions of southern Poland and of Germany, which controlled the immigration and spread of the Danubians, the earliest agriculturalists of the area (Schliz, 1906, pp. 334 ff.). The survival of Tardenoisian man in areas relatively undesirable to peoples with a different economy can, thus, be accepted on *a priori* grounds. The displacement of one culture by another is never achieved in an instant; in this particular case the overlap in time was probably a long one[1].

Direct archaeological evidence is hard to come by, since the Tardenoisians and the incoming Neolithic folk dwelt apart, preserving their economies in separate natural zones, but indications of contact are not lacking in the equipment of the final Tardenoisian. The polishing of flint is one of the distinguishing features of the Neolithic and Early Bronze Age in Northern Europe, and the discovery of Tardenoisian flint forms made from re-worked

---

[1] Ekami and Midzuno (1935) show a very similar state of affairs in Mongolia, where a microlithic culture on sand regions survived side by side with a polished stone culture on loess; their map (section 55 and fig. 27) illustrates a zone of geographical overlap between Kansu and Vladivostok. I am indebted to Professor Minns for this reference.

fragments of polished flint axes may therefore be taken as indicating contact with cultures of one or other of these periods. Such finds have been made in Belgium and in Poland. The upper level at Zonhoven produced a final Tardenoisian mixed with Neolithic material; the dominant feature of the industry was the abundance of trapezes, some of which were made from flakes derived from broken polished flint axes (Hamal-Nandrin and Servais, 1909). Kostrzewski is certain that the Tardenoisian continued until a late stage of the Neolithic in Poland and cites (1931, p. 408) the trapeze made from a flake from a polished flint axe, found by Sawicki on the Tardenoisian site at Ostrowo. Another technique, foreign to the earlier phases of the Tardenoisian, but common in the Neolithic and Bronze Age industries, is that of shallow pressure-flaking; this also is found in the final Tardenoisian of the Low Countries, on the small lanceolate points flaked over one face (*e.g.* Fig. 72, no. 3, from the upper level at Zonhoven). Similar pressure-flaking is found on some of the flints of the developed Tardenoisian of Scotland, as at Shewalton Moor, Ayrshire (Clark, 1932 (*a*), fig. 27, nos. 19–22). The Shewalton Moor industry also includes a tanged flint arrowhead of a form found in the Bronze Age but executed in typical microlithic style with steep edge-trimming (*ibid.* no. 26), a phenomenon also found at the final Tardenoisian station of Vielles, Eure, France (Octobon, 1929, pl. VIII, nos. 209, 215, 228).

The survival of the microlithic tradition into periods later than the Meso-lithic, which is supported both by the distribution of settlement and by the evidence of contact to be traced in the latest phase of the Tardenoisian, is paralleled by the survival of both the other major traditions of the Meso-lithic; the tanged-point tradition survived in Norway and Sweden into the Bronze Age, and the axe tradition survived as a delayed and peripheral Maglemose culture to the same period in Norway, and as the Ertebølle, Limhamn, Lower Halstow and Campignian cultures to the Neolithic period.

THE AZILIAN[1]

The chief areas of the distribution of the Azilian culture, as defined by the flat harpoons barbed on both edges, and the painted pebbles, lie outside the

[1] Had the Azilian culture occupied more than one edge of our region of study I should not have relegated it to an appendage of this chapter. Essentially it is, in contradistinction from the Tardenoisian, a forest culture—witness the bone axes from the Scottish sites and the stone axes of Falkenstein; but it has no connection, apart from possible contact in North Britain, with the axe cultures of the plain of Northern Europe, described in chapter III.

THE MICROLITHIC CULTURES

limits of our region of special study, in Santander, on the slopes of the Pyrenees, in Ariège, the Dordogne, and north-west Britain. The harpoon at Whitburn, near Newcastle, and the midden at Inch Keith in the Firth of Forth are on the edge of our area, and there is a stray harpoon from near Liége. The eastern slopes of the Alps show some traces of Azilian in the French departments of the Drôme and the Isère, and farther north there are traces near Basle in the painted pebbles of Birseck (Sarasin, 1912). The famous nests of skulls, accompanied by red-ochre and perforated teeth and shells, from Ofnet in Bavaria are often assigned without any particular reason to the Azilian; the only well-defined flints found with the skulls are two small scalene triangles which might equally well be Azilian or Tardenoisian. Of the measurable skulls eight were brachycephalic, eight more were mesocephalic and five were dolichocephalic; whether Azilian or Tardenoisian, they demonstrate the presence in southern Germany, probably in period II, of a strong broad-headed element.

It is probable that the Azilian was fairly strongly developed in the upper valley of the Danube, as recent finds by E. Peters (1934) well illustrate. His excavations in Falkensteinhöhle, near Tiergarten, Hohenzollern, have produced flat harpoons with both edges barbed, microlithic triangles and flat stone axes or adzes with ground edges, one of which is inset into an antler haft. The form of the harpoons is not of the earliest style, resembling the MacArthur's Cave examples rather than that from Victoria Cave, Settle (Clark, 1932 (*a*), fig. 1). I suggest that the Falkenstein find is late, probably belonging to period III, but it carries on an older tradition and itself helps to explain the occurrence of rather similar harpoons at still later dates lower in the Danube area (*e.g.* Childe, 1929, fig. 17) as well as in Switzerland (Reinerth, 1926, abb. 2).

CHAPTER VI

GENERAL SUMMARY AND RETROSPECT

The general plan adopted in this book has been to describe the evolution of each of the three main cultural groups of Mesolithic times in Northern Europe in separate chapters, sub-dividing the history of each in terms of the natural chronology established in the first chapter. Perhaps it may now be useful to rearrange the material and summarise it as a chronological sequence.

PERIOD I (PRE-BOREAL)

Geochronology. 8300–6800 B.C.

Geography. The lowland plain of Northern Europe stretched unbroken from Britain to the Swedish province of Småland and those parts of Esthonia as yet emerged from the waters of the Baltic. At the beginning of the period the Baltic formed an arm of the sea (*Yoldia*), but the emergence of Götland, Svealand and south-east Norway gradually converted it into a lake (*Ancylus*). The Scandinavian ice-sheet withdrew from the Fenno-Scandian moraines and finally divided into two in the province of Jämtland.

Climate. Temperature rose fairly rapidly from the cold of the Sub-arctic period, July temperatures rising from 8° to 12° C.

Forests. Willow, birch and pine the only forest trees.

Fauna. Lemming absent, but reindeer and other tundra forms survived to mix with incoming forest forms.

Cultures:

(*a*) *Tanged-point cultures.* Dominant over the plain of Northern Europe from Belgium to the Ukraine, manifest in the Remouchamps, Ahrensburg-Lavenstedt and Swiderian cultures, which seem to have originated in Upper Palaeolithic cultures of Magdalenian age, such as those of Elspeet, Hamburg and Mielnik.

Another branch of the tanged-point culture-group seems to have reached Scandinavia by way of Russian Carelia and to have flourished on the Arctic and Atlantic sea-boards as the Komsa and Fosna cultures.

(*b*) *Axe cultures.* A new tradition was cradled in Denmark, north Germany and south Sweden in response to the development of forests. It is evinced in this period by the Lyngby culture, which, though not very important in itself, is significant as the primary root of a tradition that was to play a leading part in future development.

GENERAL SUMMARY AND RETROSPECT

(c) *Microlithic civilisation.* A rather shadowy pre-Tardenoisian or Early Tardenoisian, represented by the lower culture at Zonhoven, marks the beginning of microlithic cultures in the area. Upper Palaeolithic cultures were also running to seed at this time, as at Creswell.

PERIOD II (BOREAL)

Geochronology. 6800–5000 B.C.

Geography. At first the lowland plain of Northern Europe, as it existed in period I, remained intact, but gradually the sea transgressed the North Sea bed and the Danish-Swedish land-bridge, until Britain became separated from the Continent and the *Ancylus* Lake was transformed into the *Litorina* Sea.

Climate. Temperature rose rapidly to reach a maximum at the end of the period of 17° C. (some 2½° C. above that of the present day). Climate was warm but at the same time dry and continental (Boreal).

Forests. Forest dominated by birch or pine, but alder and the components of the oak-mixed-forest (elm, oak and lime) come in and rise in importance throughout the period. Towards the end of the period hazel reaches high values in many parts of the area.

Fauna. Predominantly forest forms, but reindeer survived in many parts. Elk was particularly common.

Cultures:

(a) *Tanged-point cultures.* Diminished in importance very greatly on the plain of Northern Europe, but may have survived and mingled with the Tardenoisian locally in sand areas.

The Komsa and Fosna cultures of Scandinavia continued to flourish and absorbed influences from the axe cultures.

(b) *Axe cultures.* A rich culture, the Maglemose, developed from a coalescence of the Lyngby tradition, a microlithic element of Middle Tardenoisian origin, and possibly some lingering traditions of Magdalenian culture. The Maglemose is found over the whole plain of Northern Europe from eastern Britain to Esthonia and Poland and from southern Norway and Sweden to central Germany. Over this wide area a remarkable homogeneity of culture is to be observed, resulting from the geographical unity of the earlier stages of the period. Local variations of culture are subservient, but do exist. The Zealand sites exhibit a local facies which is rather later than the earlier spreads as found at Broxbourne, Sandarna, Duvensee and Kunda. The culture shows a marked adaptation to forest environment, and reflects hunting, collecting, and fishing on inland waters. The art is described in a separate chapter.

(c) *Microlithic cultures.* The Middle Tardenoisian, deriving from an Upper Palaeolithic origin outside our area and almost certainly outside Europe, is

PERIOD III (ATLANTIC)

found distributed over areas where forest was of little importance. Such areas include sandy tracts and exposed alpine regions with little depth of soil. The culture has produced no art and shows little or no adaptation to forest.

PERIOD III (ATLANTIC)

Geochronology. 5000–2500 B.C.

Geography. It is probable that by now England was separated from the Continent, though the coasts of both sides of the North Sea were still a little farther out than they are to-day. The Baltic was reunited with the sea, the level of which rose in certain regions above modern sea-level at the maximum of the *Litorina* transgression (4500–4000 B.C.).

Climate. The rise of temperature during period II reached a maximum which lasted for the early stages of period III. Precipitation increased and the climate tended to be more oceanic in character.

Forests. Alder and the components of the oak-mixed-forest rose to dominance, pine and birch diminishing in importance. Locally beech started to make its appearance.

Fauna. Reindeer completely disappeared and elk became rare.

Cultures:

(a) *Tanged-point cultures.* The Komsa and Fosna cultures continued to flourish, and the tradition survived throughout the Neolithic period and into the Bronze Age.

(b) *Axe cultures.* The Maglemose culture spread to outlying parts of Scandinavia and its influence survived throughout period III and into the Bronze Age. In the centre of our area, in Denmark and north Germany, the Ertebølle culture evolved, by way of intermediate stages such as those of Oldesloe, Gudenaa River, Kolindsund, and the lower levels of Brabrand Sø and Bloksbjerg, from the Maglemose tradition. Certain elements, such as pottery, arrived by way of borrowing (?) at the time of the *Litorina* maximum. The sites were mainly coastal and shell-middens are common in Denmark, though by no means universal. In southern Sweden and southern Norway local dwelling-place cultures, related to the Ertebølle, arose in period II (Nøstvet, Lihult and Limhamn), and formed the basis of the Arctic dwelling-place culture, which persisted side by side with the megalithic civilisation of Denmark and south Sweden. The Lower Halstow culture of south-eastern Britain differs from the Ertebølle culture in several important respects; the 'Thames pick', an important feature of the culture, survived very late in flint regions. Belated survivals of the axe tradition persisted in the Lietzow culture of Rügen and the 'Campignian' of northern France.

221

GENERAL SUMMARY AND RETROSPECT

(c) *Microlithic cultures.* The final phase of the Tardenoisian is characterised by
greater local variations than was the middle phase. Trapezes dominated the
microlithic cultures of the continental cultures, as they did the microlithic
element of the Ertebølle culture. The final Tardenoisian of the Low Countries
is distinguished by a special form of lanceolate point. Occupying areas of
negligible agricultural or pastoral value, it is certain that the Tardenoisian
people maintained their traditions until late in the Neolithic, and locally, no
doubt, even later. The first Neolithic colonisers of the loess belts must have
advanced without serious opposition as they were not occupied by the
Tardenoisian folk.

FAUNA LISTS

A. Fauna from Early, Middle and Late Magdalenian, and Azilian levels of the caves of southern Germany. Taken from R. R. Schmidt, 1912.

B. Fauna from sites of period I of the Mesolithic:
Remouchamps, after Rahir, 1920.
Hohlen Stein, after Andree, 1932 (2).
Lyngby, after Jessen, A. and Nordmann, V., 1915.

C. Fauna from sites of period II of the Mesolithic:
Holmegaard, after Broholm, 1926–31, pp. 29–31.
Mullerup, after Sarauw, 1903, pp. 194–8.
Svaerdborg, after Friis-Johansen, 1918–19, pp. 261–4.

D. Fauna from sites of period III of the Mesolithic:
Aamølle, Ertebølle, Faareveile, Havnø and Klinteso, after Madsen, Müller, Neergaard, Petersen, Rostrup, Steenstrup and Winge, 1900, pp. 179–82.
Bloksbjerg, after Westerby, 1927, p. 203.
Brabrand Sø, after Thomsen and Jessen, A., 1902–7.

N.B. In lists A, C, and D the occurrence of a species will be marked by ×, and its absence by —. In list B similar signs are used, but some attempt is made to indicate quantitative values.

LIST A. MAGDALENIAN—AZILIAN. SOUTH GERMANY

FAUNA	SITES			
	Sirgenstein Wildscheuer Ofnet	Sirgenstein Wildscheuer Hohlefels bei Hutten Schussen- quelle Andernach Munzingen	Hohlefels Schmiech- enfels Propstfels	Ofnet Istein
	MAGDALENIAN			AZILIAN
	EARLY	MIDDLE	LATE	
Frog (*Rana* sp.)	×	×	—	—
Toad (*Bufo*)	—	×	—	—
Wild duck (*Anas boscas*)	—	×	×	—
(*A. creca*)	—	—	×	—
Black grouse (*Tetrao tetrix*)	—	×	×	—
Hazel-hen (*T. bonasia*)	—	×	—	—
White grouse (*Lagopus albus*)	×	×	×	—
Partridge (*Perdrix cinerea*)	—	—	×	—
Ptarmigan (*Lagopus alpinus*)	×	×	×	—
Crane (*Grus cinerea*)	—	×	—	—
Whooper swan (*Cygnus musicus*)	—	×	—	—
(*Brachyotus palustris*)	—	×	—	—
Mammoth (*Elephas primigenius*)	×	—	—	—
Wild horse (*Equus caballus*)	×	×	×	—
Wild pig (*Sus scrofa ferus*)	—	—	—	×
Red deer (*Cervus elaphus*)	—	×	×	×
Roe deer (*C. capreolus*)	—	—	×	×
Reindeer (*Rangifer tarandus*)	×	×	×	—
Cave bear (*Ursus spelaeus*)	×	—	—	—
Brown bear (*U. arctos*)	—	—	—	×
Arctic fox (*Canis lagopus*)	×	×	×	—
Wolf (*C. lupus*)	×	×	—	—
Fox (*C. vulpes*)	×	×	×	—
Glutton (*Gulo luscus*)	—	×	—	—
Lynx (*Lynchus lynx*)	—	×	—	×
Wild cat (*Felis catus fera*)	—	—	×	—
Ox (*Bos* sp.)	—	—	×	×
Beaver (*Castor fiber*)	—	—	×	×
Arctic hare (*Lepus variabilis*)	×	×	×	—
Wild rabbit (*L. cunniculus*)	—	—	×	—
Common marten (*Mustela vulgaris*)	—	×	—	—
(*M. martes*)	—	—	—	×
Ermine (*Foetorius erminea*)	×	×	×	—
Weasel (*F. nivalis*)	×	×	—	—
Pole-cat (*Mustela putorius*)	—	×	—	—
Otter (*Lutra vulgaris*)	—	—	×	—
Mole (*Talpa europaea*)	×	×	×	—
Pika (*Lagomys pusillus*)	×	×	×	—
Squirrel (*Sciurus vulgaris*)	—	×	—	—
Obi lemming (*Myodes obensis*)	×	—	—	—
Banded lemming (*M. torquatus*)	×	×	×	—
Ibex (*Capra ibex*)	—	—	×	—
Shrews, mice and rats (various sp.)	×	×	×	—

FAUNA LISTS

LIST B. MESOLITHIC PERIOD I

FAUNA	REMOUCHAMPS × = up to 2 × × = 3 or 4 × × × = 5 or more	HOHLEN STEIN (layer II) × = very rare × × = rare × × × = common	LYNGBY (fresh-water deposits)
White grouse (*Lagopus albus*)	× ×	×	×
Reindeer (*Rangifer tarandus*)	× × ×	× × ×	×
Red deer (*Cervus elaphus*)	×	× ×	—
Roe deer (*C. capreolus*)	—	× ×	—
Elk (*Alces machlis*)	—	×	—
Aurochs (*Bos taurus urus*)	×	×	—
Wild horse (*Equus caballus*)	×	× ×	—
Goat (*Capra*)	×	—	—
Wild pig (*Sus scrofa ferus*)	×	× × ×	—
Cave bear (*Ursus spelaeus*)	—	×	—
Wolf (*Canis lupus*)	—	× ×	—
Fox (*Canis vulpes*)	×	× × ×	—
Arctic fox (*C. lagopus*)	×	×	—
Beaver (*Castor fiber*)	—	×	×
Wood marten (*Martes sylvatica*)	—	× ×	—
Badger (*Meles taxus*)	—	× × ×	—
Wild cat (*Felis catus fera*)	×	× × ×	—
Arctic hare (*Lepus variabilis*)	×	× ×	×
Field mouse (*Mus* sp.)	—	—	×
Water-rat (*Arvicola amphibius*)	—	× ×	×

APPENDIX I

LIST C. MESOLITHIC PERIOD II

Fauna	Holmegaard	Mullerup	Svaerdborg
Pike (*Esox lucius*)	×	×	×
Tortoise (*Emys orbicularis*)	×	×	×
Wild duck (*Anas boscas*)	×	×	×
The shoveller (*A. clypeata*)	×	—	—
The pintail (*A. acuta*)	—	×	—
Mute swan (*Cygnus olor*)	—	×	×
Tufted duck (*Fuligula cristata*)	—	—	×
Coot (*Fulica atra*)	×	—	—
Goosander (*Mergus merganser*)	—	—	×
Grey lag-goose (*Anser cinereus*)	—	—	×
Grouse (*Tetrao urogallus*)	—	—	×
Black stork (*Ciconia nigra*)	×	—	—
Great crested grebe (*Podicipes cristatus*)	×	×	×
Crane (*Grus cinerea*)	×	×	×
Long-tailed duck (*Pagonetta glacialis*)	—	×	—
Great black-backed gull (*Larus marinus*)	—	—	×
Black-headed gull (*L. ridibundus*)	—	×	—
Heron (*Ardea cinerea*)	—	×	×
Black-throated diver (*Colymbus arcticus*)	—	×	—
Bittern (*Botaurus stellaris*)	—	×	×
Cormorant (*Phalacrocorax carbo*)	×	×	×
White-tailed eagle (*Haliaëtus albicilla*)	×	×	×
Kite (*Milvus ictinus*)	—	×	—
Osprey (*Pandion haliaëtus*)	—	—	×
Great black woodpecker (*Picus martius*)	—	×	—
Jay (*Garrullus glandarius*)	—	×	—
Roe deer (*Cervus capreolus*)	×	×	×
Red deer (*C. elaphus*)	×	×	×
Elk (*Alces machlis*)	×	×	×
Aurochs (*Bos taurus urus*)	×	×	×
Wild pig (*Sus scrofa ferus*)	×	×	×
Brown bear (*Ursus arctos*)	—	×	×
Beaver (*Castor fiber*)	×	×	×
Squirrel (*Sciurus vulgaris*)	—	×	×
Wild cat (*Felis catus fera*)	×	×	×
Hare (*Lepus europaeus*)	—	×	—
Wood marten (*Martes sylvatica*)	×	×	×
Badger (*Meles taxus*)	×	×	×
Otter (*Lutra vulgaris*)	×	—	×
Fox (*Canis vulpes*)	×	×	×
Wolf (*C. lupus*)	—	—	×
Dog (*C. familiaris*)	×	×	×
Hedgehog (*Erinaceus europaeus*)	×	—	—

LIST D. MESOLITHIC PERIOD III

Fauna	Aam-ølle	Bloks-bjerg	Bra-brand Sø	Erte-bølle	Faare-veile	Havnø	Klin-tesø
Tortoise (*Emys orbicularis*)	—	×	—	—	—	—	—
Spur-dog (*Acanthias vulgaris*)	—	×	—	—	—	—	—
Pike (*Esox lucius*)	—	—	—	—	—	—	×
Eel (*Anguilla vulgaris*)	—	—	—	×	—	—	—
Roach (*Leuciscus rutilus*)	—	—	—	×	—	×	—
Rudd (*L. erythrophthalmus*)	—	—	—	×	—	—	—
Garfish (*Belone rostrata*)	—	—	—	×	—	—	—
Cod (*Gadus morrhua*)	—	× (?)	—	×	—	—	×
Flounder (*Pleuronectes* sp.)	—	×	—	×	—	—	×
Perch (*Perca fluviatilis*)	—	×	×	×	×	×	×
Stickleback (*Gasterosteus aculeatus*)	—	—	—	×	—	—	×
Widgeon (*Anas penelope*)	—	—	—	×	—	—	—
Wild duck (*A. boscas*)	—	×	—	×	—	—	—
Bewick's swan (*Cygnus minor*)	—	×	—	×	—	—	×
Whooper swan (*C. musicus*)	—	×	×	×	—	×	—
Scaup-duck (*Fuligula marila*)	×	×	×	×	—	×	×
Goldeneye (*Clangula glaucion*)	—	—	—	—	—	×	×
Long-tailed duck (*Pagonetta glacialis*)	—	×	—	—	—	—	×
Common scoter (*Oedemia nigra*)	—	—	—	×	×	×	×
Velvet scoter (*O. fusca*)	—	—	—	×	—	×	×
Eider-duck (*Somateria mollissima*)	×	×	—	×	—	×	×
Red-breasted merganser (*Mergus serrator*)	×	—	—	—	×	×	×
Goosander (*M. merganser*)	—	—	—	—	—	—	×
Grey lag goose (*Anser cinereus*)	×	—	—	—	—	—	×
Brent goose (*A. torquatus*)	—	—	—	×	—	—	×
Grouse (*Tetrao urogallus*)	×	—	—	×	—	×	—
Little grebe (*Tachybaptes minor*)	—	—	×	×	—	—	—
Great crested grebe (*Podicipes cristatus*)	—	—	—	×	—	—	—
Red-necked grebe (*P. griseigena*)	—	—	—	×	—	×	×
Black-throated diver (*Colymbus arcticus*)	—	—	—	×	—	—	—
Red-throated diver (*C. septentrionalis*)	—	×	—	×	—	—	×
Common gull (*Larus canus*)	—	×	—	×	—	×	×
Herring-gull (*L. argentatus*)	—	—	—	×	—	—	×
Great black-throated gull (*L. marinus*)	×	—	—	×	×	×	×
Guillemot (*Uria triole*)	×	—	×	×	—	—	×
Razorbill (*Alca torda*)	×	×	×	—	—	—	×
Great auk (*A. impennis*)	—	—	—	×	—	—	—
Heron (*Ardea cinerea*)	—	—	—	×	—	×	×
Cormorant (*Phalacrocorax carbo*)	—	—	—	×	—	—	—
Dalmatian pelican (*Pelecanus crispus*)	—	×	×	×	—	×	×
Gannet (*Sula bassana*)	—	—	×	—	—	×	—
Honey-buzzard (*Pernis apivorus*)	×	—	×	×	—	—	—
White-tailed eagle (*Haliaëtus albicilla*)	—	—	—	—	—	—	—
Tawny owl (*Syrnium aluco*)	—	—	—	×	—	—	×
Great woodpecker (*Dendrocopus major*)	—	—	—	×	—	—	—
Crow (*Corvus cornix*)	—	—	—	×	—	—	—
Roe deer (*Cervus capreolus*)	×	×	×	×	—	×	—
Red deer (*C. elaphus*)	×	×	×	×	×	×	×
Elk (*Alces machlis*)	—	×	—	×	×	×	×
Wild pig (*Sus scrofa ferus*)	×	×	×	×	×	×	×

LIST D. MESOLITHIC PERIOD III (*contd.*)

Fauna	Aam-ølle	Bloks-bjerg	Bra-brand Sø	Erte-bølle	Faare-veile	Havnø	Klin-tesø
Aurochs (*Bos taurus urus*)	×	×	×	×	—	×	—
Brown bear (*Ursus arctos*)	—	—	×	—	—	—	—
Fox (*Canis vulpes*)	×	×	×	×	×	×	×
Wolf (*C. lupus*)	×	×	—	×	×	×	×
Dog (*C. familiaris*)	×	×	×	×	×	—	×
Beaver (*Castor fiber*)	—	×	—	—	×	—	×
Squirrel (*Sciurus vulgaris*)	—	—	—	×	—	×	×
Wild cat (*Felis catus fera*)	×	—	×	×	—	—	—
Lynx (*F. lynx*)	—	—	—	×	—	—	—
Wood marten (*Martes sylvatica*)	—	×	×	×	×	×	×
Pole-cat (*Mustela putorius*)	—	—	—	×	—	—	—
Badger (*Meles taxus*)	×	×	—	×	—	—	×
Otter (*Lutra vulgaris*)	×	×	—	×	×	—	—
Brown rat (*Mus decumanus*)	—	×	—	—	—	—	—
Water-rat (*Arvicola amphibius*)	—	×	—	—	—	—	—
Bank vole (*Hypudaeus glareola*)	—	—	—	×	—	—	—
Common seal (*Phoca vitulina*)	—	× (?)	—	—	—	—	×
Ringed seal (*P. foetida*)	—	—	—	×	—	—	—
Greenland seal (*P. groenlandica*)	—	×	—	—	—	—	—
Dolphin (*Lagenorhynchus albirostris*)	—	—	×	—	—	—	—
Hedgehog (*Erinaceus europaeus*)	—	—	—	×	—	—	×
Grey seal (*Halichoerus gryphus*)	×	×	×	×	—	×	—
Killer whale (*Orca gladiator*)	—	—	—	×	—	—	—
Porpoise (*Phocaena communis*)	—	×	—	×	—	—	×

FIND-LIST OF OBJECTS OF THE LYNGBY CULTURE (Fig. 28)

Reindeer antler axes, adzes and hafts

Site	Type	Nature of find	Reference
1. Bara lilla mosse, Malmö, Sweden	Haft	Bog find: Pre-boreal by pollen-analysis	Isberg, 1930, fig. 3 Lund Museum, no. 22952
2. Briest, Havelland, Germany	Axe	Accidental find at 5·3 m. in Havel clay, topped by 0·4 m. of sand and 0·3 m. humus	Stimming, 1917, taf. V, no. 10
3. Fähre Rüsterbergen, Schleswig-Holstein	Broken		Schwantes, 1923, p. 17, abb. 1 Kiel Museum
4. Fauderup, Schleswig-Holstein	Broken		Schwantes, 1923, p. 17, abb. 2 Kiel Museum, no. 11209
5. Langenfelde, near Hamburg, Germany	Axe (Fig. 27, no. 1)	Probably from freshwater marl, underlying peat and dating from the Pre-boreal period	Schwantes, 1923, p. 17 Geol. mineral. Inst., Hamburg
6. Lyngby, North Jutland	Haft (Fig. 27, no. 3)	Probably from freshwater deposits of Pre-boreal age	Müller, S., 1896, fig. 1 Jessen and Nordmann, 1915 Schwantes, 1923, p. 17 Copenhagen Museum
7. Murowana, near Posen, Poland	Axe	In *wiesenkalk* at a depth of 1½ m. under peat	Schwantes, 1923, abb. 4 Posen Museum, no. 1898, 352
8. Odense, Fünen, Denmark	Adze (Fig. 27, no. 2)	Found in the excavation of a canal	Müller, S., 1896, fig. 2 Copenhagen Museum
9. Pritzerber See, Havelland, Germany	Adze		Stimming, 1917, taf. IV, no. 9
10. Scania, Sweden	Broken	Dated by pollen-analysis of sample from specimen itself to the very beginning of the Boreal period	Isberg, 1930, fig. 4 Lund Museum, no. 22955
11. Sickingsmühle, near Haltern, Westphalia	Axe	Dredged from bed of the river Lippe	Brandt, 1933, fig. 2
12. Vejleby, Zealand, Denmark	Haft	Contained mud—not peat	Sarauw, 1903, p. 303 Copenhagen Museum

APPENDIX II

Deer antler axe-clubs

Site	Nature of find	Reference
13. Gahle, Silesia	—	Seger, 1922, p. 1 Schles. Museum, Breslau
14. Mondschütz, Silesia	Found in a gravel-pit	Seger, 1922, p. 2 Schwantes, 1923, taf. 1, abb. 5 Schles. Museum, Breslau

Worked reindeer antlers

Site	Nature of find	Reference
15. Dagstorps mosse, near Lund	—	Ekholm, 1925, fig. 2
16. Gross-Wusterwitz, Havelland, Germany	From clay bed beneath 0·3 m. of humus, 1·5 m. of sand and 0·3 m. of marl	Stimming, 1917, taf. IV, no. 8
17. Hylteberga, Scania, Sweden	Dated by pollen-analysis of sample from the specimen itself to the end of the Boreal period	Isberg, 1930, figs. 5 and 6 Lund Museum, no. 22951
18. Popelken, Labiau, East Prussia	Found by the bank of the river Melawa at a depth of 2·35 m. Probably from a marl deposit (*wiesenmergel*)	Gaerte, 1926, abb. 3 Prussia Museum, Konigsberg
19. Schlutup, near Lübeck, Germany	From *Dryas* clay of Pre-boreal age	Schwantes, 1928 (*c*), p. 167

(Folding-map)

LIST OF MAGLEMOSE SITES AND FINDING-PLACES

arranged alphabetically under countries

Sites dated to Period II on geological evidence indicated †.
Sites dated to Period II on pollen-analytical or other botanical evidence indicated *.

BELGIUM

Brussels (to the north of). Fragment of barbed bone point of Kunda type (form 6). Bog find.

    Breuil, 1926, fig. 1. Mus. d'Histoire naturelle de Bruxelles.

La Haine, Hainault. Slotted bone point with flint insets.

    Breuil, 1926, p. 310.

Ninove. Bone point.

    Breuil, 1926, p. 310.

Wichelen, Flanders. Fragment of barbed bone point of Kunda type (form 6). From the river Escaut.

    Hasse, 1924, fig. 2.

DENMARK

Birkemose, Jutland. Barbed bone point of Kunda type (form 6). Bog find.

    Sarauw, 1903, p. 248. Copenhagen Museum, no. A 3321.

Bornholm Island. A barbed bone point of Mullerup type (form 7) and two barbed points of atypical form, one of them being barbed on both edges. Bog find.

    Friis-Johansen, 1918–19, pp. 325–6. Copenhagen Museum, nos. A 22392–4.

Copenhagen. A slotted bone point (form 23), decorated in *style pointillé*. From Winther's bathing establishment.

    Müller, S., 1918, fig. 23. Copenhagen Museum, no. A 5864.

Denmark (probably).

  (*a*) Three amber pendants decorated by drilled ornament.

    Müller, S., 1918, figs. 36, 37 and 39.

  (*b*) Slotted bone implement decorated by incision.

    Madsen, 1868, pl. 40, no. 5.

Ellemose, Zealand. Slotted bone point (form 21) and worked flints.
    Bog find.
        Sarauw, 1903, p. 256. Århus Museum, no. 5003.
Fjellenstrup mose, Zealand. Barbed bone point of Kunda type (form 6).
    Bog find.
        Sarauw, 1903, p. 249. Copenhagen Museum, no. A 12200.
Fünen Island (probably). Bone net-pricker decorated by drilled ornament.
        Müller, S., 1918, fig. 35. Odense Museum.
Grenå, Jutland. Barbed bone point of Kunda type (form 6).
        Sarauw, 1903, p. 249. Ålborg Museum, no. 2684.
Gøvlev, Zealand. Three barbed bone points of Kunda type (form 6).
        Sarauw, 1903, p. 249. Copenhagen Museum, nos. A 3029, A 6463,
        A 10721.
Hammelev, Schleswig-Holstein. Bone point of Törning type (form 9).
    Bog find.
        Müller, S., 1914–15, fig. 1.
Hassing Østerkaer, Jutland. Barbed bone point of Kunda type (form 6).
        Sarauw, 1903, p. 248. Copenhagen Museum, no. A 16966.
Haubølle, Langeland Island. Barbed bone point of Kunda type (form 6).
    Bog find.
        Sarauw, 1903, p. 249. Copenhagen Museum, no. A 4032.
Herlufmagle, Zealand. Seven single-barbed bone points (form 5).
    Bog find.
        Broholm, 1926–31, p. 60.
Hillerød, Zealand. Two barbed bone points of Kunda type (form 6) and one of Törning
    type (form 9); also a perforated adze of elk antler.
        Sarauw, 1903, p. 249. Copenhagen Museum, nos. A 8523–6.
Hinge Sø, Silkeborg, Jutland. Barbed bone point of Kunda type (form 6).
    Lake find.
        Sarauw, 1903, p. 248. Copenhagen Museum, no. A 17363.
*Holmegaard, Zealand. Two settlement sites (east and west). Flint microliths, micro-
    burins, a burin, scrapers, numerous core axes or adzes, and a few *spalter*. Per-
    forated antler adzes and axes, perforated antler sleeves, bone adzes or axes with
    perforation sunk into the articular end, bone handles, bone awls, bone points of
    single-barbed and Mullerup types (forms 5 and 7). A perforated stone adze,
    wooden javelins and clubs, a wooden paddle-rudder and other wooden objects.
    Bog find.
        Broholm, 1926–31. Copenhagen Museum.
†Horsens fjord, Jutland. Antler object, decorated by incision.
    Dredged from the sea.
        Broholm, 1926–31, fig. 28.

LIST OF MAGLEMOSE SITES

Horsø, Zealand. Perforated antler axe, decorated by incision, and an antler with incised scars.
Found in digging a canal.
Broholm, 1926–31, pp. 101–2.
Illebølle, Langeland Island. Bone fragment with incised decoration.
Müller, S., 1918, fig. 19.
Jonstrup Vang, Zealand. Two single-barbed bone points (form 5).
Bog find.
Sarauw, 1903, p. 242. Copenhagen Museum, nos. A 8143–4.
Kalundborg, Zealand. Perforated antler with incised decoration.
Bog find.
Friis-Johansen, 1918–19, fig. 51. Kalundborg Museum.
†*Koldingfjord, Jutland.* Three antler fragments, decorated by drilled ornament.
Dredged from the sea.
Müller, S., 1896, figs. 14–16.
Kolindsund, Jutland. Slotted bone point (form 21).
Sarauw, 1903, p. 252. Århus Museum, no. 3377.
Kongsted, Zealand, Denmark. Five bone points of Törning type (form 9) and one of Kunda type (form 6).
Bog find.
Broholm, 1926–31, p. 59.
Langeland Island. A slotted bone object, decorated by incision.
Madsen, 1868, pl. 40, nos. 1 *a* and *b*.
Løjesmølle, Zealand.
(*a*) Two single-barbed bone points (form 5).
Bog find.
Sarauw, 1903, p. 242, note 1.
(*b*) Two barbed bone points of Mullerup type (form 7), one of Kunda type (form 6), and one of Törning type (form 9). Also a perforated antler axe and a perforated dog's tooth.
A group find made in 1907 in a bog.
Friis-Johansen, 1918–19, p. 326.
*Mullerup, Zealand. A settlement site. Flint microliths, scrapers, numerous core axes and adzes, and a few *spalter*. Perforated antler axes and adzes, perforated antler sleeves, bone axes or adzes with perforation sunk into the articular end, bone handles, awls and barbless fish-hooks, slotted bone points (form 24), single-barbed bone points (form 5), numerous barbed bone points of Mullerup type (form 7) and one of Kunda type (form 6). Knives of wild boar incisors.
Bog find.
Sarauw, 1903. Copenhagen Museum.

233

Odense, Fünen. Barbed bone point of Törning type (form 9).

    Madsen, 1868, pl. 40. fig. 7.

Randers (neighbourhood of), Jutland. Slotted bone point (form 21).

    Sarauw, 1903, p. 252. Copenhagen Museum, no. 21852.

Refsvindinge, Fünen. Bone handle, decorated by incision.

    Müller, S., 1918, figs. 18, 27. Copenhagen Museum, no. A 24289.

Rerslev, Zealand.

    (*a*) Barbed bone point of Mullerup type (form 7) found complete with wooden shaft.

    Found in Aamosen bog.

        Friis-Johansen, 1918–19, p. 322. Copenhagen Museum, no. A 22010.

    (*b*) Group of five barbed bone points of Mullerup type (form 7) found together.

    From Aamosen bog.

        Broholm, 1926–31, p. 59.

Resen mose, Jutland. Amber figurine and perforated amber lump, both decorated by incision.

    Bog find.

        Müller, S. 1918, figs. 24, 29. Copenhagen Museum, nos. A 8411 and A 6853.

†*Ringkjøbing fjord, Jutland.* Perforated antler pendant, decorated by drilled ornament.

    Dredged from the sea.

        Müller, S., 1918, fig. 38. Copenhagen Museum, no. 28384.

Ringsted Aa, Zealand. Bone object with incised decoration.

    Müller, S., 1918, fig. 1.

Silkeborg Sø, Jutland. Antler, decorated by drilled ornament.

    Dredged from the lake.

        Müller, S., 1896, fig. 12.

Skalstrup, Zealand. Perforated antler with incised decoration.

    Broholm, 1926–31, figs. 14, 15.

Skottemarke, Lolland Island. Fourteen bone points of Kunda type (form 6), six flint core axes or adzes, nine *spalter*, and flakes and cores.

    Bog find.

        Friis-Johansen, 1918–19, pp. 324–5. Copenhagen Museum, nos. A 20341–64.

Slagelseegnen, Zealand. Two barbed bone points of Mullerup type (form 7).

    Sarauw, 1903, p. 246.

Stensby, Zealand. Bone object with incised decoration.

    Müller, S., 1918, figs. 22, 26. Copenhagen Museum, no. A 17368.

Store Vildmose, Jutland. Barbed bone point of Kunda type (form 6).

    Sarauw, 1903, p. 248. Copenhagen Museum, no. A 4763.

LIST OF MAGLEMOSE SITES

Svaerdborg, Zealand. Settlement site. Flint microliths, micro-burins, burins, scrapers, many core axes or adzes and a few *spalter*. Quartzite pebble with hour-glass perforation. Perforated antler axes and adzes, perforated antler sleeves, bone axes or adzes with perforation sunk into the articular end, bone handles, awls, fish-hooks, single-barbed bone points (form 5) and barbed bone points of Mullerup type. Perforated animal teeth. Boar incisor knives. Amber pendants.
> Bog find.
> Friis-Johansen, 1918–19, and Broholm, 1926–31. Copenhagen Museum.

Svedstrup, Zealand. Three barbed bone points of Kunda type (form 6). The points were found close together.
> Sarauw, 1903, p. 249. Copenhagen Museum, no. A 8230.

Søborg Sø, Zealand. Slotted bone point (form 24) with incised decoration.
> Müller, S., 1918, fig. 9.

Søholm, Zealand. Slotted bone point (form 24) with incised decoration.
> Westerby, 1927, fig. 45.

Taaderup, Falster. Barbed bone point of Kunda type (form 6).
> Bog find.
> Ødum, 1920, fig. 3.

Taarbaek, Zealand. Antler with incised scars.
> Müller, S., 1918, fig. 6.

Tange, Jutland. Barbed bone point of Kunda type (form 6).
> From the river Gudenaa.
> Broholm, 1926–31, p. 59, note.

Tissø, Zealand. Barbed bone point of Mullerup type (form 7).
> Lake find.
> Sarauw, 1903, p. 246. Copenhagen Museum, no. A 6769.

Törning, Schleswig. Bone point with recurved barbs of Törning type (form 9).
> Bog find.
> Mestorf, 1885, pl. XVI, no. 123. Kiel Museum.

Vadsted, Jutland. Barbed bone point of Kunda type (form 6).
> From 1¼ metres deep in *kalkmergel* under 2½ metres of peat.
> Sarauw, 1903, p. 248. Århus Museum, no. 3097.

Vejby, Zealand. Barbed bone point of Kunda type (form 6).
> Sarauw, 1903, p. 248. Copenhagen Museum, no. 22390.

Vibygaard, Zealand. Barbed bone point of Kunda type (form 6).
> Broholm, 1926–31, p. 59, note.

Vig, Zealand. Two microliths found with a flake in the breast region of an aurochs skeleton, in the ribs of which flint splinters were found.
> Found at the base of a peat layer 2·20 metres thick.
> Hartz and Winge, 1906.

APPENDIX III

Århus (neighbourhood), Jutland. Two barbed bone points of Kunda type (form 6).
Sarauw, 1903, p. 248. Copenhagen Museum, no. A 8565.

ENGLAND

Battersea, London. Barbed bone point.
Dredged from the Thames.
Westerby, 1931, pp. 45–6. London Museum, no. A 19788. Clark, 1932 (*a*),
p. 18.

**Broxbourne, Hertfordshire.* Settlement site. Flint microliths, micro-burins, burins,
scrapers, core axes, axe sharpening flakes, quartzite hammerstones.
On a sand and gravel ridge, sealed by peat and clay, on the flood-plain of the river
Lea.
Warren, Clark, Godwin and Macfadyen, 1934. S. H. Warren collection and
the British Museum.

Hornsea, Yorkshire. Barbed bone point of Kunda type (form 6).
From under 12 feet of peat.
Armstrong, 1922, 1923. Clark, 1932 (*a*), pp. 16, 17. Hull Museum.

Kelling, Norfolk. Flint chipping site. Microliths, burins, scrapers, core axes, and axe
sharpening flakes.
On gravel, immediately below modern surface.
Sainty, 1924, 1925, 1928. Clark, 1932 (*a*), pp. 54–7. Norwich, Cambridge
and British Museums.

†**Leman and Ower Banks, North Sea.* Barbed bone point of Kunda type (form 6).
Dredged in a lump of 'moorlog' from the North Sea bed between the Leman and
Ower Banks.
Clark, 1932 (*a*), p. 115. Godwin, 1933, pp. 42–3. Norwich Museum.

Newbury, Berkshire. Flint chipping site. Flint microliths, burins, scrapers and core axes.
Under peat and shell-marl on the flood-plain of the river Kennet.
G. B. Bull collection.

Romsey, Hampshire. Red deer tine with heavily incised decoration.
From a depth of 20 feet in muddy sand mixed with gravel on the flood-plain of the
river Test.
Smith, 1934. British Museum.

Royston, Hertfordshire. Fragment of barbed bone point of Kunda type (form 6).
A stray find, lacking exact provenance.
Westerby, 1931, pp. 45–6. Clark, 1932 (*a*), p. 18. British Museum.

**Skipsea, Yorkshire.* Barbed bone point of Kunda type (form 6), and flint implements,
including a flint core adze.
From the bed of an extinct mere.
Armstrong, 1922, 1923. Clark 1932 (*a*), pp. 16, 17. Godwin, 1933, pp. 38–
42. Hull Museum.

LIST OF MAGLEMOSE SITES

Thames. Perforated adze of ox-bone, decorated by heavily incised chevrons.
Dredged from the Thames.
Smith, 1934. British Museum.

Thatcham, Berkshire. Settlement site. Flint microliths, scrapers and core axes and adzes.
Under peat and shell-marl on the flood-plain of the river Kennet.
Crawford and Peake, 1922. Clark, 1932 (*a*), pp. 65–7. Newbury Museum.

Uxbridge, Middlesex. Flint chipping site. Microliths and debris of a flint industry akin
to that from Thatcham.
Under peat and shell-marl on the flood-plain of the river Colne.
Clark, 1932 (*a*), p. 67. F. N. Haward collection.

Wandsworth, London. Notched bone point of Istaby type (form 3).
Dredged from the Thames.
Westerby, 1931, pp. 45–6. Clark, 1932 (*a*), p. 18. London Museum, no.
A 4907.

FRANCE

Béthune, Artois.
(*a*) Barbed bone point of Kunda type (form 6).
Bog find.
Mortillet, G. and A. de, 1881, pl. xlii, no. 374. Saint-Germain Museum,
no. 17523.
(*b*) Barbed antler point.
Probably a bog find.
Breuil, 1926, fig. 2. British Museum.

Crouy, Somme. Perforated antler sleeve with a crack marked by short transverse incisions.
Dredged from the river Somme.
Picard, 1836, figs. 1, 5.

Isbergues, Artois. Barbed bone point of Kunda type (form 6).
From a depth of 3 metres in the alluvium of the river Lacque.
Lartet and Christy, 1875, p. 50, fig. 10.

GERMANY

Amrum Island. Barbed bone point of Kunda type (form 6).
Kiel Museum.

Barnewitz, kr. Karthaus, West Prussia. Barbed bone point of Gohra-Worle type
(form 10), and perforated antler axe.
From *wiesenmergel.*
La Baume, 1924, p. 7 and fig. 6. W. P. Prov. Mus., Danzig, no. 1, 445.

Barnow, Pomerania. Barbed bone point of Gohra-Worle type (form 10).
Bog find.
Z. f. Ethn., *Verhandl.* 1888, p. 343.

APPENDIX III

Brodersby, kr. Eckernförde, Schleswig-Holstein. Bone point with recurved barbs of Törning type (form 9).

Schwantes, 1934, abb. 116, no. 4.

Calbe a.d. Milde, near Stendal, Saxony.

(a) Numerous bone objects, including notched points (form 2) of Duvensee type.

From grey sandy clay deposit overlying sand and underlying peat. Elk and fish-bones came from the same deposit, dated to period II by Wiegers (1929) on pollen-analytical evidence.

Z. f. Ethn., Verhandl. 1886, pp. 125–9. Stendal Museum.

(b) Flint implements, including core axes, *spalter*, microliths, burins and scrapers.

Mainly from surface of sand area a few feet higher than the moor area. Unsatisfactory pollen-analytical evidence gave an early Atlantic (period III) date to an axe found recently (Andree, 1932 *(b)*, pp. 62–74).

Kupka, 1906, 1907, 1919.

Dobbertin, Mecklenburg. Two single-barbed bone points (form 5) and one notched point of form 4.

Found on the margin of an ancient lake under a layer of *wiesenkalk*.

Beltz, 1910, taf. 2, nos. 1–3.

Döhren, Hanover. A barbed bone point of Kunda type (form 6).

Probably from the river Leine.

Hanover Prov. Mus., no. 26491.

Dümmer, kr. Diepholtz, Hanover. Barbed bone point of Havel type (form 12 A).

From the Dümmersee.

Hanover Prov. Mus., no. 24654.

Duvensee, nr. Lübeck. Settlement site. Flint core axes, *spalter*, burins, microliths, micro-burins and scrapers. Notched bone points (form 2). Wooden paddle-rudder.

Moor site, overlying reed peat and mud and sealed by peat.

Schwantes, 1928 *(c)*, pp. 201–12. Hamburg and Kiel Museums.

? ?, East Prussia. Bone point with recurved barbs of Törning type (form 9), and a barbed point of Kunda type (form 6).

Voss, 1880, section 1, taf. 6, nos. 170, 171.

Elbing, West Prussia. Slotted bone point, broken but of the narrow type.

Reinecke, 1908, abb. 1, *q*. Mainz Museum.

Fernewerder, kr. Westhavelland, Brandenburg. Bone points (forms 1, 5, 8), a bone fish-hook and a bone net-pricker decorated by engraving.

Found during excavations at a brick-works.

Z. f. Ethnologie, Nachr. über deutsche Alterthumskunde, 1902, p. 28. Königl. Mus. f. Völkerkunde, Berlin.

Fienerode, Saxony. Bone point (form 2).

Königl. Mus. f. Völkerkunde, Berlin, no. Ig, 67.

LIST OF MAGLEMOSE SITES

Flatow, Pomerania. Bone point.
  Bog find.
    Lissauer, 1887, p. 40. Prov. Mus. Konigsberg, no. 2212.
Froser Seelandereien, kr. Bernberg, Anhalt. Bone point (form 1) and perforated antler axe.
    Voss, 1880, sect. IV, taf. 17.
Før Island. Barbed bone point of Kunda type (form 6).
  Found on the beach.
    Müller, S., 1914–15, fig. 2.
Gnewin, Pomerania. Single-barbed bone point (form 5).
  From *Seekreide* under peat.
    Sarauw, 1903, p. 244.
Gohra-Worle, kr. Neustadt, West Prussia. Notched point of Dobbertin type (form 4), barbed points of forms 5, 6, 10, and bone axes or adzes with perforations sunk into the articular end.
  From lacustrine deposits under 2 metres of peat.
    La Baume, 1924, pp. 6–7; 1933, taf. 5. Danzig Museum.
Gr. Rönnau, kr. Segeberg, Schleswig-Holstein. Antler axe of celtiform type.
    Schwantes, 1934, abb. 119.
Gr. Steegen, kr. Pr.-Eylau, East Prussia. Lanceolate bone point of Pentekinnen type (form 17).
    Reallexikon, ix, taf. 206, *e.*
?, kr. Gumbinnen, East Prussia. Conical tipped bone point (form 16).
    Reallexikon, ix, taf. 208, *k.*
Havelland, Brandenburg (numerous sites including *Pritzerber See, Wachow, Gross-wusterwitzer See,* etc.). Bone points (forms 1, 2, 5, 6, 8, 12 A, 12 B, 15, 17, 19; and a broken slotted bone point), bone fish-hooks, perforated axes and adzes, celtiform antler axes, bone awls, bone net-prickers, and perforated amber beads. Two bone pieces are decorated by the drill technique.
  Dredged from Havel clay at various times.
    Stimming, 1925.
Karby, kr. Eckernförde, Schleswig-Holstein. Two barbed bone points of Kunda type (form 6).
    Schwantes, 1934, abb. 116, nos. 1, 2.
Kl. Machnow, near Berlin. Perforated antler decorated by incision.
    Kossinna, 1921, fig. 28.
Kösuchen, kr. Lötzen, East Prussia. Slotted bone point (form 21).
    Reallexikon, ix, taf. 206, 1.
Krampkewitz, kr. Lauenburg, West Prussia. Barbed bone point of Sorbehnen type (form 11).
    Lissauer, 1887, p. 47. Prov. Mus. Danzig, no. 1, 364.

APPENDIX III

Kusserow, kr. Schlawe, Pomerania. Two bone points (form 1).
From an ancient lake deposit (*wiesenkalk*) under peat at a total depth of 6 metres.
Antiq. Mus. d. Gesell. f. Pomm. Gesch. u. Alterthumskunde, Stettin, Kat. p. 319, nos. 4 and 5.

'*Lattmoor*', *Muggenburg, Wismar, Mecklenburg-Schwerin.* Barbed bone point (broken), perforated antler axe and two flint core axes, from a pile-dwelling site.
Reinecke, 1908, abb. 4, *c.*

Magdeburg. Single-barbed bone point (form 5).
From the Elbe.
Sarauw, 1903, p. 244. Hanover Prov. Mus., no. 693.

Mitteldorf, kr. Mohrungen, West Prussia. Bone point. Lissauer, 1887, p. 40.

Mölln, Schleswig-Holstein. Flint adze hafted in perforated wooden sleeve.
Dredged from the Elbe-Trave canal.
Schwantes, 1934, abb. 97. Lübeck Museum.

Neu Jucha, kr. Lyck, East Prussia. Bone point of Havel type (form 12 A).
Reallexikon, IX, taf. 206, *a.*

Neu-Strelitz, Mecklenburg. Notched bone point (form 2).
From an ancient lake deposit (*Seekreide*) under 5 feet of peat.
Z. f. Ethn., Verhandl. 1871, pp. 3–4.

Peitschendorf, kr. Sensburg, East Prussia. Lanceolate bone point of Pentekinnen type (form 17). Decorated.
Reallexikon, IX, taf. 206, *f.*

Penken, kr. Pr.-Eylau, East Prussia. Barbed bone point.
Reallexikon, IX, taf. 206, *b.*

Pentekinnen, kr. Fischausen, East Prussia. Lanceolate bone point (form 17).
Reallexikon, IX, taf. 206, *d.*

Perkallen, East Prussia. Slotted bone point (form 21).
Mus. f. Völkerkunde, Berlin, no. II, 5916.

Sorbehnen, East Prussia. Barbed bone point (form 11).
Lissauer, 1887, taf. 11, fig. 11. Prov. Mus. Danzig, no. 1, 27.

Szirgupönen, kr. Gumbinnen, East Prussia. Barbed bone point of Kunda type (form 6), and tanged bone point of triangular section (form 13).
Reallexikon, IX, taf. 206, *g* and *c.*

Travenort, Schleswig-Holstein. Decorated bone net-pricker.
Verh. d. Berliner Ges. f. Anthr., Ethn., u. Vorgeschichte, 1892, p. 249.

Waren, Mecklenburg. Fragment of barbed bone point (form 6).
Under peat and *Wiesenkalk.*
Beltz, 1910, taf. 2, no. 5.

Wendhausen, kr. Hildesheim, Hanover. Barbed bone point (form 6).
Reinecke, 1908, abb. 1, *b.* Hanover Prov. Mus., no. 28033.

LIST OF MAGLEMOSE SITES

Wilsleben, kr. Aschersleben, Anhalt. Barbed bone point (form 6).
 Z. f. Ethn., Verhandl. 1880.

ESTHONIA

*Kunda. A variety of bone points, including many finely barbed specimens (form 6) and forms 16, 18, 20 and 25. Also pointed elk metatarsals.
 Obtained over a long period of time from a deposit of lake-chalk.
  Grewingk, 1882. Stjerna, 1911. Tallgren, 1922. Thomson, 1930.

Lohusu, Torma. One complete and one fragmentary barbed bone point, and one lanceolate point (form 18).
  Ebert, 1913, p. 520.

Pernau. Barbed, lanceolate and slotted bone points (forms 5, 6, 17, 18, 21), bone hooks with drilled pit ornament, and a bone fragment with elaborate pattern in the drill technique.
 Dredged (with other presumably later material) from the lower course of the Pernau river; possibly washed out of a site or sites.
  Ebert, 1913, pp. 510–20. Schwantes, 1928, pp. 214–16. Thomson, 1930, p. 243. Pernau Museum.

FINLAND

†*Esbo* (5 miles north-west of). A pointed elk metatarsal of the type found at Kunda.
 From a depth of 1·6 metres, under 0·45 metre of peaty soil and 1·15 metres of clay. Clay dated by Lindberg on phytopalaeontological evidence to period II.
  Europaeus, 1922, pl. II, no. 4.

†*Korpilahti, Antrea.* Traces of a net with pine bark floats and pebble sinkers.
 At a depth of 90 cm. under plough soil and peat, and on soft clay or loam (*Lehmgrund*). Dated to period II by Lindberg on phytopalaeontological evidence. This is disputed by many archaeologists.
  Pälsi, 1920. Alio, 1922, pp. 7–8.

NORWAY

†*Oslo.* A bone net-pricker.
 Found in digging foundations in clay.
  Øyen, 1920, fig. 1.

POLAND

Lachmirowice, Strzelno. A barbed bone point of Havel type (form 12 B).
  Kozłowski, 1926, fig. 5, no. 3.

Marzenin, kr. Witkowo. A tanged bone point of triangular section (form 13).
  Reallexikon.

Mazowsze, kr. Konstantynow. A perforated antler branch with engraved decoration.
  Kozłowski, 1926, fig. 5.

APPENDIX III

Morgi, Lida. A barbed bone point of Kunda type (form 6).

Kozłowski, 1926, fig. 5, no. 6.

Nowa, Erekcja. Two plain points (form 1), a barbed bone point of Törning type (form 9), a bone awl, and a perforated elk antler haft with blade of the same material.

Kozłowski, 1926, fig. 5, no. 5.

Ossowo, Hohenreiche. Nine bone points, some single-barbed (form 5), others with two barbs.

Kozłowski, 1926, fig. 5, no. 2.

Ostrolęka. A perforated antler branch with engraved decoration.

Sawicki, 1921, pl. I *a*.

SWEDEN

Aggarps mosse, Svedala, Scania. A barbed bone point of Törning type (form 9).

Bog find.

Lund Museum, no. 4469.

*Bare mosse, Scania. Settlement site with flint implements.

Bog site.

von Post, 1929, p. 148.

*Bussjö mosse, Scania. A slotted bone point with barbs (form 25).

Bog find.

von Post, 1929, p. 148. Stockholm Museum, no. 13075.

Esperöds mosse, Tranäs, Scania. A barbed bone point of Kunda type (form 6), found in immediate connection with the skeleton of a pike.

From a bog at a depth of 1, 2 metres.

Ymer, 1917, p. 453. Lund Museum, no. 17. 533.

Fäls mosse, Scania. Notched bone point with notches and traces of binding marks at the lower end.

Bog find.

Lund Museum, no. 5094.

Hofderup, Scania. A slotted bone point with barbs (form 25).

Krause, 1897, fig. 56. Mus. f. Völkerkunde, Berlin, no. VI*c*, 412.

*Hylteberga mosse, Skurups, Scania. A slotted bone point.

Bog find.

von Post, 1929, pp. 145 ff. Stockholm Museum, no. 14053.

Härryda, Västergötland. Perforated stone mace of Kungsladugård type.

Sarauw and Alin, 1923, fig. 18. Göteborg Museum, no. 7598.

Hästefjorden, Dalsland. Bone objects.

Sarauw, 1919, p. 149.

†**Höganäs, Scania.* Perforated antler axe with incised decoration.

From a depth of between 3·5 and 3·7 metres under sand and clay deposits. Below oak-mixed-forest and *Litorina* maximum levels.

Rydbeck, 1929. von Post, 1929 (*a*).

LIST OF MAGLEMOSE SITES

***Hörninge mosse, Öland I.*
(a) Bone leister prong (form 14).
  Bog find.
  Lundquist, 1928, p. 76. Kalmar Museum, no. 603.
(b) Bone leister prong (form 14).
  Bog find.
  Lundquist, 1928, p. 76. Kalmar Museum, no. 602.
(c) Barbed bone point.
  Bog find.
  Lundquist, 1928, p. 76. Kalmar Museum, no. 604.
†*Istaby, Blekinge.* Three notched bone points (form 3), and one of similar type but notched on both edges.
  From the base of peat, above fresh-water clay, but below salt-water *Litorina* clay.
  Erixon, 1913, pp. 130–5. Stockholm Museum, nos. 13181, 5660 A and 9015 : 17.
†*Kungsladugård, near Göteborg.* Stone mace with hour-glass perforation.
  At depth of between 1·2 and 1·5 metres in mud.
  Sarauw and Alin, 1923, p. 73. Niklasson, 1934, p. 137.
**Källingemöre mosse, Öland I.*
(a) Barbed bone point of Kunda type (form 6).
  Bog find.
  Lundquist, 1928, pp. 76 ff. Stockholm Museum, no. 6219.
(b) Bone net-pricker.
  Bog find.
  Lundquist, 1928, pp. 76 ff. Stockholm Museum, no. 8138.
Källstads, Östergotland. Barbed bone point (form 10).
  Montelius, 1917, fig. 50. Stockholm Museum, no. 11495:492.
†*Limhamn, Scania.* A net-pricker decorated with drilled pits.
  From under the Jära Bank, the old beach of the *Litorina* Sea.
  Rydbeck, 1927–8, fig. 1. Lund Museum, no. 14175.
Lörby, Blekinge. Notched bone point of Istaby type (form 3).
  Bog find.
  Erixon, 1913, p. 138 and fig. 3. Kalmar Museum.
Mjällby mosse, Blekinge. Notched bone point of Istaby type (form 3).
  Bog find.
  Erixon, 1913, p. 132, fig. 5.
Multorp, Bohuslän. Slotted bone point (form 21).
  Montelius, 1917, fig. 65.
Oxie, Scania. Barbed bone point, notched near the base.
  Bog find.
  Montelius, 1917, fig. 49. Stockholm Museum, no. 3217:4.

Ringsjön, Scania. Notched bone point.

Lund Museum, no. 24719.

Råbelovsjön, Blekinge. Objects of various periods including broad slotted bone points (form 24).

Sundelin, 1922. Montelius, 1917, fig. 50. Stockholm Museum, no. 13900.

Rönneholms mosse, Scania. Barbed bone point of Gohra-Worle type.

Bog find.

Lund Museum, no. 17, 532.

Scania (S.W.). Barbed bone point of Kunda type (form 6).

Montelius, 1917, fig. 45. Stockholm Museum, no. 13675.

Siretorp, Mjällby, Blekinge. A pair of barbed bone points.

Found close together, at the base of 1·7 metres of peat on fresh-water clay (*snäckgyttja*).

Erixon, 1913, p. 271. Stockholm Museum, no. 14942.

****Stora Dode mosse, Scania.*

*(*a*) Slotted bone point (form 21).

Found in peat-cutting.

Bring, 1921, p. 6. von Post, 1929, p. 141. Simrishamn Museum, no. 1728.

*(*b*) Slotted bone point (form 21).

Found in peat-cutting.

Bring, 1921, p. 6. von Post, 1929, p. 141. Simrishamn Museum, no. 2173.

*(*c*) Perforated antler adze.

Found in peat-cutting.

Bring, 1921, p. 6. von Post, 1929, p. 141. Simrishamn Museum, no. 2727.

Tjörn, Bohuslän. Slotted bone point (form 21).

Montelius, 1917, fig. 61. Stockholm Museum, no. 2898.

Torup, Scania. Slotted bone point (form 21).

Sarauw, 1903, p. 252. Copenhagen Museum, no. 21850.

Vejle (Lake), Scania. Barbed bone point (form 10).

From peat.

Lund Museum, no. 5092.

Viken (Lake). Slotted bone point (form 21).

Found in cutting a canal at a depth of 8 feet, under clay.

Sarauw, 1903, p. 253.

Väby, Blekinge. One notched bone point (form 3), and another barbed.

Erixon, 1913, p. 134 and figs. 9, 10. Stockholm Museum, nos. 9015: 16 and 18.

**Åmossen, Slågarps, Scania.* Nineteen slotted bone points of the narrow form, of which three have been pollen-dated.

Bog finds.

von Post, 1929, pp. 145 ff. Stockholm Museum, nos. 2918, 3191 *a*, 3191 *b*.

KEY TO THE DISTRIBUTION MAP OF CERTAIN FORMS OF BONE POINTS (Fig. 47)

Notched bone points of Duvensee type (form 2) from Calbe, Duvensee, the Havelland, and Neu-Strelitz.

Notched bone points of Istaby type (form 3) from Istaby, Lörby, Väby and Wandsworth.

Single-barbed bone points (form 5) from Dobbertin, Gnewin, Gohra-Worle, the Havelland, Holmegaard, Jonstrup Vang, Løjesmølle, Magdeburg, Mullerup, Ossowo, Pernau, and Svaerdborg.

Barbed bone points of Kunda type (form 6) from Amrum, Béthune, Birkemose, Bjeresjö, Brussels, Calbe, Döhren, Esperöds mosse, Fjellenstrup, Før, Gohra-Worle, Gøvlev, Grenå, Hassing Østerkaer, Haubølle, the Havelland, Herlufmagle, Hillerød, Hinge Sø, Hornsea, Hörninge mosse, Karby, Kongsted, Kunda, Källinge mosse, Leman and Ower Banks, Løjesmølle, Morgi, Mullerup, Pernau, Royston, Skipsea, Skottemarke, Store Vildmose, Svedstrup, Szirgupönen, Taaderup, Tange, Vadsted, Vejby, Vibygaard, Väby, Waren, Wendhausen, and Wilsleben.

Barbed bone points of Mullerup type (form 7) from Bornholm, Holmegaard, Løjesmølle, Mullerup, Rerslev, Slagelse, Svaerdborg, Tissø.

Barbed bone points of Havel type (forms 12 A and 12 B) from Dümmersee, the Havelland, Lachmirowice, and Neu Jucha.

Lanceolate bone points of Pentekinnen type (form 17) from Gr.-Steegen, the Havelland, Peitschendorf, Pentekinnen, and Pernau.

Slotted bone points of various types (forms 21–25) from Åmossen, Bussjö mosse, Copenhagen, Elbing, Ellemose, the Havelland, Hofderup, Hylteberga mosse, Kolindsund, Kösuchen, Kunda, La Haine, Mullerup, Multorp, Pernau, Perkallen, Randers, Råbelövsjön, Søholm, Stora Dode, Svaerdborg, Søborg, Tjörn, Torup, and Viken.

SUMMARY OF POLLEN-ANALYSES CORRELATING THE MAGLEMOSE CULTURE WITH THE DEVELOPMENT OF FOREST HISTORY

(See folding map)

The samples, from which the spectra have been obtained, have, as a general rule, been taken, in the case of settlement sites, from the middle of the archaeological stratum; the Duvensee sample, however, was taken from the main or lower culture stratum, and the Mullerup sample from the base of the archaeological deposit. In the case of single specimens, most of the samples have been taken from the objects themselves, often many years after their original discovery, but certain exceptional cases must be noted. The barbed bone point from between the Leman and Ower Banks was broken out of a piece of 'moorlog', but the pollen-analyses were taken from samples removed from the top and bottom of another lump trawled from the same place. The Taaderup point was associated with part of an elk's skeleton which had evidently sunk by $c. \frac{1}{5}$ of a metre, and the analyses quoted probably represent the limits between which its true horizon must be placed. The Kunda spectra represent the possible range of the culture; the bone point, from which von Post analysed a sample, may have sunk, but the objects as a group are unlikely to be younger than the top of the '*bleke*' deposit of the ancient lake.

The symbols used for the different trees in this table are:

> W. Willow (*Salix*).
> B. Birch (*Betula*).
> P. Pine (*Pinus*).
> A. Alder (*Alnus*).
> O.M.F. Oak-mixed-forest:
> > Lime (*Tilia*), Elm (*Ulmus*), Oak (*Quercus*).
> H. Hazel (*Corylus*).

N.B. The forest trees are each calculated as percentages of the total. The shrub Hazel is calculated separately as a percentage of the total forest tree pollen.

CORRELATIONS WITH FOREST HISTORY

Site	Type of evidence	Pollen percentages						Reference
		W.	B.	P.	A.	O.M.F.	H.	
Bare mosse	Settlement site	2	39	58	—	1	47	von Post, 1929 (a), p. 148
Broxbourne	,,	—	—	65	14	21	102	Warren, Clark, Godwin, and Macfadyen, 1934, p. 126
Bussjö mosse	Slotted bone point (form 25)	—	31	40	21	8	48	von Post, 1929 (a), p. 148
Duvensee	Settlement site	—	17	78	—	5	60	Schwantes, 1934, p. 93
Holmegaard:								
East	Settlement sites	—	7	52	26	15	31	Broholm, 1926–31, p. 25
West		—	15	48	21	16	41	,,
Hylteberga	Slotted bone point	—	21	26	27	26	15	von Post, 1929 (a)
Höganäs	Perforated antler axe	—	18	23	24	35	34	von Post, 1929 (a)
Hörning mosse:								
A	Leister prong	—	36	42	15	7	44	Lundquist, 1928, p. 76
B	Barbed bone point (form 6)	—	24	47	20	9	31	,,
Källingemöre mosse:								
A	Barbed bone point (form 6)	—	43	37	13	7	41	Lundquist, 1928, p. 76
B	Net-pricker*	—	36	27	24	12	27	,,
Kunda:	Many stray finds:							
Minimum	Top of 'bleke'	—	53	37	5	5	9	Thomson, 1930, p. 240
Maximum	Barbed bone point (form 6)	—	30	70	—	—	2	Thomson, 1930, p. 239, note 1
Kungsladugård	Perforated stone mace	—	36	62	1	1	48	Sarauw and Alin, 1923, p. 73
Leman and Ower Banks†	Barbed bone point (form 7)	{ — /) 2	30 / 75	69 / 23	1 / —	— / —	4 / 7	Godwin, 1933, p. 43
Mullerup	Settlement site	1	39	50	3	7	47	Broholm, 1926–31, p. 25
Stora Dode mosse:								
A	Slotted bone point (form 21)	—	19	30	24	27	36	von Post, 1929 (a)
B	,,	—	25	35	27	13	32	,,
C	Perforated antler adze	—	24	53	21	1	28	,,
Svaerdborg	Settlement site	1	31	44	14	11	22	Broholm, 1926–31, p. 25
Taaderup:								
Minimum	Barbed bone point (form 6)	0·8	50·8	21·3	3·3	22·2	53·4	Ødum, 1920
Maximum	,,	1·7	25·4	40·6	3·4	29	66·6	
Åmossen:								
A	Slotted bone point	—	41	43	10	6	47	von Post, 1929 (a)
B	,,	—	31	33	19	17	53	
C	,,	—	18	19	42	21	20	

* Kallingemöre mosse (B) gave 1 per cent. of spruce (Picea) pollen.
† Two spectra are given for the 'moorlog' from the Leman and Ower Banks, one for the top and the other for the ottom of the block.

LIST OF DECORATED OBJECTS OF THE MAGLEMOSE CULTURE

The objects are tabulated in the alphabetical order of their finding-places. The list summarises the style and kind of decoration by abbreviations:

I = incision.
P = *ornementation pointillée.*
B = *bohrornament.*

The motives are indicated by small letters (*a–x*) in reference to the key of patterns given on Fig. 60.

No.	Locality	Type of object	Decoration and technique	Our fig. reference	Reference
I	Bohuslän, Sweden	Net-pricker	(I); motives *j* and *n*	Fig. 59, no. 3	Stjerna, 1911, fig. 23
II	Brabrand Sø, Jutland	Antler axe or adze (damaged)	(I); motive *q* (P); straight lines	—	Thomsen, 1902–7, fig.
III	Copenhagen	Bone point (form 2)	(P); straight lines	—	Müller, S., 1918, fig. 2 Nat. Mus. Denmark, A 5864
IV	Crouy, Somme, North France	Perforated antler haft	A split accentuated by short incisions	—	Picard, 1836–7, figs. and 5
V	Fernewerder, West-havelland, North Germany	Net-pricker	(I); motive *s*	—	Krause, 1902, fig. 8 Mus. f. v. Berlin
VI	Thames r., South-East England	Perforated antler axe or adze	(I); motive *x*		Smith, 1934, pl. xlvi
VII	Havel region, North Germany	Bone disc with central perforation	(B); complex 'star-fish' pattern	Fig. 57, no. 6	Stimming, 1925, fig. 16
VIII	„	Net-pricker	(B); irregular pattern	Fig. 57, no. 3	Stimming, 1925, fig. 14
IX	Holmegaard, Zealand	Bone handle	(I); motive *h*	—	Broholm, 1926–31, fig.
X	„	Perforated antler tine	(I); motive *e*	—	Broholm, 1926–31, fig.
XI	Horsens fjord, Jutland	Antler implement; possibly a heavy harpoon	(I); motives *d*, *n* and *w*	Fig. 61, no. 7	Broholm, 1926–31, fig.
XII	Horsø, Mariager fjord, Zealand	Perforated antler axe	(I); motive *r*	—	Broholm, 1926–31, p. 1
XIII	„	Antler with two tines removed	Scars accentuated by short incisions	—	Broholm, 1926–31, 101–2
XIV	Höganäs, Scania, South Sweden	Perforated antler axe	(I); motives *a*, *b*, *c*, *d* and *q*	—	Rydbeck, 1929, fig. 2
XV	Illebølle, Langeland I., Denmark	Bone fragment	(I); motive *a*	Fig. 62, no. 2	Müller, S., 1918, fig. 1
XVI	Kalundborg, Zealand	Perforated antler	(I); motives *d*, *o*, *u* and *v*	Fig. 61, no. 3	Friis-Johansen, 1918– fig. 51 Kalundborg Museum

LIST OF DECORATED OBJECTS

No.	Locality	Type of object	Decoration and technique	Our fig. reference	Reference
XVII	Klein-Machnow, nr. Berlin	Perforated antler	(I); motives c and d	Fig. 59, no. 4	Kossinna, 1921, fig. 28
XVIII	Koldingfjord, Jutland	Antler fragment	(B); irregular network pattern, possibly biomorphic in character	—	Müller, S., 1896, fig. 14
XIX	,,	,,	,,	Fig. 57, no. 2 b	Müller, S., 1896, fig. 15
XX	,,	,,	(B); motive i associated with biomorphic pattern	Fig. 57, no. 2 a	Müller, S., 1896, fig. 16
XXI	Langeland I., Denmark	Slotted bone object	(I); motive q, and stylised animal	Fig. 59, no. 1	Madsen, 1868, pl. 40, nos. 1 a and b
XXII	Langø, Fünen, Denmark	Perforated antler axe	(B); haphazard	—	Broholm, 1928, fig. 15
XXIII	Limhamn, South Sweden		(B); interrupted lines	Fig. 57, no. 1	Rydbeck, 1927–8, fig. 1
XXIV	Mazowsze, kr. Konstantynow, Poland	Perforated antler	(I); motives a and h	Fig. 62, no. 4	Lund Hist. Museum, 14175 Kozłowski, 1926, fig. 5
XXV	Mendrienen, kr. Allenstein, East Prussia	Bone net-pricker	(B); simple arrangement of lines	—	Ebert, Reall. IX, taf. 207c and d
XXVI	Mullerup, Zealand	Bone fragment	(I); motive h	Fig. 62, no. 7	Sarauw, 1903, fig. 45
XXVII	,,	Bone handle	(I); motives a and h	Fig. 62, no. 6	Sarauw, 1903, fig. 44
XXVIII	,,	Bone fragment	(I); motive n	Fig. 59, no. 6	Sarauw, 1903, fig. 37
XXIX	,,	Bone point (form 22)	(I); motives h and l	Fig. 62, no. 1	Sarauw, 1903, fig. 31
XXX	Orust I., Bohuslän, Sweden	Perforated stone mace	(I); motives h and n	—	Montelius, 1917, abb. 341
XXXI	Ostrołęka, Poland	Perforated antler	(I); motives h, l and u	Fig. 62, no. 5	Sawicki, 1921, pl. I a and c
XXXII	Pernau, Esthonia	Bone fragment	(B); motive i	Fig. 57, no. 9	Ebert, 1913, taf. 23
XXXIII	Refsvindinge, Fünen	Bone handle	(I); motive a on one face (P); biomorph on the other face	Fig. 61, no. 4	Müller, S., 1918, figs. 18, 27 Nat. Mus. Copenhagen, A 24289
XXXIV	Remouchamps, Belgium	Bone fragment	(B); clusters of five pits	Fig. 57, no. 7	Rahir, 1920, fig. 8
XXXV	Resen Mose, Jutland	Amber lump with perforations	(I); motive t	—	Müller, S., 1918, fig. 29 Nat. Mus. Copenhagen, A 6853
XXXVI	,,	Amber figurine	(I); motives g and r	Fig. 59, no. 7	Müller, S., 1918, fig. 24 Nat. Mus. Copenhagen, A 8411
XXXVII	Ringkjøbing fjord, Jutland	Perforated amber pendant	(B); simple arrangement of straight lines	—	Müller, S., 1918, fig. 38 Nat. Mus. Copenhagen, A 28384
XXXVIII	Ringsted Aa, Zealand	Bone implement	(I); motive h	—	Müller, S., 1918, fig. 1
XXXIX	Romsey, Hampshire, South England	Antler tine	(I); motive x	—	Smith, 1934, pl. XLVI
XL	Silkeborg Sø, Jutland	Antler	(B); motives i, m, n and p	Fig. 57, no. 8 a, b	Müller, S., 1896, fig. 12

APPENDIX VI

No.	Locality	Type of object	Decoration and technique	Our fig. reference	Reference
XLI	Skalstrup, Zealand	Perforated antler	(I); motive o, together with conventionalised fish, etc.	Fig. 61, no. 2	Broholm, 1926–31, figs. 14, 15
XLII	Sollerön, Dalarne, Sweden		(I); motives a and h	Fig. 62, no. 3	Stjerna, 1911, fig. 24
XLIII	Stensby, Zealand	Bone object	(I); on one face motive f; on the other a biomorph	Fig. 61, no. 5	Müller, S., 1918, figs. 22, 26 Nat. Mus. Copenhagen, A 17368
XLIV	Svaerdborg, Zealand	Perforated antler adze	(B); five double rows of pits	Fig. 57, no. 4	Friis-Johansen, 1918–19, fig. 35
XLV	,,	Bone handle	(B); haphazard	—	Friis-Johansen, 1918–19, fig. 61
XLVI	,,	Perforated antler	(I); motive k	—	Broholm, 1926–31, fig. 49
XLVIII	,,	Fragment of bone point; type 22	(I); motive h	—	Broholm, 1926–31, fig. 58
XLIX	,,	Perforated antler	(I); motive c	—	Broholm, 1926–31, fig. 51
L	,,	Perforated antler	(I); motive a	—	Broholm, 1926–31, fig. 54
LI	,,	Perforated antler sleeve	Split accentuated by short incisions	Fig. 59, no. 5	Friis Johansen, 1918–19, fig. 36
LII	,,	Antler handle	(I); motive x	Fig. 59, no. 2	Broholm, 1926–31, fig. 61
LIII	,,	Pointed bone implement	(P); simple arrangement of lines (I); motive w	—	Broholm, 1926–31, fig. 55
LIV	,,	Fragment of bone point; type 22	(I); simple arrangement of short incisions	—	Broholm, 1926–31, fig. 59
LV	Søborg Sø, Zealand	Bone point; type 22	(I); motive u	—	Müller, S., 1918, fig. 9
LVI	Søholm, Zealand	Bone point; type 24	(I); motive a	—	Westerby, 1927, fig. 45
LVII	Taarbaek, Zealand	Antler	(I); scar accentuated by incisions	Fig. 59, no. 8	Müller, S., 1918, fig. 6
LVIII	Travenort, Holstein	Bone net-pricker	(I); motives l, n and o	Fig. 61, no. 1	Verh. d. Berliner Ges. f Anth., Ethn., u. Vorgeschichte, 1892, p. 249
LIX	Ystad, Scania, South Sweden	Perforated antler haft	(I); motives o and w, together with outlines of two cervids	Fig. 61, no. 6	Montelius, 1906, p. 96 Stockholm Museum o Nat. Ant.
LX	Lost provenances: Probably Fünen, Denmark	Bone net-pricker	(B); biomorphic motives	Fig. 57, no. 5	Müller, S., 1918, fig. 35 Odense Museum
LXI	Probably Denmark	Amber pendant	(B); irregular lines	—	Müller, S., 1918, fig. 39
LXII	,,	,,	(B); biomorphic design	Fig. 57, no. 11	Müller, S., 1918, fig. 37
LXIII	,,	,,	,,	Fig. 57, no. 10	Müller, S., 1918, fig. 36
LXIV	.,	Bone object with flint insets	(I); motives a, k and u	—	Madsen, 1868, pl. 40, no 5

APPENDIX VII (CHAPTER V)

LIST OF CHIEF TARDENOISIAN SITES AND AREAS
OF SETTLEMENT IN THE REGION STUDIED

BELGIUM
For a list of sites with references see Dursin, 1931.

BRITAIN
The bulk of the sites in that part of Britain within our field of study is included in the areas separately mapped by Figs. 66 and 67. The sites within Fig. 67 are listed and described by Raistrick (1933 (*a*)), and those on Fig. 66 are described by Clark (1932 (*a*), chapter v), with the exception of a newly discovered and as yet unpublished group of sites near Farnham, Surrey. Other sites shown on our map are:

Banchory, Kincardine. Patterson, 1913.
Budle Bay, Northumberland. Buckley, 1925.
Dryburgh Mains, Mertoun, Berwickshire. Callander, 1927.
Grantham (district), Lincolnshire. Sand sites. Clark, 1934 (*d*), p. 422.
Mother Grundy's Parlour, Creswell, Derbyshire. Armstrong, 1925.
Newbiggin-on-Sea, Northumberland. Raistrick, 1933 (*b*).
Peacock's Farm, Shippea Hill, Cambridgeshire. Stratified in post-glacial deposits. Clark, 1934 (*c*).
Sandy, Bedfordshire. Lower Greensand site. Clark, 1934 (*d*), p. 422.
Scunthorpe, Lincolnshire. Dune sites. Clark, 1932 (*a*), p. 35.
Selkirk, Berwickshire. Mason, 1931.
Wangford-Lakenheath region. Dune sites. Clark, 1932(*a*), pp. 32–5.
West Keal, Lincolnshire. On Spilsby sandstone. Clark, 1932 (*a*), p. 36.
Willoughton, Lincolnshire. Armstrong, 1931, p. 339.
Woodhall Spa, Lincolnshire. Clark, 1934 (*d*), p. 422.

FRANCE (NORTH-EAST CORNER OF)
Berru, Marne. Coutil, 1912, p. 310.
Fère-en-Tardenois, Aisne. de Mortillet, 1896.
Hédouville, Seine-et-Oise. de Mortillet, 1881, pl. xxxiv.
Montbani, Aisne. Dune site. Octobon, 1920, pp. 107–23.
Ostel, Aisne. Octobon, 1928.
Vielles, Eure. Octobon, 1929.

GERMANY
Aken, kr. Kalbe a. Saale. Surface find on sandy eminence on the margin of the valley of the Elbe. Engel, 1928, p. 220.
Ansbach, Franconia. Group of sites mainly on sandstone heights at elevations between 450 and 520 metres. A dwelling-pit at Eyb belongs to this group. Gumpert, 1927.
Biederitz, kr. Jerichow. Inland dune in the Elbe valley. Engel, 1928, p. 220. Magdeburg Museum.

APPENDIX VII

Boberg, near Hamburg. Dune site. Schwantes, 1928 (*c*), pp. 221–2.
Borgholzhausen and Ravensburg (between), Teutoburger Wald. Adrian collection.
'*Breit', between Pottenstein and Tuchersfeld, Franconia.* Rock-shelter; deposit disturbed by Hallstatt and La Tène folk. Gumpert, 1929, pp. 263–4.
Brunswick (north of). Sand-dunes between Bienrode and Dovesee. Lampe, 1922, p. 28.
Celle (south of). Sand-dunes between the Aller and the Fuhse rivers. Lampe, 1922.
Chwalim, kr. Bomst. Rothert and Dobrindt, 1934, p. 231.
Darlaten Moor, nr. Uchte, Hanover. Dune site. Adrian, 1931 (*b*).
Ensdorf, nr Bieden, Bavaria. Rock-shelter above the Vils. Important stratification (see p. 207). Gumpert, 1933.
Fellbach, Stuttgart. Site on the Kappelberg at 469 metres. Maier, 1932, p. 186.
Fienerode, kr. Jerichow. Numerous sand-dune sites. Bicker, 1934.
Flatow, kr. Osthavelland. Dune site. Bicker, 1933, p. 253.
Flötz, kr. Jerichow. Dune site. Müller, O., 1928, taf. 16–20.
Freisack, Havelland. Dune sites. Schneider, 1932.
Geisskirchfelse, Pottenstein, Franconia. Rock-shelter. Under Late Hallstatt-La Tène layer. Gumpert, 1929, pp. 257–61.
Gifhorn. Numerous sites on sandy heaths in the district. Lampe, 1922, pp. 24 ff.
Gross-Bokermann, Bielefeld. Sandy site. Adrian, 1934.
Haltern (between Hullern and), Westphalia. Münster Museum.
Hängelsberge, south-west of Magdeburg. Engel, 1928, p. 220.
Hermannsburg, nr. Celle. On a sandy terrace 4–4½ metres above the water-meadows of the Oerze, a tributary of the Aller. Piesker, 1932.
Hindenburg, Eastern Upper Silesia. Rothert and Dobrindt, 1934, p. 234.
Hohlefels, Happburg, Franconia. Surface site. *Reallexikon*, I, p. 305.
Holzheim, Neumarkt, Bavaria. Sandy eminence round which flows the Schwarzach. Birkner, 1923.
Hörste, Lippe. Adrian collection.
Istein, kr. Lorrach, Baden. Lais, 1929.
Katznase, kr. Marienburg. La Baume, 1933, p. 8.
Kl.-Vorwerk, kr. Glogau. Zotz, 1932, abb. 10, p. 35.
Klus mountains, south of Halberstadt. Magdeburg Museum.
Köterberg, nr. Holzminden. Sauermilch, 1928.
Lichtenfels, Franconia. Birkner, 1925, abb. 2.
Martinshöhle, nr. Letmathe. Cave find. Schmidt, 1912, p. 90.
Nagold, Ostschwarzwald. Three sites at heights of 610, 575 and 519 metres respectively in exposed situations. Stoll, 1932.
Neumühl, kr. Konitz. La Baume, 1933, p. 8.
Nordhemmern, nr. Minden. Sand site. Adrian, 1928.
Sagemühl, kr. Deutsch-Krone. La Baume, 1933, p. 8.
Salzburg, Bavaria. Only traces. Hell, 1929.
Schmöckwitz, Brandenburg. Museum f. Völkekunde, Berlin.
Schönbuch, nr. Tübingen. Schloss Museum, Tübingen.
Schwerte, Westphalia. Spiegel, 1929.
Stapelage, nr. Bielefeld. Sand site. Adrian collection.
Stimmberg i. d. Hardt. Münster Museum.
Willenberg, kr. Stuhm. La Baume, 1933, p. 8.
Wüste Scheuer, nr. Dobritz. Cave site, disturbed in early historic times. Schmidt, 1912, p. 103

TARDENOISIAN SITES

HOLLAND

A list of sites is given by Dursin, 1931, where further references may be found.

POLAND

A very large number of sites are known in Poland, especially in the middle valley of the Vistula. Only a small number are shown, owing to the fact that relatively few sites have been mapped and published (Kostrzewski, 1931). The sites on Fig. 65 are:

> *Amalienfelde, kr. Putzig.* La Baume, 1933, p. 8.
> Borku Fałęckim, Podgórski. Czapkiewicz, 1929, p. 294.
> *Kelpin Abbau, kr. Tuchel.* La Baume, 1933, p. 8.
> *Neugut, kr. Kulm.* La Baume, 1933, p. 8.
> *Rudnidk, kr. Graudenz.* La Baume, 1933, p. 6.
> Zakrzów, arr. Wieliczka. Czapkiewicz, 1930, pp. 65 ff.

> * Indicates that the old German place-names are used.

LIST OF WORKS TO WHICH REFERENCE IS MADE
IN THE TEXT

The following list does not pretend to constitute a bibliography of the subject, though it will be found to contain many of the relevant works. It is designed to eliminate bibliographical footnotes from the text, statements being documented between brackets by authors' names and the dates of their publications, details of which can then be found in this list. Author's initials are given in the text only where two or more of the same name occur. In cases where an author has published several works in a given year, these are distinguished by small letters, *e.g.* 1931 (*a*), 1931 (*b*).

Where possible the abbreviations recommended in the Oxford *World List of Scientific Periodicals* have been adopted. In cases where the periodical is absent from this list the most customary abbreviation has been adopted.

ADRIAN, WALTHER. Beiträge zur Vorgeschichte Minden-Ravensbergs, *Mannus*, xx, 1928, 384–408.
—— Der mesolithische Fundplatz Kirchdorf bei Uchte i. Hannover, *Germania*, 1931 (*a*), p. 137.
—— Die Tardenoisienstation Darlaten-Moor bei Uchte in Hannover, *Prähist. Z.* 1931 (*b*), p. 77.
—— Flammenmergel als Rohstoff für mesolithische Geräte, *Germania*, 1932, p. 265.
—— Fundübersicht der vorgeschichtlichen Bodenaltertümer der Kreise Bielefeld u. Halle i.Westf., *Aus der Vorzeit in Rheinland, Lippe und Westfalen*, I, Heft 7/8, 1934, 113–23.
ALIN, J. (with SARAUW). *Götaälvsområdets fornminnen.* 1923.
ALIO, J. Die geographische Entwicklung des Ladogasees in postglazialer Zeit und ihre Bezeihung zur steinzeitlichen Besiedelung, *Bull. Comm. Géol. Finl.* no. 45, 1915.
—— Fragen der Russischen Steinzeit. I. Die frühesten neolithischen Funde Russlands. *Finska Fornm. Fören. Tidskr.* XXIX, 1922, 3–14.
ALMGREN, O. Uppländska Stenåldersboplatser, *Fornvännen*, 1906, p. 101.
—— Nordiska Stenåldersskulpturer, *Fornvännen*, 1907, pp. 113–25.
—— Ett Karelskt Stenvapen med Alghufudfunnet i Uppland, *Fornvännen*, 1911, pp. 152–75.
ANDERSSON, G. Hasseln i Sverige fordom och nu, *Sverig. geol. Unders. Afh.* series C*a*, no. 3, 1902.
—— Die Entwicklungsgeschichte der skandinavischen Flora, *Résultats scientifiques du Congrès int. d. Bot.* Vienne, 1905.
ANDREE, J. Die frühmesolithische Fauna aus den Hohlen Stein bei Callenhardt, kr. Lippstadt, *Abh. westfäl. ProvMus. Naturk.* II, 1931.
—— Zur Stellung des westfälischen Mesolithikums, *Germania*, XVI, 1932 (*a*).
—— Beiträge zur Kenntnis des norddeutschen Paläolithikums und Mesolithikums, *Mannus-Bibl.* no. 52, 1932 (*b*).
ANTEVS, E. Shell Beds on the Skagerack, *Geol. Fören. Stockh. Förh.* L, 1928, 479–750.
—— *The Last Glaciation.* 1928.
ARMSTRONG, A. L. Two East Yorkshire Bone Harpoons, *Man*, no. 75, 1922.
—— The Maglemose remains at Holderness and their Baltic counterparts, *Proc. prehist. Soc. E. Angl.* IV, 1923.
—— Explorations at Mother Grundy's Parlour, Creswell Crags, Derbyshire, *J. R. anthrop. Inst.* LV, 1925, 146.

LIST OF WORKS

ARMSTRONG, A. L. A late Upper Aurignacian station in North Lincolnshire, *Proc. prehist. Soc. E. Angl.* VI, 1931, 335–9.

ASPELIN, J. R. *Antiquités du Nord Finno-Ougrien.* Helsingfors, 1877.

AUER, V. (with M. SAURAMO). On the Development of Lake Höytiäinen in Carelia and its Ancient Flora, *Bull. Comm. géol. Finl.* no. 81, 1928.

BELTZ, R. *Die vorgeschichtlichen Altertümer des Grossherzogtums Mecklenburg-Schwerin.* 1910.

BERGHOLT, E. Das ehemalige Vorkommen der Sumpfschildkröte in Schweden und damit zusammenhängende klimatische Erscheinungen, *Ark. Zool.* XXI, A, no. 3, 1929.

BERTSCH, K. Klima, Planzendecke und Besiedlung in vor- und frühgeschichtlicher Zeit, *XVIII Bericht d. Röm.-German. Komm. d. Deutschen Archäolog. Instituts,* 1928.

—— Die Vegetation Oberschwabens zur Zeit der Schussenrieder Rentierjäger, *Jber. oberrhein. Geol. Ver.* 1926.

BEZAAN, J. (with POPPING). Elspeet II, *Levende Nat.* February and March, 1932.

BICKER, F. K. Mesolithisch-neolithische Kulturverbindungen in Mitteldeutschland?, *Mannus,* XXV, 1933, 249–70.

—— *Dünenmesolithikum aus dem Fiener Bruch.* Halle, 1934.

BIRKNER, F. Steinzeitliche Funde aus Lithauen, *Beiträge zur Natur- und Kulturgeschichte Lithauens und angrenzender Gebiete, Abh. bayer. Akad. Wiss.* Suppl.-Band. 2.–5. Abhandl. München, 1923.

—— Das Mesolithikum in Bayern, *Atti Accad. 'Nuovi Lincei',* Ann. LXXIX, Sess. I del 27 Decembre 1925, p. 99.

BJØRN, A. Studier over Fosnakulturen, *Bergens Mus. Aarb., Hist.-Antiqu. Rekke,* no. 2, 1929.

—— Noen bemerkninger om Komsakulturen *Fornvännen,* 1920, pp. 342–50.

BLACKBURN, K. B. (with RAISTRICK). Late Glacial and Post-glacial Periods in the Northern Pennines. Part III. The Post-glacial peats. *Trans. North. Nat. Un.* 1932, p. 79.

BLYTT, A. Die Theorie der wechselnden kontinentalen und insularen Klimate, *Bot. Jb.* XI, 1882.

BOULE, M. (with BREUIL, LICENT and TEILHARD). *Le Paléolithique de la Chine.* 1928.

BRANDT, K. Die ersten bearbeiteten Rentiergeweihe aus Westfalen, *Mannus,* XXV, 1933, 325–31.

BREUIL, H. Station de l'âge du renne de Saint-Marcel, *Anthropologie, Paris,* 1902.

—— La dégénérescence des figures d'animaux en motifs ornementaux à l'époque du Renne, *C. R. Acad. des Inscriptions,* 1905, p. 105.

—— Exemples de figures dégénérées et stylisées à l'époque du Renne, *Congr. int. Anthrop. Archéol. préhist.* Monaco, 1906, pp. 394–403.

—— Le gisement quaternaire d'Ofnet et sa sépulture mésolithique, *Anthropologie, Paris,* 1909, p. 207.

—— Les subdivisions du paléolithique supérieur et leur signification, *Congr. int. Anthrop. Archéol. préhist.* Genève, 1912.

—— Notes de voyage paléolithique en Europe centrale, II. Les industries paléolithiques du lœss de Moravie et Bohême, *Anthropologie, Paris,* 1924, p. 515.

—— Harpon maglemosien trouvé à Béthune en 1849, *Anthropologie, Paris,* 1926, pp. 309–12.

—— (with CARTAILHAC). Les œuvres d'art de la collection de Vibraye au muséum national, *Anthropologie, Paris,* 1907.

—— (with SAINT-PÉRIER). Les poissons, les batraciens et les reptiles dans l'art quaternaire, *Arch. Inst. Paléont. hum.* Mémoire 2, Paris, 1927.

—— (with BOULE, LICENT and TEILHARD). *Le Paléolithique de la Chine.* 1928.

BRING, J. Bidrag till Sydöstra Skånes bebyggelsehistoria före megalitgravfarnas tid, *Fören. Forniminnes- och Heinbygdsvård i Sydöstra Skåne,* Skr. I, 1921.

LIST OF WORKS

Brinkmann, A. (with Shetelig). Ruskenesset. En stenalders jagtplass, *Norske Oldfund*, iii, Kristiania, 1920.

Broholm, H. C. Nouvelles trouvailles du plus ancien âge de la pierre. Les trouvailles de Holmgaard et de Svaerdborg, *Mém. d. Ant. du Nord*, 1926–31, p. 1.

—— Langøfundet. En Boplads fra den Aeldre Stenalder paa Fyn, *Aarbøger*, 1928, p. 129.

Brückner, E. (with Penck). *Die Alpen im Eiszeitalter*. 1901–9.

Brøgger, A. W. *Vistefundet*. Stavanger, 1908.

—— *Den Arktiske Stenalder i Norge*. Christiania, 1909 (*a*).

—— Et Fund av en Benpil med Flintegger fra Yngre Stenalder, *Norsk Geol. Tidsskr.* no. 12, 1909 (*b*).

—— Eine Renntierhornwaffe aus dem Westhavellande, *Prähist. Z.* ii, 1910, 39–45.

—— Stenaldersbostedet ved Garnes, *Bergens Mus. Aarb.* no. 2, 1913.

—— *Kulturgeschichte des Norwegischen Altertums*. Oslo, 1926.

—— Die Arktischen Felsenzeichnungen und Malereien in Norwegen, *IPEK*, 1931, pp. 11–24.

Brøgger, W. C. Om de senglaciale og postglaciale nivåforändringar i Kristianiafeltet, *Norg. geol. Unders.* no. 31, 1901.

—— Strandliniens beliggenhed under stenalderen i det sydöstlige Norge, *Norg. geol. Unders.* no. 41, 1905.

Buckley, F. *A microlithic industry of the Pennine Chain. Related to the Tardenois of Belgium.* 1924.

—— The microlithic industries of Northumberland, *Archaeol. aeliena*, series iv, i, 1925, pp. 42–7.

Burchell, J. P. T. The Shell Mound Industry of Denmark as represented at Lower Halstow, Kent, *Proc. prehist. Soc. E. Angl.* v, 1925, 73–8.

—— Further report on the Epi-Palaeolithic Factory site at Lower Halstow, Kent, *Proc. prehist. Soc. E. Angl.* v, 1927, 217–23.

—— A final account of the investigations carried out at Lower Halstow, Kent, *Proc. prehist. Soc. E. Angl.* v, 1928, 288–96.

—— Early Neoanthropic Man and his relation to the Ice Age, *Proc. prehist. Soc. E. Angl.* vi, 1931, 253–303.

—— Some Littoral Sites of Early Post-glacial times, located in Northern Ireland, *Proc. prehist. Soc. E. Angl.* vii, 1934, 366–72.

Burkitt, M. C. *Prehistory*. Cambridge, 1921; 2nd ed. 1925.

—— A Maglemose Harpoon dredged up recently from the North Sea, *Man*, no. 138, 1932.

Bøe, J. *Felszeichnungen im westlichen Norwegen*, i. Bergen, 1932.

Callander, J. G. A collection of Tardenoisian implements from Berwickshire, *P.S.A.S.* lxi, 1927, 318.

Childe, V. G. The Forest Cultures of Northern Europe: A study in Evolution and Diffusion, *J. R. anthrop. Inst.* lxi, 1931, 325–48.

—— *The Danube in Prehistory*. 1929.

—— *The Prehistory of Scotland*. 1935 (*a*).

—— Prehistory in the U.S.S.R., *Proc. Prehistoric Soc.* 1935 (*b*), p. 151.

Christy, H. (with Lartet). *Reliquiae Aquitanicae*. 1875.

Clark, J. G. D. *The Mesolithic Age in Britain*. 1932 (*a*).

—— A microlithic flaking site at West Heath, West Harting, Sussex, *Sussex Archaeol. Coll.* lxxiii, 1932 (*b*), 145–55.

—— The Classification of a microlithic culture, *Arch. J.* xc, 1934 (*a*), 52–77.

—— A Late Mesolithic settlement site at Selmeston, Sussex, *Ant. J.* xiv, 1934 (*b*), 134–58.

LIST OF WORKS

CLARK, J. G. D. Recent Researches on the Post-glacial deposits of the English Fenland, *Irish Nat., Quaternary Research Number*, 1934 (*c*).

—— (with WARREN, GODWIN and MACFADYEN). An Early Mesolithic site at Broxbourne sealed under Boreal peat, *J. R. anthrop. Inst.* LXIV, 1934, 101–28.

—— Some unrecorded finds of microliths from England, *Proc. prehist. Soc. E. Angl.* VII, Part III, 1934 (*d*), 421.

COMMONT, V. Note sur les Tufs et les Tourbes de divers âges de la Vallée de la Somme. Mode de formation et chronologie d'après la faune et l'industrie que renferment ces dépôts, *Ann. Soc. Géol. Nord*, XXXIX, Lille, 1910, 210–48.

COUTIL, L. Tardenoisien, Captien, Gétulien, Ibéro-Maurusien, Intergétulo-Néolithique, Tellien, Loubirien, Geneyenien (Silex à formes géométriques, silex Pygmées et micro-silex géométriques), *Congr. int. Anthrop. Archéol. préhist.* I, Genève, 1912, pp. 301–6.

CRAWFORD, O. G. S. (with PEAKE). A flint factory at Thatcham, Berkshire, *Proc. prehist. Soc. E. Angl.* IV, 1922, 499–514.

CZAPKIEWICZ, BOLESLAW. Trouvailles de l'âge de la pierre de Zakrzów, arrondt. de Wieliczka, *Ksiega Pamiatkowa*, Poznań, 1930, p. 65.

—— Rapport sur les Recherches archéologiques (1924–5), *Wiad. Archeolog.*, X, 1929, p. 294.

D'ACY, M. Marteaux, Casse-tête et Gaines de Hache Néolithiques en bois de cerf ornamentés, *Anthropologie, Paris*, 1893, pp. 385–401.

DÉCHELETTE, J. *Manuel d'archéologie préhistorique*, I. 1908.

DE GEER, G. Om Skandinaviens Geografiska Utveckling efter Istiden, *Sverig. geol. Unders. Afh.* series C, no. 161 *a*, Stockholm, 1896.

—— A Geochronology of the last 12,000 years, *Int. Geol. Congr.* Stockholm, 1910, fasc. I, 241–57.

—— On the determination of Geochronology by a study of laminated deposits, *Science*, LII, no. 1352, November 26th, 1920, 502–3.

—— Forhistoriska tidsbestamningar och kulturutvecklingen, *Ymer*, 1925, pp. 1–34.

—— Geochronology as based on solar radiation, and its relation to archaeology, *Antiquity*, 1928, pp. 308–18.

DE MORGAN, J. *Prehistoric Man.* 1924.

DIDON, L. Faits nouveaux constatés dans une station Aurignacienne des environs de Sergeac, *Congr. int. Anthrop. Archéol. préhist.* I, Genève, 1912, 337.

DOBRINDT, C. (with ROTHERT). Neue Fundplätze des Swiderio-Tardenoisien in Ostdeutschland, *Mannus*, 1934, pp. 220–36.

DOKTUROWSKY, W. S. Pollenanalyse aus der Kulturschicht bei Lialovo, Gouv. Moskau, *J. russe Antropol.* XIV, Moscou, 1925.

DUBOIS, G. Recherches sur les terrains quaternaires du Nord de la France, *Mém. Soc. Géol. Nord*, VIII, i, Lille, 1924, 1–355.

DURSIN, L. La question tardenoisienne en Belgique et aux Pays-Bas, *Institut Intern. d'Anthropologie, Session de Paris*, 1931, pp. 389–400.

EBERT, M. Die baltischen Provinzen Kurland, Livland, Estland, 1913, *Prähist. Z.* V, 1913, 490.

EISNER, JAN. Outillage microlithique dans la Slovaquie, *Ksiega Pamiatkowa*, Poznań, 1930, p. 57.

EKAMI, N. (with MIDZUNO). Inner Mongolia and the Region of the Great Wall, *Arch. Orientalis*, I, Tokyo, 1935.

EKHOLM, G. Det brakycefala elementet i Nordens stenålders-befolkning, *Ymer*, 1924, pp. 45–56.

—— Die erste Besiedelung des Ostseegebietes, *Wien. prähist. Z.* 1925 (*b*), pp. 1 ff.

—— War Skandinavien während der letzten Zwischeneiszeit besiedelt? *Wien. prähist. Z.* 1926, pp. 20 ff.

LIST OF WORKS

EKHOLM, G De Skandinaviska Hällristningarna, *Ymer*, 1916.
—— Människor i Skandinavien under sista interglacialen? *Ymer*, 1925 (*a*), pp. 416–22.
ENGEL, C. Übersicht der mittelsteinzeitlichen Fundplätze im Mittelelbegebiet, *Abh. Mus. Nat.- u. Heimatk. Magdeburg*, v (Festschrift), 1928, 216.
—— Mesolithische Fundplätze aus der näheren Umgebung Magdeburgs, *Abh. Mus. Nat.- u. Heimatk. Magdeburg*, v (Festschrift), 1928, 209.
ENGELSTAD, E. S. *Østnorske Ristninger og Malinger av den Arktiske Gruppe.* 1934.
ENQUIST, F. Sambandet mellan klimat och växtgränser, *Geol. Fören. Stockh. Förh.* 1924, pp. 202–13.
—— The Relation between Dune-form and Wind-direction, *Geol. Fören. Stockh. Förh.* 1932, p. 19.
ERDTMAN, G. Studies in Micro-Palaeontology. II. Moorlog from the Dogger-Bank, *Geol. Fören. Stockh. Förh.* XLVI, 1924.
—— Notes on Pollen-Statistics, *Svensk. bot. Tidskr.* XXI, 1927.
—— Studies in the post-arctic history of the forests of north-western Europe: I. Investigations in the British Isles. II. Untersuchungen in Nordwestdeutschland und Holland. III. Recherches dans la Belgique et au Nord de la France, *Geol. Fören. Stockh. Förh.* L, 1928.
—— Some aspects of the post-glacial History of British Forests, *J. Ecol.* XVII, 1929.
ERIXON, S. Stenåldern i Blekinge, *Fornvännen*, 1913, pp. 125–212.
EUROPAEUS, A. Fornfynd från Kyrkslätt och Esbo socknar, *Soumen Muinaismuistoyhdistyksen Aikakauskirja—Finska Fornm. Fören. Tidskr.* XXXII, no. 1, 1922, 3–208.
—— Stenålderskeramik från kustboplatser i Finland, *Soumen Muinaismuistoyhdistyksen Aikakauskirja—Finska Fornm. Fören. Tidskr.* XXXVI, no. 1, 1926, 45–77.
EVANS, Sir JOHN. *The Ancient Stone Implements, weapons, and ornaments of Great Britain.* 2nd ed., 1897.
FEURSTEIN, S. P. Geschichte des Viller Moores und des Seerosenweihers an den Lanser Köpfen bei Innsbruck, *Beih. bot. Zbl.* LI, Abt. II, 477–526.
FIRBAS, K. (with RUDOLPH). Die Hochmoore des Erzgebirges, *Beih. bot. Zbl.* XLI, Abt. II, 1924.
FRANZ, L. Bemerkungen zur Steinzeit Nordeuropas, *Mitt. Anthrop. Ges. Wien*, LVII, 1927, 1.
—— Alteuropäische Wurfhölzer, *Festschrift; publication d'hommage offerte à P. W. Schmidt*, Vienna, 1928, edited by W. Koppers, pp. 800–8.
FRIIS-JOHANSEN, K. En Boplads fra den aeldste Stenalder i Svaerdborg Mose, *Aarbøger*, 1919, p. 106.
—— Une Station du plus ancien Âge de la Pierre dans la Tourbière de Svaerdborg, *Mém. d. Ant. du Nord*, 1918–19, p. 241.
FÜRST, C. M. Stångenäskraniets renässans, *Fornvännen*, 1925, p. 289.
GAERTE, W. Auf den Spuren der ostpreussischen Mammut- u. Renntierjäger, *Mannus*, XVIII, 1926, pp. 253–7.
GAMS, H. (with NORDHAGEN). Postglaziale Klimaänderungen und Erdkrustenbewegungen in Mitteleuropa, *Landesk. Forsch. München*, Heft 25, 1923.
GAVELIN, A. Studier öfver de postglaciala nivå- och klimatförändringarna på norra delen, *Sverig. geol. Unders. Årsbok*, no. 1, 1907.
GEIKIE, J. Discovery of an ancient canoe in the old alluvium of the Tay at Perth, *Scot. Nat.* v, 1879, 1–7.
—— *Prehistoric Europe.* 1881.
GEINITZ, E. Das Quartär Nordeuropas, *Lethaea geognostica*, III, 2, 1904.
GJESSING, G. *Arktiske Hellristninger i Nord-Norge.* Oslo, 1932.

LIST OF WORKS

GJESSING, H. To benredskaper fra Stenalderen, *Oldtiden*, IX, 1920 (*a*), 139–43.

—— *Rogalands Stenalder.* Stavanger, 1920 (*b*).

GODWIN, H. and M. E. British Maglemose harpoon sites, *Antiquity*, March, 1933, pp. 36–48.

—— Pollen Analysis. An outline of the problems and potentialities of the method. Part I. Technique and Interpretation, *New Phytol.* XXXIII, no. 4, 1934.

—— *Ibid.* Part II. General Applications of Pollen Analysis, *New Phytol.* XXXIII, no. 5, 1934.

—— —— (with CLARK and MACFADYEN). Report on an Early Bronze Age Site in the South-Eastern Fens, *Ant. J.*, April, 1933, pp. 266–96.

—— —— (with WARREN, CLARK and MACFADYEN). An Early Mesolithic site at Broxbourne sealed under Boreal peat, *J. R. anthrop. Inst.* LXIV, 1934, 101–28.

GOODCHILDE, H. H. (with REID and WHITEHEAD). Some notes on 'Moorlog', a peaty deposit from the Dogger Bank in the North Sea, *Essex Nat.* XVI, 1909–10, 51.

GREWINGK, C. Die neolithischen Bewohner von Kunda in Estland, *Verh. gelehr. estn. Ges.* XV, 1884.

—— Geologie und Archäologie des Mergellagers von Kunda in Estland, *Arch. Naturk. Liv-, Esth-, u. Kurl.* IX, Dorpat, 1882.

GROSS, H. Das Problem der nacheiszeitlichen Klima- und Florentwicklung in Nord- und Mitteleuropa, *Beih. bot. Zbl.* XLVII, Abt. II, 1931, 1–110.

GUMPERT, C. Fränkisches Mesolithikum, *Mannus-Bibl.* XL, 1927.

—— Der Tardenoisienmensch in der Fränkischen Schweiz als Höhlen- und Abrisbewohner, *Mannus*, XXI, Hefte 3/4, 256, 1929.

—— Der Rennerfels, *Bayer. Vorgeschichtsblätter*, X, 1931–2, 60.

—— Der madeleinezeitliche 'Rennerfels' in der Fränkischen Schweiz. *Prähist. Z.* XXII, 1931, 56.

—— Eine paläolithische und mesolithische Abri-Seidlung bei Ensdorf..., *Mannus*, XXV, Heft 2, 1933, 176.

—— Die Abrisiedlung Steinbergwand bei Ensdorf..., *Bayer. Vorgeschichtsblätter*, XI, 1933, 57.

—— Eine mesolithische Wohngrubenstation bei Pottenstein..., *Bayer. Vorgeschichtsblätter*, XI, 1933, 70.

HALLEZ, P. Sur les fonds du Détroit du Pas-de-Calais, *Ann. Soc. Géol. Nord*, XXVIII, 1899, 4–23.

HALLSTRÖM, G. Nordskandinaviska Hällristningar, *Fornvännen*, 1907, pp. 160–89; 1908, pp. 49–86; 1909, pp. 126–59.

HAMAL-NANDRIN, J. (with SERVAIS). Contribution à l'étude du préhistorique dans la Campine limbourgeoise, *Féd. archéol. et hist. de Belgique, Annales du XXIe Congrès*, II, 1909.

HARTZ, N. (with WINGE). Om Uroxen fra Vig, *Aarbøger*, 1906, pp. 225 ff.

HASSE, G. Quelques vestiges du paléolithique en Flandre, *Bull. Soc. Anthrop. Paris*, XXXIX, 1924, 176–81.

HEDE, J. E. (with VON POST and MUNTHE). Gotlands Geologi, *Sverig. geol. Unders. Årsbok*, 18, 1924.

HEDSTRÖM, H. Om ändmoräner och strandlinier i trakten af Vaberget, *Geol. Fören. Stockh. Förh.* XXIII, 1901, 163–79.

HELL, M. Mesolithformen aus Salzburg, *Germania*, XIII, 1929, 158–62.

HOHMANN, K. Ein neues Vorkommen der Lyngbystufe in der Mark Brandenburg, *Prähist. Z.* XVIII, 1927, 186–207.

HOOPER, W. The Pigmy flint industries of Surrey, *Surrey Archaeol. Coll.* XLI, 1933, 50.

HULTH, J. M. Über einige Kalktuffe aus Westgötland, *Bull. Geol. Inst. Univ. Upsala*, IV, 1898.

LIST OF WORKS

HÄGG, R. Stånganäskraniets skalbank, *Geol. Fören. Stockh. Förh.* 1924, pp. 443 ff.

ISBERG, O. Till frågan om människans och renens första uppträdande på den skandinaviska halvön under postarttisk tid, *Ymer*, 1930, pp. 381–402.

JACOB-FRIESEN, K. H. Die Steinkammern in Moore von Hammah, Kreis Stade, *Prähist Z.*, 1924, 28–40.

JAESCHKE, J. Zur postglazialen Waldesgeschichte des nördlichen Schwarzwaldes, *Beih. bot. Zbl.*, LI, Abt. II, 1934, 527–65.

JESSEN, A. Langøfundet. Den geologiske Undersøgelse, *Aarbøger*, 1928, pp. 141–51.

—— (with NORDMANN). Ferskvandslagene ved Nørre Lyngby, *Danm. geol. Unders.* 2nd series, no. 29, 1915.

—— (with THOMSEN). Une trouvaille de l'ancien âge de la pierre. La trouvaille de Brabrand, *Mém. d. Ant. du Nord*, 1902–7, pp. 161–232.

JESSEN, K. Moseundersøgelser i det nordøstlige Sjaelland, *Danm. geol. Unders.* 2nd series, no. 34, 1920.

—— (with MILTHERS). Interglacial Fresh-water Deposits in Jutland and North-west Germany, *Danm. geol. Unders.* 2nd series, no. 48, 1928.

JOHANSEN, A. C. Om Temperaturen i Danmark og det sydlige Sverige i den Senglaciale Tid, *Medd. dansk geol. Foren.* no. 12, 1906, 7–22.

—— (with LYNGE). Om Land- og Ferskvandsmolluskerne i holocaene Lag ved Strandgaarden SSO for Kalundborg, og deres Vidnesbyrd om Klimaforandringer, *Medd. dansk geol. Foren.* V, no. 11, 1917.

KADNER, A. Homo Kiliensis, *Mannus*, XVII, 1925, 257–70.

KALDHOL, H. Nordfjords kvartaeravleiringer, *Bergens Mus. Aarb.* 1912, no. 3.

KEILHACK, K. Die grossen Dünengebiete Norddeutschlands, *Z. dtsch. Geol. Ges.* 1917, Mon. Ber. pp. 2–17.

KELLER, P. Pollenanalytische Untersuchungen an Schweizer Moor und ihre florengeschichtliche Deutung, *Veröff. geobot. Inst. Rübel*, 1928.

—— Beiträge zur Kenntnis der nacheiszeitlichen Waldentwicklung in der Ostschweiz, *Beih. bot. Zbl.* XLV, Abt. II, 1929, 181–219.

—— Postglaziale Waldperioden in den Zentralalpen Graubündens, *Beih. bot. Zbl.* XLV, Abt. II, 1930.

—— Die postglaciale Entwicklungsgeschichte der Wälder von Norditalien, *Veröff. geobot. Inst. Rübel*, 1931.

KJELLMARK, K. Öfversikt af Sveriges stenåldersboplatser, *Ymer*, 1904, pp. 187–225.

—— En stenåldersboplats i Järavallen vid Limhamn, *Antikvarisk Tidskr. Sverige*, 1903.

KLINGHARDT, Prof. F. *NachrBl. dtsch. Vorzeit*, 1926, p. 47.

KOCH, L. Nye Bidrag til Mullerupkulturens geologiske Alder, *Medd. dansk geol. Foren.* V, no. 6, 1916.

KOSSINNA, G. Der Ursprung der Urfinnen und der Urindogermanen und ihre Ausbreitung nach dem Osten: I. Urfinnen und Nordindogermanen, *Mannus*, I, 1907, 17–52.

—— Die Indogermanen, *Mannus-Bibl.*, no. 26, 1921.

—— *Ursprung und Verbreitung der Germanen.* 1926–7.

KOSTRZEWSKI, M. J. Nouvelles fouilles et découvertes en Poméranie Polonaise, *Rev. anthrop.* XXIX, 1929, 383–97.

—— Quelques observations sur le Tardenoisien en Grande Pologne, *Inst. Int. Anthrop.* Paris, 1931, pp. 400–9.

KOZŁOWSKI, L. L'époque mésolithique en Pologne, *Anthropologie*, Paris, XXXVI, 1926, 47–74.

—— Die Steinzeit im Dünengebiet der kleinpolnischen Höhe, *Arch. Nauk Antrop.* 1923.

LIST OF WORKS

KRAUSE, E. *Globus*, 1897, p. 271. Wildgruben und Jagdgeräthe aus der Steinzeit von Ferne-werder, *NachrBl. dtsch. Alterthumsfunde*, 1902, Heft 2, 28 ff.

KRUKOWSKI, S. Importance des zones de recession de la dernière glaciation en Pologne pour la connaissance des plus anciennes industries sur le terrain de cette glaciation, *Wiad. Archeol.* VII, 1922, p. 92.

KUPKA, P. Über einen Fund der älteren Steinzeit bei Calbe a. d. Milde. *Z. Ethn.* XXXVIII, 1906, 744 ff.

—— Das Campignien im norddeutschen Glazialgebiet, *Z. Ethnol.* XXXIX, 1907, 192 ff.

—— Das Campignien von Calbe a. d. Milde und seine Bedeutung für das norddeutsche Mesolithi-kum, *Beitr. Gesch. Landesk. Altmark*, IV, 1919.

LA BAUME, Prof. Dr W. Zur Kenntnis der frühesten Besiedelung Nordostdeutschlands, *Elbinger Jb.* Heft 4, 1924.

—— (with LANGENHEIM). Die Steinzeit im Gebiet der unteren Weichsel, *Bl. dtsch. Vorgesch.* Heft 9/10, 1933.

LAGERHEIM, G. (with WITTE). *Stratiotes aloides* L. funnen i Sveriges post-glaciala aflagringar, *Geol. Fören. Stockh. Förh.* XXVII, 1905.

LAMPE, W. Die frühneolithische Besiedlung des Allertals, *NachrBl. niedersächs. Vorgesch.* III, Hannover, 1922.

—— Ein frühsteinzeitlicher Siedlungsplatz von Wustrow an der Jeetzel, *Niedersächs .Jb.* III, Hannover, 1926.

LANGENHEIM, R. (with LA BAUME). Die Steinzeit im Gebiet der unteren Weichsel, *Bl. dtsch. Vorgesch.* Heft 9/10, 1933.

LARTET, E. (with CHRISTY). *Reliquiae Aquitanicae.* 1875.

LEQUEUX, L. Stations Tardenoisiennes des Vallées de l'Amblève, de la Vesdre, et de l'Ourthe, *Bull Soc. Anthrop. Brux.* XXXVIII, 1923 (*a*), 37–122.

—— Contribution à l'étude de l'industrie tardenoisienne évoluée de la Campine, *Bull. Soc. Anthrop. Brux.* XXXIX, 1924, 248–77.

LEWIS, F. J. The Plant Remains in the Scottish Peat Mosses since the Pleistocene Period, *Trans. Roy. Soc. Edinburgh*, 1905–7.

—— The Changes in the Vegetation of British Peat Mosses since the Pleistocene Period, *Proc. Geol. Assoc. Liverpool*, 1908, pp. 24–30.

LICENT, E. (with BOULE, BREUIL and TEILHARD). *Le Paléolithique de la Chine.* 1928.

LINDBERG, H. Die Schichtenfolge auf dem steinzeitlichen Fundplatz bei Korpilshti, Kirchspiel Antrea, Län Wiborg. Phytopaläontologische Untersuchungen, *Finska Fornm. Fören. Tidskr.* XXVIII, Helsingfors, 1920.

LINDQUIST, S. Nordens benålder och en teori om dess stenåldersraser, *Rig*, 1918, pp. 65 ff.

LISSAUER, A. *Die prähistorischen Denkmäler der Provinz Westpreussen und der angrenzenden Gebiete.* 1887.

LUNDQUIST, G. Studier i Ölands Myrmarker, *Sverig. geol. Unders.* series C, no. 353, 1928.

LYNGE, H. (with JOHANSEN). Om Land- og Ferskvandsmolluskerne i holocaene Lag ved Strand-gaarden SSO for Kalundborg, og deres Vidnesbyrd om Klimaforandringer, *Medd. dansk geol. Foren.* V, no. 11, 1917.

MACFADYEN, W. A. The Foraminifera of the Fenland Clays at St Germans, near King's Lynn, *Geol. Mag. Lond.* LXX, 1933 (*a*), 182–91.

—— Report on the Silts and Clay. Plantation Farm excavation report. *Ant. J.* XIII, 1933 (*b*), 289.

—— (with WARREN, CLARK and GODWIN). An Early Mesolithic site at Broxbourne sealed under Boreal peat, *J. R. anthrop. Inst.* LXIV, 1934, 101–28.

LIST OF WORKS

MADSEN, A. P. *Afbildninger af danske Oldsager.* Kjøbenhavn, 1868.

—— Undersøgelse af Kjøkkenmøddingen ved Meilgaard i 1888, *Aarbøger*, 1888, p. 299.

—— (with MÜLLER, NEERGAARD, PETERSEN, ROSTRUP, STEENSTRUP and WINGE). *Affaldsdynger fra Stenalderen i Danmark.* 1900.

MAIER, P. Mesolithikum aus Stuttgart, *Germania*, 1932, p. 186.

MARR, J. E. (with SHIPLEY). *The Natural History of Cambridgeshire.* 1904.

MASON, W. D. Prehistoric man at Tweed Bridge, Selkirk, *P.S.A.S.* LXV, 1931, 414–17.

MATHIASSEN, T. Blubber lamps in the Ertebølle Culture? *Acta Archaeologica*, vol. VI, 1935, pp. 139 ff.

MENGHIN, O. Die mesolithische Kulturentwicklung in Europa, *Deutsches Archäologisches Institut, Rom.-Germ. Komm. Bericht*, XVII, 1927, 154.

—— *Weltgeschichte der Steinzeit.* Wien, 1931.

MESTORF, J. *Wohnstätten der älteren neolithischen Periode in der Kieler Föhrde.* Kiel, 1904.

—— *Vorgeschichtliche Alterthümer aus Schleswig-Holstein.* Hamburg, 1885.

MIDZUNO, S. (with EKAMI). Inner Mongolia and the Region of the Great Wall, *Arch. Orientalis*, I, Tokyo, 1935.

MIEG, M. Stations préhistoriques de Kleinkems, *Bull. Soc. Sci. Nancy*, 1904.

—— Note sur une station de l'époque paléolithique découverte à Istein, *Bull. Soc. Sci. Nancy*, 1901.

MILTHERS, V. Nordostsjaellands Geologi, *Danm. geol. Unders.* 5th series, no. 3. 1922.

—— (with JESSEN, K.). Interglacial Fresh-water Deposits in Jutland and North-west Germany, *Danm. geol. Unders.* 2nd series, no. 48, 1928.

MONTELIUS, O. *Kulturgeschichte Schwedens.* Leipzig, 1906.

—— *Minnen från vår forntid.* Stockholm, 1917.

—— Dolkar, spjut- och pilspetsar av ben och flinta, särskilt inom det germanska området, *Antikvarisk Tidskr. Sverige*, Del. XXII, no. 2, 1917–24.

MORTILLET, A. DE. Les petits silex taillés à contours géométriques trouvés en Europe, Asie et Afrique, *Rev. mens. Éc. Anthrop.* 1896, pp. 337–405.

MORTILLET, G. and A. DE. *Musée préhistorique.* Paris, 1881.

MÜLLER, O. Mesolithische Fundplätze bei Flötz, *Abh. Mus. f. Nat- u. Heimatk. Magdeburg*, V (Festschrift), 1928, 195.

MÜLLER, SOPHUS. *Ordning af Danmarks Oldsager*, I. *Sten- og Bronzealderen.* 1888–95.

—— Nye Stenalders Former, *Aarbøger*, 1896, pp. 303–419.

—— L'âge de la pierre en Slesvig, *Mém. d. Ant. du Nord*, 1914–15, pp. 1 ff.

—— Archaeologisk Udbytte af Mosearbeidet i Krigsaaret 1917, *Aarbøger*, 1917, p. 148.

—— *Oldtidens kunst i Danmark*, I. *Stenalderens Kunst.* 1918.

—— (with MADSEN, NEERGAARD, PETERSEN, ROSTRUP, STEENSTRUP and WINGE). *Affaldsdynger fra Stenalderen i Danmark.* 1900.

MUNTHE, H. Studies in the Late-Quaternary history of Southern Sweden, *Geol. Fören. Stockh. Förh.* XXXII, 1910, 1197–1293. (Gives bibliography of earlier works.)

—— Studier över Ancylussjöns Avlopp, *Sverig. geol. Unders. Årsbok*, 21, no. 1, pp. 1–107, 1929.

—— (with VON POST and HEDE). Gotlands Geologi, *Sverig. geol. Unders. Arsbok*, 18, 1924.

NANSEN, F. The Strandflat and Isostasy, *Christiania Vidensk.-Selsk. Skr., I. Mat.-Naturv. Kl.* no. 11, 1921.

NEERGAARD, C. (with MADSEN, MÜLLER, PETERSEN, ROSTRUP, STEENSTRUP and WINGE). *Affaldsdynger fra Stenalderen i Danmark.* 1900.

NIELSEN, H. A. Fund i Svaerdborg og Mullerup Moser af Skeletdele af Mennesker fra den aeldste Stenalder, *Aarbøger*, 1921, p. 205.

LIST OF WORKS

Nihlén, J. *Gotlands Stenåldersboplatser.* Stockholm, 1927.

Niklasson, N. (with Alin and Thomasson). *Stenåldersboplatsen på Sandarna vid Göteborg,* Göteborg, 1934.

Nordhagen, R. *De Senkvartaere Klimavekslinger i Nordeuropa og deres Betydning for Kultur-forskning.* Oslo, 1933.

—— (with Gams).Postglaziale Klimaänderungen und Erdkrustenbewegungen in Mitteleuropa, *Landesk. Forsch. München,* Heft 25, 1923.

Nordman, C. A. Skaldyngernes Stenyxor, *Aarbøger,* 1918, pp. 137–50.

Nordmann, V. On Remains of Reindeer and Beaver from the commencement of the Postglacial Forest Period in Denmark, *Danm. geol. Unders.* 2nd series, no. 28, 1915 (*a*).

—— (with Jessen, A.). Ferskvandslagene ved Nørre Lyngby, *Danm. geol. Unders.* 2nd series, no. 29, 1915.

Nummedal, A. Nogen primitive stenaldersformer i Norge, *Oldtiden,* 1921, pp. 145 ff.

—— *Stone Age Finds in Finnmark.* Oslo, 1929.

Obermaier, H. Das Paläolithikum und Epipaläolithikum Spaniens, *Anthropos,* xiv/xv, 1919–20, 143–79.

—— *Fossil Man in Spain.* New Haven, 1925.

Octobon, le Commandant. La question Tardenoisienne. Ateliers des buttes de sable près de la ferme Montbani (Commune de Mont-Notre-Dame, Aisne), *Rev. anthrop.* 1920, pp. 107–23.

—— La question Tardenoisienne (Ostel), *Bull. Soc. Préhist. France,* 1928, p. 158.

—— La question Tardenoisienne. La station de Vielles, commune de Beaumont-le-Roger (Eure), *Bull. Soc. Préhist. France,* 1929, p. 227.

Overbeck, F. (with Schmitz). Zur Geschichte der Moore, Marschen und Wälder Nordwest-deutschlands. I. Das Gebiet von der Niederweser bis zur unteren Ems, *Mitt. Provinzial-stelle für Naturdenkmalpflege Hanover,* Heft 3, 1931.

Owen, R. *A History of British Fossil Mammals.* 1846.

Patterson, H. M. L. Pygmy flints in the Dee Valley, *Man,* no. 58, 1913.

Peake, H. J. E. (with Crawford). A flint factory at Thatcham, Berkshire, *Proc. prehist. Soc. E. Angl.* IV, 1922, 499–514.

Penck, A. (with Brückner). *Die Alpen im Eiszeitalter.* 1901–9.

—— Schwankungen des Meeresspiegels, *Jb. geogr. Ges. München,* VII.

Petch, J. A. *Early Man in the district of Huddersfield.* 1924.

Peters, E. Deutsches Höhlen- und Freilandmesolithikum, *NachrBl. dtsch. Vorzeit,* 1932, pp. 52 ff.

—— Das Mesolithikum der oberen Donau, *Germania,* xviii, 1934, 81–8.

Petersen, C. G. J. (with Madsen, Müller, Neergaard, Rostrup, Steenstrup and Winge). *Affaldsdynger fra Stenalderen i Danmark.* 1900.

Petersen, J. Stenaldershelleristninger i det sydøstlige Norge, *Naturen,* 1917.

Petersen, T. Solsemhulen paa Leka, *Oldtiden,* iv (Rygh-heftet), 1914.

—— Fra hvilken tid stammer de naturalistiske helleristninger, *Naturen,* 1922.

Petzsch, W. *Die Steinzeit Rügens.* 1928.

Phillips, C. W. The present state of archaeology in Lincolnshire. *Archaeol. J.* xc, 1933, 106–49.

Picard, C. Notice sur quelques instruments celtiques, *Mém. Soc. Émul. Abbeville,* 1836–7, p. 238 and figs. 1, 5.

Piesker, H. *Vorneolithische Kulturen der südlichen Lüneburger Heide* Leipzig, 1932.

Piette, E. *L'Art pendant l'Âge du Renne.* Paris, 1907.

Popping, H. J. Een Magdalenien-station op de Veluwe, *Levende Nat.,* March, 1931.

—— (with Bezaan). Elspeet II, *Levende Nat.,* February and March, 1932.

LIST OF WORKS

POST, L. VON. Einige südschwedischen Quellmoore, *Bull. geol. Instn. Univ. Upsala*, 1916, pp. 219–78.
—— Föredrag om skogsträdpollen i sydsvenska torfmosselagerfjölder, *Geol. Fören. Stockh. Förh.* Stockholm, 1917, p. 392.
—— Ur de sydsvenska skogarnas regionala historia under post-arktisk tid, *Geol. Fören. Stockh. Förh.* 1924, pp. 83–128.
—— Gotlands-agen (*Cladium mariscus*) i Sveriges postarktikum, *Tidskr. Svenska sällskapet Antrop. Geogr.* 1925.
—— Ornerad skafthålsyxa av hjorthorn funnen i Höganäs; Pollenanalytisk undersökning, *Fornvännen*, 1929 (*a*), p. 141.
—— (with MUNTHE and HEDE). Gotlands Geologi, *Sverig. geol. Unders. Årsbok*, 18, 1924.
—— Svea Ælvs Geologiska Tidsställning, *Sverig. geol. Unders. Årsbok*, 21, no. 2, pp. 1–132, 1929.
PÄLSI, S. Ein steinzeitlicher Moorfund, *Finska Fornm. Fören. Tidskr.* XXVIII, Helsingfors, 1920.
RAHIR, E. L'habitat Tardenoisien des Grottes de Remouchamps, Chaleux et Montaigle. L'industrie tardenoisienne et son évolution en Belgique, *Bull. Soc. Anthrop. Brux.* 1920, pp. 31–89.
—— La station tardenoisienne du Sougné, *Bull. Soc. Anthrop. Brux.* 1924, pp. 18–31.
RAISTRICK, A. The distribution of Mesolithic sites in the North of England, *Yorks. Archaeol. J.* XXXI, 1933 (*a*), 141.
—— Mesolithic sites of the North East Coast of England, *Proc. prehist. Soc. E. Angl.* 1933 (*b*), p. 188.
—— (with BLACKBURN). Late Glacial and Post-glacial periods in the Northern Pennines. Part III. The Post-glacial peats. *Trans. North. Nat. Un.* 1932, p. 79.
RAMSAY, W. Nivåförändringar och stenåldersbosättning i det baltiska området, *Fennia*, XLVII, no. 4, 1926 (1), 68.
—— Eustatic changes of level and the Neolithicum, *Finska Fornm. Fören. Tidskr.* XXXVI, no. 2, 1926 (2).
RAU, C. *Prehistoric Fishing.* 1884.
RECHE, O. Die Schädel aus der Ancyluszeit vom Pritzerber See und ihre Beziehungen zu den steinzeitlichen Rassen Europas, *Arch. Anthrop.* XXI, 1925, 122–90.
REID, C. *Submerged Forests.* Cambridge, 1913.
—— (with GOODCHILDE and WHITEHEAD). Some notes on 'Moorlog', a peaty deposit from the Dogger Bank in the North Sea, *Essex Nat.* XVI, 1909–10, 51.
REINECKE, P. Zur Kenntnis der frühneolithischen Zeit in Deutschland, *Mainzer Z.* 1908, p. 44.
REINERTH, H. *Das Federseemoor als Siedlungsland des Vorzeitmenschen.* Augsburg, 1929.
—— *Die Jüngere Steinzeit der Schweiz,* 1926.
REUTERSKIÖLD, E. Ett Karelskt Stenvapen med Älghufud funnet i Uppland. 2. Till frågan om älgbildens användning, *Fornvännen*, 1911, pp. 164–71.
REVERDIN, L. La station préhistorique du "Sälihöhle Oben" près d'Olten (Soleure, Suisse), *Anz. Schweiz. Altertumskunde*, XXVI, 1924, 1–19.
RICHTHOFEN, Frhr. B. VON. Zur Kunst des nordostischen Kulturkreises der jüngeren Steinzeit, *Congr. Sec. Archaeologorum Balticorum Rigae*, 1931.
RIVIÈRE, E. Les dessins gravés de la grotte de la Mouthe, *Bull. Soc. Anthrop. Paris*, 1901.
ROSENKJAER, H. N. Fra Frihavnen, *Naturen og Mennesket*, IX, 1893.
ROSTRUP, E. (with MADSEN, MÜLLER, NEERGAARD, PETERSEN, STEENSTRUP and WINGE). *Affaldsdynger fra Stenalderen i Danmark.* 1900.

LIST OF WORKS

ROTHERT, L. (with DOBRINDT). Neue Fundplätze des Swiderio-Tardenoisien in Ostdeutschland, *Mannus*, 1934, pp. 220–36.

RUDOLPH, K. Die bisherigen Ergebnisse der botanischen Mooruntersuchungen in Böhmen, *Beih. bot. Zbl.* XLV, Abt. II, 1929, 1–180.

—— Grundzüge der nacheiszeitlichen Waldgeschichte Mitteleuropas, *Beih. bot. Zbl.* XLVII, Abt. II, 1931, 111–76.

—— (with FIRBAS). Die Hochmoore des Erzgebirges, *Beih. bot. Zbl.* XLI, Abt. II, 1924.

RUTOT, M. A. Le cannibalisme à l'époque des cavernes en Belgique, *Bull. Soc. Préhist. de France*, 1907.

RYDBECK, O. Några iakttagelser beträffande vissa yxtyper från stenåldern, *Fornvännen*, 1916.

—— Stenåldershavets nivåförändringar och Nordens äldsta bebyggelse, *Kungl. Human. Vetenskaps. Årsber.* 1927–8.

—— Ornerad skafthålsyxa av hjorthorn funnen i Höganäs, *Fornvännen*, XXIV, 1929, 129.

—— The Earliest Settling of Man in Scandinavia, *Acta Archaeologica*, 1930.

—— Aktuelle Steinzeitprobleme, *Kungl. Human. Vetenskaps. Årsber.* 1933–4.

SAINT-PÉRIER, R. DE. Le burin Tardenoisien, *Rev. anthrop.* 1922, p. 314.

—— (with BREUIL). Le poissons, les batraciens et les reptiles dans l'art quaternaire, *Arch. Inst. Paléont. hum.* Mémoire 2, Paris, 1927.

—— La Grotte de Gouerris à Laspugue, *Anthropologie, Paris*, 1927, pp. 233 ff.

SAINTY, J. E. A flaking site on Kelling Heath, Norfolk, *Proc. prehist. Soc. E. Angl.* IV, 1924, 165–78.

—— Further Notes on the flaking site on Kelling Heath, Norfolk, *Proc. prehist. Soc. E. Angl.* V, 1925, 56–61.

—— The Kelling flaking site, *Proc. prehist. Soc. E. Angl.* V, 1928, 283–7.

SALMONY, A. Die Kunst des Aurignacien in Malta (Siberien), *IPEK*, 1931, pp. 1–6.

SANDEGREN, R. *Najas flexilis* i Fennoskandia under postglacialtiden, *Svensk bot. Tidskr.* 1920.

SARASIN, F. Les galets coloriés de la grotte du Birseck près Bâle, *Congr. int. Anthrop. Archéol. préhist.*, Genève, 1912.

SARAUW, G. F. L. En Stenalders Boplads i Maglemose ved Mullerup, *Aarbøger*, 1903, p. 148.

—— Maglemose, *Prähist. Z.* V–VI, 1913–14.

—— Fynd i Västra Sverige av Maglemosetidens Redskapstyper, *Rig*, 1919, p. 149.

—— (with ALIN). *Götaälvsområdets fornminnen.* 1923.

SAUERMILCH, C. Eine Fundstätte mikrolithischer Kultur bei Holzminden a. Weser, *Mannus*, XX, 1928, 175–8.

SAURAMO, M. The quaternary geology of Finland, *Bull. Comm. géol. Finl.* no. 86, 1929.

—— (with AUER). On the Development of Lake Höytiäinen in Carelia and its Ancient Flora, *Bull. Comm. géol. Finl.* no. 80, 1928.

SAWICKI, L. Zabytki archeologiczne w Okoloicy Ostrokeki w ziemi Łomzyńskiej, *Wiad. Archeol.* VI, 1921, 47.

—— Wydmy jako środowisko występowania zabytków kulturowych, *Wiad. Archeol.* VIII, 1923, 139.

—— L'âge de l'industrie swidérienne à la lumière de la géomorphologie de la vallée de la Pré-Vistule aux environs de Varsovie, *Księga Pamiątkowa*, Poznań, 1930, p. 9.

SCHLIZ, A. Der schnurkeramische Kulturkreis und seine Stellung zu den anderen neolithischen Kulturformen in Südwestdeutschland, *Z. Ethn.* 1906, pp. 312–45.

—— *Die diluviale Vorzeit*, III. *Anthropologischer Teil.* 1912.

SCHMIDT, R. R. *Die diluviale Vorzeit Deutschlands.* 1912.

LIST OF WORKS

SCHMIDT, R. R. Die spätpaläolithischen Bestattungen der Ofnet. Beitrag zur Paläethnologie des Azilien-Tardenoisien, *Mannus*, 1910.

SCHMITZ, H. (with OVERBECK). Zur Geschichte der Moore, Marschen und Wälder Nordwestdeutschlands, *Mitt. Provinzialstelle für Naturdenkmalpflege Hanover*, Heft 3, 1931.

SCHNEIDER, M. Die Urkeramiker, *Mannus-Bibl.* 1932.

SCHNELL, I. Strandlinjebestämningar och Markanalys, *Fornvännen*, 1932, pp. 40–7.

SCHWANTES, G. Das Beil als Scheide zwischen Paläolithikum u. Neolithikum, *Arch. Anthrop.* N.F. xx, Heft 1, (1923), 13.

—— Der frühneolithische Wohnplatz von Duvensee mit Beiträgen von K. Gripp und M. Beyle, *Prähist. Z.* xvi, 1925, 173.

—— Eine Zivilisation von paläolithischem Gepräge in Holstein. *Mitt. anthrop. Ges. Wien*, 1926–7, p. 158.

—— Der eiszeitliche Mensch bei Hamburg, *Hamburg Ges. Heimatbl.* 1928 (*a*), p. 1.

—— Schleswig-Holsteins älteste Bewohner, *Nordelbingen*, vi, 1928 (*b*).

—— Nordisches Paläolithikum und Mesolithikum, *Mitt. Mus. Völkerk.* Hamburg, xiii, 1928 (*c*), 159.

—— Die Bedeutung der ältesten Siedlungsfunde Schleswig-Holsteins für die Weltgeschichte der Steinzeit, *Festgabe für Anton Schifferer*. Breslau, 1931.

—— *Geschichte Schleswig-Holsteins*, i, 1–160. 1934.

SERNANDER, R. On the evidences of Postglacial changes of climate furnished by the peat-mosses of Northern Europe, *Geol. Fören. Stockh. Förh.* xxx, 1908, 465–73.

SERVAIS, J. (with HAMAL-NANDRIN). Contribution à l'étude du préhistorique dans la Campine limbourgeoise, *Féd. archéol. et hist. de Belgique, Annales du XXIe Congrès*, ii, 1909.

SHETELIG, H. *Primitive Tider i Norge*. Bergen, 1922.

—— *Préhistoire de la Norvège*. Oslo, 1926.

—— (with BRINKMANN). Ruskenesset. En stenalders jagtplass, *Norske Oldfund*, iii, Kristiania, 1920.

SHIPLEY, A. E. (with MARR). *The Natural History of Cambridgeshire*. 1904.

SIMPSON, G. C. World Climate during the Quaternary Period, *Quart. J. Roy. met. Soc.* 1934, pp. 425–78.

SKERTCHLY, S. B. J. *The Geology of the Fenland*, Geological Memoir. 1877.

SMITH, R. A. Examples of Mesolithic Art, *B.M. Quarterly*, viii, no. 4, 1934, 144.

SONDER, W. Prähistorische Siedlungen an den Oldesloer Salzquellen, *Mitt. geogr. Ges. Lübeck*, 2nd series, Heft 31, 1928, 187.

SPIEGEL, J. Eine mesolithische Fundstelle an der Ruhr bei Schwerte, *Mannus*, xxi, 1929, 265 ff.

STEENSTRUP, K. J. V. (with MADSEN, MÜLLER, NEERGAARD, PETERSEN, ROSTRUP and WINGE). *Affaldsdynger fra Stenalderen i Danmark.* 1900.

STIMMING, R. Die Renntierzeit in der märkischen Havelgegend, *Mannus*, viii, 1917, 233–40.

—— Die Ancyluszeit in der märkischen Havelgegend, *Arch. Anthrop.* xxi, 1925, 109–21.

STJERNA, K. Före Hallkisttiden, *Antikvarisk Tidskr. Sverige*, Del xix, No. 2, 1911.

STOLL, H. Mesolithikum aus dem Ostschwarzwald, *Germania*, xvi, 1932, 91.

STOLLER, J. Moorgeologische Untersuchung im Havellandischen Luche nordwestlich von Friesack zur Feststellung des Alters einer mesolithischen Kulturschichte an der dritten Rhinbrucke, *Jb. preuss. geol. Landesanst.* xlviii, 1927.

SUNDELIN, U. Råbelövssjöns och Nosabykärrets Senkvartära historia och de där gjorda stenåldersfynden, *Geol. Fören. Stockh. Förh.* xliv, 1922, 553–90.

SZMIT, Z. Badania Osadnictwa Epoki Kamiennej Na Podlasiu, *Wiad. Archeol.* x, 1929, 36.

TALLGREN, A. M. L'âge du cuivre dans la Russie centrale, *Finska Fornm. Fören Tidskr.* xxxii, no. 2, 1920.

LIST OF WORKS

TALLGREN, A. M. Zür Archäologie Eestis, *Acta Univ. dorpat.* 1922.

TANNER, V. Om nivåförändringarna och grunddragen av den geografiska utvecklingen efter istiden i ishavsfinland samt om homotaxin av Fennoskandias kvartära marina avlagringar, *Bull. Comm. Géol. Finl.* no. 88, 1930.

TAYLOR, H. King Arthur's Cave, near Whitchurch, Ross-on-Wye, *Proc. Speleol. Soc. Bristol,* III, no. 2, 1927, 59–83.

TEILHARD, P. (with BOULE, BREUIL and LICENT). *Le Paléolithique de la Chine.* 1928.

THOMASSON, H. Baltiska tidsbestämningar och baltisk tidsindelning vid Kalmarsund, *Geol. Fören. Stockh. Förh.* XLIX, 1927, 19.

THOMSEN, T. (with JESSEN, A.). Une trouvaille de l'ancien âge de la pierre. La trouvaille de Brabrand, *Mém. d. Ant. du Nord,* 1902–7, pp. 161–232.

THOMSON, P. W. Pollenanalytische Untersuchungen von Mooren und lakustrinen Ablagerungen in Estland, *Geol. Fören. Stockh. Förh.* XLVIII, 1926, 489–97.

—— Geologische Datierungen archäologischer Funde in Estland, *Fornvännen,* 1930, pp. 238–45.

TOMS, H. S. Pigmy flint implements found near Brighton, *Brighton and Hove N. H. Soc.* 1907.

VIRCHOW, R. Besuch der westfälischen Knockenhöhlen, *Z. Ethn.* 1870, p. 358.

—— *Z. Ethn.* 1880, p. 300, fig. 3.

VOLKOV, T. Nouvelles découvertes dans la station paléolithique de Mézine (Ukraïne), *Congr. int. Anthrop. Archéol. préhist.* Genève, 1912, pp. 415 ff.

—— Industrie en os de la station paléolithique de Mizyn, *Académie des Sciences d'Ukraine.* Kiev, 1931.

VOSS, A. *Photographisches Album der Ausstellung praehistorischer und anthropologischer Funde Deutschlands, Berlin.* 1880.

WARREN, S. H. The Classification of the Prehistoric Remains of Eastern Essex, *J. R. anthrop. Inst.* XLII, pp. 91 ff.

—— (with CLARK, GODWIN and MACFADYEN). An Early Mesolithic site at Broxbourne sealed under Boreal peat, *J. R. anthrop. Inst.* LXIV, 1934, 101–28.

WEBER, C. A. Ueber Litorina- u. Prälitorina-Bildungen der Kieler Forde, *Bot. Jb.* XXXV, no. 1, 1904, 1–54.

—— Aufbau und Vegetation der Moore Norddeutschlands, *Bot. Jb.* 1907.

—— Über spät- und postglaziale lakustrine und fluviatile Ablagerungen in der Wyhraniederung bei Lobstädt und Borna und die Chronologie der Postglazialzeit Mitteleuropas, *Abh. naturw. Ver. Bremen,* XXIX, 1918.

—— Das Moor des Steinkammergrabes von Hammah, *Prähist. Z.* 1924, pp. 40 ff.

—— Grenzhorizont und Klimaschwankung, *Abh. naturw. Ver. Bremen,* 1928, pp. 97–106.

WEGEWITZ, W. Ein Flintplatz aus der mittleren Steinzeit in der Feldmark Ahlerstedt, Kr. Stade, *Stader Arch.* N.F. Heft 18, 1928, 128.

—— Zur Siedlungsgeschichte der Feldmark Ahlerstedt, Kr. Stade, *Stader Arch.* N.F. Heft 19, 1929, 94.

—— *Ibid. Stader Arch.* N.F. Heft 19, 1930, 70.

WENNERSTEIN, O. V. Boplats från Stenåldern i Visby, *Fornvännen,* 1909, pp. 198–212.

WERNERT, P. Figuras humanas esquemáticas del Maglemosiense. *Notas Com. paleont. prehist. Madr.* 1917.

—— Figures biomorphes schématiques de l'ancien âge de la pierre du Danemark, *Anthropologie,* Paris, XXX, 1920, 503–12.

WERTH, E. Zur Kenntnis des postglazialen Klima- und Vegetationswechsels, *Ber. dtsch. bot. Ges.* XLVI, 5, 1928.

WESTERBY, ERIK. *Stenalderbopladser ved Klampenborg*. København, 1927.

—— Den mesolitiske Tid i Norden, *Ymer*, Heft 1, 1931, 41.

—— Nogle Stenalderfund fra tørlagt Havbund, *Medd. dansk geol. Foren.* VIII, Heft 33, 1933, 231–48.

WHELAN, C. B. The tanged flake industry of the River Bann, County Antrim, *Ant. J.* 1930, pp. 134–8.

WHITEHEAD, H. (with REID and GOODCHILDE). Some notes on 'Moorlog', a peaty deposit from the Dogger Bank in the North Sea, *Essex Nat.* XVI, 1909–10, 51.

WIEGERS, F. Über Gliederung und Alter des Magdeburger Diluviums und die Zahl der Eiszeiten in Norddeutschland, *Jb. preuss. geol. Landesanst.* L, 1929.

WINGE, H. (with HARTZ). Om Uroxen fra Vig, *Aarbøger*, 1906, pp. 225 ff.

—— (with MADSEN, MÜLLER, NEERGAARD, PETERSEN, ROSTRUP and STEENSTRUP). *Affaldsdynger fra Stenalderen i Danmark.* 1900.

WITTE, H. (with LAGERHEIM). *Stratiotes aloides* L. funnen i Sveriges postglaciala aflagringar, *Geol. Fören. Stockh. Förh.* XXVII, 1905.

WOLDSTEDT, P. *Das Eiszeitalter.* 1929.

WOODHEAD, T. W. History of the Vegetation of the Southern Pennines, *J. Ecol.* XVII, 1929.

WRIGHT, W. B. *The Quaternary Ice Age.* 1914.

ZOTZ, L. F. Das Tardenoisien in Niederschlesien, *Altschlesien*, III, Heft 2/3, 1931, 121.

—— Kulturgruppen des Tardenoisien in Mitteleuropa, *Prähist. Z.* XXIII, Heft 1/2, 1932, 19.

—— Neue Erwerbungen aus der mittleren und jüngeren Steinzeit, *Altschlesien*, IV, Heft 4, 1934, 229.

ØDUM, H. Et Elsdyrfund fra Taaderup paa Falster, *Danm. geol. Unders.* 4th series, I, no. 11, 1920.

ØYEN, P. A. Nogle bemerkninger om stenaldersfund omkring den indre del av Kristianiafjorden, *Oldtiden*, IX, 1920, 125–38.

Addendum

JESSEN, K. (with JONASSEN, H.)[1]. The Composition of the Forests in Northern Europe in Epipalaeolithic Time, *Kgl. Danske Videnskab. Selskab. Biolog. Medd.* XII, 1, 1935.

[1] This work appeared too late to influence my text.

INDEX

Aamosen, Rerslev, 122, 234
Aamølle, 46, 51, 140, 156, 223, 227
Adimonia tanaceti, 48
Adrian, W., x, xi, 61, 192, 203, 204, 252
adzes, absence of, 201; antler, 111, 150; antler
(Lyngby), 79 ff.; antler (perforated), 112, 232,
233, 239, 244, 247 ff.; bone (perforated), 112,
237; flint, 102 ff., 142, 155, 232 ff.; perforated
stone, 105, 148, 232
Africa, North, 132, 144, 190, 215
Aggarps mosse, 242
agriculture, *see* economy
Ahrensburg, 54 ff., 65
Ahrensburg-Lavenstedt culture, 54 ff., 62, 65, 68,
73 ff., 213, 219
Aisne, 190, 251
Aken, 251
alder, 31 ff., 83, 129 ff., 136, 158, 211, 220, 221,
246, 247
Algeria, 144, 200
Alin, J., 72, 73, 106, 242, 243, 247
Alio, J., 109, 241
Allenstein, kr., 249
Aller, river, 192, 252
Almgren, O., 72, 185
Alps, 30, 31, 218; *see also under* ice-sheet
Alster, river, 74
Alta fjord, 66
Alunda, 185, 186, Pl. VIII
Amalienfelde, 253
amber, 110, 162, 171, 174, 175, 231, 234, 235, 239,
249, 250
Amblève, river, 198, 204, 209
America, 6, 50
American Indians, 84
Amrum island, 237, 245
amulets, 128, 162
Ancylus Lake, 9 ff., 16, 19, 39, 40, 49, 70, 83, 87,
88, 107, 109, 136, 167, 171, 219, 220
Andernach, 224
Andersson, A., xi, 24, 26 ff.
Andree, J., xi, 47, 57, 223
Anhalt, 239, 241
animal-headed implements and weapons, 185, 186,
Pl. VIII
Ansbach, x, 194, 199, 203, 204, 213
Antevs, E., 25
Antiquaries, Society of, ix
antlers, perforated, 112, 171, 233, 234, 239, 248 ff.;
see also adzes, axes, sleeves
Antrea, 109, 185, 241, Pl. IV
Arca glacialis, 25
Archangel, 185

Arctic art, 166, 180 ff.; style A, 4, 16, 181, 182,
184; style B, 4, 16, 181, 182, 184
Arctic coast, 66, 68, 70, 219
Arctic culture, 161, 221
Argentine, 6
Ariège, 217
Armstrong, A. L. A., xi, 197, 215, 236, 251
Arne, Dr T. J., ix
Arrhenius, 21
arrowheads, flint, concave base type, 137; flint,
flake type, 72 ff.; leaf, 158; slate, 67, 71, 185;
transverse, 142, 144, 149, 153, 155, 157, 204
art, Arctic, 16, 166; Ertebølle, 153, 154; Maglemose, 88, 110, 128, 153, 162 ff., 214, 248 ff.
Artois, 87, 118, 237
Aschersleben, 241
ash, 149
Asia, 50; Central, 78
Aspelin, J. R., 185
aspen, 136
Atlantic climate phase, 23 ff., 29, 31, 35, 37, 49,
51, 81, 189, 211, 221
Auer, V., 32
auk, great, 51, 227
Aurignacian culture, 74, 76, 78, 163, 187 ff., 207
aurochs, 47 ff., 59, 61, 89, 96, 204, 225, 226, 228,
235
Australian aborigines, 107
Auvergne, 31
awls, bone, 60, 113, 232, 233, 235, 242; flint,
145
axe civilisation, 79 ff., 214 ff., 219 ff.
axes, absence of, 54, 57, 84, 201; animal-headed,
185; antler, 111, 239; antler (perforated), 112,
149, 150, 154, 232, 233, 235, 237, 239, 242,
247 ff.; bone, 112, 232 ff.; flint (core), 102 ff.,
142, 155, 157, 158, 198, 232 ff., 240; flint
(flake), see *spalter*; origins of, 84 ff., 131, 132;
stone, 16, 67, 71, 137; transversely sharpened
flint, 102 ff.; *see also* battle-axe, *geröllebeil*,
hand-axe, Limhamn, Lyngby, Nøstvet, *walzenbeil* (stump-butted)
Ayrshire, 217
Azilian, 180, 217, 218, 223
Ålborg Museum, 232
Åloppe, 185
Åmossen, 88, 131, 244, 247
Ångerman, river, 6
Ångermanland, 185
Ånnsjöns, 186
Århus, 140, 236; Museum, 232, 233
Åsele, 185
Åskollen, 182, 184, 188

INDEX

Baden, 252
badger, 208, 226, 228
Bakkebölle, 81
Balcombe, 197
Baltic, 9, 10 ff., 27, 39; for early phases of, *see Ancylus* Lake, Baltic ice-dammed lake, *Litorina* Sea and *Yoldia* Sea
Baltic ice-dammed lake, 10, 16
Banchory, 251
Bann river culture, 81
Bara lilla mosse, 83, 229
Bardal, 182 ff., 187
Bare mosse, 88, 242, 247
Barnewitz, 237
Barnow, 237
barrows, Bronze Age, 41
bâtons de commandement, 113
Battersea, 118, 236
battle-axe, 16
Bavaria, x, 201, 218, 252
Bay-Bonnet caves, 197
beach, ancient, *see* sea-level, old
beakers, 152
bear, 182, 186; cave, 224, 225; brown, 224, 226, 228
beaver, 47 ff., 59, 136, 224 ff., 228
Bedfordshire, 251
beech, 42 ff., 221, 243
beetles, 13, 48
Belgium, xi, 29, 32, 47, 61, 69, 76, 87, 115, 118, 128, 144, 164, 190, 197, 198, 204, 207 ff., 216, 217, 219, 231, 249, 251; *see also* Low Countries
Beltz, R., 139, 238, 240
Bergen, 66, 71, 136, 137
Bergholt, E., 26
Berkshire, 193, 236
Berlevåg, 67, 68
Berlin, x, 113, 174, 239, 249; Museum für Völkerkunde, x, 238, 240, 242, 248, 252
Bernberg, 239
Berru, 251
Bertsch, K., xi, 30, 32, 41 ff., 212, 213
Berwickshire, 251
Béthune, 118, 237, 245
Betula nana, 26, 39, 80
Bewick's swan, 227
Bezaan, J., 78
Bicker, F., xi, 192, 252
Bieden, 252
Biederitz, 251
Bielefeld, x, 192, 252
Bienrode, 252
'Binsen keramik', 206
biomorphs, 127, 162, 163, 171, 175, 180, 249, 250
birch, 24, 31 ff., 73, 77, 83, 92, 109, 112, 129 ff., 136, 138, 158, 198, 219 ff., 246, 247
bird-catchers, 115, 120
birds, 136, 182; *see also* auk, Bewick's swan, bittern, brent goose, coot, cormorant, crane, crow, diver, duck, eagle, gannet, goldeneye, goosander, goose, grebe, grouse, guillemot, gull, heron, honey-buzzard, jay, kite, lag-goose, merganser, mute-swan, osprey, owl, pelican, pintail, razorbill, scaup-duck, scoter, shoveler, stork, swan, whooper-swan, widgeon, woodpecker
Birkemose, 231, 245
Birkner, Prof. F., x, xi, 252
Birseck, 218
bittern, 226
Bjørn, A., xi, 68 ff., 78
Blackburn, K. B., 32
Blackdown, Hants., 206
Blackstone Edge, 41
Blackwater, river, 37
blades, flint, 76, 145
Blasensandstein, 194
'bleke', 246, 247
Blekinge, 36, 87, 121, 123, 127, 243, 244
Bloksbjerg, 51, 141, 142, 145, 147, 148, 150 ff., 157, 161, 221, 223, 227
Blytt, A., 231
boar's tusks, as axe or adze blades, 110, 112; as knives, 110
Boberg, 252
bog finds, 79, 86, 88, 90, 231 ff., 242 ff.; *see also* fens
Bogge, 181, 182, 184
Bohemia, 135
bohrornament, 61, 88, 110, 114, 127, 128, 154, 163 ff., 175, 231 ff., 239, 241, 243, 248 ff.
Bohuslän, 10, 22, 87, 97, 107, 114, 135, 136, 168, 171, 181 ff., 243, 248, 249
Bomst, Kr., 61, 65, 252
bone, *see* adzes, awls, axes, dagger(s), hooks, leister prongs, points
bones, decay of, 21
Boreal climate phase, 23 ff., 29, 31, 35 ff., 39, 40, 44, 49, 50, 83, 85, 109, 154, 211, 220, 229, 230
Borgholzhausen, 252
Borgsdorf, 61
Borku Faleckim, 253
Bornholm, 125, 231
Boule, Prof. M., 78
bow, 148, 149
bow-drill, 163, 177
Brabrand Sø, 19, 21, 51, 112, 140, 142, 145 ff., 161, 171, 221, 223, 227, 248
bracelets, bone, 152 ff.
brachycephalic, *see* skulls
Brandenburg, 22, 61, 64, 87, 119, 165, 174, 212, 239, 252
Brandt, K., 229
'Breit', 252
Bremen, 9, 10, 42
Brennermoor bei Oldesloe, 155
brent goose, 227
Breuil, Prof. H., xi, 22, 78, 118, 165, 178, 231, 237

INDEX

Briest, 83, 229
Brighton, 190
Bring, J., 112, 244
Britain, 9, 10, 15, 32, 49, 50, 160, 190, 206, 207, 210 ff., 219 ff., 236, 237, 248, 249, 251; south-eastern, 22, 87, 118, 124 ff., 160, 165, 174, 214
British Museum, 236, 237
Brittany, 12, 15
Bro, 135
Brodersby, 238
Broholm, H. C., xi, 48, 90, 106 ff., 152, 223, 232 ff., 247 ff.
Bronze Age, 16, 41, 81, 134, 137, 181, 182, 216, 217, 221, 222; Early, 38, 41, 210; Late, 42, 114
Broxbourne, 41, 86, 88, 92 ff., 100, 102, 214, 216, 236, 247
Bruniquel, 178, 179
Brunswick, 252
Brussels, 118, 231, 245
Brøgger, A. W., xi, 71, 136, 137, 181 ff., 186
Brøgger, W. C., xi, 12, 16
Brønsted, Dr, x
Buchau, xi, 199, 202
Buckley, F., xi, 96, 198, 203, 251
Budle Bay, 251
Bug, river, 62
Bühl, see ice-sheet, retreat of Alpine
Bull, G. B., 236
Burchell, J. P. T., xi, 158 ff.
burials, 156; absence of, 128; ceremonial, 59
burins, 57 ff., 62, 68, 69, 76, 77, 96 ff., 132, 133, 145, 146, 153, 155, 158, 198, 199, 202, 204, 232, 235, 236, 238; use of, 100
Burkitt, M. C., xi, xii, 15, 178, 180
Bussjö mosse, 131, 242, 245, 247, Pl. V
Butter, J., x, xi
buzzard, see honey-buzzard
Byttingsvik, 68
Böla, 181, 184
Bøe, J., xi, 181, 184
Bøgenaes, 104
Børselvneset, 67

Calbe a.d. Milde, 88, 92, 102, 120, 238, 245
Callander, Dr J. G., 251
Cambridge, Faculty of Archaeology and Ethnology at, ix; Fenland Research Committee at, xi; University Museum of Archaeology and Ethnology, 122
Cambridgeshire, 37, 38, 41, 50, 210 ff., 251, Pl. III
Campignian, 85, 160, 161, 217, 221
Campine, 208
Canada, 6
cannibalism, 128
canoe, dug-out, 109
Capsian culture, 144, 180
Cardium edule, 140
Carelia, Russian, 78, 185, 219
Carpathians, 31

carse clays, 9, 109
cat, wild, 224 ff., 228
Catalonia, 176
causeway, wooden, 42
cave art, 22, 187 ff.
cave-dwellers, 22
caves, 45 ff., 57, 59, 81, 128, 164, 195, 197, 200, 207, 223, 252
Celle, kr., 252
Chaleux, 76, 197
Champion, G. C., 13
Chancelade skull, 135
Channel, English, 12
charcoal, 44 ff., 136, 198
chequer pattern, 127, 170, 174, 176
chert implements, 198
Childe, Prof. V. G., xi, 86, 114, 124, 218
Chile, 6
China, 78
chipping-places, see flint chipping-places
chisels, slate, 67
Chlebowice, 62
Chlebowician culture, see Swiderian culture
Christiania, see Oslo
Christiansund, 68 ff.
Christies Minde, 68, 69
Christy, H., 84, 163, 237
chronology, 15, 41, 44, 57 ff., 61, 65 ff., 69, 77, 83, 114, 128 ff., 154 ff., 170, 171, 182, 207 ff., 215, 216, 219 ff.; see also geochronology
Chwalim, 61, 252
cist, stone, 185
Cladium mariscus, 27
Clark, J. G. D., 9, 15, 37, 41, 54, 94, 100, 102, 104, 107, 118, 159, 197, 198, 203, 206, 210, 217, 218, 236, 247, 251
clay deposits, 9, 10, 12, 19, 32, 37, 41, 70, 109, 129, 134, 137, 141, 148, 152, 158, 165, 210, 211, 229, 230, 241, 243, 244; see also carse clays
climate, 23 ff., 30, 31, 197, 200, 215, 219 ff.; 'continental', 23, 24; 'oceanic', 23, 24; optimum, 49; sub-arctic, 23, 24, 219; see also Atlantic, Boreal, Pre-boreal, Sub-atlantic, Sub-boreal
clubs, 84
coastal settlement, 18, 19, 22, 23, 118, 136 ff., 161
cod, 51, 227
Cogul, 176
coil-built pottery, 152, 157
Colinda, trawler, 15
collecting, see economy
Colne valley, 88, 236
combs, bone, 152 ff.; see also pottery, comb-decorated
composite implements, 89, 96, 124
'continental' climate, see climate
conventionalisation, 178, 182
coot, 226

INDEX

Copenhagen, ix, 141, 163, 172, 231, 245, 248; Ethnological Museum, 121; free harbour, 39; National Museum of Antiquities at, 93, 99 ff., 106, 142, 143, 145 ff., 152, 229, 231 ff., 244, 248 ff., Pls. V, VI

core-dressings, 94

cores, 69, 199

cormorant, 48, 226, 227

cotton-grass peat, 24, 41

Coutil, L., 192, 251

Covesea, 114

crane, 48, 49, 224, 226

Crawford, O. G. S., xi, 237

Cree Indians, 84

Creswell, 197, 207, 208, 215, 220, 251

Crouy, 88, 167, 237, 248

crow, 227

Cyril Street, Kiev, 177

Czapkiewicz, B., 63, 253

Czecho-Slovakia, 32

Czerwony Borek, 63

d'Acy, M., 165

dagger, bone, 113; flint, 137

Dagstorps mosse, 230

Dalarne, 88, 114, 250

Dalsland, 242

Danube area, 218; see also Danubian culture

Danubian culture, 195, 216

Danzig, museum at, xi, 237, 239, 240

Darlaten, 203, 252

Daun, see ice-sheet, retreat of Alpine

decay, varying degrees of, 54, 91, 92, 148, 149, 200, 214

Déchelette, J., 59

decoration, see bohrornament, ornementation pointillée, patterns, rillenornamentik

deer, red, 47 ff., 85, 208, 224 ff.; roe, 47 ff., 59, 90, 200, 208, 224 ff.

de Geer, Baron G., xi, 1, 3, 5, 6

Delsbo, 185

De Morgan, J., 12

Denmark, ix ff., 1, 8, 18, 22, 23, 25, 26, 32, 36, 44, 45, 50, 70, 79 ff., 87, 88, 110, 113, 115, 127, 132, 134, 136, 138, 148, 158, 160, 164, 165, 175, 179, 185, 211, 214, 219 ff., 231 ff., 248 ff.

Derbyshire, 197, 251

Deutsch-Krone, kr., 252

Deventer, x

diatomite, 81

diatoms, 9, 11, 40, 112, 129

Didon, L., 163

Diepholtz, 238

distribution maps, 14, 18, 20, 27, 28, 35, 55, 82, 125, 126, 166, 191; distribution, 130, 174, 186, 190 ff.

diver, black-throated, 227; red-throated, 227

Dobbertin, 86, 88, 120, 238, 245; culture, 86; race, 133 ff.

Dobrindt, C., 61, 65, 252

Döbritz, 197, 252

dog, 49, 51, 124, 226, 228

Dogger Bank, 15

Döhren, 88, 112, 238, 245

Dokturovsky, W. S., 32

dolichocephalic, see skulls

dolmens, 184

dolomite, implements of, 67

dolphin, 51, 117, 228

Dom Bosco monastery, x

domesticated animals, 49, 51, 124, 137; absence of representations of, 182

Dömitz skull, 134

Dordogne, 217

Dovesee, 252

drainage, effect of modern, 41

drainage (modern), 41

Drammen, 16, 184

drilled ornament, see bohrornament

drilling apparatus, 131, 132, 163

Drôme, 218

Dryas clay, 83, 230

Dryas octopetala, 26

Dryburgh Mains, 251

Drynjesundet, 69

Dubois, G., 12

duck, eider-, 51, 227; long-tailed, 48, 51, 226, 227; scaup-, 51, 227; tufted, 226; wild, 224, 226, 227

Dullenried, 45

Dümmersee, 88, 238, 245

dunes, 54, 62, 65 ff., 192, 200, 212, 213, 216, 251, 252

Dungeness, 12

Dursin, L., 192, 207, 251, 253

Duvensee, 41, 86, 89 ff., 98, 100, 102 ff., 120, 130, 131, 142, 214, 216, 220, 238, 245 ff.

dwelling-place cultures, 17, 23, 74, 157

dwelling-places, 16, 17, 19 ff., 41, 71 ff., 90 ff., 129, 185, 195 ff., 232, 233, 235, 242, 246, 247; see also caves, huts, pile-dwelling, pit-dwelling, rock-shelter, wind-break

eagle, white-tailed, 48, 226, 227

East Anglia, 192

Ebert, M., 241, 249

Eckernförde, 238

economy, food-gathering (hunting, fishing, fowling and collecting), 23, 89 ff., 92, 124, 127, 132, 139, 140, 160, 182, 204, 216; food-producing (agriculture), 137, 195, 216

edaphic conditions, 30

eel, 227

Egypt, 142; chronology of, 6

eider-duck, 51, 227

Ekami, N., 216

Ekeberg, 182, 184

Ekholm, G., 4, 230

Elaphrus lapponicus, 48

272

INDEX

Elbe, river, 88, 134, 192, 240, 251
Elbe-Trave canal, 104, 107, 240
Elbing, 238, 245
elk, 44, 48 ff., 136, 152, 182, 185, 186, 220, 221, 225 ff., 232, 238, 241, 242, 246
Ellemose, 232, 245
Ellerbek, 138, 139, 151, 152, 156
Ellierode, 61
elm, 27, 83, 158, 220, 246
Elspeet, 78, 219
Ely, 31, 37
Embach, river, 88
Emys orbicularis, 26, 27
Engel, C., 251, 252
Engelstad, E. S., 181
England, *see* Britain
Ensdorf, x, 195, 197, 200, 201, 203, 204, 208, 213, 252
Epping Forest, 198
Erdtman, G., 12, 32, 36, 39, 81, 109, 158
Erekcja, 242
Erixon, S., 243, 244
Erlanic, 12
ermine, 224
Ertebølle, 46, 51, 112, 113, 134, 138 ff., 165, 211, 216, 221 ff., 227; culture, 16, 29, 102
Erzgebirge, 29
Esbo, 17, 241
Esbovik, 17
Escaut, river, 118
Esperöds mosse, 122, 242, 245
Esquimaux, 162, 163
Essex coast, 9, 15, 37
Esthonia, xi, 11, 22, 32, 34, 35, 49, 87, 88, 114, 124 ff., 127, 160, 164, 165, 171, 219
Eure, 217
Europaeus, A., xi, 17, 241
eustatic rise of sea-level, 7 ff., 11
Evans, Sir John, 142
Evenhus, 182, 184
Eyb, 199, 251

Faareveile midden, 46, 51, 140, 147, 152, 223, 227
Fähre Rüsterbergen, 229
Falkensteinhöhle, 218
Falster, x, 44, 50, 131
Fannerup midden, 156
Farnham, 190, 251
Fatyanovo culture, 186
Fauderup, 229
Faulschlamm, 76, 133
fauna, 46 ff., 57, 61, 80, 89, 137, 140, 165, 213, 219 ff., 223 ff.; absence of, 16; dating of by pollen-analysis, 40
Federsee, xi, 41 ff., 45, 195, 196, 199, 204, 213; Museum, 202
Fellbach, 252
fenland, English, 9, 37, 41, 50
Fenland Research Committee, Cambridge, xi

Fenno-Scandian moraines, *see* moraines
fens, 13, 15, 40, 41, 87, 88, 211; *see also* bogs, fenland
Fère-en-Tardenois, 190, 251
Fernewerder, 114, 174, 238, 248
fertility amulets, 128
Fiener Bruch, 192
Fienerode, xi, 238, 252
figurines, 162, 171, 185, 234, 249
finger-nail decoration, 152
Finiglacial, *see* ice-sheet, retreat of Scandinavian
Finland, xi, 6, 11, 15, 16, 17, 27, 32, 87, 185, 186, Pl. I
Finnmark, 12, 16, 66
Firbas, K., 29
fire, as method of carpentry, 107
Fischausen, kr., 240
fischschuppmesser, 114
fish, 15, 22, 51, 136, 238; *see also* cod, eel, flounder, garfish, perch, pike, roach, rudd, salmon, shell-fish, spur-dog, stickleback
fish-hooks, bone, 113 ff., 119, 121, 137, 150, 153, 174, 204, 233, 235, 237, 238, 241
fishing, *see* economy, fish-hooks, leister prongs, net
Fjellenstrup mose, 232, 245
Flanders, 118, 231
Flatow, 239, 252
flint, mining of, 161; scarcity of, 204; trade in, 207
flint chipping-places, 66 ff., 139, 155, 203, 204, 236, 238
flint implements, importance of, 92; *see also* adzes, arrowheads, awls, axes, blades, burins, core-dressings, cores, lanceolate points, micro-burins, microliths, picks, pseudo-awls, saws, scrapers, tanged flakes, tanged points
floats, net, 109, 241, Pl. IV
Flötz, 252
flounder, 51, 227
fonds de cabanes, 198
Font Robert, 74
foraminifera, 9, 10, 37
forests, composition of, 26, 29 ff., 77, 219 ff., 246, 247; effect on culture of, 30, 79, 84, 124, 160, 214; effect on fauna of, 47 ff., 59, 61, 219 ff.; *see also* pollen-analysis
Forgandenny, 39
Forselv, 182, 188
Forth, firth of, 9, 39, 218
Fosna culture, xv, 16, 23, 66, 73, 78, 219 ff.
fowling, *see* economy
fox, 208, 224 ff., 228; arctic, 47, 59, 61, 224, 225
France, xi, 74, 115, 161, 190, 217, 237; north of, 12, 13, 165, 221, 248; north-eastern, 87, 118, 125, 174, 251
Franconia, x, 190, 194, 195, 199, 203, 251, 252
Franz, L., 107, 128, 148, 152
Freisack, 212, 252
Friarton brickworks, 109

INDEX

Friis-Johansen, K., xi, 48 ff., 104, 110, 115, 119, 122, 128, 155, 223, 231, 233 ff., 248, 250
Frisian islands, 12
frog, 224
Froser Seelandereien, 239
Fuencaliente, 175, 180
Fuhse, river, 252
Fykanvatn, 182, 184, 187
Fäls mosse, 122, 242
Fünen, 79, 80, 113, 114, 142, 164, 165, 175, 232, 234, 249, 250
Fürst, C. M., 135
Før island, 239, 245

Gaerte, W., 230
Gahle, 230
Gams, H., xi, 24
gannet, 51, 227
Garcibuey, 175
garfish, 51, 227
Garnes, 71 ff.
Garrod, Miss D. A. E., 215
Gavelin, A., 24
Geikie, A., xi, 10, 109
Geisskirchfels, 197, 252
geochronology, 4 ff., 11, 219 ff.
geometric art motives, 167 ff., 178 ff.
Germany, ix ff., 8, 11, 12, 32, 197, 199 ff., 206, 237 ff., 251, 252; eastern, 65; northern, 22, 24, 25, 49, 61, 69, 70, 74, 79 ff., 87, 88, 115, 120, 127, 132, 160, 161, 164, 168, 174, 190, 214, 219 ff., 248; north-western, 37; southern, 30, 46 ff., 194, 213, 223
geröllebeil, 105, 153
Geschnitz, *see* ice-sheet, retreat of Alpine
Gifhorn, 252
Ginding Herred, 142
Gironde, 187
Gjeithus, 181, 182
Gjessing, G., 181, 188
Gjessing, H., 71 ff., 106
Glogau, kr., 61, 252
Glösa, 4, 182, 188
glutton, 47, 77, 224
Gnewin, 239, 245
goat, 225
Godsted, 142, 152
Godwin, Dr H., xi, xii, 32, 33, 36, 37, 41, 43, 49, 211, 236, 247
Gohra-Worle, 88, 112, 120, 239, 245
goldeneye, 227
Goodchild, H. H., 13
goosander, 226, 227
goose, 77; brent, 227; grey, 227; lag, 226
Gorge d'Enfer, 163
Gossa island, 68
Gotland island, 9, 19, 20, 39, 73, 157, 185, 219, Pl. II
Gottsche, C., 82

Gourdan, 178
Grantham (district), 251
Graudenz, 253
grave, *see* burial, passage-graves, single-graves
grebe, great crested, 48, 226, 227; little, 227; red-necked, 227
Greenland, East, 122, Pl. VI
greenstone axes, 67
Grenå, 232, 245
Grenzhorizont, 24
Grewingk, C., 241
Gris Nez, Cap, 12
Gr.-Bokermann, 252
Gr.-Rönnau, 111, 239
Gr.-Steegen, 239, 245
Gr.-Wusterwitz, 230
Grossenmeer, 37
Grosswusterwitzer See, 110, 239
Grotte des Espélugues d'Arudy, 178, 179
Grottes des Enfants, 215
Grottes des Fées, Marcamp, 178
grouse, 227; black, 224; white, 47 ff., 59, 61, 77, 224, 225
Gudenaa, river, 155, 161, 221, 235
guillemot, 51, 227
Gulf Stream, 23
gull, black-headed, 226; black-throated, 227; common, 227; great black-backed, 48, 51, 226; great black-throated, 227; herring, 227
Gullrum, 73, 185
Gumbinnen, kr., 239, 240
Gumpert, K., x, xi, 194, 197, 199, 201, 204, 210, 213, 251, 252
Göteborg, 88, 105, 129, 243; Museum, 242
Gøvlev, 232, 245

Haapajärvi, Pl. I
hafting, 86, 96, 104, 112, 120 ff., 144, 145, 149, 200, 204, 242
hafts, antler (Lyngby), 79 ff.; for Maglemose examples *see* sleeves
Hainault, 231
Halberstadt, 252
Halden, 105, 129
halibut, 182
Halland, 72
Halle, xi
Hallehög, 72, 73
Hallez, 12
Hallstatt culture, 207, 252
Hallström, G., 181 ff., 186 ff.
Haltern, 252
Hamal-Nandrin, J., xi, 208, 217
Hamburg, 54, 79, 219, 252; culture, 74 ff., 132; museum at, x, 238
Hammelev, 232
hammer (bone), 113; (stone), 105, 199, 204
Hammersmith, 112
Hampshire, 193, 206, 236, 249

274

INDEX

hand-axe, 85
handles, antler, 250; bone, 113, 232, 233, 235, 248 ff.
Hängelsberge, 252
Hanover, 41, 54, 87, 88, 125, 203, 238, 240, 252; museum at, x, 238, 240
Happburg, 252
hare, 208, 226; arctic or variable, 47, 59, 61, 224, 225
'harpoons', 115 ff., 218
Hartz, N., 89, 235
Hasse, G., 118, 231
Hassing Østerkaer, 232, 245
Hassocks, 198, 214
Hastings, 203
Haubølle, 232, 245
Havelland, 77, 79, 88, 112 ff., 119, 125, 164, 165, 174, 239, 245, 248, 252
Havel clay, 83, 110, 134, 229
Havelse midden, 148
Havnø, 51, 140, 151, 223, 227
Haward, F. N., 237
hazel, 26, 28, 31 ff., 83, 90, 198, 211, 213, 220, 246, 247
hazel-hen, 224
Heathery Burn, 114
Hede, J. E., 9, 20, 39
hedgehog, 226, 228
Hédouville, 251
Heim, A., 2
Helgeland, 68
Hell, M., 181, 188, 252
Helsingland, 185
Herlufmagle, 232, 245
Hermannsburg, 252
heron, 226, 227
herring-gull, 227
Hertfordshire, 95, 118, 236
Hildesheim, 240
Hillerød, 232, 245
Himalayas, 6
Hindenburg, 252
Hinge Sø, 232, 245
Hofderup, 242, 245
Hohenreiche, 242
Hohenzollern, 218
Hohlefels, 195, 252
Hohlefels bei Hutten, 224
Hohlen Stein, 47 ff., 57 ff., 223, 225
Hohmann, K., 61, 64, 73
Holbæk midden, 156
Holderness, 36, 87
Holeheien, 71, 73
Holland, x, xi, 12, 74, 78, 190, 207, 253; see also Low Countries
Holmegaard, 41, 45 ff., 88 ff., 142, 148, 162, 170, 216, 223, 226, 232, 245, 247, 248
Holstein, 61
Holzheim, 195, 252

Holzminden, 252
Homo Kiliensis, 133
honey-buzzard, 227
hooks, see fish-hooks
Hornsea, 118, 122, 236, 245
horse, wild, 47, 59, 61, 77, 224, 225
Horsens fjord, 88, 128, 171, 172, 176, 232, 248
Horsø, 167, 233, 248
Hoveenge, 39
Huddersfield, 194, 198, 204
Hudson's Bay, 122, 123
Hull Museum, 236
Hullern, 252
Hulth, J. M., 23
human skeletal material, 128, 133 ff., 156
hunting, see economy
huts, 45, 199
Hvittis, 185
Hylteberga, 83, 131, 230, 242, 245, 247
Hägg, R., 135
Härryda, 242
Hästefjorden, 242
Höganäs, 19, 40, 104, 112, 129, 170, 171, 242, 247, 248
Hörninge mosse, 88, 107, 122, 131, 243, 245, 247, Pl. VI
Hörste, 252
Høilandsvandet, 137

ibex, 224
Iceland, 6
ice-sheet, 78, 185, 219; bi-partition of the Scandinavian, 2, 3, 5, 6, 219; melting of, 7, 195; retreat of Alpine, 29, phases of: Bühl, 1, 2, Daun, 1, 2, Geschnitz, 1, 2; retreat of Sandinavian, 29, phases of: Daniglacial, 1, 2, Finiglacial, 2, 4, 11, Götiglacial, 2, 10, Post-glacial, 2
Illebølle, 173, 233, 248
Inch Keith, 217
incised technique, 162 ff., 182, 248 ff.
Ireland, northern, 9, 81
Iron Age, Early, 43, 57, 200
Isberg, O., 40, 49, 229, 230
Isbergues, 237
Ise fjord, 18
Isère, 218
Islandmagee, 81
Isobases, 8
Isostatic rise of land, 7 ff., 11, 16
Istaby, 88, 127, 129, 243, 245, Pl. V
Istein, 224, 252
Italy, north, 30

Jacob-Friesen, K. H., 41
Jade, estuary, 12
Jaeschke, J., 32
jaws, human, 134, 135
jay, 226
Jerichow, kr., 251, 252

Jerzmanowska-Höhle, 78
Jessen, A., xi, 21, 47 ff., 50, 71, 80, 140, 145, 223, 229
Jessen, K., xi, 32, 39, 141
Johansen, A. C., 25, 26
Johnstrup, 48
Jonstrup Vang, 233, 245
Jura, 31
Jutland, 10, 12, 15, 19, 23, 26, 36, 47, 71, 79, 87, 110, 127, 128, 140, 144, 155, 162, 164, 168, 171, 172, 174, 231 ff., 248, 249
Jyderup, 89
Jämtland, 4, 5, 6, 182, 186, 219
Jära Bank, ix, 9, 114, 129, 157, 165, 243

Kadner, A., 133
Kalajoki, river, Pl. I
Kalbe a. Saale, kr., 251
Kaldhol, H., 184
Kalkmergel, 235
Kalmar Museum, xi, 243, Pl. VI
Kalmarsund, 39
Kalundborg, 26, 171, 233, 248; Museum, 233, 248
Kansu, 216
Kappelburg, the, 252
Karby, 239, 245
Karthaus, kr., 237
Kassemose midden, 150, 156
Kattegatt, 11
Katznase, 252
Kehdinger Moor, 41
Keilhack, K., 192
Keller, P., 29, 30, 321
Kelling, 92, 94, 100, 102, 236
Kelpin Abbau, 253
Kennet, river, 88, 236, 237
Kent, 158, 193
Kernbeil, see axe, flint (core)
Kersten, K., x
key-pattern, 177
Kiel, x, 54, 133, 138, 139, 156; Museum, 98, 102, 229, 237, 238
Kiev, 177
Kincardine, 251
King Arthur's Cave, 215
Kirchdorf, 61
Kirkenes, 67, 68, 70
Kirlelandsøen, 68
kitchen-middens, 18, 19, 23, 46, 50, 51, 138 ff., 154, 156, 157; *see also* Ertebølle culture
kite, 226
Kjellmark, K., 157
Kl.-Machnow, 113, 168, 174, 239, 249
Kl.-Vorwerk, 61, 252
Klercker, Dr John af, ix
Klinghardt, Prof. F., 139
Klintesø midden, 51, 140, 157, 223, 227
Klobich-See, 64, 65
Klubba, 182, 184

Klus mountains, 252
knives (boar's tusk), 110, 233, 235; fish-scaling, 114
Koch, L., 91
Koldingfjord, 88, 128, 152, 164, 171, 175, 233, 249
Kolindsund, 155, 161, 221, 233, 245
Kolvik, 67
Komsa culture, xv, 16, 23, 66 ff., 73, 78, 219 ff.
Kongsted, 233, 245
Konigsberg, Prussia museum at, 230, 239
Konitz, kr., 252
Konstantynow, kr., 241, 249
Korpilahti, 109, 170, 241
Kossinna, Prof. G., 86, 133 ff., 151, 156, 239, 249
Kostrzewski, M. J., 63, 192, 217, 229, 253
Kösuchen, 239, 245
Köterberg, 252
Kozłowski, L., xi, 62, 78, 241, 242, 249
Krampkewitz, 239
Krause, E., 242, 248
Krukowski, S., 62
Kulm, 113, 253
Kunda, 49, 50, 86, 88, 121, 122, 131, 220, 241, 245 ff.
Kungsladugård, 105, 106, 129, 243, 247; mace type, 148
Kupka, P., 238
Kusserow, 240
Källingemöre mosse, 107, 114, 243, 245, 247
Källstads, 243

Laag, C., 54
La Baume, Prof. W., 112, 114, 237, 239, 252, 253
Labiau, 230
Lachmirowice, 241, 245
Lacque, river, 237
ladle, wooden, 185
Ladoga, lake, 16
Lagerheim, G., 32
lag-goose, grey, 226
La Haine, 231, 245
lake-chalk, 241
Lake Fjord, 122, Pl. VI
Lakenheath, 192, 212, 251
lakes, 48, 88, 232, 234, 235; ancient lakes, 79, 88, 131, 133, 138, 195, 196, 201, 236, 238 ff., 243, 264; fluctuations in levels of, 24; *see also* Seekreide
Lammefjord, 155
La Mouthe, 188
Lampe, W., 61, 252
lanceolate points with pressure flaking, 208, 222
land-bridge, 22, 79, 87, 124 ff., 160, 219 ff.
land-movement (relative), 7 ff., 15, 22, 25, 36 ff., 128, 141, 183, 184, 211, 219 ff.
Landverk, 4, 182, 185, 188, Pl. VIII
Langeland island, x, 168, 173, 175, 233, 248, 249
Langenfelde, 80 ff., 229
Langø, 142, 150, 152, 154, 165, 249

INDEX

Lappland, 185
Lartet, E., 84, 163, 237
La Tène culture, 252
'Lattmoor', 240
Latvia, 11
Lauenburg, kr., 239
Laugerie-Basse, 179
Laugerie-Haute, 178
Laukaa, 186
Lavenstedt, 54 ff.
Lea river valley, 88, 236
Lebus, kr., 64
Le Campigny, 161
Leiknes, 182, 185
Leine, river, 88, 112, 238
leister prongs, 115 ff., 121 ff., 243, 247, Pl. VI
Leman and Ower Banks, 15, 87, 88, 118, 122, 128, 131, 236, 245 ff.
lemmings, 77, 219; banded, 47, 224; Obi, 47, 224
Lequeux, L., xi, 197 ff., 203, 204, 206, 208, 209
Lerida, 176
Lespugue, 178
Letmathe, 197, 252
Lewis, F. J., 31
Licent, E., 78
Lichtenfels, 195, 252
Lida, 242
Lidén, R., 6
Liége, 218
Lietzow, 139, 221
Lihult culture, 157, 161, 221
lime, 31 ff., 158, 211, 220, 246
Limhamn, 9, 88, 114, 129, 157, 161, 164, 165, 217, 221, 243, 249; type of axe, 148, 154, 157
Lincolnshire, 190, 251
Lindberg, H., 109, 241
Lindquist, S., xi, 86
Lippe, 252; river, 229
Lippstadt, kr., 57
Lissauer, A., 114, 239, 240
Lithuania, 11, 194
Litorina, littorea, 140; oceanic phase, 70; Sea, ix, 9 ff., 17 ff., 25, 39, 40, 88, 136, 138, 156, 157, 243, Pls. II, V
loess, 74, 190, 192, 195, 216, 222
Lohusu, 241
Lolland island, 234
London, 88, 237; Museum, 236, 237; Society of Antiquaries of, ix
long-tailed duck, 48, 51, 226, 227
Lorrach, kr., 252
Los Gavilanes, 175
Lötzen, kr., 239
Loughton, 198
Low Countries, ix, 87, 206, 217, 222; see also Belgium *and* Holland
Lower Greensand, 190, 198, 204, 214, 251
Lower Halstow, 158 ff., 217, 221
Lübeck, 54, 79, 238; museum at, xi, 240

Lucerne, lake, 2
Luchow, kr., 61
Lund, 230; Museum, ix, 122, 229, 230, 242 ff., 249
Lundquist, G., 39, 243, 247
Lyck, kr., 240
Lyngby culture, 50, 70, 71, 79 ff., 160, 214, 219, 220, 229, 230; see also Nørre-Lyngby
Lynge, H., 26
lynx, 224, 228
'Lyonesse surface', 9, 15
Lörby, 127, 243, 245
Løjesmølle, 130, 233, 245, Pl. V

MacArthur's Cave, 218
mace-heads, 105 ff., 129, 145, 148, 155, 185, 242, 243, 247, 249
Macfadyen, W. A., 10, 236, 247
Madsen, A. P., xi, 51, 111, 140, 151, 223, 231, 233, 234, 249, 250
Magdalenian culture, 47 ff., 74 ff., 160, 178, 189, 197, 208, 209, 219, 220, 223, 224; Early, 47, 224; Middle, 47, 224; Late, 47, 132, 224
Magdeburg, x, 88, 240, 245, 252; Museum, 251, 252
magic, 182, 186; see also amulets
Maglemose culture, 29, 86 ff., 140, 142, 145, 150, 153 ff., 162 ff., 189, 190, 192, 214 ff., 220, 221
Maier, P., 252
Mainz, museum at, 238
Malmo, 83, 229
Malta (Siberia), 163
mammoth, 224
Mariager fjord, x, 248
Marienburg, kr., 252
Marne, 251
Marr, Prof. J. E., 40
Marsoulas, 178, 179
marten, 208, 224; wood, 226, 228
Martinshöhle, 197, 252
Marzenin, 241
Mason, W. D., 251
Mathiasson, T., 91
Mazowsze, 113, 173, 241, 249
Mecklenburg, 26, 87, 133, 139, 238, 240
Medway estuary, 158
megalithic civilisation, 185, 188; axe types of, 16; tomb types of, 73; see also dolmens, passage-graves
Meiendorf, 74, 75
Meilgaard, 140, 142, 148, 150, 152, 153
Meinersdorf, 133
Melania lactea, 59
Melawa, river, 230
Mendrienen, 114, 249
Menghin, Prof. O., xv, 200
Mentone, 215
merganser, red-breasted, 227
Mertoun, 251
mesocephalic, *see* skulls

INDEX

Mestorf, J., 235
metal, 186
Mézine, 177
micro-burins, 54, 94 ff., 132, 197 ff., 214, 215, 232, 235, 238; absence of, 57, 62, 65
microlithic civilisation, 190 ff., 220 ff.
microliths, 65, 92 ff., 132, 133, 153, 155, 158, 198 ff., 232, 233, 235 ff.; methods of hafting, 89, 96, 200, 203; methods of manufacture, 203; types of: blunted down all one side, 59, 94, 142, 203, 208, crescents, 61, 94, 155, 197, 203, 208, 216, obliquely blunted, 89, 94, 142, 203, 208, 210, points with concave base, 57, 58, 197, 203, 208, 210, 216, rhomboids, 203, trapezes, 61, 94, 142, 155, 197, 203, 208, 210, 215, 222, trapezoidal, 94, triangles, 59 ff., 155, 197, 200, 203, 208, 210, (isosceles), 94, (scalene), 61, 94, 142, 216, 218
middens, 45; see also kitchen-middens
Middlesex, 237
Midzuno, S., 216
Mielnik, 63, 78, 219
Milthers, V., 18
Minden, 252
Minns, Prof. E. H., xii, 216
Mitteldorf, 240
Mjällby, 121, 123, 127, 243
Mohrungen, kr., 240
mole, 224
Mölln, 107, 240
molluscs, freshwater, 26; marine, 25, 141
'Monastirien', see raised beaches
Mondschütz, 230
Mongolia, 216
Montaigle, 197
Montbani, 251
Montelius, O., xi, 176, 243, 244, 249, 250
'moorlog', 8, 13 ff., 36 ff., 131, 236, 246
moraines, Baltic end, 1, 65; Fenno-Scandian, 2, 219; north German, 1
Moravia, 74
Morbihan, 12
Morgi, 242, 245
Mortillet, A. de, xi, 190, 237, 251
Mortillet, G. de, 237, 251
Mother Grundy's Parlour, 197, 207, 215, 251
mouse, 224, 225
Mugem, 144
Muggenberg, 240
Müller, O., 252
Müller, S., ix, xi, 81, 84, 113, 140, 163, 223, 229, 231 ff., 248 ff.
Müller-Brauel, J., 54
Mullerup, 41, 45 ff., 86, 88 ff., 101 ff., 119, 125, 128, 130, 135, 163, 168, 170, 171, 216, 223, 226, 233, 245 ff.
Multorp, 243
Muncheberg Museum, 64
Münchehofe, 64, 65
Munich, x

Münster Museum, x, 252
Munthe, H., xi, 9, 10, 20, 39, Pl. II
Munzingen, 224
Muota delta, 2
Murowana, 229
mute-swan, 226
Mytilus edulis, 140

Nagold, 195, 252
Najas flexilis, 27
Nassa reticulata, 140
Natica Parisiensis, 59
naturalism, 176, 178 ff.
navigation, 22, 107 ff., 207
Neagh, Lough, 81
Neanderthaloid traits, 133
Near East, 6
needles, absence of, 113
Neergaard, C., 91, 140, 223
Neolithic A culture of Britain, 37, 38, 41, 210
Neolithic civilisation, 65, 67, 81, 134, 156, 158, 160, 161, 176, 195, 208, 210, 211, 216, 217, 222
net, 109, 132, 170, 241, Pl. IV; pattern, 114, 127, 132, 136, 170, 174, 177, 179; -prickers, 129, 165, 171, 175, 232, 238 ff., 243, 247 ff.; see also nätstickor
Neu Bukow, 139
Neugut, 113, 253
Neu Jucha, 240, 245
Neumarkt, 252
Neumühl, 252
Neustadt, kr., 239
Neu-Strelitz, 240, 245
Newbiggin-on-Sea, 251
Newbury, 88, 236; museum at, 237
Newcastle, 217
Newlyn, Ordnance Datum, 37, 38
Nielsen, H. A., 135
Nihlén, J., 73, 157, 185
Nijni-Novgorod, 186
Niklasson, N., xi, 97, 100, 104, 128, 243
Nilsson, S., 135
Ninove, 231
Nivaagaard midden, 150
Nordfjord, 184
Nordhagen, R., 4, 10, 24, 25, 27
Nordhemmern, 252
Nordic, 135; proto-, 156
Nordman, C. A., xi, 109, 148
Nordman, V., xi, 47 ff., 50, 71, 80, 229
Norfolk, 87, 128, 236
Normandy, 12
North Sea, 8, 12 ff., 22, 36 ff., 87, 118, 125, 160, 211, 220, 221, 236
Northumberland, 251
Norway, xi, 15, 17, 25, 74, 160, 181 ff., 217; north and north-western, 4, 16, 66 ff., 70 ff.; southern, 136, 157, 219

Norwich Museum, 236
Nowa, 242
Nüesch, 3
Nummedal, A., xi, 67 ff.
nuts, 90, 198
Nyland, 17
Nämnforsen, 4
nätstickor, 114; *see also* net-prickers
Nørre-Lyngby, 47, 70, 71, 79 ff., 223, 225
Nøstvet culture, 16, 157, 161, 184, 221

oak, 31 ff., 136, 158, 220
oak-mixed-forest, 26, 31 ff., 83, 129 ff., 138, 141, 213, 220, 221, 242, 246, 247
Obermaier, Prof. H., 177, 180
Oberpfalz, 197
Obi, *see* lemmings
'oceanic' climate, *see* climate
Ochertye Moss, 39
Octobon, le Capitaine, xi, 217, 251
Odense, 80, 114, 234; museum at, 232, 250
Oder, river, 192
Oedenbühl, 42
Oerze, river, 252
Ofnet, 218, 224
Oldenbroker Moor, 12
Oldenburg, 12, 37, 142, 144
Oldesloe, culture, 155, 161, 221; Museum, 56
Olonetz, 185
origins, 74 ff., 131 ff., 153 ff., 213 ff.
ornementation pointillée, 154, 162, 163, 175, 177, 231, 248 ff.
Orust island, 249
Osieck, 63
Oslo, 11, 12, 16, 26, 87, 114, 182, 184, 241
osprey, 226
Ossowo, 242, 245
Ostel, 251
Östergötland, 10, 26, 243
Ostrobothnia, Pl. I
Ostrołęka, 113, 171, 173, 242, 249
Ostrowo, 63, 217
Ostschwarzwald, 252
otter, 224, 226, 228
Ottersberg, 42
Oulu, river, 6
Ourthe, river, 199, 204, 209
Overbeck, F., 9, 10, 12, 32, 37, 42
Overyssel, x
Owen, R., 50
Ower, *see* Leman and Ower Banks
owl, tawny, 227
ownership marks, 77
ox, 208, 224
Oxie, 243
oyster, 25
Öland island, 26, 39, 88, 107, 114, 122, 131, 243, Pl. VI
Ødum, H., 44, 50, 235, 247

Øyen, P. A., xi, 70, 241

paddle-rudder, 22, 107, 108, 232, 238
Padosero, 185
painted pebbles, 180, 218
paintings, *see* rock-paintings
Pair-non-Pair, 187
palaeolithic civilisation, lower, 84; upper, 22, 29, 59, 69, 74, 76, 78, 81, 84, 85, 96, 113, 124, 127, 128, 131, 132, 145, 187 ff., 195, 197, 207, 215, 219, 220; art of, 177 ff.
Palestine, 132, 215
partridge, 224
passage-graves, 19, 20, 70, 73, 185
patterns, classification of, 169 ff.; *see also* chequer, key, net
Patterson, H. M. L., 251
Peacehaven, 102
Peacock's Farm, 37, 38, 41, 210 ff., 251, Pl. III
Peake, H. J. E., xi, 237
peat, 9, 10, 12, 19, 23, 24, 31, 32, 37 ff., 41, 76, 77, 79, 82, 89, 105, 109, 121, 129, 133, 134, 141, 158, 194, 204, 210 ff., 231 ff., 241, 243, 244; see also cotton-grass peat, *Phragmites* peat, *Sphagnum* peat
pebbles, with counter-sunk hollows, 105, 158; with hour-glass perforation, 105, 145, 155, 158, 206, 235
pecking technique, 105, 148, 182
Peitschendorf, 240, 245
pelican, Dalmatian, 227
Penck, A., 1, 7
pendants, 110, 231, 235, 249, 250
Penken, 240
Pennines, 41, 96, 194, 198, 204, 210
Pentekinnen, 120, 125, 240, 245
perch, 227
Perkallen, 240, 245
Pernau, 88, 114, 121, 125, 164, 165, 171, 241, 245, 249; Museum, 241
Perth, 39, 109
Petch, 194
Peterhouse, governing body of, x
Peters, E., 218
Petersen, C. G. J., 140, 223
Petersfehner Moor, 142, 144
Petitville, 12
Petrosavodsk, 185
phalange, perforated (aurochs), 113; (reindeer), 58 ff., 113
Phillips, C. W., xii, 192
Pholas stage, 70
phosphate analysis, 19 ff.
Phragmites peat, 39
physical types, *see* human skeletal material
Picard, C., 167, 237, 248
Picardy, 87
picks, flint, 102 ff.; Thames type, 158 ff., 221
Piesker, H., 252

INDEX

Piette, E., 178, 179
pig, wild, 47 ff., 59, 61, 136, 152, 224 ff.
pika, 47, 224
pike, 48, 77, 89, 122, 226, 227, 242
pile-dwelling, 15, 134
Pils, Dr, x
pine, 24, 31 ff., 73, 77, 80, 83, 89, 92, 109, 129 ff.,
136, 138, 141, 158, 211, 213, 219 ff., 246,
247
pins, bone, 200
pintail, 226
Pinus cembra, 185
pit-dwelling, 198 ff.
pit-ornament, see *bohrornament*
Placard, Le, 178, 179
Plau, 134
plough-scenes, absence of, 182
Podgorz, 63
points, bone, 201, 202, 231; classification of
Maglemose, 115 ff.; forms of Maglemose:
(1) 119, 174, 238 ff.; (2) 119, 120, 125, 130, 238,
245, 248; (3) 118, 127, 129, 237, 243 ff., Pl. V;
(4) 120, 239; (5) 120, 121, 130, 174, 232, 233,
238 ff., 245, Pl. V; (6) 13, 50, 87, 118 ff., 128,
130, 231 ff., 247, Pl. V; (7) 125, 130, 174, 231 ff.,
245, 247, Pl. V; (8) 119, 239; (9) 120, 125,
232 ff., 238, 242, Pl. V; (10) 120, 125, 237, 239,
243, 244; (11) 125, 239; (12) 119, 125, 238 ff.,
245; (13) 120, 125, 240, 241; (14) 243, Pl. VI;
(15) 119, 239; (16) 121, 125, 239; (17) 119, 120,
121, 239 ff., 245; (18) 121, 241; (19) 119, 121,
239; (20) 121, 125; (21) 121, 122, 232 ff., 243,
244, 247; (22) 122, 249, 250; (23) 122, 125, 231;
(24) 122, 125, 233, 235, 244, 250; (25) 121, 122,
242, 247, Pl. V; (21)–(25) 137, 245, 247
Poland, xi, 22, 63, 64, 69, 79, 87, 113, 124 ff., 127,
144, 160, 171, 173, 174, 179, 190, 192, 203, 216,
217, 220, 249, 252
polecat, 224, 228
polished flint or stone implements, 84, 148, 208,
216, 217
pollen-analysis, 15, 32 ff., 49, 50, 77, 78, 81, 83,
105, 107, 112, 114, 122, 125, 129 ff., 141, 158,
210 ff., 229 ff., 246, 247, Pls. III, V
pollen spectra, 14, 82, 129 ff.
Pomerania, 26, 87, 114, 125, 139, 237, 239,
240
Popelken, 230
Poppenbrugge, 133
Popping, H. J., 78
population, pressure of, 195; sparseness of, 127
porpoise, 51, 228
Porsanger fjord, 67
Portlandia arctica, 25
Portugal, 144
Posen Museum, 229
Post, L. von, x, 9, 20, 26, 27, 32, 34, 35, 39, 40, 105,
242, 244, 246, 247
Pottenstein, 195, 197, 207, 252

pottery, 137, 152 ff., 156, 157, 221; absence of,
17, 124, 199, 206; cord-impressed, 17; comb-
decorated, 71
Pre-boreal climate phase, 24, 25, 31, 35, 36, 49, 77,
83, 219, 229, 230
precipitation, 23 ff.
Předmost, 74, 78, 177
Pr.-Eylau, kr., 239, 240
prickly sedge, 27
Pritzerber See, 88, 110, 111, 134, 239
Propstfels, 224
Prussia, East, 79, 87, 114, 120, 125, 238 ff., 249;
West, 237 ff.
pseudo-awls, 76
ptarmigan, 224
Puck-â-maugan, 84
Putzig, 253
Pyrenees, 31, 217
Pälsi, S., 109, 241

quartz implements, 67
quartzite implements, 67, 105, 107, 145, 155, 206,
207; *see also* pebbles
Quillebœuf, 12

rabbit, 224
Rahir, E., xi, 29, 47, 59, 60, 197, 198, 223, 249
raised beaches, 9, 16, 23; 'Monastirien', 12
Raistrick, A., xi, 32, 194, 203, 251
Ramsay, W., 11
Randers, 234, 245
rats, 224; brown, 228; water, 225, 228
Rau, C., 123
Ravensburg, 252
Raymonden, 179
razorbill, 51, 227
Reche, Prof. O., 133 ff.
Reckenwalde, 65
Reddis, 114
Refsvindinge, 113, 163, 172, 175, 234, 249
Reid, Clement, xi, 13
reindeer, 40, 47 ff., 58 ff., 61, 77, 81, 82, 182, 219 ff.,
224, 225; difference between tundra and forest
types, 50
Reinecke, P., 238, 240
Reinerth, Prof. H., xi, 41 ff., 45, 195, 196, 199, 206,
212
religion, 127
Remonchamps, 47 ff., 164, 165, 208, 213, 219,
223, 225, 249; culture, 59 ff., 68, 73
Rennerfels, 197, 207
Repvåg, 67
Rerslev, 122, 234, Pl. V
Resen Mose, 110, 168, 171, 174, 234, 249
Reuterskiöld, E., 186
Rhineland, 25
Rhinluch, 212
Rieseberg, 61
rillenornamentik, 77

Ringkjøbing fjord, 234, 249
Ringsjön, 244
Ringsted Aa, 234, 249
Rivière, E., 188
roach, 227
Roche-aux-Faucons, 199, 203, 204, 206
rock-engravings, 180
rock-paintings, 175, 176, 185
rock-shelter, 45, 136, 195, 197, 207, 252
Roman road, 41
Romsdalen, 68
Romsey, 100, 162, 175, 236, 249
Roskilde fjord, 18, 19, 104, 140, 154
Ross-on-Wye, 215
Rostock, 139
Rostrup, E., 140, 223
Rothert, L., 61, 65, 252
Royston, 118, 236, 245
rudd, 227
Rüder Moor, 152
Rudnidk, 253
Rudolph, K., xi, 29, 32
Rudynsky, M., 65
Rügen, 139, 221
Ruskenesset, 137
Russedalen, 67
Russia, xiii, 32, 87, 122, 185, 186
Rust, A., 76
Rutot, M. A., 128
Rydbeck, O., ix, xi, 104, 136, 156, 157, 242, 243, 248, 249
Rymill, J., 122
Råbelovsjön, 244, 245
Rönneholms mosse, 244

Sagelven, 182, 184
Sagemühl, 252
Saint-Germain, museum at, xi, 237
Saint-Marcel, 178
Saint-Périer, R. de, 22, 178, 214
Sainty, J. E., 236
Salamanca, 175
Salix herbacea, 26
Salix polaris, 26, 80
Salix reticulata, 26
salmon, 122
Salmony, A., 163
Salzburg, 252
sand, control over settlement of, 190 ff., 251, 252; *see also* dunes
Sandarna, 86, 88, 94, 97, 100, 102, 104 ff., 128, 129, 135, 142, 145, 148, 220
Sandegren, R., 27, 105, 129, 216
Sandy, 251
Santander, 217
Sarasin, F., 218
Sarauw, G. F. L., xi, 48, 72, 73, 81, 105, 106, 111, 119, 128, 130, 163, 223, 229, 231 ff., 242 ff., 247, 249, 250

Saskatchewan, 84
saucers, 152
Sauermilch, C., 252
Sauramo, M., xi, 1, 6, 10, 32, Pl. I
Sawicki, L., xi, 63, 65, 66, 217, 242, 249
saws, flint, 145, 204
Saxony, 87, 238
Scania, ix, 5, 9, 19, 22, 26, 40, 44, 49, 79, 83, 112, 114, 122, 129, 136, 242 ff., 248 ff.
scaup-duck, 51, 227
schleiftechnik, 182
Schleswig-Holstein, 87, 88, 111, 114, 125, 138, 152, 155, 171, 229, 239, 240
Schliz, A., 134, 216
Schlutup, 83, 230
Schmidt, R. R., xi, 46, 178, 197, 223, 252
Schmiechenfels, 224
Schmitz, H., 9, 10, 12, 32, 37, 42
Schneider, M., 61, 206, 252
Schnell, I., 21, 22
Schönbuch, 252
Schubert, E., 42
Schussenquelle, 224
Schwantes, Prof. G., x, xi, 54, 57, 73 ff., 80 ff., 84, 85, 96, 102, 111 ff., 150, 155, 229, 230, 238 ff., 247, 252
Schwarzach, river, 252
Schwerte, 252
scoter, common, 51, 227; velvet, 51, 227
Scotland, 9, 10, 31, 216
scrapers, 57 ff., 62, 68, 69, 71, 76, 100, 144 ff., 158, 199, 204, 232, 233, 235
sculptures, 162, 171, 177, 180, 186
Scunthorpe, 192, 251
seal, 10, 51, 117; common, 228; Greenland, 228; grey, 228; ringed, 228
sea-level, old, 9 ff., 16, 19, 22, 67, 68, 70, 88, 102, 129, 136, 154, 157, 183, 184, 211, 219 ff., 243, Pl. II; relation of peat-beds to, 44, 129
seasonal, economy, 138, 182; settlement, 49, 51, 90, 127, 160
Seekreide, 88, 122, 239; *see also* lake-chalk
Segeberg, kr., 239
Seger, H., 230
Seïma, 186
Seine, river, 12
Seine-et-Oise, 251
Selkirk, 251
Selmeston, 144, 198, 204, 205, 214
Sensburg, kr., 240
Sergeac, 163
Sernander, R., xi, 23, 24
serrated flakes, *see* saws
Servais, J., 208, 209, 217
settlement, geographical control of, 86 ff., 190 ff.; seasonal, 49, 51, 90, 127, 160; for settlement sites *see* dwelling-places
Seward, Prof. A. C., xii
shell-banks, 25, 135

shell-fish, 15, 22, 136, 140
shell-marl, 236, 237
shell-mound, *see* kitchen-middens
shells, perforated, 59
Shetelig, H., xi, 69, 71, 137, 181, 184, 188
Shewalton Moor, 217
Shipley, 40
Shippea Hill, 37, 38, 210 ff., 251, Pl. III
shoveler, 226
Siberia, 78, 140, 163
Sickingsmühle, 229
Sidingefjord, 155
Sierra Morena, 175, 180
Silesia, 85, 135, 230, 252
Silkeborg Sø, 88, 163, 164, 171, 234, 249
silver-fir, 31 ff.
Simpson, G. C., 24
Simrishamn Museum, 244
single-graves, 73
sink-stones, net, 109, 241, Pl. IV
Siretorp, 121, 123, 244
Sirgenstein, 224
Skagerack, 25
Skalstrup, 172, 176, 234, 250
Skarås, 106
Skeldelev, 39
skeletal remains, *see* human skeletal material
Skertchly, S. B. J., xi, 31, 40, 50
Skipsea, 49, 88, 102, 118, 236, 245
Skodje, 69
Skogerveien, 184
Skottemarke, 50, 130, 234, 245
skulls, brachycephalic, 133 ff., 218; dolichocephalic, 134 ff., 218; mesocephalic, 218
Skurups, 242
Slagelseegnen, 234, 245
slate implements, 67, 71, 72, 137, 185
sleeves, (antler), 112, 232, 233, 235, 237, 248, 250; (wooden), 104, 107
Sletjord, 182
Słochy Annopolski, 203
Słochy Ogrodinki, 144
Slågarps, 244
Smiatchka XIV, station of, 65
Smith, R. A. S., 236, 237, 248, 249
Småland, 10, 219
social groups, 92
social outlook, 127, 128
solar, cult, absence of, 182; radiation, 7, 24
Sollerön, 114, 136, 173, 250
Solsem, 185
Solutrean, 78
Somme, 237, 248; river, 88, 167, 174, 237
Sonder, W., 155
Sorbehnen, 240
Sougné, 198
South Downs, 160, 190, 192
Sotra, 68
Spa, 59

Spain, 175, 215
spalter, 104, 139, 142, 153, 155, 157, 158, 232 ff., 238
Spandau skull, 134
Spanish art group III, 175, 180
Sphagnum peat, 24, 41
Spiegel, J., 252
Spilsby sandstone, 192, 251
Spitzbergen Sea, 25
Spree, river, 134, 192
spruce, 31 ff., 247
spur-dog, 51, 227
squirrel, 208, 224, 226, 228
Stade, 41
Stala, 107
Stańkowice, 62 ff.
Stapelage, 252
Stavanger, 71, 136
Steenstrup, K. J. V., 48, 140, 150, 223
Stellmoor, 54
Stendal, 238; Museum, 238
Stensby, 171, 172, 175, 234, 250
Stenseng, 67, 68
steppe, 29, 84; fauna, 46 ff., 59
stickleback, 227
Stimmberg i. d. Hardt, 252
Stimming, R., 77, 110 ff., 119, 134, 229, 230, 239, 248
Stirling, 39
Stjerna, K., 130, 241, 248, 250
Stockholm, ix; Museum, 242 ff., 250, Pl. V; University, 32
Stoll, H., 195, 252
Stoller, J., 212
stone circles, 12
stone types, *see* mace-heads, pebbles with countersunk hollows, pebbles with hour-glass perforation
Stora Dode mosse, 88, 112, 131, 244, 245, 247
Storbukta, 67, 68
Store Vildmose, 234, 245
stork, black, 226
Stour, river, 37
Strand, 182
stratigraphy, archaeological, 141, 148, 150, 152 ff., 207, 208, 210; *see also* superposition
Struckhausen, 37
Strzelno, 241
Stuhm, kr., 252
Stuttgart, 195, 252
Stångenäs, 135, 156
Sub-atlantic climate phase, 23, 24, 39, 41, 42
Sub-boreal climate phase, 23, 24, 39, 81
subsistence, *see* economy
Suffolk, 144
Sundelin, U., 244
Suomusjärvi culture, 17
superposition, 183
Surrey, 193, 251

INDEX

survival of culture, 61, 66, 70 ff., 85, 136 ff., 216, 217
Sussex, 144, 193, 197, 198, 203, 204, 214
Svaerdborg, 45, 48 ff., 86, 88, 94 ff., 128, 131, 135, 142, 144, 162, 164, 165, 167, 168, 170, 171, 174, 214, 216, 223, 226, 235, 245, 247, 250
Svealand, 11, 219
Svedala, 242
Svedstrup, 119, 234, 245
swan, wild, 77, 89; Bewick's, 227; mute, 226; whooper, 224, 227
Sweden, ix ff., 2, 5 ff., 11, 22, 26, 27, 34 ff., 70, 72, 79, 81, 83, 85, 87, 88, 105, 115, 121 ff., 125, 127, 129, 137, 138, 157, 160, 164, 167, 170 ff., 179, 182, 185, 186, 214, 219 ff., 248 ff.
Swiderian culture, 62 ff., 73, 78, 213, 219
Swidry, 62
Switzerland, 29, 32
Szirgupönen, 120, 240, 245
Szmit, Z., 62 ff., 203
Säkkijärvi, 185, 186
Søborg Sø, 235, 245, 250
Søholm, 235, 245, 250
Sølager, midden, 140, 148, 150, 152, 157

Taaderup, 44, 50, 131, 235, 245 ff.
Taarbaek, 167, 168, 235, 250
Tallgren, A. M., xi, 49, 186, 241
Tange, 235, 245
tanged flakes, 71, 79 ff.
tanged point cultures, 54 ff., 213, 217, 219 ff.; see also flint implements
tanged points, 54 ff., 68, 69, 71 ff., 213; with inverse retouch, 62
Tanner, V., 7, 16, 67, 68, 70
Tannstock, 199 ff., 213
Tapes decussatus, 25
Tapes shore-line, 67, 88, 105, 129, 134, 137, 185
Tardenoisian, 65, 78, 92, 132, 133, 192 ff., 220 ff., 251 ff.; settlement, 29, 190; Early, 206, 208, 210; Middle, 61, 206, 208, 210; Late, 41, 61, 94, 206, 208, 210
Taubried, 45
Tawastland, 186
Tay, firth of, 10, 39; river of, 109
Taylor, H., 215
Tebessa, 200
teeth, perforated for adornment, 58, 110; used as implements, 110
Teilhard, P., 78
temperature, 23, 25 ff.
Tennes, 182
Test, river, 236
Teutoburger Wald, 192, 252
Thaingen, 178
Thames, 88, 100, 112, 118, 127, 160, 162, 237
Thatcham, 88, 94, 102, 237
Thomasson, H., 39
Thomsen, T., xi, 21, 51, 140, 147 ff., 223, 248

Thomson, P. W., 32, 34, 35, 122, 241, 247
throwing-sticks, 107, 148, 149
Thuringia, 197
Tidelski, 138
Tiergarten, 218
Tirlemont, 207
Tissø, 88, 235, 245
Tjörn, 244, 245
toad, 224
Tollevik, 67, 68
Toms, H. S., 198
Toome, 81
Torma, 241
tortoise, 26, 27, 226, 227
Torup, 244, 245
Törning, 125, 235
trade, 22, 207
Tranäs, 122, 242
tranchet, grand, see spalter; petit, see arrowheads, transverse; technique, see axes, transversely sharpened flint
transverse arrowhead, see microliths, trapezes, and arrowheads
Trapa natans, 27
trapeze, see microliths
Trave, river, 88, 113, 155
Travenort, 114, 171, 240, 250
tree-limit, 29
trees, see forests
Trondhjem fjord, 68, 181, 185
Tübingen, xi, 195, 252
tufa, calcareous, 23
tufted duck, 226
Tunbridge Wells sand, 190
tundra, 29, 47, 59, 77, 84; fauna, 46 ff., 59, 219
Tutilik, 122, Pl. VI
Tvaermose, 142, 144

Uchte, 252
Ukraine, 64, 65, 69, 190, 215, 219
United States, 6
Uppland, 185, 186
Uxbridge, 88, 237

Vadsted, 235, 245
Vamlingbo, Pl. II
varve, 4 ff.
Vatne, 69
Vedbotneidet, 67, 68
Vejby, 235, 245
Vejle, lake, 244
Vejleby, 229
Vermeer-Louman, G. G., 36
Vesdre, river, 197, 198, 204, 209
Vester Ulslev, 143, 152
Vesterborg, 81
Viborg, 109
Viby, 81
Vibygaard, 235, 245

Victoria Cave, Settle, 218
Vielles, 217
Vig, 89, 96, 204, 235
Viken, lake, 244, 245
Vils, river, 197, 252
Vingen, 182, 184
Visby, 73
Vissenberg, 142
Viste, 136
Vistula, river, 62, 66, 192, 253
Vitträsk, 17
Vladivostok, 216
vole, 228
Volkov, T., 177
Vorfinnen, 133 ff., 156
Voss, A., 139, 238, 239
Väby, 127, 244, 245
Vänern, lake, 11
Västergötland, 242
Vättern, lake, 87

Wachow, 239
walzenbeil (stump-butted axes), 16, 145, 147, 153, 154
Wandsworth, 118, 127, 237, 245
Wangeroog, 37
Wangford, 144, 192, 212, 251
Waren, 240, 245
Warren, S. H., 15, 37, 94 ff., 100, 107, 198, 236, 247
water-nut, 27
wattle and daub construction, 199, 200, 206
Weald, the, 190, 192
weasel, 224
Weber, C. A., xi, 24, 138, 139
Wegnez, 198
Wellingsbüttel, 74, 75
Wendhausen, 240, 245
Wennerstein, O. V., 73
Wentorf, 80
Wernert, P., 175, 176, 180
Werth, E., 24, 25
Weser, river, 8, 12, 192; estuary, 12
Weseram, 77
Westerby, E., x, xi, 51, 141, 142, 145, 151, 152, 155, 223, 235 ff., 250
Westhavelland, 238
West Keal, 251
Westphalia, 47, 57, 79, 197, 252
whales, 10, 117, 182; killer, 51, 228
Whelan, Blake, 81
whistle, 58 ff., 113
Whitburn, 217

Whitehead, H., 13
White Hill, 96, 204
White Sea, 25
whooper-swan, 227
Wichelen, 118, 231
widgeon, 227
Wiegers, F., 238
Wieliczka, 253
wiesenkalk, 229, 238, 240
wiesenmergel, 88, 230, 237
Wildscheuer, 224
Wilhelmshaven, 37
Wilke, W., 64
Willenberg, 252
Willoughton, 25
willow, 31 ff., 73, 83, 219, 246, 247
Wilsleben, 241, 245
wind-break, 198
Windmill Hill pottery, 37, 41
Winge, H., xi, 48, 89, 140, 223, 235
Wismar, 240
Witkowo, kr., 241
Witte, H., 32
wolf, 224 ff.
Wolletz, 61
Wommersom, 207
wooden, bow, 148, 149; clubs, 232; handle, 112, 149; paddle-rudder, 107, 232, 238; sculpture, 185; shaft, 122, 142; sleeve, 104, 107; throwing-sticks, 107, 148, 149
Wood Fen, 31
Woodhall Spa, 251
Woodhead, T. W., 32, 41
woodpecker, great, 227; great black, 226
Woolwich Beds, 190
Wright, W. B., 2, 11, 50
Wümme river, 8, 12
Württemberg, 41, 190, 199, 213
Wüste Scheuer, 197, 252
Wustrow, 61

Yoldia Sea, 11, 40, 79, 184, 219
Yorkshire, 23, 118, 194, 236; East, 49
Ystad, decorated antler haft from, ix, 171, 172, 176, 177, 179, 189, 250

Zakrzów, 63, 253
Zealand, 18, 19, 26, 39, 49, 50, 79, 86 ff., 93, 94, 130, 140 ff., 155, 164, 165, 168, 170 ff., 216, 220, 231 ff., 248 ff.
Zeven, 54
Zonhoven, 144, 208, 209, 213, 217, 220, 222
Zotz, L. F., xi, 61, 65, 252